THE JEWISH
BOOK OF
WHY

THE TORAH

ALSO BY ALFRED J. KOLATCH

Best Baby Names for Jewish Children
A Child's First Book of Jewish Holidays
Classic Bible Stories for Jewish Children
The Complete Dictionary of English
and Hebrew First Names
The Concise Family Seder
El Libro Judio del Por Que
The Family Seder
How to Live a Jewish Life
Great Jewish Quotations
The Jewish Book of Why
The Jewish Child's First Book of Why
The Jewish Heritage Quiz Book
The Jewish Mourner's Book of Why
The Jonathan David Dictionary of First Names
Let's Celebrate Our Jewish Holidays!
Masters of the Talmud
The New Name Dictionary
The Presidents of the United States & the Jews
The Second Jewish Book of Why
Today's Best Baby Names
What Jews Say About God

THE JEWISH
BOOK OF
WHY

THE TORAH

ALFRED J. KOLATCH

jD | JONATHAN DAVID PUBLISHERS, INC.
MIDDLE VILLAGE, NEW YORK 11379

The Jewish Book of Why
THE TORAH

Copyright © 2004
by Alfred J. Kolatch

Originally published in 1988 under the title
This Is the Torah.

JONATHAN DAVID PUBLISHERS, INC.
68-22 Eliot Avenue
Middle Village, New York 11379

www.jdbooks.com

2 4 6 8 10 9 7 5 3 1

Library of Congress Cataloging-in-Publication Data

Kolatch, Alfred J.
    [*This is the Torah*]
    The Jewish book of why—the Torah / Alfred J. Kolatch.
        p. cm.
    Includes index.
    ISBN 0-8246-0454-7
    1. Bible. O.T. Pentateuch—Miscellanea. 2. Judaism—
Customs and practices. 3. Tradition (Judaism). I. Title.

    BS1225.5.K65 2004
    222'.1061—dc22

                                                            2003062737

Book design by Arlene S. Goldberg

Printed in the United States of America

For
ERWIN ZIMET
— rabbi extraordinaire —
whose love of Torah
is exceeded only by
his love of man

In Appreciation

Thanks are due many colleagues and associates for their help in preparing this manuscript. The task was far greater than it seemed at the outset, and without their advice and assistance this book could not have been published.

To my brother, Rabbi Arthur J. Kolatch, and to Rabbi William Dalin, both of San Francisco, my heartfelt thanks for their careful and critical review of all questions and answers and for their many valuable suggestions.

Thanks are also due longtime friends and colleagues who have read parts or all of the manuscript and have made important observations: Dr. Tony Buono of Jamaica, New York; Rabbi Baruch Silverstein of Atlantic Beach, New York; Rabbi Edward M. Tenenbaum of Los Angeles, California; Rabbi Marvin Weiner of Forest Hills, New York; and Rabbi Erwin Zimet of Poughkeepsie, New York.

Although they did not review the actual manuscript, Professor Harry Orlinsky, editor-in-chief of the Jewish Publication Society's new translation of the Bible, and Rabbi Solomon B. Freehof, master of the responsa literature and author of many books on the subject, have always been available for consultation. Their guidance was invaluable.

To my secretary, Florence Weissman, for patiently typing and retyping the many drafts of the manuscript, my sincere thanks.

Three people in particular are deserving of special mention, and to them I am deeply indebted. Each has pored over the entire contents of the manuscript with great diligence and has made many valuable comments and recommendations.

First, thanks to Rabbi Ephraim Bennett of Netanya, Israel, who, because of his thorough knowledge of Bible and Talmud, was able to pinpoint inaccuracies in the text and footnotes. His painstaking effort and interest in this work is greatly appreciated.

Second, I am most grateful to my son Jonathan for his keen insights and observations which led to the pruning of unnecessary material. His exceptional abilities at organization have, indeed, enhanced the quality of this work.

To my son David, who worked closely with me for over a year, I owe very special thanks. His uncanny ability at recognizing ambiguity and refining language has resulted in the information being presented in a more attractive way for laymen, for whom this book is intended. Without his energy this book, which has been three years in the writing, would not have reached fruition in this form.

Contents

Note on Transliteration

The Hebrew words in this volume are transliterated to correspond to modern Israeli pronunciation. For the most part, the system of transliteration used is that found in most scholarly works. Exceptions were made here when it was felt that a person unfamiliar with Hebrew might be more likely to mispronounce a word if it were presented in the established scholarly manner. Consequently, the guttural **ch,** as in *chutzpa,* is spelled with a **ch,** not with an **h.** The final **h** in words such as *Chanuka, aliya,* and *sidra* has been dropped in keeping with the system established by *The Jerusalem Post.* The sole exception is the word *Torah,* where the established spelling has been retained because it is so familiar and recognizable.

In this volume transliterated words are italicized except in cases where the words appear repeatedly—such as sidra, aliya, and Kohayn. These words are italicized only when they are first introduced.

* * *

When a tractate of the Talmud is mentioned, the reference is to the Babylonian (Bavli) Talmud rather than the Jerusalem or Palestinian (Yerushalmi) Talmud.

General Introduction

In Jewish tradition the word *Torah*, which literally means "teaching," is often used to describe the entire gamut of Jewish religious learning. When so used, Torah refers not only to the Five Books of Moses but also to the Prophets, Holy Writings, Talmud, and Midrash—in fact, to all religious writings from earliest times to the present.

Basically, however, the term Torah applies to the Five Books of Moses, the first five books of the Bible. The word *Pentateuch*, a Latin word derived from the Greek, meaning "five books," is commonly used to refer to these five books. Pentateuch corresponds to the Hebrew word *Chumash*, meaning "five."

In addition to the five books that are collectively called the Torah, there are two other parts to the Bible: the Prophets *(Neviim)*, which consists of twenty-one books, and the Holy Writings or Hagiographa *(Ketuvim* or *Ketubim)*, which consists of thirteen books. This biblical triad is often referred to as the *Tanach*, a Hebrew acronym fashioned from the first letter of the Hebrew words *Torah* (Pentateuch), *Neviim* (Prophets), and *Ketuvim* (Holy Writings).

The following are the thirty-nine books of the Bible:

The Torah: Genesis, Exodus, Leviticus, Numbers, Deuteronomy.

The Prophets: Joshua, Judges, I Samuel, II Samuel, I Kings, II Kings, Isaiah, Jeremiah, Ezekiel, Ho-

1

sea, Joel, Amos, Obadiah, Jonah, Micah, Nahum, Habakkuk, Zephaniah, Haggai, Zechariah, Malachi.

The Holy Writings: Psalms, Proverbs, Job, Song of Songs, Ruth, Lamentations, Ecclesiastes, Esther, Daniel, Ezra, Nehemiah, I Chronicles, II Chronicles.

According to an early talmudic method of counting the books of the Bible, the figure was set at twenty-four. This number was arrived at by counting the twelve Minor Prophets as one book (in Aramaic the group is called *Tray Asar,* "twelve") and by counting each of the following as one book: First Samuel and Second Samuel; First Kings and Second Kings; First Chronicles and Second Chronicles; and Ezra and Nehemiah. (Thus, the thirty-nine count is reduced by fifteen.) The term often used to designate these books in classical literature is *Esrim V'arba* or *Esrim V'arba'a.*

The Centerpiece of Judaism

The Torah is the centerpiece of Judaism and the key to Jewish survival. Although not every Jew is familiar with the contents of the Torah or observes its commandments, all Jews recognize the centrality of the Torah in Jewish religious life and its function as the moral guide of the Jewish people.

The role played by the Torah in the lives of individual Jews varies considerably. Some Jews have studied the Torah sufficiently to appreciate its message; some have learned to read the Hebrew text; some have learned to chant the unvocalized script of the Torah scroll; some have been called to the Torah on Sabbaths or holidays and are able to recite the Torah blessings. Many Jews, perhaps the majority, however, have had minimal contact with the Torah.

What made it possible for this relatively brief book to achieve such a high level of importance? How did one book come to be so revered that Jews in every century have been willing to sacrifice their lives rather than violate its teachings?

The answers to these questions may be found in the attitudes of the Rabbis of the Talmud and their successors toward the unique historical event generally referred to as the Revelation, or *Mattan Torah,* the giving of the Torah on Mount Sinai over three thousand years ago. The Torah itself describes the scene dramatically: Amidst thunder and lightning, a quaking mountain is engulfed by fire and clouds of smoke. Then the piercing sound of a *shofar* is heard as God appears atop Mount Sinai and reveals the Ten Commandments (and, according to tradition, the entire Torah) to Moses, who then transmits it to the people-at-large.

The Rabbis chose to embellish the scant text and thus add to the mystery surrounding the event. Rabbi Abahu, for example, notes that when the Torah was given, the world lapsed into silence. No one spoke. Total silence. Birds did not chirp; fowl did not fly; oxen did not low. Even the heavenly angelic choir that always serenaded God with "Holy, holy, holy . . ." lapsed into silence and withheld its never-ending praises of the Lord.

It was at this point, says Rabbi Abahu, that the intense stillness was suddenly pierced by a powerful, thunderous Voice proclaiming the first of the Ten Commandments: "I am the Lord your God!"[1]

Other Rabbis proposed that the Torah was not intended for Israel alone but was to be the property of the entire world. Commenting on Exodus 20:15, "And all the people saw the Voices," one Rabbi asked, "Why is the plural, Voices, used in this verse when quite clearly the reference is to the Voice of God. The singular, Voice, should have been used."

Rabbi Yochanan explains that we are to understand from the plural usage that the one Voice, the Voice of God, divided itself into seven, and the seven grew and expanded and emerged as seventy Voices so that all seventy nations of the world would receive the message at the same time. To Rabbi Yochanan the Torah was a universal document, the heritage of all mankind.[2]

Other Rabbis of the Talmud and Midrash present a

scenario in which the Torah was offered to nation after nation. Each refused to accept the Torah when it became aware that the scroll's teachings were in conflict with the nation's lifestyle. Some could not countenance the ban against stealing; others against murder; still others objected to the prohibition against adultery.[3]

Not all Rabbis were convinced that the Torah was eagerly accepted by the Israelites either. In fact, said one Rabbi, God had to force the Torah upon them.[4] In commenting on the verse "And they [the Israelites] stood at the foot of the mountain," Rabbi Avdimi bar Chama declared, "This verse teaches us that God lifted up the mountain and held it over the heads of the Israelites and said to them: 'If you accept the Torah, fine and good; if not, this place will be your burial site. You will be buried under this mountain.'"

In the end, tradition has it, the Israelites did accept the Torah willingly and eagerly, and when it was offered to them, they immediately said, *"Na'aseh ve-nishma* [We will do and we will listen]." So anxious were they to accept the Torah that they agreed to observe its commandments even before they were aware of exactly what those commandments were.[5]

The statement in Deuteronomy 33:4 that the Torah is "the inheritance of the Congregation of Jacob" became a widely accepted doctrine. The Torah became the legacy of the Jewish people. They took the Torah to their hearts. They loved it and guarded it. They studied it and taught it and interpreted it, passing on its teachings from generation to generation.

How the Torah Survived

The Rabbis sought to insure that the sanctity of the Torah would be preserved. They did so by "building a fence [*seyag*] around it."[6] This "fence" is constructed of laws and regulations designed to preserve the message of the Torah and safeguard its teachings. The Rabbis also sought to encourage respectful treatment of the Torah by mandating how each scroll was to be written, and by whom, and upon what kind of material. They also established regulations governing public readings: when the Torah should be read, how much of it should be read, and by whom. And they specified precisely how the Torah should be housed and how it should be dressed.

Perhaps the greatest factor contributing to the longevity of the Torah is the conscious effort made by great Jewish intellectuals to prevent it from becoming obsolete or irrelevant, as has happened to many famous documents of antiquity. In a perpetual search for new meaning, the Torah was constantly studied, analyzed, probed. Every sentence, every word, every letter was dissected and examined. Was a word missing in a sentence? Was a letter missing in a word? Was a word or a phrase repeated unduly? If so, what was the significance of this occurrence? Was there a hidden, deeper meaning to the text?

According to some scholars, it was Ezra the Scribe, of the fifth century B.C.E., who initiated this analytical method of Bible study. They base this on the statement "Ezra had dedicated himself to study the Torah of the Lord so as to observe it and to teach laws and rules to Israel" (Ezra 7:10). The word "study," say the scholars, implies that Ezra analyzed the Torah text in order to determine what the words were intended to teach.

Scholars of the next ten centuries, through the end of the talmudic period (fifth century C.E.), followed in the footsteps of Ezra. Through constant examination they extracted new meaning from old words and learned profound lessons from episodes that had hitherto been unexplored. The result was that the Torah became a *Torat Chayim,* a living Torah, as it has often been called.

Early Interpreters

The most eminent of the early scholars who interpreted the Torah and made it a relevant, living document were Hillel and Shammai of the first century B.C.E. These two giants and their disciples continually clashed in their interpretations of Torah law, Shammai being extremely rigorous and Hillel taking a more liberal and sympathetic approach. Hillel, for example, would permit an *aguna* (one whose husband has disappeared) to remarry even if only indirect evidence of the husband's death has surfaced, while Shammai would insist that witnesses come forward with direct testimony before a new marriage would be allowed.[7]

The interpretations of these scholars and their contemporaries, known as *tannaim,* meaning "teachers," are recorded in the first part of the Talmud, known as the Mishna. In compiling the Mishna, which was completed around the year 220 C.E., Judah the Prince, his co-editor Nathan, and their associates sifted through, evaluated, and edited a vast number of legal opinions that had been expressed over the centuries in the academies of learning, primarily in Palestine.

The second part of the Talmud, known as the Gemara, is a commentary on the Mishna. The scholars whose views are presented in the discussions in the Gemara are known as *amoraim,* meaning "interpreters" or "speakers." For the most part they lived in Babylonia, where the great academies were situated following the destruction of the Temple and the continuing Roman occupation of Palestine. The Gemara of the Babylonian scholars was edited and finalized by Rabina and Ashi and their associates around the year 500 C.E. Together with the Mishna it comprises the Babylonian Talmud.

A second Talmud, the Palestine (or Jerusalem) Talmud, was also created. The Mishna of Rabbi Judah the Prince is the central text of this work as well. However, the Gemara of the Palestinian Talmud consists of the discussions that took place among the *amoraim* in the academies of learning in Palestine. The academies that continued to flourish in Palestine, primarily in Tiberias, during the Roman occupation in the early centuries C.E. were not equal in stature to those of Babylonia, and the Palestinian Talmud therefore enjoys a lesser status than the Babylonian Talmud.

The Palestinian Talmud, which is often called by its Hebrew name, Yerushalmi, meaning "of Jerusalem," is only about one-third the size of the Babylonian Talmud, which is often referred to as the Bavli, meaning "of Babylonia." Only in recent centuries have scholars begun to study the Yerushalmi.

Analysis of Scripture did not cease with the final editing of the Babylonian and Jerusalem Talmuds, and the most important Bible commentary to emerge from the post-talmudic period is a library of books called the Midrash.[8] Each of these books records random comments on the Bible by scholars who lived during the talmudic period. The earliest midrashic volume is Genesis Rabba, composed some time after the final editing of the Talmud in the sixth century, and the last is Yalkut Shimoni, a compilation by Simon Kara, also known as Shimon Ha-darshan, a thirteenth-century scholar who lived in southern Germany. These volumes contain primarily the wisdom and insights of the scholars of Palestine, although many of the sayings, parables, legends, and interpretations were culled from the teachings of Babylonian scholars who were no less ardent students of the Bible.

Classical Commentators

Not until the eleventh century did commentators begin to address themselves to the text of the Torah in sequential fashion. The greatest of these commentators of the Middle Ages was undoubtedly the French scholar *Rabbi Shlomo Yitzchaki* (1040-1105), popularly known as Rashi. He interpreted the Bible literally and achieved renown because of his manner of explaining difficult words and phrases, enabling the student to understand the simple meaning of the text.

Rashi's commentary is profusely illustrated with quotations from the Talmud and Midrash that have a bearing on verses being discussed. All of this earned Rashi the honorary title *parshandata*, Aramaic for "supreme commentator."

Four other medieval commentators, along with Rashi, are considered to be *the* classical Bible commentators. The first of these is a grandson of Rashi, *Rabbi Samuel ben Meir*

(1085-1158), often referred to by the acronym Rashbam. He revered his grandfather and followed his method of presenting the direct, simple meaning of the text. But he avoided interpreting the text in a homiletical (sermonic) manner because, he believed, this might distort the true meaning of the Torah.

Abraham ibn Ezra (1089-1164) was a scholar and poet who lived in Spain until he was fifty years of age and then spent the balance of his life traveling. Ibn Ezra ("son of Ezra"), as he is often called, was an astrologer, physician, and grammarian with a special interest in etymology. Like the Rashbam, he concentrated on uncovering the primary meaning of the text while avoiding homiletical interpretation.

Rabbi David Kimchi (1160-1235), known by the acronym Redak or Radak, was the most prominent member of a family of Hebrew grammarians and translators who were originally from Spain but later settled in southern France. Although primarily concerned with grammar and etymology, Radak's commentary often speculates on moral lessons implicit in the stories of the Bible.

Rabbi Moses ben Nachman (1194-1270), often referred to by the Greek name Nachmanides, "son of Nachman," is best known by the acronym Ramban. Born in Gerona, Spain, he spent his last three years in Acre, Palestine. Extremely well versed in languages, the natural sciences, philosophy, and mysticism, Ramban was a scholar's scholar and earned the approbation "the great lion in the lair of lions." Although in his interpretations of Scripture he favored following the literal meaning of the text, he often interjected a rational or mystical explanation.

Modern Commentators

Outstanding scholars continued to write Torah commentaries in the centuries that followed the classical period. However, none of these individuals reached the stature of the five classical interpreters just described.

In the middle of the eighteenth century biblical scholars produced commentaries that were distinguished by their comprehensiveness and that have been widely accepted by students and laymen alike. Among the most noteworthy are:

Moses Mendelssohn (1729-1786), born in Germany, was highly educated in philosophy, mathematics, and languages. His German translation of the Pentateuch with Hebrew commentary, called *Biur,* meaning "explanation, exposition," was completed in 1783. Mendelssohn's disciples collaborated with him in preparing the commentary, which turned out to be a work of great significance.

Samson Raphael Hirsch (1808-1888), the German-born, university-educated leader of Orthodoxy and rabbi of the Frankfurt-am-Main Jewish community, is regarded as the progenitor of neo-Orthodoxy. Among his scholarly contributions is a five-volume *Translation and Commentary on the Pentateuch,* which appeared in 1878. Hirsch, a strict constructionist, believed that the validity of the Torah is not dependent on time or place and that no commandment or observance may be renounced.

Meir Leibush (Loeb) ben Yechiel Michael (1809-1879), better known by the acronym Malbim, was born in Volhynia, Russia, and served as rabbi of congregations in major European cities. Although he insisted that in interpreting the Torah the literal meaning of the text must not be distorted, he was not averse to interjecting talmudic legal discussions that he felt applied to the actions of a particular biblical character.

Arnold B. Ehrlich (1848-1919), born in Poland, migrated to Germany, where he studied Oriental languages in Berlin. There he helped the Hebrew scholar Franz Delitzsch translate the New Testament into Hebrew. In 1878 he migrated to the United States. Ehrlich's commentary on the Torah and the rest of the Bible, entitled *Mikra Ki-pheshuto* (published in Berlin in 1901), is marked by great originality and displays an extensive knowledge of linguistics.

Joseph Herman Hertz (1872-1946), born in Slovakia, was the first graduate of the Jewish Theological Seminary of America (1894). After serving congregations in New

York and South Africa, he was appointed Chief Rabbi of the British Empire in 1913. His widely used commentary, *Pentateuch and Haftorahs,* was published in England in 1961. Written in English, the Hertz commentary explicates the text by drawing on statements from the Talmud and Midrash, as well as modern sources.

W. Gunther Plaut (1912-) migrated to the United States from Germany. In 1939, he was ordained at Hebrew Union College in Cincinnati and subsequently served Reform congregations in Chicago, St. Paul, and Toronto. His commentary, *The Torah,* reflects a liberal point of view but includes gleanings from the Talmud, Midrash, and classical commentaries, plus insights and observations of modern scholars and commentators.

Nehama Leibowitz (1904-), born in Riga, Latvia, settled in Palestine in 1935. In 1968 she was appointed Professor of Bible at Tel Aviv University. Her six-volume *Studies in the Bible* brings together classical and modern scholarship as it probes some of the more thought-provoking verses and sections of each portion of the Torah. It was originally published in Hebrew, and an English translation by Aryeh Newman appeared in 1973.

Methods of Interpretation

At the very end of the thirteenth century (1291), the Bible scholar Bachya ben Asher of Saragossa noted that there are four ways of interpreting Scripture. These came to be known by the acronym *pardess,* spelled *pay resh dalet samech.*

The *pay* of *pardess* stands for *peshat,* meaning "literal explanation of the text." The commentator seeks to explain the plain meaning of the text and no more.

The *resh* of *pardess* stands for *remez,* meaning "allusion, allegory, symbolism." The commentator compares words and phrases in one part of the Bible to similar words and phrases in other parts of the Bible and draws inferences from them.

The *dalet* of *pardess* stands for *derash,* a form of the

word *midrash,* meaning "interpretation." Here the commentator probes beneath the literal meaning of a word or phrase in order to uncover an ethical or moral lesson that is thought to be implicit in the text.

The *samech* of *pardess* stands for *sod,* meaning "mystery, secret." Kabbalists (mystics) in particular are fond of probing the stories of the Bible to uncover the secrets of the Torah and of life itself.

These methods of interpretation are used in varying degrees and combinations by biblical commentators. The selected verses that follow show how some of these authorities have used these methods of interpretation to resolve obscurities and contradictions in the biblical text and to extract moral lessons from it.

Commentary on Abraham and His Visitors

Genesis 18 tells the story of Abraham and the three men who come to visit him within days after he was circumcised at the age of ninety-nine (Genesis 17:24). Genesis 18:1-2 reads:

> The Lord appeared to him [Abraham] by the oaks of Mamre; he was sitting at the entrance of his tent as the day grew hot. Looking up, he saw three men standing near him; as soon as he saw them, he ran from the entrance of the tent to greet them, bowing to the ground.

Abraham offers the visitors water to bathe their feet and a morsel of food to eat. He then rushes off to arrange for a more elaborate meal of tender calf meat and curds and milk to be served his visitors. Abraham waits upon them as they eat and refresh themselves. The visitors then ask Abraham about his ninety-year-old wife Sarah and promise him that next year at this time she will give birth to a son.

The Rabbis of the Talmud and later scholars found both the details and the language of this episode puzzling.

Commentators were bothered by the first two verses of Chapter 18. The first verse says that God appeared to Abraham; the second, that when Abraham looked up, he saw three men standing near him. Was it God Himself who visited Abraham, they wondered, or was it three men?

Quoting the Talmud,[9] Rashi notes that only three days earlier Abraham had been circumcised, and as he was sitting in the hot sun ("in the heat of the day") recuperating from the procedure, he felt neglected, having had no visitors. God, explains the Talmud,[10] had brought forth a sun so hot that visitors would be discouraged from disturbing Abraham during his recovery period; and here, in Genesis 18:1, Abraham is yearning for company. So God Himself comes to visit the sick. He makes his appearance, however, in the form of three angels dressed as humans.

Maimonides, the famous twelfth-century philosopher and codifier of Jewish law, expressed the belief that in Scripture angels are only seen or heard in a "vision of prophecy" or in a dream. The reader must assume this whether or not it is explicitly stated in the text. In Chapter 18 of Genesis, Maimonides notes, the first verse begins with a general statement: God appears to Abraham in a prophetic vision. Then, as the story unfolds (beginning with the second verse) and Abraham looks up to find three men standing near him, it becomes clear to Abraham that these three men are angels representing God. Verse 2 concretizes the general statement made in the first verse.[11]

Nachmanides is so perturbed by Maimonides' interpretation that he refers to him not by name but only as "the author of the *Moreh Nevuchim* [*Guide for the Perplexed*]." Nachmanides objects to Maimonides' view that the events described in two verses of Genesis are to be taken figuratively: that the conversations did not actually take place as reported but were only part of the prophetic vision experienced by Abraham. The Torah, says Nachmanides, must be taken literally in this instance. Although his interpretations of Scripture are often a combination of the literal and the mystical, here he believed that one must accept the plain text as true.

Ibn Ezra points out that some commentators are of the opinion that in this story God and the three men are one and the same and may not be separated. They fail to note, he says, that later two of these three men (in the form of angels) go on to visit Sodom (Genesis 19:1). Ibn Ezra accepts the view of other classical commentators that God appeared to Abraham in a prophetic vision.

Kabbalists interpret the story of Abraham allegorically. Biblical accounts are not to be taken literally, for they have profound mystical implications.

It is the kabbalistic belief that stories such as those relating to the patriarchs Abraham, Isaac, and Jacob reflect aspects of God's creativity. They exude "sparks" or "emanations" *(sefirot)* which are ten in number and which are the foundation upon which the world rests. In the story of Abraham the emanation called *chesed,* or "lovingkindness," is demonstrated. This is evident in the manner in which Abraham treats his three visitors.[12]

Commentary on the Golden Rule

The language used in Leviticus 19:18, the Golden Rule, raises many questions and invites much commentary.

The verse ends with the admonition *Ve-ahavta lerayacha kamocha,* "And you shall love your neighbor as yourself." What is meant by "neighbor"? A fellow Jew? One's countryman? A fellow human being?

And what is meant by the imperative "love"? How can one be commanded to love?

Thirdly, what is meant by the words "as yourself"? Is it possible to love another as one loves oneself?

Various commentators have chosen to interpret various aspects of the wording of the Golden Rule, although none addresses all of the questions raised above.

In his commentary *Mikra Ki-pheshuto,* Arnold Ehrlich observes that it is a serious error for anyone to assume that the word "neighbor" refers to anyone but an Israelite. He argues that when the Torah says "Love your neighbor as yourself," it means love only your neighbor who is like yourself—namely, "one who is an Israelite, just as you are an Israelite."[13]

Nachmanides comments extensively on Leviticus 19:18

and considers it to be an overstatement. He generally sees the concept of loving one's neighbor as oneself as an ideal, but he cautions against taking the words of the Torah literally. Commenting on "as yourself," he expresses doubt that Jewish law would obligate an individual to endanger his life for another person. Nachmanides points to the statement of Rabbi Akiba, who said that when it comes to a choice between saving one's own life and the life of another, one's own life comes first.[14] However, the commentator adds that man should rejoice for the good fortune of his neighbor. He must never feel jealousy or envy.

Ibn Ezra's interpretation of the commandment, similar to that of Nachmanides, is that the Golden Rule should be understood as meaning that one must wish for his neighbor all the good fortune he wishes for himself.

Nehama Leibowitz, in her commentary,[15] addresses the issue of being *commanded* to love one's fellow man. She notes that Moses Mendelssohn, in his *Biur,* says that "it is hardly conceivable that the Almighty would command that which is beyond human capacity. Feelings such as hate and love are hardly the objects of commands, since they are not under human control." She goes on to point out that Mendelssohn considered Hillel's negative interpretation of the verse, "What is hateful unto you do not do to your neighbor,"[16] to be correct. If one cannot *love* his neighbor, he should at the very least do nothing to him that he would not like done to himself.

The Rashbam also confronted the problem of observing a commandment that demands the impossible—to love one's neighbor as oneself—by saying that this really means that man must love his neighbor only if he is good, but that if he is evil, man has no obligation to do so. What the Rashbam read into the text was not shared by other commentators.

* * *

The range of interpretation that has been given the

Torah by commentators from earliest talmudic times to the present is vast and impressive. And yet, diverse as the interpretations sometimes are, they all fall within the authentic Judaic tradition.

There are numerous legitimate approaches to achieving an understanding and appreciation of the Torah. The Midrash put it very well when it said, "There are seventy faces [facets] to the Torah."[17] To which other Rabbis later added: Whatever any diligent student offers as an interpretation of the Torah may be considered as if it, too, came from Sinai. Professor Abraham J. Heschel summed up those sentiments in this pithy statement: "Judaism is a minimum of revelation and a maximum of interpretation."

* * *

The Torah continues to serve as the moral guide of the Jewish people and as a blueprint for humanity as a whole. In *The Jewish Book of Why: The Torah*, we will explore the origins of this unique document, the methods of interpretation and analysis used in its study, and the many laws and customs that have evolved to preserve its sanctity as the centerpiece of Jewish life.

Chapter 1

The Torah and Its Roots

INTRODUCTION

The primary source of information about the origin of the Torah is the Torah itself.

Chapter 19 of the Book of Exodus gives the following account: After being enslaved in Egypt for centuries, the Children of Israel escape from the "house of bondage" and are miraculously guided in safety through the Sea of Reeds (often confused with the Red Sea). They approach Mount Sinai seven weeks later, in the third month after leaving Egypt.

Moses ascends the mountain while the Children of Israel are encamped below. God speaks to Moses and tells him that the Israelites will be His Chosen People, a holy nation, if they will conduct their lives in purity and be steadfast in their loyalty to Him. This loyalty is to be manifested by the observance of the Torah's commandments *(mitzvot)*.

Moses comes down from the mountain and delivers God's message to the Israelites assembled below, and they respond in unison, "All that God has spoken, we will do." Moses returns to the mountaintop and conveys this response to God. Whereupon God instructs Moses to return to his people and lead them through three days of ritual preparation, at which point God will "come down and appear before them."

Early on the third day there is thunder and lightning, and

17

a thick cloud appears on the mountain. A thunderous blast of the *shofar* is heard, and everyone in the camp trembles.

God descends from the heavens and appears on the summit of Mount Sinai. He calls to Moses, and Moses goes up to meet Him. Moses receives the Ten Commandments and takes them down from the mountaintop to transmit them to the Children of Israel.

This is the essence of the Revelation on Mount Sinai as described in the Bible and as accepted by traditionally minded Jews: God revealed Himself to Moses and then revealed the Torah to the Children of Israel through Moses.

But do all traditionally minded Jews accept this narrative exactly as presented?

Do all believe that what happened at Sinai occurred precisely as the Torah describes?

Did God actually speak to Moses as one man talks to another?

Did Moses actually hear God's voice?

Did God actually hand Moses the Ten Commandments?

Although not all traditionalists describe the Revelation in the same way, their accounts share a common element: the belief that an awesome event transpired at Mount Sinai, an event that defies human understanding. They believe that in that wilderness of Sinai the Jewish people came into possession of the Torah. The precise nature of its original form, how it was received by Moses from God, and how it was transmitted by Moses to the people of Israel are left open to speculation.

The Rabbis of the Talmud offer a wide range of views about the origin of the Torah. There are those who believe that the Torah is older than the world itself, that it existed for 947 generations before the world was created.[1] Others maintain that since the Torah is the epitome of wisdom, God consulted it, in fact was guided by it, when He decided to create the world.[2]

At the other end of the spectrum are traditionalists who

believe that the Torah is a God-inspired document, that its truths are divinely revealed and that it consists of a record of how the earliest Jews conceived of the creation of the world and how they view the relationship between man and his Creator. To them, its essential purpose is to explain how God manifested His presence in history.

The traditionalists can be divided into three groups:

1. *The loose constructionists.* Theirs is the approach to Scripture of the twelfth-century Moses Maimonides. While Maimonides affirmed that what took place on Sinai is beyond human comprehension, he insisted that all biblical descriptions of God as hearing, seeing, speaking, and making appearances must not be taken literally. "To anthropomorphize God is an act of sacrilege," said Maimonides, adding that "whoever conceives of God as a corporeal being is an apostate."[3]

2. *The strict constructionists,* as represented by Rabbi Samson Raphael Hirsch (1808-1888), a German scholar and the founder of neo-Orthodoxy. While Hirsch agrees with Maimonides that what took place at Sinai is incomprehensible, he maintains that every word of the Written Law (Torah) and the Oral Law (Talmud) must be taken literally because both were supernaturally revealed. To the strict constructionists, when the Bible says "And the Lord spoke to Moses," it is to be taken to mean that the Lord actually spoke.[4]

3. *The modernists.* Included in this group are contemporary Orthodox, Conservative, Reform, and Reconstructionist Jews who believe that the Torah is divinely inspired and was written by God-inspired men of exceptional spirituality, men of the caliber of Moses. While modernists believe that the Torah is divine and in that sense comes "from heaven" *(min ha-shama'yim),* they do not necessarily believe that every word or phrase or sentence in the Torah need be taken literally, just as Maimonides did not take the anthropomorphisms literally. They remind us of the statement of Rabbi Jose, a disciple of Rabbi Akiva, that the verse in Exodus (19:3) which describes Moses as "going up" and God as "coming down" to the mountaintop is to be taken figuratively, not literally. In the view of Rabbi Jose, Moses did not go up and God did not come down.[5]

Traditionalists have never spoken with one voice. All authorities do agree, however, that an extraordinary event took place at Mount Sinai, one that transformed the Jewish people from an idolatrous nation into a God-loving one.

———————B———————

Why was it necessary for three months to elapse from the Exodus to the Revelation on Mount Sinai?

The Bible informs us that the Revelation took place in the third month (Sivan) after the Exodus. This amount of time was needed, say the Rabbis, in order to prepare an enslaved people to accept the Torah and to agree to adhere to its commandments.[6]

The Rabbis compared the Children of Israel at that juncture in their history to three types of people: a female proselyte, a woman who had just been freed from captivity, and an emancipated (female) slave. By law, each of these women was not permitted to marry until she had lived for at least three months as a free Jewess. Similarly, say the Rabbis, God insisted that three months had to pass after the deliverance of the Israelites from Egyptian bondage before their state of mind would be such that they might receive the Torah. Only persons free of the slave mentality could appreciate the Torah and enter into a covenant with God.

Why did Jewish mystics believe that there is special astrological significance in the choice of the third day of the third month for God's appearance on Mount Sinai?

Many of the Rabbis of the Talmud were strong believers in astrology, and they saw special meaning in the fact that Chapter 19 of the Book of Exodus reports that the Revelation took place on the third day of the third month (Sivan) following the escape from Egyptian bondage. The Children of Israel had reached Mount Sinai, and Moses is instructed by God to have the Israelites cleanse and purify themselves in preparation for the momentous event that would take place on the third day after their arrival (Exodus 19:11).

Jewish mystics believe that the third day of the third month of the Hebrew calendar (which falls in May-June) was chosen for the physical appearance of God (theophany) and the sixth day of the month (two times three) was chosen for the Revelation of the Torah because they coincide with the appearance of Gemini in the zodiac. A constellation containing the stars Castor and Pollux, Gemini is represented as twins sitting together. That the theophany and the Revelation took place under the twins' sign indicates that the Torah does not belong to the descendants of Jacob (Israel) alone but also to those of his twin brother, Esau, and hence to all mankind.[7]

Why does Jewish tradition claim the Sabbath to be the day on which the Torah was given?

The number seven, like the number three, occupies an important place in Jewish law and lore.[8] It figures prominently in events leading up to the Revelation on Mount Sinai and in various procedures associated with the writing and reading of the Torah.

A strong association is made between the Revelation and the number seven because it was on the seventh day of the week, the Sabbath, that the Rabbis believe the Torah was given. The Talmud[9] states: "All agree that the Torah was given to Israel on the Sabbath Day." And the Rabbis confirm this view by bringing proof from Scripture: When Exodus 20:8 ("Remember the Sabbath Day and keep it holy") refers to the Sabbath, it uses the word "day." We must assume therefore that when Exodus 13:3 ("Remember this day on which you came out of Egypt . . .") uses the word "day" in connection with the Israelites' departure from Egypt, which led to the day of Revelation, it is referring to the Sabbath as well.

Why was Mount Sinai selected as the site of the Revelation?

Mount Sinai, located in the wilderness of Sinai, is the smallest and least significant mountain in the region. Why, then, was Sinai chosen over the other mountains as the site where Moses was to receive the Ten Commandments?

The Rabbis of the Talmud[10] discussed this subject and concluded that the choice of Sinai was not accidental, that it was arrived at after much deliberation, and that its selection was meant to convey a message. The Rabbis envisioned a scenario in which the various mountains in the area carried on a dispute.

Mount Tabor said to Mount Hermon, "I am most deserving to have God's Presence [the *Shechina* in Hebrew] rest upon me because in the days of Noah, when the earth was inundated by flood, only my peak remained above water while all other mountaintops were submerged."

Mount Hermon replied to Mount Tabor, "I am the one upon whom God's Presence should rest, for when the Children of Israel passed through the Sea of Reeds, it was I who enabled them to accomplish this remarkable feat. I placed myself in the middle of the sea, making it possible for the Israelites to pass through on dry land. Even their clothes did not get wet."

Mount Carmel was silent. It settled down partly on the shore and partly in the sea, thinking to itself, "If the *Shechina* appears on the sea, it will rest upon me; and if it will come to the mainland, it will rest upon me."

A voice then rang out from heaven: "The *Shechina* will not rest upon high mountains that are so proud. It will rest upon a low, modest mountain that does not look upon others with disdain. It will rest upon Sinai because it is the smallest and most self-effacing of all."

When this decision was announced, the other mountains protested, "Are we to receive no reward for our good intentions?"

"You too will be rewarded," God replied. "Upon you, Mount Tabor, I will aid Israel in the days of Deborah, and upon you, Mount Carmel, I will support Elijah in his battle with Baal."

The Rabbis add that Mount Sinai was shown preference over the other mountains not because of its humility alone, but also because it had never been used for idol worship. Idol worshipers established altars only on tall mountains, hoping thereby to be closer to their gods.

Why was the Torah given to Israel in the wilderness of Sinai rather than in the Land of Israel?

The Rabbis were puzzled that the Torah was given to the Children of Israel on the top of a small mountain in the midst of the wilderness of Sinai rather than in the Promised Land, the future Land of Israel. They concluded that the wilderness was purposely selected so as to indicate that the teachings of the Torah were not intended exclusively for Israel but for the benefit of all mankind.[11]

Why is the Revelation at Mount Sinai a reaffirmation of God's Covenant with Abraham?

Genesis 12:1-3 describes the Covenant God made with Abraham (Abram): Abraham is instructed to go forth and spread God's name throughout the world, and as a reward he and his descendants will be blessed forever. Centuries later, during the course of the Revelation at Sinai, the Covenant was reaffirmed and its terms restated (Exodus 19:5-6): If Israel will be faithful to God and obey the commandments, God will treasure them and reward them. As God's Chosen People, they will become a kingdom of Priests and a holy nation.

In Jewish tradition, the Covenant is regarded as a permanent link between the past and the present. It can never be dissolved. All Jews come under its umbrella by virtue of the fact that they are of the "seed of Abraham."[12] The Jewish people thus became the "holy seed" (zera kodesh), and the members of this holy fellowship became known as the Covenant People. It matters not whether an individual Jew remains fully observant of Jewish law. Membership in the holy fellowship cannot be denied one who is of the seed of Abraham.

Why is the mountain on which the Revelation took place known by a variety of names?

The mountain on which the Revelation took place is known by six different names, each based upon one of the names given to the desert in which Mount Sinai is located. Using homiletical license, the Talmud[13] explains the reason behind the selection of each name. The mountain is called

- Tzin because God announced His commandments there. The name Tzin is connected to the word *tziva,* meaning "He commanded."
- Kadesh because Israel was sanctified there. The name Kadesh is connected with the word *kadosh,* meaning "holy, sanctified."
- Kadmut because the Torah, which had existed from the time of Creation, was finally revealed there. The name Kadmut is connected with the word *kodem* or *keduma,* meaning "early, ancient."
- Paran because it was there that the numbers of Israelites greatly increased. The name Paran is connected with the word *paru,* meaning "and they multiplied."
- Sinai because it was there that God's hatred of heathens began. The name Sinai is connected with the word *sin'a,* meaning "hatred [toward idolators]."
- Chorev (Horeb) because the annihilation of heathens was decreed there by God. The name Chorev (Horeb) is connected with the word *churba* or *churban,* meaning "desolation, destruction."

Why did Moses remain atop Mount Sinai for forty days and forty nights?

Surely, said the Rabbis, it did not require forty days and forty nights to inscribe the Ten Commandments on the two tablets of stone. And if it did not, they questioned, why did Moses stay on Mount Sinai for so long?

By way of explanation, these talmudic scholars point out that Moses tarried on the mountaintop for forty days because not only were the Ten Commandments received by him at that time but the entire Torah was communicated to him as well. This included the Pentateuch, also called the Written Law *(Torah She-bichtav)*, and its commentary the Talmud, also called the Oral Law *(Torah She-be'al Peh)*.[14]

Two scholars of the first century C.E., Rabbi Yochanan and his favorite pupil, Rabbi Elazar ben Arach, give a more mystical reason for Moses having remained atop Mount Sinai for forty days and forty nights.[15] The Torah is the essence of the Jewish people, they said, just as the embryo is the essence of the human being. Because forty days are required for the embryo to become viable, it was required that Moses spend forty days on Mount Sinai to establish the Torah.[16]

Why did Moses go to the top of Mount Sinai a second time?

After spending forty days and forty nights atop Mount Sinai, Moses received two stone tablets inscribed by God with the Ten Commandments (Exodus 31:18). God then tells Moses that the Israelites had sinned, that in his absence they had erected and were worshiping a Golden Calf (Exodus 32:7-8).

Moses rushes down from the mountaintop, and upon seeing the Golden Calf, he smashes the two tablets, sets the Golden Calf afire, and grinds the molten remains into a powder. He then spreads this powder upon the drinking water and makes the people drink it (Exodus 32:20).

After pleading with God to forgive the Israelites, Moses

is told to return to the mountaintop with two new tablets and to inscribe on them the same words as appeared on the first tablets. Once again Moses remains on the mountain for forty days and forty nights, during which time, he (this time Moses) inscribes the words of the Ten Commandments on the tablets (Exodus 34:28).

Why have many theories been advanced as to the precise words uttered on Mount Sinai?

Since it is widely (although not universally) accepted that when the Bible refers to the voice of God it speaks metaphorically rather than literally, there has been much speculation as to what was actually uttered by the Voice and heard by the people at the base of Mount Sinai.

Among the theories advanced are:

- The whole of the Ten Commandments were heard.
- Only the first two of the Ten Commandments were heard.
- Only the first word *(anochi)* of the first commandment was heard.
- Only the first letter *(alef)* of the first word of the Decalogue was heard.

Why is a scholar sometimes referred to as a Sinai?

In Jewish tradition a scholar who is thoroughly versed in Torah and in Jewish law *(halacha)* is sometimes called a Sinai.[17] The reason, of course, is that the Torah comes from Sinai, and he who has thoroughly mastered its contents in the order given at Sinai merits this appellation.

In recent times a celebrated Austrian scholar, Harry Torczyner, who moved from Vienna to Palestine in 1910, assumed the name (Naphtali Herz) Tur Sinai. *Tur* is Aramaic for "mountain."

Why do kabbalists compare the marriage ceremony to events that transpired on Mount Sinai?

Jewish mystics (kabbalists) believe that the formal marriage ceremony is an imitation of what transpired at Mount Sinai when the Torah was given to Israel. Exodus 19:17 says, "Moses led the people out of the camp toward God, and they took their place at the foot of the mountain." God (the bridegroom) then came down from heaven to meet His bride (the Children of Israel). Mystics therefore taught that just as God came down from heaven and reached the top of Mount Sinai before Moses (who represented the Israelites), so must a bridegroom always take his place under the wedding canopy first and there await his bride.

In some communities the Sabbath before Shavuot is called Shabbat Kalah, "The Bridal Sabbath," while in other communities (this was true especially in earlier centuries) any Sabbath that precedes a wedding is referred to by this name.[18]

Why was Moses selected as the one through whom the Torah was to be revealed?

Just as the Rabbis believed that Mount Sinai was chosen as the site of the Revelation because of its unassuming presence, so was Moses selected to be the transmitter of the Torah because of his humility.

The Rabbis envisioned a scenario in which God says to Moses, "Go forth and set Israel free."

Moses in his humility replies, "Who am I that I should be selected to lead the Children of Israel out of Egypt (Exodus 3:11)? There are more noble and more worthy ones than I to be assigned such a task!"

But God replies, "You are a great man, and you have I chosen!"

However, Moses, true to his modest nature, persists in refusing, until God says to him, "If Israel is to be liberated, you are the one to do it. No one else can free them."[19]

Why has Moses not been deified?

Moses, the great Lawgiver and emancipator, the master Prophet in Jewish history, was the man who, the Bible says, received the Ten Commandments directly from God. Yet, in Jewish tradition Moses is just another mortal, with no divine attributes. The Torah (Numbers 12:3) refers to him simply as "the man Moses."

The Sages explain that the precise burial place of Moses was kept secret so that future generations would not be tempted to worship at his grave, leading ultimately to his deification. Throughout the ages the Rabbis were concerned about the possible overglorification of any mortal, particularly Moses. This is why in the entire Passover Haggada, which tells the story of the Exodus (in which Moses is the principal figure), the name of Moses appears only once and then merely as part of a biblical reference.

Maimonides summed up the traditional Jewish attitude toward Moses the Prophet when he wrote that Jews do not believe in the *man* Moses; they believe only in the *prophecy* of the man Moses.[20]

Why has it been said that Israel was not actually chosen by God to receive the Torah?

The first-century leader of Palestinian Jewry, Rabbi Yochanan, says that Israel was not actually chosen by God to receive the Torah. Israel, he says, did the choosing. He bases this view on verses in Deuteronomy (33:2) and Habakkuk (3:3) which he interprets to mean that God offered the Torah to every nation and they refused it. He then offered the Torah to the Children of Israel, who accepted it. Thus, Israel chose God.[21]

Why was the Torah rejected by many peoples before it was accepted by Israel?

According to an early Jewish legend,[22] before God gave the Torah to Israel he offered it to many tribes so they would never be able to say, "Had God given us the Torah, we would surely have accepted it."

God approached the Children of Esau and asked, "Will you accept the Torah?"

"What is written in it?" they queried.

"You shall not murder," God replied.

The Children of Esau asked, "Do you plan to deny us the blessing bestowed upon our father Esau? He was blessed with the words, 'By your sword shall you live.' We cannot accept the Torah [because it denies us the right to commit murder]."

God then went to the Children of Lot and offered them the Torah. "What is written in it?" they asked.

"You shall not commit unchastity," God replied.

"We are descended from unchastity," they responded. "We cannot accept the Torah."

Then God approached the Children of Ishmael and said, "Will you accept the Torah?"

"What is written in it?" they asked.

"You shall not steal," God replied.

"Will you deny us the blessing of our father?" they responded. "Our father was promised that 'his hand will be against every man.' We cannot accept the Torah."

Then God came to Israel and said, "Will you accept the Torah?"

"What is written in it?" they asked.

God answered, "It contains 613 commandments [mitzvot]."

The Children of Israel responded, "All that the Lord has commanded we shall do and obey."

Why is the carrying of candles in a wedding procession associated with the giving of the Torah?

Among the Jews of the first century, the bride was accompanied by bridesmaids carrying torches. (An essential part of the marriage ceremony among Romans of that time was the passing of a torch. Light was a symbol of purity.) In some communities today it is customary for the escorts of the groom to carry lighted candles down the aisle during the marriage ceremony. One interesting explanation relates the tradition of carrying lighted candles to the giving of the Ten Commandments by God to Israel at Mount Sinai. "There were voices and lightning and a thick cloud on the mountain," says the Bible (Exodus 19:15). The candles are thought to be reminders of the lightning that filled the sky when Israel (the bride) accepted God (the bridegroom).

Why did the Rabbis link Shavuot with the Revelation on Mount Sinai?

The Bible does not associate the holiday of Shavuot with God's Revelation on Mount Sinai, but the Talmud does. The connection was made after the Rabbis observed that the agricultural festival of Shavuot and the events at Mount Sinai occurred in the same season of the year.

Possibly the first Rabbi of the Talmud to refer to Shavuot as "the time of the giving of the Torah [*Zeman Mattan Toratenu*]" is the third-century C.E. scholar Rabbi Eleazar. He noted that all authorities agree on the necessity of rejoicing with good wine and food on Atzeret (the talmudic name for Shavuot) because on that day the Torah was given to Israel.[23]

After the association between Shavuot and the Revelation on Mount Sinai had been firmly established, the one-time agricultural holiday became the annual occasion to celebrate the giving of the Torah. Torah study sessions were held all through the night of the holiday, and the holiday was highlighted as a time for Jewish affirmation.

Why is a special Torah study period held on the night of Shavuot?

An old custom, now growing in popularity, is for members of a congregation to assemble on the first night of Shavuot and to study the Torah far into the night.

The origin of this practice dates back to the sixteenth

century when, while the noted kabbalist and mystic Solomon Alkabetz of Safed was studying the Torah with his colleague Joseph Caro on the night of Shavuot, the *maggid* (a heavenly power that reveals secrets to a kabbalist) appeared to Caro in a vision. This was taken as a sign that it was desirable to stay awake on the night of Shavuot and study the Torah. The custom became popular from that time onward.

The all-night study period, the purpose of which was to achieve self-improvement, became known as *tikun layl shavuot* (*tikun* means "improvement"). A book entitled *Tikun Layl Shavuot* was later composed for use during the night. The anthology contains selections from the beginning and the end of each of the books of the Bible, the tractates of the Talmud, and the *Zohar* as well as poetic prayers *(piyyutim)* referring to the 613 *mitzvot* (commandments).[24]

Why is Shavuot called *Zeman Mattan Toratenu?*

Zeman Mattan Toratenu means "the time of the *giving* of the Torah." Some chassidic teachers have wondered why the Shavuot holiday was not called *Zeman Kabbalat Toratenu*, meaning "the time of the *receiving* of the Torah." Rabbi Menachem Mendel of Kotzk, a nineteenth-century chassidic Polish leader, explained that that which was *given* was the same for everyone but that which was *received* differed from person to person. Each experienced the Revelation in his own way.

Why is Confirmation celebrated on Shavuot?

In the nineteenth century, Reform congregations in Germany substituted a ceremony they called Confirmation (probably inspired by practices of the Christian Church) for the Bar Mitzva ceremony. They contended that age thirteen, when the Bar Mitzva is celebrated, is too early for a boy to be ushered into the Jewish fold. They felt that at age sixteen or seventeen a teenager is better equipped to understand the teachings of the Torah.

Today, quite appropriately, Confirmation is celebrated on Shavuot, the holiday associated with the giving of the Torah. The ceremony is held in Reform, Conservative, and occasionally in modern Orthodox congregations. Boys and girls between the ages of thirteen and eighteen participate, depending on the custom of each individual synagogue.

Why are dairy foods associated with the day on which the Torah was given?

According to an ancient legend, dairy foods are eaten on Shavuot, the day on which the Torah was given, because when the Israelites reached their homes after receiving the Torah at Mount Sinai, they had little time to prepare a meat meal (a good deal of time is required for the slaughtering of an animal). Instead, they hastily put together a dairy meal, which could be prepared more quickly.[25]

Why are *blintzes* associated with the Ten Commandments?

Traditionally, two *blintzes* are served on Shavuot, and these are said to represent the two tablets on which the Ten Commandments were inscribed. Because *blintzes* are usually made with a cheese filling, they have become associated with Shavuot, the day on which the Torah was given, in fulfillment of the words of the Song of Songs (4:11), "honey and milk under thy lips." This is said to imply that just as milk products are pleasant and good for our spirits, so too are the words of the Torah.[26]

Why is the color green associated with the giving of the Torah?

According to an ancient tradition, Mount Sinai was once a green mountain with trees and shrubs. This led to the custom of decorating the synagogue with greenery on

Shavuot, the holiday associated with the giving of the Torah.[27]

Not all authorities approved of this practice, considering it to be an imitation of Gentile customs. Chief among its opponents was the famous eighteenth-century Gaon of Vilna. He recognized the use of greenery in home and church rites as symbolizing the birth and growth of Christianity. Not only was the custom of using Christmas trees and wreaths widespread in Christian homes, but the Church itself introduced greenery on Pentecost Sunday (fifty days after Easter) to symbolize new growth. On this Sunday, called Whitsunday (short for White Sunday), candidates for baptism were robed in white to symbolize forgiveness from sins and were then baptized. Some European churches still schedule the majority of their baptisms on this Sunday.

Being well aware of this association, the Gaon of Vilna forbade the introduction of greenery into the synagogue. His view, however, did not prevail, for to other authorities greenery carried positive symbolism in Judaism. To many, greenery was associated with the baskets of first fruits brought to the Temple on Shavuot. To others, trees symbolized the Torah itself, for in Scripture the Torah is spoken of as a "tree of life."

On Shavuot today, almost all synagogues are decorated with greenery.

Why is it possible for scholars to believe that Moses was the author of the Torah despite obvious internal inconsistencies?

Since talmudic times, one of the major problems with which traditionalists have had to deal concerns the closing verses of the Book of Deuteronomy (34:5-12), which describe the death of Moses. How could Moses, the sole author of the Bible according to tradition, have described his own death?

Many answers to this question have been proposed.

The Talmud says[28] that Moses did not write Deuteronomy's concluding verses. They were written by Joshua, the successor of Moses. This, of course, does not sustain the view that Moses authored the *entire* Torah.

Other talmudic scholars proposed that God dictated the entire Torah to Moses, who wrote the verses describing his death word for word. And, they add, as Moses wrote, tears streamed from his eyes; he was overcome by grief.[29]

The second-century C.E. Jewish philosopher Philo believed that the spirit of God enveloped Moses and that he was able to foresee his own death. Thus, it is conceivable that Moses was able to write the description of his last days, as found in Deuteronomy 34.[30]

Why do traditionalists believe that every word in the Torah has many facets?

Kabbalists, particularly from the sixteenth century onward, were fond of probing every word and letter of the Torah, searching for new insights and ferreting out new meanings. In examining verse 37 of Exodus 12, which states that 600,000 adult Israelites were freed from Egypt, the kabbalists concluded that that number also applies to the number of interpretations possible for every word in the Torah. "Every word in the Torah has 600,000 facets," they said, a conclusion arrived at based on the biblical statement that each person present in the Sinai wilderness (Exodus 12:37) experienced the Revelation in his own way.

This interpretation was first expressed in the Talmud by Rabbi Levi.[31] In commenting on Psalms 29:4, which reads, "The voice of the Lord is power," he explained that "power" means "according to the power of each individual; according to the individual power of the young, the old, and the small children." That the voice of God reached every individual and was understood in accordance with the power (ability) of each to perceive and comprehend has become a popular way of interpreting the happenings at Mount Sinai.

The Maharal of Prague, Rabbi Judah Loew ben Betzalel (1512-1609), creator of the Golem, was an advocate of

Rabbi Levi's view. In commenting on the verse in the Bible which says that God *descended* to the top of Mount Sinai, the Maharal points out that because God is generally conceived of as being without physical form, the thought of God *descending* is absurd. Each individual will therefore interpret the term "descending" based on his own experience and in keeping with the powers of his own imagination.[32]

Why was Baruch (Benedict) Spinoza excommunicated?

Baruch Spinoza (1632-1677), a Dutch philosopher who was descended from a family of Portuguese Marranos, was excommunicated in 1656 by the Sephardic rabbinate of Amsterdam, Holland, for denying the Mosaic authorship of the Torah. Spinoza was one of the earliest initiators of biblical criticism, and his book *Tractatus Theologico-Politicus* pointed to internal biblical contradictions. He is generally regarded as the founder of Higher Criticism (see next question).

The action of the rabbinical court was consistent with the view of talmudic scholars who had been quite explicit in their condemnation of all who did not believe that the Torah was dictated by God to Moses.[33] Their condemnation included all those who, like Spinoza, would suggest that the Torah was not revealed in its totality from Heaven (God).

Why do some scholars subscribe to the Documentary Theory of the Bible?

Scholars like Spinoza, who question the theology and literary makeup of the Bible, belong to what is known as the School of Higher Criticism, sometimes referred to as the School of Historical Criticism. They are concerned less with the accuracy of the language of the Bible text than with authorship, dates of writing, and concepts. The work of the Higher Critics is rejected by most traditionalists, who maintain that the Torah was divinely given.

One of the chief concerns of Higher Criticism is the composition of the Bible. It does not accept as fact the authorship of the Bible attributed to Moses in the Book of Exodus. Instead, this school subscribes to what has come to be known as the Documentary Theory of the Bible. As explained below, this theory conceives of the first five books of the Bible as having been drawn from various sources composed in different time periods. This material, these scholars contend, was brought together by editors who created what today is referred to as the Pentateuch, Torah, Five Books of Moses, or Chumash. According to this theory, the Pentateuch achieved its final form at about the time of Ezra the Scribe, in the middle of the fifth century B.C.E.

The Documentary Theory grew out of the observation that because of the many internal contradictions in the biblical text, the Torah must have come from more than one source.[34] As an example, the Higher Critics cite Genesis, Chapters 5 to 9, which tell the story of the flood in the time of Noah, and point to the large number of contradictory statements found there:

- Genesis 6:19 says that Noah took one pair of all animals into the ark, whereas Genesis 7:2 says that seven pairs of all clean animals and one pair of unclean animals were taken in.
- Genesis 7:17 and 8:6 narrate that the rain that flooded the earth lasted for forty days, whereas in Genesis 7:24 it is written that "the waters swelled on the earth for 150 days."
- Genesis 8:8-12 writes of Noah sending out a dove to see if the flood had ended, whereas Genesis 8:7 speaks of a raven having been sent out.

Why do traditionalists generally reject the Documentary Theory of the Bible?

Most traditionalists dismiss out of hand the Documentary Theory advocated by the Higher Critics. They believe that the Bible comes from a divine source despite the anachronisms and inconsistencies that it may contain. And they reject outright the contention that some sections of the Torah, primarily the Book of Leviticus, were written much later than others.

Leviticus, say the traditionalists, is a continuation of the narrative in the Book of Exodus. They argue that the fact that Leviticus deals with concepts and institutions that were common to the post-wilderness period and the fact that it uses language associated with the Babylonian exile and post-exile periods (after the sixth century B.C.E.) does not constitute proof that the book was written by anyone other than Moses.

Traditionalists do not feel compelled to explain every inconsistency that may be found in the Bible. What may appear contradictory, they contend, may indeed be contradictory *only to us* because we cannot comprehend the deeper meaning of the text. If words appear in the Bible, goes the traditional view, they are there because that is what God dictated to Moses.

In studying the Bible, traditionalists generally believe that one must accept the following as axiomatic:

- The Bible does not follow an exact chronology: what is detailed earlier may have actually happened later and vice versa.[35]
- The Torah speaks in the language of man. Words and concepts must not be analyzed scientifically. Their sole purpose is to explain God's law.[36]

Why do most traditionalists generally accept the scholarship of Lower Critics?

Scholars who are concerned primarily with establishing a correct text of the Bible are called Lower Critics or Textual Critics, as opposed to the Higher Critics mentioned above. Their work is accepted by most traditionalists because their concern is in establishing the correct original text of the Bible as they believe it was given by God through Moses.

One of the leading Lower Critics was Samuel David

Luzzatto (1800-1865), better known by the acronym Shadal. Shadal was an Italian scholar who, as a professor at the Padua Rabbinical College, taught Bible, Hebrew grammar, philology, philosophy, and liturgy. Drawing on the commentaries of earlier scholars, he emended the biblical text to eliminate errors that had crept in over the centuries. Shadal called attention particularly to the incorrect separation of words, transposed letters (metathesis), and incorrect vocalization and cantillation (musical notation).

Why do the letters J and E have special significance to Higher Critics?

The letters J and E are used by Higher Critics to identify two categories of documents of which they believe the Torah was composed.[37]

The letter J stands for the English word Jehova, which in Hebrew is spelled and pronounced *Yehova*. Since Jewish tradition considers *Yehova* to be the real name of God, it placed a ban on its use to avoid its being pronounced in vain, and whenever that name appears it is read as *Adonai*.

The letter E stands for *Elohim*. In the Torah, particularly in the Book of Genesis, both *Adonai* and *Elohim* are names used for God.

The first chapter of Genesis uses the name *Elohim* exclusively. The second chapter of Genesis introduces the name *Adonai* as well as the compound name *Adonai Elohim*. The third chapter continues this trend, with the exception of verse 1, which uses the name *Elohim* alone. Chapter 4 employs only the word *Adonai* when referring to God. Chapter 5 refers back to *Elohim*. Chapter 6 uses both *Adonai* and *Elohim*.

This is the pattern of the use of the divine name in the Book of Genesis.

In 1753, the French biblical scholar Jean Astruc, who was also physician to King Louis XIV, took note of the usage of the words *Adonai* and *Elohim* in Genesis. Citing this as proof, he maintained that the narrative in Genesis in fact came from two independent sources. One source used *Elohim* for God, and its documents became known as the E documents. The other source employed Jehova *(Yehova)*, and its writings became known as the J documents.

Jean Astruc is considered by many to be the first of the Higher Critics.

Why are the letters P and D significant in biblical scholarship?

In the years following Jean Astruc's discovery, Higher Critics pursued his line of research and uncovered two more categories of biblical documents. These categories were named P and D, and together with J and E they are said to form the backbone of the entire Pentateuch.

The letter P stands for priestly because the category of documents to which it refers is known as the Priestly Code. Much of this material comprises the Book of Leviticus, which details the rules pertaining to the functioning of the Priests in the sanctuary and discusses man's relationship with God.

Material ascribed to the P documents is not found exclusively in Leviticus, however. Passages from other parts of the Bible, such as the rainbow representing the Covenant between God and man as described in Genesis (9:1-17) and the genealogies in various parts of the Torah, are ascribed to this priestly source as well because they bear a stylistic kinship with Leviticus. Some nineteenth-century scholars believe that the P documents were written in the sixth century B.C.E. and that they are the oldest source from which the Pentateuch was derived.[38]

The letter D represents the fourth category of documents of the Pentateuch. This category is so named because it is the source from which Deuteronomy, the fifth book of the Bible, is basically drawn. It should also be noted that scholars claim that other parts of the Torah are also written in the style of the D documents and hence are assumed to be derived from this source.[39]

Chapter 2

Sanctifying the Torah Scroll

INTRODUCTION

The teachings of the Torah, and Jewish tradition in general, are directed toward one primary purpose: to encourage the Jewish people to achieve a state of holiness by emulating God. Verse 2 in Chapter 19 of Leviticus spells out this goal in precise, unmistakable language: "You shall be holy, for I the Lord your God am holy."

This concept is repeated in Leviticus 22:31-32:

> You shall observe My commandments diligently; I am the Lord. You shall not profane My holy name that I may be sanctified in the midst of the people of Israel. I am the Lord Who sanctifies you.

The German-Austrian Bible scholar Adolf Jellinek (1821-1893) categorized these verses as "Israel's Bible in miniature."

The third-century Babylonian scholar Rabbi Chama interpreted these various verses in Leviticus to mean that one must imitate God, a concept which later popularly came to be known by the Latin term *imitatio Dei*. Rabbi Chama said that to believe in God means to behave like God: "Just as He is righteous, so must you be righteous; just as He is compassionate, so must you be compassionate. . . ."[1]

To impress this concept of holiness upon all Jews for all time the Rabbis created a ladder of holiness, and they placed on the very top rung the Torah itself. The Torah scroll that is written specifically for reading at public services is the most sanctified object in Jewish life, and any other article that is associated with it, even remotely, is likewise invested with a degree of sanctity.

But not all religious articles are of equal rank. Thus, the Talmud tells us[2] that one may not sell a Torah scroll to purchase secondary books of the Bible (those in the Prophets or Holy Writings). Nor may one sell these secondary books of Scripture to buy Torah wrappings (mantle, *gartl,* and so on). Nor may one sell these wrappings to buy an ark to house the Torah. Nor may one sell an ark and use its proceeds to buy a synagogue building.

The rule governing this hierarchy of sanctity established by the Rabbis is: One may raise a religious article from one level of sanctity to another, but one may not lower the status of an article. This rule governs not only the buying and selling of holy articles, as mentioned above, but also their use and disposition. Thus, one may not salvage any part of the parchment of a Torah scroll and use it to write *tefilin* or *mezuzot. Tefilin* are of lower sanctity than a Torah; *mezuzot* of lower sanctity than *tefilin.*[3]

This chapter discusses the variety of laws and traditions that were established to sanctify the Torah and everything associated with it.

---□---

Why must the Torah scrolls used in the synagogue today be handwritten on parchment?

From earliest times, the Torah scrolls used for public synagogue readings were handwritten on parchment, and that tradition has become law. The Sages were opposed to any deviation from practices instituted by earlier generations—anything that would diminish the sacredness of the Torah. To further enhance the holy character of the scrolls used in the synagogue, the Rabbis insisted that the parchment and ink used be specially prepared and that a precise method of writing be employed.[4] Above all, the scribe must address his task with conscious intent. See Chapter Four, Writing the Torah.

Why is it forbidden to use metal instruments to write a Torah?

Instruments made of iron and steel were generally associated with war and violence, and the Rabbis therefore forbade the use of metal instruments when writing a Torah scroll. They based their ruling on Scripture (Exodus 20:21-22), which prescribes that the altar upon which sacrifices are offered not be built of hewn stones. Whole stones had to be used, "for by wielding your tool [made of iron] upon them [the stones] you have profaned them."

The purpose of the altar, say the Rabbis, is to bring peace between Israel and God, and nothing should be used in its construction that is used for destructive purposes. The Rabbis explain: "Iron was created to shorten man's life; the altar was created to prolong man's life."[5]

Following similar reasoning, later Rabbis extended this ban to the use of printing presses for the printing of Torah scrolls, *tefilin,* and *mezuzot* because metal type makes contact with the parchment. Only a quill taken from a kosher fowl, such as a goose or turkey, is acceptable as the writing instrument for religious articles.

Why is it forbidden to use an incomplete Torah scroll at a public reading?

Handwritten scrolls which included only one of the Five Books of Moses rather than the entire Pentateuch were often prepared for purposes of study because it would have been cumbersome to carry around a heavy scroll containing all five books. The Rabbis ruled that such scrolls could not be used for public readings because an incomplete scroll is less holy than a scroll containing all Five

Books of Moses. To use an incomplete scroll would show disrespect for the congregation.[6]

In addition, the Rabbis forbade the use of individual scrolls of the Torah in place of a single scroll containing all five books because, they believed, use of individual scrolls might represent an indignity to the Torah itself, for it might convey the idea that an individual book of the Torah is as important as all five books.[7]

Why do many congregations read from the same Torah scroll each week?

Although in the arks of most congregations there are many Torot, one scroll is generally read from week after week. A particular Torah may be favored because it has large script and is easier to read or because it is lighter in weight and easier to lift and carry.

While these reasons are valid, in the opinion of some authorities reading from one scroll does not accord with the tradition that every scroll in an ark is of equal sanctity and should therefore be given equal recognition. In addition, reading from the same scroll each week makes it impossible to detect errors that may be present in the other scrolls in the ark and that should be corrected as required by law.[8]

Why is it improper to place a prayerbook on a Bible?

Jewish law established degrees of sanctity that apply to religious articles. The Torah scroll ranks highest, and therefore no other object may be placed on it.

The same applies to printed books. A printed Chumash is the most sacred of all books, and accordingly the Prophets, the Holy Writings, the tractates of the Talmud, or any other book of lower status may not be placed on it.

The principle of Jewish law followed here was first stated in the Talmud: "One may elevate [upgrade] sacred articles [to a higher degree of sanctity], but one may not lower [downgrade] them."[9]

The Talmud,[10] in discussing the relative sanctity of the Pentateuch, the Prophets, and the Holy Writings, notes specifically that *megillot,* which are part of the Holy Writings, may not be placed on top of the Torah or the Prophets.

Why is the Torah carried with the right arm?

The Rabbis of the Talmud[11] ruled that a Torah must be carried with the right arm and, when passed from one person to another, must be received on the right side.

Perhaps this rabbinical ruling is simply a reflection of the fact that most people are right-handed and that the right arm is therefore stronger. However, Jewish tradition generally bases its rulings on Scripture.

In the case of carrying the Torah, the Rabbis base their ruling on Deuteronomy 33:2, which reads: "The Lord came from Sinai . . . lightning flashing from His right." The Rabbis believed that this refers to the side from which God handed the Torah to Moses on Mount Sinai. This view is also expressed in the *Zohar,* where Rabbi Judah declared that the Torah was given from the side of power, the right side.[12]

Any number of examples are to be found in Scripture to support the view that the right hand and right side are preferred to the left. In Genesis 48, Joseph brings his sons Manasseh and Ephraim to his father, Jacob, for a blessing. Joseph stations Manasseh, the older son, opposite Jacob's right side so that Jacob will be forced to bless him with his right hand. But Jacob preferred Ephraim to Manasseh, and so he crossed his hands, resting his right hand on Ephraim, the younger son.

Leviticus 8:22-26 reveals the importance of the right hand and the right side as it describes one of the ceremonies connected with the sacrificial system. Moses dabbed the blood of the sacrificial ram on the lobe of Aaron's right ear, on the thumb of his right hand, and on the big toe of his right foot. Moses then followed the same procedure with the sons of Aaron.[13]

Over the centuries the right side has continued to assume great significance in Jewish law, so much so that the *Code of Jewish Law*[14] prescribes that one must put on his right shoe first. When washing one's hands before pronouncing a blessing, water is to be poured on the right hand first. When putting on "hand" *tefilin*, it is placed on the left arm (by right-handed persons), leaving the right hand free to wrap the *tefilin* straps around it. When affixing a *mezuza*, it is to be attached to the right doorpost.

It is interesting to note that for many centuries the Christian Church considered left-handed persons to be deviants.

See page 155 for more on the importance of the right side in Torah tradition.

Why is one forbidden to touch a Torah scroll with bare hands?

The *Code of Jewish Law* specifies that one may not touch a Torah scroll with bare hands,[15] but it offers no reason for this prohibition. The rule was probably instituted to instill an attitude of respect toward the Torah.

It has become accepted Torah etiquette that when one is required to touch the Torah parchment, as before reciting the Torah blessings, the touching be done with a prayerbook or Bible or with the fringe of a talit or the edge of a Torah mantle. The Torah reader uses a Torah pointer in order to avoid touching the parchment.

Why do some people believe that if a menstruant touches a Torah scroll, the Torah becomes unfit for further use?

Many people mistakenly believe that since a menstruant may not cohabit with her husband because she is considered to be in a state of impurity, any holy object she touches—especially a Torah—becomes unclean and unfit for use. That this is not the case is clearly implied in the statement of Rabbi Judah ben Bathyra, who said, "Words of the Torah are not susceptible to uncleanness."[16] No individual, not even one who is ritually impure, can defile a Torah by touching or handling it.

A woman in a state of ritual impurity may hold or kiss a Torah, just as she is permitted to touch and kiss a *mezuza*, which contains a parchment with writings from the Torah.

Why is it permissible to allow non-Jews to handle a Torah scroll?

In many communities it is customary for groups of non-Jewish schoolchildren and adults to visit synagogues in order to learn about Jewish customs and ceremonies. On such occasions a Torah scroll is often removed from the ark so that the visitors may inspect it. While some authorities oppose this practice, the Talmud states clearly that a Torah scroll cannot be made ritually unclean regardless of who handles it.[17] This is emphasized by Moses Maimonides, who wrote that anyone may handle a Torah scroll and read from it, even a non-Jew.[18]

Why did the Rabbis permit the Torah to be translated into Greek?

In the Babylonian Talmud, some rabbis expressed the view that while *tefilin* and *mezuzot* may be written in any language, the Torah may be written only in Hebrew. However, Rabbi Simeon ben Gamaliel, first-century C.E. president of the Sanhedrin, said that the Torah may be written in Greek as well as in Hebrew. He reasoned that this should be done out of respect for King Ptolemy, the Greek ruler of Palestine who in the middle of the third century B.C.E. had been very kind to the Jews. The view of Rabbi Simeon prevailed.[19]

The Palestinian Talmud[20] further explains why the Rabbis agreed to make an exception in the case of the Greek language. They felt that Greek is a rich language, sufficiently elastic to capture the flavor and nuances of the Hebrew text. A Greek translation of Scripture, it was believed, would reflect honor on the Torah and help propagate its message.

Some dissidents rejected this notion and characterized the day on which the Torah was rendered into Greek as "a sad day for the Jewish people, a day comparable to the day on which Israel decided to worship the Golden Calf."[21]

In the twelfth century, Moses Maimonides emphasized that permission was given to write Torah scrolls in Greek but not in any other language.[22]

The earliest Jewish record of how the Hebrew Bible came to be translated into Greek is found in *Antiquities of the Jews,* by Flavius Josephus, who lived in Jerusalem and Rome during the first century C.E.

In this first history ever written about the Jews, Josephus tells of the beneficent King Ptolemy Philadelphus, who ruled over Palestine and Egypt in the third century B.C.E.[23] Demetrius, the king's librarian, wanted to assemble a great library and sought to gather all books that existed anywhere in the world. The king, too, was very eager that this be accomplished.

Demetrius learned that there were many books of law belonging to the Jews that should be in the king's library but were written in a language not understandable to the Greeks. How could a translation of these works be rendered?

Aristeas (Aristeus), an intimate friend of the king, had long been disturbed over the plight of the many thousands of Jewish captives who lived in lands ruled by King Ptolemy. He suggested to the king that a letter be sent to Elazar, the High Priest in Jerusalem, requesting that scholars be provided to prepare a Greek translation of the Pentateuch. As an inducement, Aristeas suggested that Ptolemy free the Jewish slaves.

Demetrius, having learned that copies of the Divine Law then in use were often carelessly transcribed, was resolved that the proposed Greek translation be done independently of all copies then available. He therefore suggested to the king that Elazar be asked to select seventy-two tal-

ented, scholarly elders, six from each of the twelve tribes of
Israel, and that they be housed in Alexandria in seventy-two
individual rooms, where each would write his own independent translation.

A letter (The Letter of Aristeas) making this request
was dispatched by the king to the High Priest. Elazar accepted King Ptolemy's proposal. The plan was executed
and, miraculously, all seventy-two translations turned out
to be identical.[24]

The story of how the Septuagint came to be written, as
detailed above, is not accepted as fact by most scholars.
Some believe that The Letter of Aristeas was actually
written during the Hasmonean period, around 165 B.C.E.
Others believe the date of writing to be around 80 B.C.E.
Later, the Rabbis of the Talmud do refer to such a letter.
They indicate their belief in its authenticity and in the fact
that the Greek translation of the Torah was composed under divine guidance.[25]

Why is the Greek translation of the Pentateuch called the Septuagint?

The Greeks named their translation of the Torah Septuagint, meaning "seventy," and the Jews translated this
word into Hebrew, calling it *Targum Ha-shivim,* meaning
"Translation of the Seventy."

Why these names should have been selected is quite in-
explicable in view of the fact that according to the accepted
traditional and historical view, as explained above, seventy-
two persons were involved in the translation.

Scholars have been baffled by this. Some theorize that
the use of the number seventy rather than seventy-two was
merely a matter of convenience, that seventy is a round
number and therefore much easier to remember. Others
hold the view that the number seventy displaced seventy-
two because it is a cardinal number and much easier to
record. Still others believe it was chosen because seventy is
a multiple of two important numbers in the Bible: seven and
ten. Seven times ten equals seventy.[26]

What seems to have been overlooked by biblical scholars is that the minor tractate Sefer Torah (1:8), whose compiler lived in the early part of the third century (before the final editing of the Mishna) records a view not noted anywhere else: that *seventy* elders translated the Torah into Greek. This would explain why the Septuagint is called *Targum Ha-shivim*.

In later centuries, when the balance of the Bible was translated into Greek, the term Septuagint was applied to the entire Bible, although originally it referred to the Torah alone.[27]

Why are some authorities opposed to the teaching of Torah to Gentiles?

Verse 33:4 in the Book of Deuteronomy reads, "Moses has commanded us the Torah, an inheritance for the community of Jacob." Moses Maimonides and other authorities interpreted this to mean that the Torah may be studied only by Jews; and for a Jew to teach a non-Jew Torah is a violation of this biblical commandment. The prohibition against teaching Scripture to non-Jews was widely enforced, especially prior to modern times.

Much of the opposition to teaching Torah to Gentiles was based on the fear that they would employ the knowledge gained for their missionary work. Nonetheless, some authorities[28] challenged this outright prohibition, favoring instead the view that judgments be made on a case-by-case basis. The more liberal authorities argued that the verse in Deuteronomy is not to be taken literally. They point to the prophecy of Isaiah (2:2-3) as the attitude that must be assumed. Isaiah foresaw the day when many nations will say:

> Come ye, and let us go up to the mountain of the Lord, to the house of the God of Jacob, and He will teach us of His ways and we will walk in His paths.

Non-Jews, in Isaiah's view, are not excluded from the obligation to learn and follow God's commandments.

In order for this to be effected, it follows that non-Jews must be instructed in Jewish teachings, and more than a century ago Rabbi Israel Salanter (1810-83) of Lithuania, founder of the Mussar Movement, actually proposed and propagated the idea that talmudic studies be a part of the curriculum of European universities. Today, throughout the world, many universities are offering courses in Jewish studies, usually taught by rabbis, to the general university population.

Why is the Torah scroll generally kept covered?

It is considered disrespectful toward a Torah scroll to leave it unrolled and uncovered when it is not being read. Some congregations therefore place a cover *(mappa)* over the scroll after each Torah portion has been read, while others use the Torah mantle itself.[29] Others, however, cover the Torah only when there is a prolonged hiatus between the reading of one portion and the reading of the next.[30] This happens when special prayers are recited between aliyot.

Why are Torah scrolls sometimes lined with silk fabric?

Eastern Sephardim, those from Iraq, Iran, Syria, Egypt, Yemen, and other countries of the Near East, lay a long piece of silk fabric along the entire underside of the Torah parchment. This prevents the scratching or erasure of the Torah's letters, which would make the Torah invalid *(pasul)*. The entire scroll is then set into a *tek* or *tik*, cylindrical metal or wooden box lined with velvet.[31]

Non-Eastern Sephardic congregations, including those of Spain, Portugal, and the North African countries, line the underside of their Torah scrolls with silk but do not house them in cylindrical containers. Rather, they cover the scrolls with cloth mantles, as do Ashkenazim.

Why do Eastern Sephardim encase their scrolls in cylindrical containers?

As mentioned above, Oriental communities in Syria, Iraq, Iran, Egypt, Yemen, and other countries of the region do not use Torah mantles to cover their scrolls. Instead they encase them in highly-decorated cylindrical containers made out of wood or metal. These containers stand vertically and, when opened, reveal the Torah scroll. The parchment can be rolled to the appropriate section by manipulating two finials *(atzay chayim)* that protrude from the top of the case. The bottom surface is flat so that the container may rest on the reading table.

The reason for encasing scrolls in containers is not definitely known, but it may have been a way of minimizing direct handling and touching of the parchment, thus showing respect for the scroll and minimizing the possibility of erasing letters.[32] The scroll is never removed from the case unless it is necessary to make corrections.

Why is the Torah covered with a mantle?

The Talmud[33] mandates that it is obligatory to write a beautiful scroll and to wrap the finished scroll in beautiful silk. Great care was taken to conform to the statement in Scripture: "This is my God and I will glorify Him" (Exodus 15:2), which was explained by the Rabbis to mean that God is glorified and honored by being served with handsome religious articles made with love and care.

The function of the Torah mantle is both to protect the scroll and to beautify it. Mantles are made of a variety of materials that come in many colors. White is used for holidays, particularly the High Holidays, and blue and maroon are the more common colors used during the year.

Mantles are embroidered by hand or by machine with a variety of symbols and biblical phrases. Among the popular decorative symbols used are the Ten Commandments, lions, crowns, Stars of David, menorahs, flowers, and wreaths. Usually the name of the individual who presented the Torah and/or the mantle to the synagogue is embroidered on the bottom of the mantle or on its lining.

Since it is not considered proper to touch the Torah parchment with bare hands, some persons receiving an aliya will touch it with the edge of the Torah mantle and then kiss the mantle before reciting the first and last blessings.

Why are white mantles used on holidays?

The *Code of Jewish Law,*[34] while discussing other aspects of Torah coverings, makes no reference whatsoever to their color.

The probable reason for using white Torah appurtenances on holidays is that white (the color used by brides) is a color of purity and celebration.[35] The Palestinian Talmud[36] offers an explanation for the use of white on such solemn days as Rosh Hashana and Yom Kippur: "Ordinarily, when a man has to face judgment, he wears black garments [to be humble in the presence of a stern judge], but [on the solemn days of Rosh Hashana and Yom Kippur] we wear white garments in joyous confidence that God will perform a miracle for us."

A reference in Isaiah (1:18) is often cited as the reason for the use of white mantles and ark curtains on Yom Kippur: "Be your sins like crimson, they can be turned snow-white."

Why is a *mappa* used as a Torah covering?

Mappa, meaning "covering," is the Hebrew word sometimes used to designate the Torah mantle itself. However, the word *mappa* is more commonly used to designate a simple piece of rectangular fabric approximately 12 by 24 inches with a decorative Star of David embroidered on it. This is used as a covering for the Torah whenever the open scroll on the reading table is not being read for a period of time. To leave the Torah exposed and unread is considered a denigration.

Mappa is also the name used for the lectern or table

covering on which the Torah is placed as well as for the Torah binder. See questions below relating to the Torah *gartl.*

Why is a silk scarf sometimes draped over the Torah parchment?

At Eastern Sephardic services the Torah is read from a vertical position, and between aliyot a silk scarf is draped over the parchment that is exposed. This serves several purposes:

- It protects against accidental erasure of letters.
- It marks the place where the Torah reading is to resume for the next aliya.
- It keeps the words of the Torah from being idly exposed between one aliya and the next.

Why is the Torah tied with a *gartl?*

After the Torah is rolled up and before the mantle is placed over it, the scroll is bound with a length of material two to three inches wide. The band is generally referred to by the Yiddish term *gartl,* although in some communities it is called *mappa.* The *gartl* serves to encircle the Torah scroll and hold it tightly together.

A *gartl* may be made of a variety of materials and colors. In fact, the swaddling clothes used at a boy's *brit* are sometimes saved and fashioned into a *gartl.*[37] Embroidered with the child's name, date of birth, and expressions of good luck, the binder is used on the Torah that is read on the day of the boy's Bar Mitzva.

Why are women sometimes seen pressing the *gartl* to their eyes?

In some Sephardic congregations the *gartl* that is removed from the Torah taken from the ark for the Sabbath reading is rolled up and passed among the women of the congregation. As each receives it, she kisses it, presses it to her eyes, and meditates for a few moments. It is hoped that the *gartl* and the holiness with which it is imbued by virtue of its having touched the Torah will assist in bringing a satisfying response to the personal prayers being uttered.

Why is the Torah kissed when it is carried in procession?

When the Torah is carried in procession through the synagogue, it is customary for the congregants to pay their respects to the scroll either by touching the Torah with one's fingers and then kissing them or by touching a *talit* or a prayerbook to the Torah and then kissing that object. Though not demanded by Jewish law, this practice is universally followed, reflecting the deep respect and adoration Jews have for the most holy of all Jewish religious objects.

The origin of the kissing custom may be found in the Song of Songs (3:11), where the Jewish people is portrayed as a bride, and God, represented by the Torah, as its bridegroom. In Temple times it was customary for a bridegroom to be crowned with flowers, and in later years this practice was transferred to the Torah by dressing it with a crown of silver rather than flowers. When paraded down the aisles of a synagogue, the crowned Torah is showered with kisses by its adoring bride, the Congregation of Israel.

Why is the Torah sometimes hugged when it is carried in procession?

It is reported that the famous sixteenth-century mystic of Safed, the Ari, would step up to the Torah when it was removed from the ark and not only kiss it but hug it as well. He would then follow the Torah in procession until it was positioned on the reading table and opened to the place where the reading was to begin. The Ari would then peer at the letters closely before returning to his seat. As a result of looking intently at the letters, he explained, he was overcome by a strong spiritual feeling.[38]

In Sephardic congregations today one still sees men and women extending open arms in huglike fashion toward the Torah as it passes in procession.

Why is it customary in some congregations to wave to the Torah as it passes?

Just as kissing the Torah is an expression of adoration and devotion, so is the custom of waving one's hand toward the Torah as it passes in procession. The handwaving practice is primarily Sephardic.

The practice developed because not all congregants were physically able to reach the Torah as it was carried past, particularly in large synagogues. Women, usually seated in a gallery or in a special section on the side or in the rear of the synagogue, were at a particular disadvantage. They could only acknowledge their adoration by waving to the passing Torah or by throwing a kiss toward it by touching their fingers to their lips and waving. Men who were not close enough to touch the Torah directly would wave the fringes of their *talit* toward the Torah and then kiss the fringes.

Why do members of a congregation sometimes rise when a rabbi or scholar approaches?

The Talmud[39] accepted Rabbi Yochanan's view that when the Nasi enters a room everyone except mourners and those who are ill should stand as a sign of respect. The Nasi was the president of the Sanhedrin (supreme court) and the spiritual leader of the Jewish community. Rising for the Nasi led to the practice of according respect to all men of superior learning by standing when they approach, for such persons represent the Torah.

In some congregations, even today, members will rise as the rabbi enters the synagogue or walks down the aisle, just as they rise to honor the Torah when it is carried in procession.

Why is the sale of a Torah discouraged in Jewish law?

Jewish law encourages every individual to own his own Torah, in fact to write one if at all possible, but discourages the sale of Torah scrolls. Selling a Torah is considered a sign of disrespect and is therefore frowned upon unless the circumstances are compelling. Communities have been known to sell a Torah in order to ransom captives.

An individual is justified in selling his personal Torah only in the event that the individual requires funds in order to pursue Torah studies or to marry.[40]

Why does a silver crown often adorn a Torah scroll?

The Torah is the holiest and most regal object in Jewish life, and it is therefore natural that it be adorned with the symbol of royalty. Some authorities ascribe the selection of a crown (in Hebrew referred to as *keter, keter Torah,* or *atara*) as the primary Torah appurtenance to a statement in *Ethics of the Fathers (Pirkay Avot):* "There are three crowns: the crown of the Law [Torah], the crown of the Priestly office, and the crown of royalty, but the crown of a good name is above them all" (4:17). The famous rabbinical scholar Hai Gaon, a tenth-century Babylonian leader, was the first to make specific reference to the use of a crown as a Torah adornment.

Today, two types of Torah ornaments are called crowns. One resembles the familiar single-unit cylindrical adornment used by kings and queens. The other consists of two tall narrow units that fit on each of the Torah finials and are commonly known as *rimmonim, kitray Torah,* and *atzay chayim* (singular, *etz chayim*). The term *atzay chayim* is also used for the wood rollers to which the Torah parchment is attached, and often—in the singular—as a name for the Torah itself.

Why are breastplates sometimes placed on top of the Torah mantle?

A breastplate is a shieldlike decoration placed on a Torah in imitation of the gold breastplate (*choshen* or *tass*)[41] worn by the High Priest (Exodus 28:15). Generally made of silver and measuring approximately 8 by 10 inches, breastplates may be decorated in a variety of ways. Some have four rows of precious or semiprecious stones, as did the High Priest's breastplate, on which was engraved the name of each of the twelve sons of Jacob. Others carry simple engravings or applied ornaments. A chain is attached to the breastplate so that it can be draped over the two finials extending from the top of the scroll.

A more elaborate breastplate sometimes has soldered to it a small silver box which contains silver plates engraved with the names of holidays and special Sabbaths. The plate bearing the name of the holiday or Sabbath being celebrated is placed up front in the box to indicate to the cantor or Torah reader which Torah has been prepared for the day's reading.

Why are bells attached to some Torah adornments?

The Bible (Exodus 28:33) informs us that when performing priestly duties the High Priest wore a breastplate, over which he wore a robe *(me'il)* with golden bells attached. The tinkling noise of the bells served notice upon those assembled in the Temple Court that the Priest was engaged in performing his holy rituals. The small bells that adorn the breastplate and the various types of crowns today were probably inspired by the bells on the High Priest's vestment.

A practical reason for introducing Torah ornaments with bells relates to the requirement that one is expected to stand when the Torah is removed from the ark. Since not everyone seated in the congregation can see what is transpiring, the tinkling of the bells is a reminder that a Torah has been removed from the ark and is in procession.[42]

In the opinion of some modern scholars, attaching bells to Torah ornaments was introduced by Oriental Jewish communities, where it was popularly believed that evil spirits are warded off by the noise of bells. In most Sephardic synagogues, it is a high honor to be called upon to place these ornaments on a Torah before it is taken in procession around the synagogue. Often the honoree allows a child to carry out this function for him.

Why do some authorities object to attaching bells to Torah ornaments?

Although in the minority, some rabbinic authorities disallow the use of crowns and breastplates with bells attached. They place bells in the category of musical instruments, arguing that while musical instruments were used in the Temple ritual on Sabbaths and holidays, after the destruction of the Second Temple in 70 C.E., their use was no longer permitted. These authorities invoke a principle of Jewish law that considers it a violation to produce sounds via musical instruments on Sabbaths and holidays.[43]

Why are Torah rollers called *atzay chayim?*

The Book of Proverbs (3:18) refers to the Torah as *etz chayim,* "a tree of life." For this reason, the wooden rollers to which the ends of the parchment scroll are attached took on the name *etz chayim* (plural, *atzay chayim*).

Why is the Torah parchment attached to rollers?

Each end of the Torah scroll is attached to a wooden roller, and attached to each end of the two rollers are finials extending approximately eight inches. These allow for the parchment to be easily rolled from one place to another without touching it with one's bare hands. They also make it possible for the Torah to be raised and made visible to the entire congregation.

Why is a Torah pointer called a *yad*?

The Torah pointer, referred to in Hebrew as *yad*, meaning "hand," consists of a piece of wood or a metal tubing approximately six to eight inches long, to which a sculpted hand is attached.

Since in Jewish tradition the right side is favored over the left, when a craftsman sculpts a Torah pointer, he uses as his model the right hand with its index finger extended. The sculpted finger is used to point to the words of the Torah.

The Torah reader always holds the Torah pointer in his right hand and stands to the left of the person being honored with the aliya, making it easier for the honoree to follow the words of the Torah as they are pointed to.

The Torah pointer probably originated in Germany in the sixteenth century. Since then pointers have been presented to congregations as gifts by members who wish to honor or memorialize relatives or friends.

Why is the professional staff of a synagogue often referred to as *klay kodesh*?

The silver ornaments that adorn the Torah scroll—such as crowns, breastplates, and pointers—are referred to in Hebrew as *klay kodesh,* meaning "holy vessels" or "holy appurtenances." This term, which applies only to objects that serve a Torah and enhance its beauty, was later applied to all persons who serve a congregation, particularly the rabbi, cantor, and sexton *(shamash).*

Why do congregations rarely sell their Torah accessories?

All ornaments used in connection with a Torah scroll—including crowns, pointers, and mantles—are considered sacred because they have been in direct contact with the holy scroll. The Rabbis therefore ruled that these articles not be sold unless the funds realized from their sale are to be expended for the purchase of a new Torah scroll or for books of the Bible. The legal principle at work here, discussed in the introduction to this chapter, is *maalin bakodesh v'lo moridin,* meaning that it is permissible to elevate the status of a sacred object but not to reduce it.[44]

Why is a Torah scroll occasionally tied with its binder around the mantle?

Generally, when an error is discovered in a Torah scroll, it must be corrected within thirty days. Upon discovery of the error, the invalid scroll is removed from service and is promptly covered with its mantle. The *gartl* is then tied around the outside of the mantle. The Torah is placed in the ark, and the binder serves as a reminder that the scroll is in need of immediate repair.[45]

Why does a Torah scroll retain its sanctity as long as eighty-five letters are in good condition?

The number eighty-five was selected because verses 35 and 36 of Chapter 10 of the Book of Numbers contain a total of eighty-five letters. These two verses were considered by the Rabbis to be a separate book of the Torah (see Chapter Eight, The Masoretic Text), and therefore any section of the Torah that contains eighty-five consecutive letters in good, readable condition is to be equated with a complete book of the Torah and is to be accorded the same degree of sanctity.

Scholars in the Babylonian academy of Sura during the third century C.E. discussed whether a Torah scroll that has been partially burned in a fire on the Sabbath retains its sanctity. Rabbi Nachman ruled that as long as eighty-five consecutive letters are clearly readable, such a scroll has not lost its holiness.[46]

Why were Torot sometimes placed in a *geniza*?

A Torah that is old and shabby or one that has been corrected so many times as to become unseemly must be buried in a cemetery as soon as practical. In earlier times a Torah awaiting burial was often stored in a special room in the synagogue building.[47] This storage room, known as a *geniza* (literally, "a place to store or hide") was a depository not only for worn-out Torot but also for all types of religious writings and objects, including the ark itself.[48]

The Cairo *geniza,* the most famous of all storage rooms, is situated on the upper floor of the Ben Ezra Synagogue in Fostat (Old Cairo), Egypt. Built in 882, the Ben Ezra Synagogue was the house of worship in which Moses Maimonides prayed in the twelfth century. But it was not until 1896 that Dr. Solomon Schechter, then on the faculty of Cambridge University, visited the synagogue and discovered the full extent of the literary treasures in the Cairo *geniza.*[49]

Why are Torah scrolls buried when they are no longer valid for public reading?

In the Jewish tradition a Torah scroll is equated with a human being. As a human must be treated with dignity, so must a Torah be treated with the utmost reverence. Just as a person is to be buried in the earth when his life is over, so must a Torah scroll be buried when its useful life has come to an end. Generally, the parchment is placed in an urn and buried in a cemetery next to an honored scholar.[50]

Other sacred writings, such as prayerbooks and tractates of the Talmud, are treated with the same reverence when they have outlived their usefulness.

Why is one required to rend his garment when he sees a Torah on fire?

Just as a Jew tears his garment (performs *keria*) when he loses a close relative, so must he rend his garment when he sees a Torah consumed by flames. As pointed out above, in Jewish tradition the same degree of respect that is accorded a human being must be accorded a Torah scroll, for the highest degree of holiness is inherent in both.[51]

Why is it forbidden to bring a Torah into a cemetery other than to bury it?

Judaism equates a poor man with a dead man. Hence, those lying in their graves are sometimes referred to as "the poor ones." Tradition considers it mockery of the dead to come into a cemetery with religious articles that the deceased may once have enjoyed.

For this reason, Jewish law prohibits one not only from bringing a Torah scroll into a cemetery but also from wearing *tefilin* or from engaging in formal prayer there. These prohibitions are based on an interpretation of the verse in Proverbs (17:5), "He who mocks the poor [figuratively, the dead. The Hebrew term is *loeg le-rash.*] blasphemes God."[52]

Why are unusable Torah mantles sometimes converted into shrouds?

The law requires that an unusable Torah mantle be treated with respect since it has been in close contact with a Torah scroll. Although the usual method of disposing of appurtenances that have come into contact with the Torah is to bury them or store them away in a *geniza,* converting mantles into shrouds became an effective and respectful way of treating them.[53]

The actual origin of this practice is mentioned in the Talmud[54] by Mar Zutra, who said, "Scroll coverings that are worn out may be used for making shrouds."

Why is it customary to fast if a Torah scroll is dropped?

While Jewish law does not demand that one fast after dropping a Torah scroll, it has been customary to do so.

The reasoning is that since one is required to fast if he drops *tefilin,* it is only logical that he should be expected to do the same if he drops a Torah, a more sacred article.

Opinions are divided as to whether only the person who dropped the Torah must fast or whether all present must do likewise. The prevailing view is that he who actually drops the scroll must fast on the next three weekdays on which the Torah is read. For example, if the Torah were dropped at a Sabbath service, the fast would be held on the following Monday, Thursday, and Monday. All others present when the Torah was dropped would be expected to fast for only one day. In all cases the fasting period is from dawn to sundown, as on minor fast days.

Since fasting after a Torah is dropped is a custom rather than a legal requirement, some authorities permit those who are unable to fast, particularly for health reasons, to make a charitable contribution instead.[55]

Chapter 3

The Ark and the Pulpit Area

INTRODUCTION

The ark was the centerpiece of the Tabernacle that the Children of Israel carried with them during their forty-year trek through the desert. In it were kept the two tablets on which were inscribed the Ten Commandments, often referred to as the Decalogue, from the Greek *deka* and *logos*, meaning "ten words." The word Decalogue corresponds precisely with the Hebrew term *Aseret Ha-dibrot*.

Bezalel, a gifted craftsman and cabinetmaker, was selected by Moses (Exodus 31:2-6) to build the ark that was to be housed in the Tabernacle. Since the Israelites were in transit, en route to the Promised Land, the tabernacle and its appurtenances were designed so they might be assembled quickly and moved about without difficulty. The sacred assignment of carrying the ark fell to the Levites, for according to biblical tradition it was they alone who did not participate in the building of the Golden Calf (Exodus 32:26, Numbers 3:27ff., and I Chronicles 15:2).

Although the ark was continually being moved from place to place, first during the wanderings of the Children of Israel in the wilderness and later when they reached Canaan, it was always treated with respect and was always carefully handled and protected. The ark represented God's holiness and presence, and disrespect toward it was tantamount to disrespect toward God.[1]

There were times in early history when the ark had to be

hidden, lest it be captured by the enemy. Such was the case when David was king of Israel. While he was busy battling the Philistines, the ark was stored for many years in the out-of-the-way home of Avinadav, who lived in the safer hilly countryside. When victory over the Philistines was accomplished, David ordered that the ark be brought to Mount Zion.

When David's son Solomon finally built the holy Temple, a permanent home was established for the ark—in the Holy of Holies (I Kings 8:6).

The ark is to this day the most sacred object in Jewish life next to the Torah itself. It is the focal point of the interior of every synagogue, and the most important rites and rituals in Judaism center about it and the pulpit area in which it is located.

This chapter explores and explains the laws, traditions, and rituals that pertain to the ark and the ceremonies that revolve about it and the area in which it is located.

Why is there a tradition that in biblical times two arks existed?

Deuteronomy 10:2 states that Moses was to build an ark in which the second set of Ten Commandments was to be stored. These new tablets were replacements for those that Moses smashed upon seeing the Golden Calf erected by the people in his absence.

Deuteronomy indicates only that an ark was built to house the set of replacement tablets. But some Rabbis believed that a second ark was built as well: to house the *broken* tablets. According to one tradition, it was the second ark—the one containing the shattered tablets—that accompanied the Children of Israel whenever they want out to battle.[2]

Another rabbinical view is that only one ark was in existence and that in it were kept not only the unbroken tablets but the shattered fragments of the set that Moses had destroyed.[3]

Why is the ark called *aron* by some Jews and *haychal* by others?

Aron, meaning "box," or *aron ha-kodesh,* meaning "holy cabinet," are terms used for the ark by Ashkenazim. The word *aron ha-kodesh,* first used in II Chronicles 35:3, is an apt description of the container that houses the Torah scrolls. *Aron* parallels in meaning the simple Hebrew word *tayva,* which is used for ark in later talmudic literature.[4]

Sephardim prefer the biblical word *haychal* for ark. *Haychal,* meaning "sanctuary," is found in I Kings 6:3 and Isaiah 6:1, among other places in the Bible. The term is also used as a synonym for the Temple built by Solomon.

Why in some synagogues is the ark placed on the eastern wall, while in others it is located on the western wall?

Traditionally, prayer by Jews, no matter where they lived, was always directed toward Jerusalem, the place where the Temple of Solomon was originally situated.

In Eastern countries, such as those located in the vicinity of Iraq (called Babylonia in ancient times) and Iran (formerly Persia), the ark is placed on the western wall of the synagogue, the direction of Jerusalem. In Western countries, such as those of Europe and America, the ark is placed on the synagogue's eastern wall, which faces the holy city. Synagogues in Israel itself place the ark on the wall that faces the Temple Mount, the site where the Temple stood in ancient times.

Why is an ark sometimes reckoned as a person in order to complete a quorum?

Throughout the centuries congregations in small towns or villages often found themselves shy one person to complete a *minyan*. Many innovations were introduced in an attempt to solve this problem.

The Palestinian Talmud[5] says in effect that if nine adults plus a minor are present, the minor together with the Torah in the ark can be considered as the tenth person.

The Babylonian Talmud[6] quotes Rav Huna as saying that if nine adults are present, the ark may be counted as the tenth person, and a full service may be held.

Why should every synagogue ark contain at least three Torot?

Since there are Sabbaths in the Jewish calendar when the Torah reading must consist of selections from three different parts of the Torah, it is advisable for every synagogue to possess at least three Torot. Should a congregation have less than that number, it would be necessary for congregants to suffer the inconvenience of waiting lengthy periods while a scroll is rolled from one place to another.

The three occasions on which readings are conducted from three scrolls at one service are described on page 325.

Why do some people say that even a Torah in the ark depends on luck?

"Everything depends on luck [*mazal*], even a Torah in the ark"[7] is a popular kabbalistic saying. This proverb has been explained in several ways, the most popular explanation being that whether a particular Torah will be chosen for a public reading on a particular day is a matter of sheer luck.

However, the proverb is more likely linked to a fact of life: in earlier centuries mice often gnawed away at the parchment of Torot stored in the ark. Such Torot were considered defective and could not be used for a public reading. If a Torah scroll was spared an attack by mice, it was indeed fortunate, for that scroll might be selected for the Torah reading.

Why does the ark sometimes house a Torah scroll that is never used?

A Torah scroll that has become frayed or otherwise very worn but is nevertheless still kosher for a public reading may be kept in the ark alongside other scrolls. It need not be stored away or buried as is the case with a scroll that is invalid for public reading. However, if the congregation wishes to bury a worn but still kosher scroll, it may do so.[8]

It is considered fitting to offer an extra scroll to a poor congregation that would be pleased to have an extra Torah on hand, even if it is not in superior condition.

Why, when no longer usable, must an ark be consigned to a storeroom or be buried?

Next to the Torah scroll itself, the ark is the holiest object in the synagogue.[9] Jewish law prohibits the sale of an unused ark even if the funds are to be used to build a synagogue.[10]

The principle invoked by the Rabbis in establishing this rule of law is that the sanctity of a religious article should never be diminished. Since Torah scrolls come into direct contact with an ark, the ark itself achieves a status of holiness second only to the Torah. Just as a Torah scroll is stored away in a *geniza* or buried when no longer usable or needed, so too is an ark. The same treatment is accorded a Torah mantle or any religious article that has been in direct contact with a Torah scroll.[11]

Rabbi Ephraim Oshry, once a leading rabbi of the Kovno (Lithuania) Jewish community, ruled that a fragment of wood from a destroyed ark that is found in a pile of rubble must be buried or stored away; it is to be treated with the same sanctity as a whole ark.[12]

Why is the ark covered with a curtain?

The special curtain that covers the ark in Ashkenazic synagogues is called the *parochet* (or *paroches*).[13] The

Book of Exodus (26:31-33) explains that this curtain was to be made of "blue, purple, and crimson yarns, and fine twisted linen . . ." and that it should serve as a partition between the Holy of Holies, in which the ark was housed, and the rest of the Tabernacle. Reference is again made to the *parochet* in Exodus 40:21, where Moses "brought the ark into the Tabernacle and set up the curtain and screened the ark." In the First and Second Temples the *parochet* was used to separate the Holy of Holies from the rest of the Temple.

Almost all Sephardic congregations and some Ashkenazic congregations do not use ark coverings at all. Instead, the ark doors are usually elaborately decorated. The reason for the establishment of this practice is not definitely known, but it may be part of an old tradition which bans the duplication of the precise form of the appurtenances used in the two Temples in Jerusalem.

See page 82 for more on this tradition, especially as it relates to the *menora*.

Why is the ark covered with a white curtain on holidays?

As is true of the Torah mantle, the *parochet* used to cover the ark throughout the year may be any color. However, blue, purple, and maroon seem to have found special favor. On holidays, particularly the High Holidays, practically all synagogues change the ark covering as well as the Torah mantles and lectern covers to white.

The choice of the color white, a symbol of purity and hope, is linked to one of the popular prophecies of Isaiah (1:18): "If your sins be like crimson, they can turn snow white." The message is that man can change and be redeemed.

The color of the *parochet* used on a particular occasion is not mandated by law. In fact, Jewish law does not require the use of an ark curtain at all, and its adoption did not become widespread until after the sixteenth century.

Why is the ark curtain removed on Tisha B'Av?

On Tisha B'Av the *parochet* is removed from the ark to accentuate the mournful mood of the day. On that day—on the ninth day of the month of Av—both the First and the Second Temples were burned to the ground, the First by the Babylonians in 586 B.C.E. and the Second by the Romans in 70 C.E.

As a further sign of mourning, the *talit* and *tefilin* are not worn at the Tisha B'Av morning service but are donned instead at the afternoon service. In some congregations, primarily Sephardic ones, Tisha B'Av worshipers sit on the floor or on low benches while the Book of Lamentations (Aycha) is chanted.

Why is a valance generally hung across the top of the ark curtain?

The short valance that is seen hanging across the top of the ark curtain is called the *kaporet* (or *kapores*). This horizontal piece of fabric, which runs the full width of the ark and is generally eight to twelve inches high depending on the length of the *parochet* itself, was created to match the ark curtain and round out the design. The *kaporet* is first mentioned in Exodus 26:34.

In Eastern Europe of the sixteenth through eighteenth centuries, it was not uncommon for ladies of a community to create a *kaporet* from clothing worn by children at a *brit* or other important occasions. This custom is being revived in some American communities.

Why is an ark covering considered to be less holy than a Torah covering?

The Torah scroll is the holiest object found in the synagogue, and the ark is second on the plane of holiness. Accordingly, the Torah mantle, which makes direct contact with the Torah, is considered more holy than the *parochet,* which covers the ark but does not make direct contact with the Torah.

Why does the congregation rise when the ark is opened?

The Rabbis of the Talmud[14] ruled that members of a congregation should rise and remain standing when the ark is opened and the Torah is exposed. The ruling is based on the verse in Leviticus (19:32), "You shall rise before the aged and show deference to the old." In the Talmud, "aged" means "old in wisdom," people who are "wise and learned." The Rabbis reasoned: If when a learned person is in our presence we must rise in deference to his wisdom and knowledge, how much more so is it required that we rise in the presence of the Torah, which is the source of all wisdom.

Why must Torah scrolls for the day's reading be prepared in advance by rolling them to the proper place before the prayer service begins?

Jewish law takes into account the feelings of the public in determining how a ritual or ceremonial practice should be carried out. This principle is known by the Hebrew term *kevod ha-tzibur,* meaning "dignity of [respect for] the public."[15]

Because a congregation might grow impatient if it has to sit and wait while a Torah is being rolled from portion to portion, the Rabbis ruled that a Torah must be rolled to the proper place before the service begins. When on any particular day two or three Torot are to be read, all must be prepared in advance.

Naturally, if a congregation owns only one or two Torot, there is no alternative but for members to wait patiently while a Torah is rolled to its proper reading place.

Why, after removing the Torah from the ark, do all on the pulpit face the ark and bow?

In the Ashkenazic service, after the Torah is removed from the ark, the cantor chants the *Shema,* which is repeated by the congregation. The cantor then recites a sentence beginning with the words *echad Elohenu,* "Our God is One," and the congregation repeats it. Then, all on the pulpit turn and face the ark, and the cantor chants the verse from Psalms 34:4 that begins with the Hebrew word *gadlu,* meaning "magnify, exalt." The full verse is "O magnify the Lord with me, and let us exalt His name together."

When the cantor sings out, "Let us exalt His name together," he is speaking not only for the congregation and the Torah that has been removed and will soon be read, but also for all the Torot in the ark. Everyone, including the person holding the Torah that was removed, bows to the other Torot in the ark by way of acknowledging that they are not being forgotten, even though they will not be used in that day's reading.

This procedure is followed only at Ashkenazic services. Sephardim, such as Moroccans, and particularly those of Oriental countries (Syria, Iran, Egypt, and others) do not recite the *gadlu* verse, nor do they recite the *Shema* when the scrolls are removed. Instead they recite a verse from the Song of Songs (3:11). See question below.

Why in Ashkenazic congregations is the *Shema* prayer chanted after the Torah is removed from the ark?

The first paragraph of the *Shema* (Deuteronomy 6:7) reads, "And thou shalt teach them [the words of the Torah] unto thy children, and shalt talk of them when thou sittest in thy house, when thou walkest by the way, when thou liest down, and when thou risest up." This important precept is introduced with the words (Deuteronomy 6:4), "Hear, O Israel [*Shema Yisrael*], the Lord our God, the Lord is One." Since the reading of the Torah was deemed to be a study period, Ashkenazic leaders considered it appropriate to use the words "Hear, O Israel" after the Torah is removed from the ark and before it is read to the public.[16]

Sephardim follow a different procedure. See the next question.

Why do Sephardim recite a passage from the Song of Songs when the Torah is removed from the ark?

Ashkenazic congregations recite the *Shema* when the Torah is removed from the ark, but Sephardim (with the exception of Egyptian congregations and possibly some others) follow a different tradition. They chant the following verse from the Song of Songs (3:11):

> Go forth, O ye daughters of Zion, and gaze upon King Solomon, even upon the crown with which his mother crowned him on the day of his wedding and on the day his heart was so very happy.

The daughter of Zion, the bride, symbolizes Israel. King Solomon, the bridegroom, symbolizes God. Just as the bride in this verse greets the bridegroom, so do the members of the congregation welcome the crowned Torah, which represents God.

To Sephardim, this joyous serenade of the Torah is a meaningful way of celebrating its centrality in Jewish life.

Why do some persons take three steps backward when retreating from the ark?

The *Code of Jewish Law*[17] cautions that one should not turn his back on the Torah. This has led to the practice of stepping backward when retreating from the ark area.

Why precisely three steps are taken is not definitely known, but it is possibly related to the fact that many important events in Jewish history are associated with the number three.[18] Once three steps backward have been taken, a person is no longer considered to be within the domain of the Torah.

Why is it important that a Torah be carried in procession after it is removed from the ark?

The Talmud tells us that "the pious men of Jerusalem acted in the following manner: When the Torah scroll was taken out of the ark and when it was returned after the reading, they followed it as a mark of respect."[19]

According to one tradition, God commanded Moses to involve the entire nation in the construction of the ark so that they might all have a share in the Torah which was to be housed in the ark. By extending their hands to touch and kiss the Torah as it passes them in procession, congregants manifest their involvement with the Torah and their adoration of it.

Why do Torah processions always leave the pulpit from the right side?

The right hand and the right side signify God's majesty and power, and they are always given preferential treatment. Tradition has it that God gave the Torah to Moses in his right hand. For this reason, whenever the Torah is carried in procession around the synagogue before the Torah reading begins, it is always taken to the right side of the synagogue first (proceeding counterclockwise as one leaves the pulpit).

After circling the synagogue once, the Torah is taken to the reading table. When the scroll is returned to the ark after the Torah has been read, the reverse order is followed.

See pages 44 and 155 for more on the importance of the right side in Jewish tradition.

Why are Torot sometimes removed from the ark only for the purpose of parading them through the synagogue?

Very elaborate synagogue processions known as *hakafot* (singular, *hakafa*) are held on two holidays: Sukkot and Simchat Torah.

Hoshana Rabba, the last day of Sukkot, is the first occasion in the Jewish year when all Torot are removed from the ark and carried around the synagogue. During this procession, congregants holding Torot circle the synagogue seven times, followed by others carrying the *lulav* and *et-rog.* All the *Hoshana* prayers that were recited during the first six days of Sukkot are repeated, thus giving the holiday its name: Hoshana Rabba, the "Great Hosanna Day."[20]

The most widely observed procession takes place on Simchat Torah. All Torot are removed from the ark and the congregation sings and dances as the scrolls are carried in procession around the synagogue seven times, or as many times as required to give all persons present an opportunity to carry a scroll. This ceremony is mentioned for the first time in a book entitled *Minhagim,* composed at the beginning of the fifteenth century by Rabbi Isaac Tyrnau, an Austrian scholar.[21]

Why is a Torah sometimes brought to the reading table for other than reading purposes?

There are at least three occasions in the course of a year when one or more Torot are brought to the reading table not for the purpose of reading from them but to add importance to the prayers about to be chanted.

On the Sabbath prior to the arrival of a new Hebrew month, a member of the congregation carries a Torah to the reader's desk and holds it upright while the cantor intones the blessing for the new month that is to be ushered in. This Sabbath is known by the Hebrew name Shabbat Mevarchim, meaning "Sabbath of the Blessing [of the new month]."

During each of the seven days of Sukkot, a Torah is removed from the ark and is held at the reading desk while appropriate prayers are recited and the congregants, holding *etrogim* and *lulavim,* march in procession around the synagogue. (On Sabbaths, in some synagogues, the procession takes place but the *etrog* and *lulav* are not carried. In others, the procession is not held at all.) The Torah is displayed because the special prayers (called *Hoshanot* in Hebrew) recited at that time by cantor and congregation include the words "Help us to live with honor and to love Thy Torah."

Another occasion during the year when Torot are brought out for display alone is on Yom Kippur, at the Kol Nidre service. In some congregations one or more scrolls are brought forth to the reading table when the cantor recites the memorial prayer at a *Yizkor* service.

Why are two Torot removed from the ark for the recitation of the *Kol Nidre* prayer?

Before reciting the *Kol Nidre* prayer on the eve of Yom Kippur, it is traditional to remove two Torot from the ark and to have two elders or distinguished members of the congregation hold the scrolls while standing at the side of the cantor as he recites the *Kol Nidre*.

Kol Nidre is a prayer for the nullification of vows made under duress, and Jewish tradition and law saw fit to establish a legal formula whereby one can be released from such vows. Since *Kol Nidre* is a legal procedure, its importance was emphasized by having the cantor recite it in behalf of the congregation in the immediate presence of two reliable witnesses: two Torot.

In some congregations it has become traditional to remove all Torot from the ark and for each to be held by a congregant while the *Kol Nidre* is recited.

Why do many congregations permit the preacher and Torah reader to turn their backs to the ark when officiating?

Rabbi Yechiel Epstein, author of the *Aruch Ha-shulchan,* a commentary on the *Shulchan Aruch,* discusses the propriety of rabbis preaching to their congregations with their backs to the ark.[22] He justifies this practice by stating that the ark is generally raised above the pulpit floor and consequently is in a separate, self-contained area. The preacher cannot therefore be charged with showing disrespect toward the Torah if he stands with his back to the ark. Rabbi Epstein also argues that by his very activities a preacher is actually showing great respect for the Torah, because in his preachments he is urging acceptance of the Torah's laws.

While almost all Orthodox congregations forbid the *baal koray* from having his back to the ark when reading from the Torah, non-Orthodox congregations, in keeping with the reasoning of the *Aruch Ha-shulchan,* permit it.

Most synagogues today are constructed so that the reading table is to the side of the ark rather than directly in front of it, which solves the problem completely.

Why is the Torah always read from a raised platform?

The platform on which the Torah reading table is located is called the *bima,* which literally means "raised platform."[23] Ashkenazim also refer to the *bima* as *almemar,* a name derived from the Arabic *al-minbar,* meaning "the platform." Sephardim generally refer to the platform as *tayva,* "box," a name they also use to designate the ark. (In the Talmud the ark is called *tayva.*)

There are two reasons why services are conducted from a *bima.* The first and more practical one is to enable congregants to see and hear the officiants with greater ease.[24] The second and more important reason for conducting the service, specifically the Torah reading, from a raised platform is grounded in Jewish law. When the Torah reading is conducted from a special raised area, Jewish law permits the congregation to remain seated during the reading because the *bima* is then considered to be in a separate domain.

Why, according to some scholars, is the ark area considered to be a separate domain?

In the sixteenth century, the question of whether one is always obligated to stand in the presence of the Torah was addressed by Joseph Caro and Moses Isserles in the *Code of Jewish Law.*

Caro was of the opinion that one must stand when a

Torah passes in procession and that one must remain standing until the Torah is placed on the reading table or until it is no longer within one's field of vision.[25]

Isserles, in his Notes, says that when the Torah is placed on the reading table (which is normally on a platform [bima] at least ten handbreadths [approximately three feet] above the floor level of the congregation), it is considered to be in a different domain or area (the Hebrew word used is *reshut*). It is therefore not necessary for the congregation to remain standing despite the fact that the Torah is visible.[26]

Using the same reasoning, David ben Samuel Halevi, the seventeenth-century author of Turay Zahav, a commentary on the *Shulchan Aruch*, says that when the Torah is in the ark it is considered to be in a different domain, and one therefore does not have to stand even when the ark is open and the Torot are visible. This authority recognizes that in many congregations worshipers do stand when the ark is open, but he points out that there is no actual obligation to do so.

Later authorities have been more strict in this matter. The eighteenth-century Dutch scholar Rabbi Meir Eisenstadt is of the opinion that congregants should remain standing when the ark is open and the Torot are visible. Rabbi Moses Sofer, the famous Hungarian authority, agrees. "If the ark is open," he says, "it is forbidden to remain seated."[27]

Rabbi Yechiel Epstein, the nineteenth-century rabbinic authority, says in his code that since *most* people rise when the ark is open, *all* people should rise. Although the law does not require that one rise (since the Torah is in another domain), Epstein feels that members of the congregation may think that the person who remains seated is acting disrespectfully toward the Torah. Only if a person is known to be weak or ill may he or she remain seated.[28]

Why have Orthodox authorities opposed changing the location of the bima?

In the First and Second Temples (from approximately

1000 B.C.E. to 70 C.E.), sacrifices were brought upon the altar that was situated more or less in the *center* of the open court. Accordingly, when the synagogue was established, Jewish tradition designated the *center* of the synagogue as the appropriate place from which religious leaders should conduct the prayer service.

Until modern times, the raised platform was located in the center, or close to the center, of the synagogue. Over the centuries rabbinic authorities had been asked for permission to move the *bima* to the front of the synagogue, closer to the ark, so that the officiants might be better seen and heard. Permission was routinely denied on grounds that Jewish tradition does not favor altering established custom.[29]

In Conservative and Reform congregations there is no special *bima* in the center of the room. Instead, the entire service is conducted from a raised platform located in front of or to one side of the ark. This pulpit area is also called a *bima*.

In some synagogues—non-Orthodox as well as modern Orthodox—a lectern is placed on either side of the pulpit, one for the rabbi and one for the cantor. The cantor's lectern is usually larger or has an extra flap so that it can be enlarged and used as a Torah reading table.

Why is a Torah scroll sometimes returned to the ark without having been read?

There is a difference of opinion among scholars as to how to handle the situation in which a Torah scroll is taken from the ark, carried in procession around the synagogue, and when opened is found not to be in the right place for the reading of the day. Should the congregation be kept waiting while the Torah is rolled to the proper place, or should the Torah be returned to the ark and be replaced with one that had been properly prepared in advance of the service?

Some authorities maintain that if the first Torah blessing has not yet been recited, the scroll should be returned to the ark and replaced with the scroll that had been properly prepared. Those who hold this view contend that it would cause inconvenience to the congregation to have to wait while the scroll is being rolled to the correct place.[30]

Other authorities disagree, reasoning that the Torah is a sacred object and that it would be demeaning to return the scroll to the ark without first having read from it. They also argue that if the Torah is returned to the ark so abruptly, some congregants may come to the erroneous conclusion that there is doubt about the validity of the scroll.[31]

Why are Torot placed in the ark in a vertical position?

As depicted in artistic renderings on the walls of the Jewish catacombs in Rome, in early times Torot were stored horizontally in wall niches.

In the Middle Ages, however, Torah scrolls began to be placed vertically in tall niches and cabinets. This eventually became the common practice, even though vertical storage was apparently not most desirable, as evidenced from the statement of the eminent thirteenth-century scholar Rabbi Meir of Rothenburg, who wrote the following to a correspondent:[32]

> You ask, "Why do we not lay the Torah horizontally in the ark, just as the Ten Commandments were kept in the Temple?" This is a good question [said Rabbi Meir]. Rabbenu Tam [the grandson of Rashi] once wrote in a responsum that it would be a good idea to lay the Torah flat in the ark . . . and had he [Rabbenu Tam] throught of it when he built his own ark, he would have made it wider [so as to be able to place his Torah horizontally rather than vertically].[33]

Although the Talmud[34] says that one Torah may be laid on top of another, implying that this is not considered an act of disrespect, adopting the vertical position for the storing of scrolls was primarily based on space considerations and ease of access.

Why is an invalid scroll permitted to be retained in a synagogue ark?

Although the *Code of Jewish Law*[35] declares that an invalid *(pasul)* scroll must be placed in an earthen jug and buried in a grave next to a scholar, many post-sixteenth-century authorities have ruled otherwise. Some have pointed out that just as the fragments of the shattered first set of Ten Commandment tablets were kept in the ark of the Tabernacle along with the second set of Ten Commandments,[36] so is it permitted to keep an invalid Torah in an ark. The Rabbis of the Talmud were of the opinion that so long as a section of this otherwise invalid scroll contains at least eighty-five consecutive correctly written letters, it must be treated with dignity.[37]

The eighteenth-century rabbinical authority Ezekiel Landau expressed the generally accepted view that the only reason for not keeping an invalid Torah in a synagogue ark is that people might forget that it is *pasul* and will use it for a public reading.[38] Others object to this reasoning, however, claiming that since it is customary to tie a Torah band around the outside of the mantle of such an invalid Torah, a mistake cannot be made.

General practice is to keep an invalid Torah in the ark for a short period of time, until it is buried or repaired.[39]

Why is a lighted candle sometimes placed in the ark?

Jewish tradition demands that an ark never be without a Torah in it. Leaving an ark empty was considered an act of disrespect to the sacred ark, which in Jewish law ranks second only to the Torah in holiness.[40]

In some communities, when all the Torot are removed from the ark in order to parade them through the synagogue on Hoshana Rabba and Simchat Torah, a lighted candle is placed in the ark. The light of the candle symbolizes the "light" of the Torah, which is referred to in the

Book of Proverbs (6:23) in the expression *Torah or* and in the Talmud in the expression *ora zo Torah,* both meaning "the Torah is light."[41]

Among Ethiopian Jews, the Torah is called *orit,* a variant form of *ora.*[42]

The practice of leaving a lighted candle in the ark was never encouraged by rabbinic authorities. Some have suggested leaving a Pentateuch in the ark.

Why is a *menora* with seven lights rarely seen in the pulpit area?

The Rabbis of the Talmud forbade duplicating the seven-branched *menora* that graced the Tabernacle in the desert and, later, the Temples in Jerusalem.[43] This type of candelabrum was reserved for Temple use only, and to copy it was considered sacrilegious. Such a *menora,* it was hoped, would again be used only when a third Temple would be built.

The Rabbis, however, did not object to the display in the synagogue of a candelabrum with five, six, or eight branches. And although many synagogue candelabrums today have seven branches, the middle branch frequently has a Star of David on it rather than the usual cup to hold a candle.

Some congregations today disregard the tradition of not using a seven-branched candelabrum in the pulpit area. They reason that modern *menorot* are electrified and are therefore quite unlike the Temple original, which needed daily attention: they had to be cleaned; the wicks had to be changed; and fresh oil had to be added.

Why does an eternal light burn perpetually above the ark?

The eternal light *(ner tamid)* that burns perpetually over the ark was introduced in the eighteenth century. The original "eternal light" was part of the seven-branched *menora* that was a centerpiece of the First and Second Temples. Actually, this special light was the westernmost arm of the original seven-branched *menora* and was therefore called *ner maaravi,* "western lamp."[44] Fed constantly with oil so that it would burn continuously, the eternal light had as its chief function to serve as a pilot from which the other six branches could be lighted. The six lights were extinguished daily for cleaning purposes, but the westernmost light was kept burning continuously.

Why are artistic renderings of any kind sometimes thought to be prohibited in the synagogue?

The second of the Ten Commandments reads: "You shall not make for yourself a sculpted image or any likeness of what is in the heavens above or on the earth below or in the waters under the earth" (Exodus 20:4). This injunction, repeated in Deuteronomy 4:16, would seem to imply that artistic renderings of any kind may not be used under any circumstances. However, such is not the case.

The actual purpose of the second commandment is explained in Leviticus 20:23, where we find the exhortation that "you shall not imitate the practices of the nations that I [God] am driving out before you. For it is because they did all these idolatrous things that I abhorred them." What is actually being condemned in the commandment is the practice of idolatry, not artistic expression.[45]

Artistic representations may be used in the synagogue so long as they are not adored or worshiped as gods.[46] Accordingly, we find the Talmud noting that in the days of the third-century C.E. scholar Rabbi Yochanan bar Naphcha (Naphacha) "men began to paint pictures on walls and he [Rabbi Yochanan] did not stop them."[47] By the Middle Ages idolatry was no longer a threat to Judaism, and it was not uncommon for synagogues to be adorned with paintings and sculpture. We know that artistic adornment was not a novelty in the twelfth century because Maimonides mentions in one of his responsa that objects of art were a distracting influence and that during prayer he would shut his eyes so as to achieve full concentration. Maimonides, however, did not impose a ban on the use of artistic renderings.

It should be noted that not all scholars have been in agreement on the use of artistic representations. The thirteenth-century scholar Rabbi Meir of Rothenberg, for example, forbade their use in the synagogue.

Why may replicas of the Ten Commandments be used to decorate the ark?

Although the Talmud[48] specifically prohibits duplicating the rooms and verandas of the Jerusalem Temples as well as the tables and the seven-branched *menorot* found within them, it says nothing about replicating the two Tablets of the Law. Why the replication of the Decalogue is permitted is not definitely known, but it may relate to the fact that people never actually saw the tablets. The Ten Commandments were stored in the Holy of Holies, an area off-limits to everyone excluding the High Priest, who visited it once a year.

Representations of the Decalogue became, in time, the most popular of all synagogue decorative motifs. Made of wood or stone, the tablets are mounted above the ark or on the outside of the synagogue building. Oftentimes Decalogue motifs are embroidered on the ark curtain or Torah mantle.

Why do lions appear as decorative symbols on arks and on Torah appurtenances?

The prophet Amos (3:8) wrote: "When a lion roars, who will not fear!" The lion, a symbol of strength, courage, and majesty, is mentioned in the Bible more times than any other animal.[49]

When blessing his sons and predicting their futures, Jacob compared his fourth son, Judah, to a lion (Genesis 49:9), and Judah indeed measured up to the prediction. By the time the Land of Canaan was divided among the Israelites, Judah had become the most powerful and important of all tribes.

David belonged to the tribe of Judah, and when he

became king, the dominance of the tribe was firmly established. Other great leaders, including Isaiah and Nehemiah, were also members of the tribe of Judah.

Given this distinguished history, it is understandable that the characteristics of the lion—strength, courage, majesty—should have become associated with the Torah, the centerpiece of Judaism, and its likeness should appear as decorative art on arks, ark curtains, and Torah covers.

Why is the Star of David used as a symbol on the ark?

The Star of David is called *Magen David,* literally "shield of David."

According to one tradition, King David used a six-pointed shield, but there is no mention of this in the Bible. In fact, hexagram-shaped figures were unheard of until Roman times, when they were used as decorative symbols on mosaic pavements.

The earliest placement of the Star of David in a synagogue dates back 1,800 years, when it appeared next to a five-pointed star (pentagram) on a synagogue frieze in Capernaum. In sixth-century Italy, the Star of David emblem appeared for the first time on a tombstone. From this time onward, we encounter the *Magen David* on a variety of religious articles, including arks and Torah mantles.

In the Middle Ages, Jewish mystics (kabbalists) used the terms "Shield of David" and "Shield of Solomon" interchangeably, usually in connection with magic.[50] But not until the seventeenth century, in Prague, do we encounter the Star of David as a specifically Jewish emblem. At that time it appeared as the official seal of the community on printed prayerbooks and on documents of various kinds. Only as recently as the nineteenth century did the *Magen David* become widely used among Jews. In 1897 the First Zionist Congress adopted the Star of David as its symbol, and in 1948 it became the central figure in the flag of the new State of Israel.

Chapter 4

Writing the Torah

INTRODUCTION

Although many of the laws pertaining to the writing of a Torah scroll are scattered throughout the Talmud, most are found in the minor tractates Soferim and Sefer Torah. In the twelfth century, Maimonides collected and systematized all talmudic laws pertaining to the writing of Torah scrolls, and these are found in his *Mishneh Torah*. These laws are also recorded in the *Shulchan Aruch*, the sixteenth-century code composed by Rabbi Joseph Caro.

The writing of a Torah scroll must be done with a reed or a quill taken from a kosher fowl. The ink must be black and specially prepared. The parchment on which the Torah scroll is written must be from the hide of a kosher animal. The size of each parchment sheet and the number of columns per sheet is prescribed, as is the width of each line of script and the size of the margins to be left on all sides.

The manner of writing particular letters, lines, sections, and poetic portions is precisely delineated and must be followed by the scribe *(sofer)* so that the finished product conforms to the laws and traditions established by the Masoretes. (See Chapter Eight, The Masoretic Text). Deviation from the prescriptions laid down by the Masoretes is reason enough to invalidate an otherwise perfectly written Torah.

The scribe is considered to be engaged in sacred work, and it is therefore customary for him to immerse himself in a ritual bath *(mikva)* on the day that he begins writing a new scroll. Before setting quill to parchment, to be mindful of the sanctity of the task he is about to undertake, the scribe declares, "I am writing the Torah in the name of its sanctity and the name of God in its sanctity." And each time, before he writes the name of God, the scribe says aloud, "I am writing the name of God in honor of His holy name."[1]

When a scribe writes a new Torah, he must have before him a corrected scroll or printed Pentateuch to serve as his guide.[2] No matter what precautions are taken, however, because of the difficulty of the scribe's task, which can take as long as a year, mistakes are inevitable. The following errors are most common:

1. *Dittographic errors,* made by writing the same letter or word twice.
2. *Haplographic errors,* made by omitting one or two identical letters or words that rightfully follow each other.
3. *Homoioteleutonic errors,* made by omitting a few words or lines because they appear further on in the passage. The scribe's eye picks up on the repeated words and as a result fails to include the words in between.

Most simple errors may be corrected by the scribe by scratching out the incorrect writing with a sharp blade. More serious errors are subject to other types of treatment, as discussed in this chapter.

The conscientious scribe, as he writes a scroll, is ever mindful of the verse in Exodus (15:2), "This is my God and I will glorify Him." The scribe proves that he is glorifying God, says the Talmud, by writing a beautiful scroll with choice ink and a fine reed pen or quill on selected, well-finished parchment.[3]

———— ❏ ————

Why is a scribe called a *sofer*?

The Hebrew word *sofer* (plural, *soferim*) means "one who counts." The Talmud informs us that some of the early scribes were called *soferim* because they used to count all the letters, words, and verses of the Torah.[4] They did so in order to make certain that letters or words were neither added nor omitted and that a Torah scroll represented as correct was indeed so.

The practice of counting words, verses, and lines was well known in the literary world of the Greeks and Romans and appears to have been introduced by the librarians of the great library in Alexandria, Egypt, in the second or third centuries B.C.E. Authors and copyists would indicate at the end of their works all or some of these vital statistics for two reasons: to help teachers and students refer to passages and to enable buyers of manuscripts to check whether the exact number of words and lines were copied—without addition or deletion.

One of the earliest Jewish authors to employ this method of recording essential statistics was the first-century C.E. historian Flavius Josephus, who indicated at the end of his *Antiquities of the Jews* that "the work consists of twenty books [major parts] and 60,000 lines."

Aside from the activity of actually counting the contents of the Torah, the more practical aspect of the work of most *soferim* involved the actual writing of scrolls as well as the writing of parchments for use in *tefilin* and *mezuzot*.

Why is a scribe sometimes called *sofer setam*?

SeTaM (also spelled *stam*) is an acronym for three words: *sefarim* (plural of *sefer*), which refers to Torah scrolls; *tefilin;* and *mezuzot* (plural of *mezuza*). A scribe is expert at writing these three types of religious objects and is therefore called a *sofer setam*.[5]

Why is it preferred that a scribe be right-handed?

In biblical times the right hand and the right side were considered superior. (See pages 44 and 155 for a full discussion.)

In accordance with this belief, the Rabbis encouraged right-handed persons to become scribes.[6] They based this on Scripture, pointing to Deuteronomy 6:8-9, which says, "And you shall bind them for a sign upon your hand. . . . And you shall write them on the doorposts of your house . . ." Although in the Pentateuch these commandments relate to *tefilin* and *mezuzot,* the Rabbis of later centuries associated them with the Torah.

Noting the juxtaposition of the words "And you shall *bind* them" and "And you shall *write* them," Rabbi David ben Samuel Halevi says in his commentary on the *Shulchan Aruch* that just as the tying (binding) of the *tefilin* around the left arm is done by the right hand, so must the writing of *tefilin* (and Torah) be done with the right hand.[7]

Today, the generally accepted view is that a left-handed person is permitted to write a Torah scroll because the left hand of a left-handed person is equal in power and strength to the right hand of a right-handed person.[8]

Why did the Rabbis forbid a scribe from writing a Torah scroll from dictation?

The Rabbis ruled[9] that a scribe, when writing a Torah scroll, must have an accurate copy of the Torah before him and must pronounce each word as he writes it. In early times the scribe referred to a handwritten scroll or codex; today he uses a printed copy of the Pentateuch. The scribe may not write from memory,[10] nor may anyone dictate the words of the Torah to him.

There are two basic reasons for this ruling: First, it ensures that the scribe will concentrate intently on the sacred words of the Torah as he writes them. By constantly referring to a correct text, his mind is prevented from wandering, which would result in words being written mechanically and possibly incorrectly.

Second, errors in spelling are less likely to occur if the scribe sees each word in print immediately before he is to write it. If the scribe were to write from dictation, frequent errors might occur as a result of mishearing or lack of familiarity with the text. For example, if the single word *aylav*, meaning "to him," were dictated in the Sephardic pronunciation, the word would be sounded as *elav*. This pronunciation could lead the scribe to believe that two separate words, *el av*, meaning "to the father," had been dictated.

Such errors can also occur very easily with the words *lo* and *hi*, which are sometimes misspelled in the accepted Torah text but have not been corrected because that would be counter to tradition. In the Torah the word *lo* is often incorrectly spelled *lamed alef*, meaning "no, not," when it should have correctly been spelled *lamed vav*, meaning "to him," as the sense of the verse would dictate.[11] And the word *hi*, pronounced *hee* and meaning "she," normally spelled *hay yod alef*, is often incorrectly spelled in the Torah as *hay vav alef*, pronounced *hu* and meaning "he."[12] If writing from dictation, the scribe might not spell the word *hay vav alef* as tradition demands.

Why do scribes consult a *Tikun* when writing a Torah?

According to one tradition, on Yom Kippur the High Priest would read from a Torah that was kept in the Temple precincts. This same scroll was used by scribes as a guide when writing new Torah scrolls.[13]

Over the centuries, scribes have always consulted a master text. Maimonides, the twelfth-century authority, revealed that when he wrote his own personal Torah he used as a guide a copy of the Torah text that had been worked on and approved by the Ben Asher family of Tiberias.[14]

When printing was introduced, a book called the *Tikun*

was published. This carefully edited printed text of the Pentateuch became the standard reference for scribes. To avoid mistakes when writing a scroll, the scribe would read aloud a sentence from the *Tikun* and then proceed to write it.

Why do scribes immerse themselves in a *mikva* before writing a Torah scroll?

Since writing a Torah scroll is highly sacred, it was considered proper for a scribe to immerse himself in a ritual bath *(mikva)* before beginning the process. Some scribes immerse themselves each day before they begin work, while others do so only on the very first day, at the beginning of the entire undertaking.

Why are women not permitted to write a Torah scroll?

Although not all authorities agree, the accepted rule is that a woman may not write a Torah scroll, and if she does, the scroll is considered invalid for public use.[15]

The main reason for invalidating a Torah written by a woman is that according to Jewish law a scroll may be read in public only if it has been written by one who is eligible to read it publicly. Since women in post-talmudic times were not permitted to read the Torah before a congregation, they were not permitted to write a Torah either.[16]

Why is it no longer necessary to split animal hide for use as Torah parchment?

Parchment on which a Torah scroll (as well as *tefilin* and *mezuzot*) may be written must come from the hide of a domestic or wild animal that has split hooves and chews its cud, as prescribed in Leviticus 11:3. The hides of sheep, goats, and calves were most popularly used.

The Talmud[17] tells us that there are three types of parchment:

The first type is called *gevil*. This is the whole hide of the animal. Before the scribe can write on it, it must be cured (see the next question).

The second and third types of parchment are created by dividing—that is, slicing—the very thick *gevil*. The two resulting pieces are called *kelaf* and *doksostos* (or *duxustus*). *Kelaf* is a Hebrew word, *doksostos* a Greek word.

The *kelaf* is that portion of the hide that is closest to the hairy surface of the animal (the exterior portion), and *doksostos* is the inside half of the split hide, the portion closest to the fleshy part of the animal. *Kelaf,* says the Talmud, is considered superior to *doksostos*. While in biblical and early post-biblical times the whole unsplit hide (the *gevil*) was used for writing a Torah scroll, in talmudic and later times the *kelaf* alone was also used for this purpose. *Kelaf* came to be preferred over *doksostos* for scroll writing primarily because it was thinner and could more easily be rolled up. For the same reason *kelaf* was used for writing *tefilin*. *Mezuzot* were not always rolled up and hence were written on the thicker *doksostos*.

Today, hides are no longer split. They can be stretched sufficiently thin so that the Torah scrolls eventually written on the parchment made from them can be easily rolled up and will not be too heavy. It should be noted that today the term *kelaf* is used to refer to the whole unsplit hide of the animal, what was formerly called the *gevil*.

When the scribe writes on the whole unsplit hide of the animal, after it has been scraped clean and cured, he writes on the exterior side, the side where the animal's hair once was. In the days when cured *kelaf* was used for scroll writing, the scribe wrote on the underside of the skin, the part that had been nearest the fleshy part of the animal. When the scribe wrote on *doksostos,* he wrote on the upper side, the side where the split had taken place.[18]

Why must the hide of an animal be cured before it can be used as Torah parchment?

Before parchment can be used by a scribe, it must be

made smooth and durable and able to accept ink. It is essential that the ink completely adhere to the parchment, for should the letters peel off, the scroll becomes invalid.

The technique of treating the hide of an animal with chemicals and other ingredients to render it suitable as a writing surface was known to the early Greeks. They were the first to create what we call parchment, a word derived from the Greek *pergamon*, named after a city in Asia Minor. From the fourth century C.E. onward parchment was widely used, and because of its greater durability it replaced papyrus as a writing surface for manuscripts.

The method of cleaning and softening animal hide has changed throughout the centuries. During talmudic times, salt and barley flour were sprinkled on the skins, which were then soaked in the juice of gallnuts.[19] Gallnuts are a source of tannic acid, and when rubbed on parchment produce a good, durable writing surface.

In modern times skins are softened by soaking them in water for two days. The hair is then removed by soaking the hides in limewater for nine days. Finally, the skins are rinsed, dried, and stretched on a frame. When necessary, creases are ironed out.[20]

Why is it permissible to write a Torah scroll on the skin of an animal that is not kosher for eating purposes?

The Rabbis ruled[21] that an undomesticated animal that is listed in Leviticus 11 as kosher but that has not been ritually slaughtered—for example, a deer found dead in a field of natural causes (called a *nevela*) or one killed by another animal (called a *terefa*)—is not kosher for eating purposes, but its skin may be used for the writing of a scroll.

Rabbi Joshua explained that such animals found in the field are to be considered as having met death by an act of God. They are forbidden to be consumed as food, as stated in Leviticus 22:8 and Deuteronomy 14:21, but this does not exclude the use of their carcasses in other ways.

Why must a Torah scroll parchment be prepared by a Jew?

When preparing the hide of an animal for the writing of a Torah scroll, the tanning must be done with *that* express purpose in mind. The Talmud says that the curing process must be performed by a Jew who expressly states that the parchment upon which he is working will be used for the writing of a Torah scroll.[22] Consequently, if the work is done by a non-Jew (and the Talmud includes Samaritans in this category), such parchment may not be used.[23]

The same rule applies to the parchment upon which *tefilin* are written but not to the parchment upon which a *mezuza* is written. *Mezuzot* are lower than *tefilin* on the scale of sanctity.

Why may the skin of kosher fish not be used to write a Torah scroll?

A scribe may write a Torah scroll on the hide of any domestic or wild animal or on the skin of any bird as long as it is of the kosher variety listed in Leviticus 11. He may not, however, use the skin of a kosher fish because, as explained by Maimonides, fish have a foul odor, and this odor does not disappear even after tanning.[24]

Why is the skin of birds rarely used for writing sacred parchments?

While the skin of kosher birds, after being properly tanned, may theoretically be used as Torah parchment, this is rarely done because the skin is so thin that perforations would be formed by the pressure the scribe must exert when writing certain letters. Perforations in the parchment would render the scroll invalid.[25]

Why must a Torah be written in scroll form on one side of a sheet of parchment?

In the first century C.E., instead of writing the books of

the Bible in scroll form—on sheets of parchment stitched together and rolled up—it became more convenient to write them in codex form. Codices were written on smaller sheets of parchment or papyrus which were then assembled and bound between pieces of wood. The codex Bible format was preferred by the new, emerging Christian Church. By the fourth century it was in common use by both Christians and Jews.

Wanting to maintain the distinctiveness of Jewish tradition, the Rabbis ruled that a Torah written for use in the synagogue must always be written on parchment rather than on papyrus, on one side of a sheet rather than on both sides, and that it must be in scroll form. Codices were used by Jews for study purposes only, not for reading in the synagogue. Most of the fragments found in the Cairo Geniza are from codices, relatively few from scrolls.

Why does a scribe use a quill to write a Torah scroll?

In talmudic times (the first five centuries C.E.) scribes used pieces of wood or reeds as pens, but when it was discovered that quills were more durable and sturdy, they became the preferred writing instrument. Quills are generally taken from geese or turkeys.

The scribe prepares the quill by shaving the thick end of the feather shaft to a fine point and then slitting the tip lengthwise. This allows the scribe to fashion sharp, fine letters or broad ones, as needed.[26]

Why did Rabbis of the Talmud express differing views about the use of vitriol in the ink for writing a Torah?

Vitriol is a chemical compound containing one of several sulphates of metals, such as iron sulphate, copper sulphate, and zinc sulphate. When vitriol is an ingredient in the ink mixture used to write Torah scrolls, the letters written with it become hard, indelible, and have a glassy appearance.

In early talmudic times there was a dispute among authorities as to whether vitriol may be added to ink used to write a Torah. In one tractate[27] vitriol is totally prohibited. In others[28] it is permitted as long as three verses in the Book of Numbers (5:21-23), which spell out the curses that will befall an adulterous woman *(sota)*, are written in ink that is erasable. If written with ink containing vitriol, it would not be possible for the Priest to erase those verses when he rubs them with the "bitter waters" (verse 23), which is required of him as part of a ceremony that must be performed before the accused wife is fed the bitter waters which will determine her guilt or innocence.[29]

When the Ordeal of Bitter Waters was canceled by the Rabbis after the destruction of the Temple in 70 C.E. (because the sacrificial system was no longer operative), vitriol (usually copper sulphate crystals) became a common ingredient of ink used for scroll writing and remains so today. The preparation is usually made by boiling a mixture of gallnuts, gum arabic, and copper sulphate crystals. Some scribes add vinegar and/or alcohol to the mixture.[30]

Why is it prohibited to write a Torah scroll with gold ink?

The Talmud[31] relates that in Alexandria, Egypt, in the early centuries B.C.E., a Torah scroll was in use in which the name of God was repeatedly written in gold. When this was brought to the attention of the Sages, they ruled emphatically that "sacred scrolls must not be written in gold" and ordered that the scroll in question be stored in a *geniza* for eventual burial.[32]

Generally, scrolls written wholly or partially with gold ink are banned because they are said to smack of ostentation, and the use of such scrolls is not considered compatible with the spirit of modesty that should pervade synagogue services. Another explanation offered is that gold lettering in a Torah reminds one of the gold that was used in fashioning the Golden Calf (Exodus 32), an irreverent act that is deplored in Jewish tradition.

It is interesting that the Talmud forbids one to paint boxes of *tefilin* with gold paint in order to make them conspicuous, because this is a practice of the *minim*. *Minim*, often translated as "sectaries," is the name used in the Talmud for Christians. It appears from this reference that for quite a few centuries after the beginning of Christianity, Christians continued to observe the Jewish law pertaining to the wearing of *tefilin*.

Why do scribes write the word "Amalek" before starting to write a Torah scroll?

To make sure that the ink is proper in color and viscosity and that the quill is properly slit at the tip to produce the desired thickness of lettering, the scribe runs a test by writing on a piece of paper the name "Amalek" and then drawing lines through it several times. The name was selected because Amalek is the nation that perpetrated a cowardly attack on the Israelites when they fled Egypt.

In Jewish history the Amalekites are recalled with disdain. The Bible (Deuteronomy 25:17-19) puts it this way:

Remember what Amalek did to you after you left Egypt . . . how he [they] surprised you on the march . . . and cut down all the stragglers in your rear. Therefore, when the Lord your God grants you safety from your enemies . . . you shall blot out their memory . . . Do not forget [to do so].

Thus, it became customary for a scribe to test his pen and ink by writing "Amalek" and then crossing it out, thus "blotting out their memory."

Why must the scribe first rule lines on the parchment sheet before starting to write a scroll?

A sloppily written Torah scroll was frowned upon by the

Rabbis. They believed that a holy scroll must be written with great care and be not only accurate but beautiful. To ensure that the words of the Torah are written straight and that there is equal space between lines, the parchment is first ruled.

A total of forty-three lines are drawn on the average-sized parchment sheet in order to accommodate forty-two lines of script. The top line serves as a guide; nothing is written above it. Two vertical lines are drawn on either side of the column to ensure that all lines will begin and end evenly.[33]

The instrument used by the scribe for drawing guidelines is called a *sargel*. For the ruling of sacred documents (a Torah scroll, *tefilin*, or a *mezuza*) the *sargel* is to be made from a reed. It is prohibited to use an instrument made of iron or steel because these metals are identified with war and violence. No ink is used in making the guidelines.[34]

Why does a scribe often turn a sheet of parchment face down as soon as it has been written?

The Talmud says, "If a scroll cannot be covered with a cloth, it may be turned over on its writing."[35] The point of the regulation is to emphasize that if a covering is not available to protect the newly written sheet of parchment from being smudged while the ink is drying, it is quite proper, not disrespectful, to turn the sheet of parchment over, face down.

It is said of the second-century C.E. scribe Rabbi Yehuda, a disciple of Rabbi Akiba, that when he wrote a Torah scroll, in order to avoid the possibility of letters becoming smudged he would add vitriol to his ink, which would cause the ink to dry more quickly. The Rabbis[36] visualized the possibility of a fly perching itself atop the crownlets *(tagin)* on the letter *dalet* in the word *echad*, the last letter of the *Shema* (Deuteronomy 6:4), while the ink was still wet. As a consequence the letter might be smudged and the *dalet* would look like a *resh*. The net effect would be that the word *echad* would be read as *acher,* meaning "other," and instead of the verse reading "Hear, O Israel, the Lord is One," it would read, ". . . the Lord is [an]other."

Why are most Torah scrolls between eighteen inches and twenty-two inches high?

Jewish law established a rule that the height of a Torah scroll and its circumference should be equal.[37]

The law also specifies[38] that the average height of a Torah be six *tefachim.* The commentaries explain that the reason for establishing six *tefachim* as the proper height of a Torah parchment is that each of the tablets *(luchot)* of the Ten Commandments which Moses brought down from Mount Sinai was six *tefachim* wide by six *tefachim* high.[39]

A *tefach* (singular of *tefachim*) is the width of an average palm, the width of four fingers of one's hand excluding the thumb. This amounts to approximately three and one-half inches (9.3 centimeters), which would make the height of an acceptable Torah approximately twenty-one inches. Most Torot today are written on parchment ranging from eighteen inches to twenty-two inches high.

Why are *gidin* used to join one parchment sheet to another in a Torah scroll?

After the scribe has finished writing all the sheets of a Torah scroll, he sews one parchment to another with *gidin,* which are made from the dried veins of a kosher animal. These veins are stretched until they are as fine as thread.

The kosher animal from which the veins are taken need not be one that has been ritually slaughtered, but it must be one of those animals listed as kosher in Leviticus. Thus, if a deer (a wild animal that is kosher) is found dead in the field and had not been slaughtered in accordance with Jewish law, the carcass may not be used as food, but its veins may be used to make thread for sewing sheets of parchment.[40]

At times, *gidin* are also made from tendons taken from the foot muscles of kosher animals.

Why is the script used by scribes known as Assyrian script?

The type of lettering used today by scribes is referred to as Assyrian script *(ketav Ashuri)*, after its place of origin.[41] This advanced form of the earlier Aramaic script which was used by Jews in the sixth century B.C.E. is sometimes called square script *(ketav meruba)* because of its shape.[42]

The law demands that a Torah scroll be written in one style and that it be consistent throughout. The accepted script is the *ketav Ashuri,* of which there are two different types, one employed by Sephardim and one by Ashkenazim.

As the illustrations below show, the primary difference between the two styles is that the Ashkenazic lettering is much thicker, requiring at times that the *sofer* make several strokes to form a letter.

ועתה כתבו לכם את
השירה הזאת ולמדה

ועתה כתבו לכם את
השירה הזאת ולמדה

Sephardic script.   Ashkenazic script.

Why did square letters become the only acceptable type of writing for sacred scrolls?

Before the Second Temple was destroyed in 586 B.C.E., leading to the dispersion of the Jews to Babylonia, the old Phoenician-Hebrew script was used to write Torah scrolls. During their years of exile in Babylonia the Jews adopted the square Assyrian (Aramaic) script used in that country. When they returned to Palestine in 538 B.C.E., the Jews replaced the Phoenician-Hebrew script with the newly adopted square style.[43] In fact, the Rabbis of the Talmud forbade the usage of the Phoenician-Hebrew script for the writing of Torot to be read publicly.[44]

One probable reason for considering the Phoenician-

Hebrew script less sacred than the Assyrian was that the Samaritans, who had not been dispersed to Babylonia and who had been rejected by the Jewish community, continued to write their scrolls in the older script. To them the introduction of the newer Assyrian script was a flagrant violation of tradition. When the Samaritans separated themselves from the Jewish community during the Maccabean period (second century B.C.E.),[45] the Rabbis banned the use of the Samaritan scrolls and the script employed in writing them.

Why are some letters in the Torah scroll embellished?

The embellishments used by the scribe to decorate the letters in the Torah are called *tagin* (singular, *tag*). *Tagin*, an Aramaic word meaning "daggers," are probably so named because these decorations, which look like small daggers, resemble the shape of the Hebrew letter *za'yin*. These embellishments are referred to in the Talmud as *ketarim* (singular, *keter*), "crowns." The New Testament (Matthew 5:18) refers to them as "tittles."

Letters with *tagin*, as described in *Sefer Ha-tagin*.

The Talmud[46] considers the *tagin* to have come directly from Sinai, to have already been in place when the Torah was transmitted to Moses. Tradition also has it that there once existed a manual known as *Sefer Ha-tagin*, which described the letters that were to be adorned with these crowns. This handbook, which was passed down through the generations, is often referred to in manuscripts from the Middle Ages.

Modern scholars tend to believe that *tagin* are nothing more than calligraphic flourishes introduced by early scribes in order to enhance the beauty of the Torah lettering. While this may be the case, it is quite possible that the fact that *tagin* are dagger-shaped—like the letter *za'yin*—has a greater significance. The dagger is a device one uses to protect himself and his property, and the early Rabbis saw it as an instrument that could protect the Torah from those who would violate it in any way.

In the Midrash[47] King Hezekiah shows some of the "precious things" of the Temple that are mentioned in Isaiah (39:2). Rabbi Yochanan comments, "He showed a dagger swallowing a dagger." And Rabbi Levi adds, "With these we fight our battles and are victorious." Interestingly, this same dagger or *za'yin* plays a significant role in the interpretation of Psalm 91.

What is significant about the words in this Psalm is that all the letters of the Hebrew alphabet appear in its sixteen verses—except for the letter *za'yin*, the "dagger." This letter was not included, say the mystics, so that it could remain a free spirit to roam and protect those who speak the words of Psalm 91.[48]

It is not inconceivable that the *za'yin*-shaped *tagin* that appear on letters of the Torah have a similar purpose—namely, to protect the words of the Torah.

The seven letters most commonly decorated with *tagin*.

Seven of the twenty-two letters in the Hebrew alphabet are decorated with *tagin*. These are the letters *shin, a'yin, tet, nun, za'yin, gimmel,* and *tzadi*. Most have three *tagin* and some have one. There is also a tradition that the letters *bet, dalet, kuf, chet, yod,* and *hay* should be adorned with one *tag*. (See illustrations.)

Scholars generally agree that when a letter has more than one branch, the *tag* is placed by the scribe on the upper left-hand corner of the left-most branch. When three strokes appear as part of the *tag,* the center stroke is drawn slightly higher than the other two.

Why is a Torah considered by some authorities to be invalid if it is written without *tagin* on the appropriate letters?

Tagin are used to beautify the writing of a Torah and, according to Maimonides, if decorations are omitted the scroll is nevertheless valid.[49] Maimonides considers a scroll fit for use if all letters and words are written clearly, without omissions or additions.

Ashkenazim, however, do not agree. The Ashkenazic authors of the Magen Avraham and the Be'er Haytayv commentaries of the *Shulchan Aruch*[50] state that a scroll is not valid if it does not have *tagin* on the appropriate letters. They consider the use of *tagin* to be a requirement that cannot be ignored because they were part of the original transmission from God to Moses.[51]

Why is the first letter of the Torah decorated with four crowns?

The Rabbis ruled[52] that the *bet* of *bereshit,* which is the first letter of the first word in the Torah, deserves special treatment. They therefore mandated that every scribe write the letter *bet* so that it is larger than the average letter. They also ruled that four *tagin* be placed on the *bet,* one more than is found on any other letter in the Torah.

Why did the early scribes introduce five final letters into the Hebrew alphabet?

The earliest manuscripts of the Torah (and the rest of the Bible) were not divided into chapters or verses. One verse ran into another, and even words had no spacing between them.

To alleviate problems faced by the *baal koray* and by students who had difficulty determining where words began or ended, the early scribes introduced final letters for the following five consonants: *mem, nun, tzadi, pay, chaf.*[53] Whenever a word ended with one of these letters, the shape of the letter was changed (usually it was elongated), thus enabling the reader to recognize where the words ended.

The need for a device to indicate the ending of words was particularly acute with two-lettered words, such as *ach, im, min, af,* and *ben.* Two-lettered words, it was found, were often mistakenly combined with the short words that preceded them.

Why does the Torah begin with the letter *bet* rather than with the letter *alef?*

Early scholars questioned why the first letter of the first word of the first book of the Bible is a *bet* (the second letter of the alphabet) rather than an *alef* (the first letter of the alphabet). Speculation continued for centuries, and a variety of explanations are offered in talmudic texts and later midrashic commentaries. The following are among the more interesting theories[54] to have been put forth: ·

- The Torah begins with a *bet* to serve as a reminder not to probe too deeply into the origin of the world because that may lead to heresy. Rabbi Levi put it this way: "Just as the letter *bet* is closed on three sides but open in the front, so are you *not* permitted to investigate matters that are above and below, what is before and what is behind." Sensing that this explanation may be misleading (since Rabbi Levi lists *four* forbidden areas of investigation, although the *bet* is sealed on only *three* sides), his colleague Bar Kappara comments: "You may speculate about things that happened after Creation, but you may not speculate about that which transpired before Creation."[55]

- *Bet* was selected because it has a numerical value of two and therefore represents the two worlds: this world and the world-to-come, that is, the Messianic Age.
- *Bet* pleaded before God that it deserved the honor of being the first letter of the Torah because it is the first letter of the word *baruch,* meaning "blessed."
- *Bet* was preferred over *alef* because *alef* is the first letter of the Hebrew word *arur,* meaning "cursed." In addition, *alef* is a weak letter. It stands on two spindly legs, while *bet* has a flat, strong base.
- *Bet* was favored because of the two points that protrude from it; the first extends from the base of the letter and points behind it; the second protrudes from the top of the letter and faces upward.

  To anyone who questions the origin of the Torah by asking "Who created you?" the *bet* can answer by pointing upward, toward God. And to anyone who asks, "What is the name of the One who created you?" *bet* can answer by pointing behind it to the letter *alef,* which is the first letter of the name of God.
- In one *midrash* the alert *alef* is portrayed as very modest. It did not push its claim to be the first letter of the Torah and was rewarded instead by becoming the first letter of the Decalogue (Exodus 20:2). (The *alef* is the first letter of *anochi,* meaning "I," and *anochi* is the first word of the Ten Commandments.)

  In a different *midrash* Rabbi Eleazar portrays the *alef* as being rather pushy: "For twenty-six generations from the time of Adam the *alef* complained to God, 'Sovereign of the universe, I am the first of the letters of the alphabet, yet you did not create the world with me!' "

  "When I reveal My Torah at Sinai," God answered, "I will place you at the head of the commandments, as the first letter of *anochi.*"

Why did the Rabbis rule that a line in the Torah should be able to accommodate thirty letters?

The Rabbis[56] said that a line in the Torah should not be so long as to confuse the Torah reader as his eyes shift from line to line, nor should it be so short as to make the Torah look like an epistle or letter. The proper line length was determined to be five "fingers." A finger *(etzba)* was reckoned as being approximately one inch, the distance from the tip of the thumb to the first joint or from the first joint to the second joint of the middle finger.

As a simple guide, the Rabbis recommended that the length of a Torah line be such that it can accommodate the longest word in the Torah three times. That word, *le-mishpechotayhem* (Genesis 8:19), meaning "to their families," contains ten Hebrew letters.[57]

The number of characters found in a given line of the Torah is dependent on the width of the letters on a particular line and on the scribe's writing style.

Why are Torah scrolls written with not less than three columns per sheet of parchment?

The Talmud[58] ruled that a scroll must contain not less than three or more than eight columns of script per sheet of parchment. Jewish tradition, in which the number three is considered special, prefers that all Torot be written with only three columns to a parchment sheet. Some commentators explain that sheets with three columns are most attractive, adding to the beauty of the Torah scroll.

Why has it become standard for Torah scrolls to contain forty-two lines in each column?

The Talmud offers the following reason for the selection of forty-two lines as an appropriate number to be contained in a Torah column. Chapter 33 of the Book of Numbers describes the itinerary followed by the Israelites after the Exodus: forty-two stops were made in the course of their journey from Sinai to the Plains of Moab on the banks of the Jordan. Since forty-two stops were made, said the Rabbis, forty-two lines should be contained in every Torah column.[59]

There was also a practical consideration for selecting forty-two lines per column—namely that when placing that number of lines in a column, a readable script size can be employed by the scribe and the resulting scroll will be neither too large nor too heavy.

Why were Torah scrolls sometimes written with more than forty-two lines in a column?

Before the number of lines in a Torah column was standardized at forty-two, some Torot were occasionally written with sixty, seventy-two, or ninety-eight lines per column.[60]

The number of lines varied with the height of the parchment sheet used and the size script employed by the scribe. The taller the parchment, the more lines it would accommodate; and the larger the script, the fewer the number of words and lines there would be in a column.

Biblical justification for writing sixty-lined columns is based on the appearance of the word "sixty" in Numbers 1:46. There we find the results of a census which reported that the number of Israelites of military age was sixty myriads and 3,550 (for a total of 603,550).

The writing of seventy-two lines in a Torah column is associated with the number of elders mentioned in Numbers 11:16. This is confusing because the number of elders referred to in the text is actually seventy, not seventy-two.[61]

The justification for writing Torot with ninety-eight lines per column is found in Deuteronomy 27:28, where the number of curses and warnings totals ninety-eight.

A Torah scroll equal in size to another scroll but with more lines per column (and hence smaller letters) will naturally be more difficult to read. Such Torot were written because they required less parchment and were consequently less costly to produce and easier to transport because of their lighter weight. This was an obvious advantage to students.

Why are the margins found in a Torah scroll precisely prescribed?

The Rabbis took great pains in prescribing the size of the margins to be left by a scribe when he writes a Torah scroll for public use. (Scrolls written for private study were not subject to restrictions.) The singular purpose behind the legislation was to enhance the appearance of publicly-used scrolls.[62]

The following rules pertaining to margins were established:[63]

1. A three-inch margin must be left from the top of the parchment to the top of the first line of script.[64]
2. A four-inch margin must be left below each column. A larger margin is required here because the bottom of the Torah is subject to more wear, and to remove the frayed portion it is necessary at times to trim off some of the parchment.
3. A full two-inch margin must be left between each column of script. Where sheets are to be sewn together, an extra "finger-width" (one inch) is allowed for the sewing. Nothing may be written in the space between columns unless it is necessary in exceptional cases to squeeze an extra letter into a line.

A space of four lines must be left between each of the books of the Pentateuch.[65]

Why did scribes begin the practice of extending the width of certain letters?

Before the ninth century the columns of Torah scrolls and codices were not justified on the left side. Some scribes felt that Torot would be more attractive if all lines ended evenly, and they therefore introduced the practice of sometimes writing letters wider than normal in order to accomplish this. Extending letters was also an aid to scribes in arranging the text so that columns would begin with the letter *vav*.

Among the letters most often extended are *tav, resh, hay, dalet, lamed,* and the final *mem.* Why these particular letters were selected is not definitely known, but it would appear that they lend themselves most readily to lateral extension. Extended letters appear most often at the end of a word, although they can also be found within a word.

Why does almost every column in a Torah scroll begin with the Hebrew letter *vav*?

Most scribes follow an old established tradition of beginning almost every column of a Torah scroll with the Hebrew letter *vav*. This tradition is based upon a phrase in the Book of Exodus (27:10) which describes the hanging of the curtains in the Tabernacle erected in the desert.[66] Made of linen, the curtains were supported by twenty posts (pillars), known in Hebrew as *amudim* (singular, *amud*), which were set five cubits (7½ feet) apart. A silver band bordered the top of the curtain, to which were attached silver hooks known as *vavim* (singular, *vav*).

The Torah uses the term *vavay ha-amudim,* meaning "hooks of the posts," in describing the hardware upon which the curtains of the Tabernacle were hung. Scribes, upon discovering this reference, believed it was a signal to start each column *(amud)* in a scroll with a *vav,* thus, in a manner of speaking, suspending each Torah column on a *vav,* just as the curtains of the Tabernacle were suspended on *vavim.*[67]

Why did the scribes insist that six particular words in the Torah must be at the head of a column?

In the years prior to the thirteenth century scribes who were engaged in Torah writing developed the practice of always placing six particular words at the head of a column. These words are:

1. *Bereshit* in Genesis 1:1.
2. *Yehuda* in Genesis 49:8.
3. *Ha-ba'im* in Exodus 14:28.
4. *Shemor* in Exodus 34:11.
5. *Ma* in Numbers 24:5.
6. *Ve-a'ida* in Deuteronomy 31:28.

The first letter of each of these words—*bet, yod, hay, shin, mem, vav*—when taken together form the acronym *be-ya shemo,* which means "by His name, Ya." *Ya* is a short form of Yehova (Jehova), the name of God.

It would appear that these particular words were singled out because they represent situations and concepts that are basic to Judaism:

- In Genesis 1:1 the word *bereshit* establishes God as the first Cause, God as Creator.
- In Genesis 49:8 the word *Yehuda* establishes the tribe of Judah, to which King David belonged, as the tribe from which the royal family and eventually the Messiah would emerge.

The shaded type is a Masoretic note indicating that the letter *yod* in the word *Yehuda* (Genesis 49:8) is to begin a new column in handwritten scrolls.

- In Exodus 14:28 the word *ha-ba'im* represents the belief that God is on the side of Israel and will save them just as He saved the Israelites who fled from the Egyptians.[68]

- In Exodus 34:11 the word *shemor* represents a renewal of the terms of the Covenant after Moses returned from the mountaintop with the second set of Ten Commandments.
- In Numbers 24:5 the word *ma* is the first word of *Ma tovu ohalecha Yaakov* ("How goodly are thy tents, O Jacob"), which was uttered by Israel's enemy Balaam, whose intention to curse Israel was unsuccessful. The curse turned into a blessing that is part of Jewish liturgy today.[69]
- In Deuteronomy 31:28 the word *ve-a'ida*, which means "And I will call forth [heaven and earth] as witnesses" confirms the eternal nature of the Covenant between God and Israel. Heaven and earth, which are also eternal, will testify to that fact.[70]

Not all authorities considered it necessary to follow the scribal practice of having the above six words begin a column. Rabbi Meir of Rothenburg, the leading scholar of the thirteenth century, stated that he personally would not follow this procedure and would place at the head of a column only the word *ve-a'ida* (Deuteronomy 31:28), which he felt represents a basic Jewish concept.[71]

Nonetheless, the practice took root, and in the centuries that followed codices used by students were always marked by an asterisk over each of the six words. The asterisk referred to a marginal notation which read *be-ya shemo*, indicating that the word is one of the six that must begin a column. This notation appears in many Hebrew texts today.

Why are scribes required to write the *Song at the Sea* so that it has the appearance of a brick wall?

The Masoretes, who designed the format of the Torah, considered certain portions of the Pentateuch to be extremely important and therefore deserving of special treatment. They established a special style for the writing of

אז ישיר משה ובני ישראל את השירה הזאת ליהוה ויאמרו

לאמר   אשירה ליהוה כי גאה גאה   סוס

ורכבו רמה בים   עזי וזמרת יה ויהי לי   לישועה

זה אלי ואנוהו   אלהי

אבי וארוממנהו   יהוה איש מלחמה יהוה   שמו

מרכבת פרעה וחילו ירה בים   ומבחר

שלשיו טבעו בים סוף   תהמת יכסימו ירדו במצולת כמו

אבן   ימינך יהוה נאדרי בכח   ימינך

יהוה תרעץ אויב   וברב גאונך תהרס   קמיך

תשלח חרנך יאכלמו כקש   וברוח

אפיך נערמו מים   נצבו כמו נד   נזלים

קפאו תהמת בלב ים   אמר

אויב ארדף אשיג   אחלק שלל תמלאמו   נפשי

אריק חרבי תורישמו ידי   נשפת

ברוחך כסמו ים   צללו כעופרת במים   אדירים

מי כמכה באלם יהוה   מי

כמכה נאדר בקדש   נורא תהלת עשה   פלא

נטית ימינך תבלעמו ארץ   נחית

בחסדך עם זו גאלת   נהלת בעזך אל נוה   קדשך

שמעו עמים ירגזון   חיל

אחז ישבי פלשת   אז נבהלו אלופי   אדום

אילי מואב יאחזמו רעד   נמגו

כל ישבי כנען   תפל עליהם אימתה   ופחד

בגדל זרועך ידמו כאבן   עד

יעבר עמך יהוה   עד יעבר עם זו   קנית

תבאמו ותטעמו בהר נחלתך   מכון

לשבתך פעלת יהוה   מקדש אדני כוננו   ידיך

יהוה ימלך לעלם ועד   כי

בא סוס פרעה ברכבו ובפרשיו בים   וישב יהוה עלהם את מי   הים

ובני ישראל הלכו ביבשה בתוך   הים

The scribe writes the *Song at the Sea* so that it has the visual effect of a brick wall.

these portions and ruled that scrolls written differently from the prescribed form are not to be used for public reading.[72]

One such portion of the Torah is the *Song at the Sea* (Exodus 15:1-19), which extols God for his miraculous intervention at the Sea of Reeds. With the Egyptians at their heels, certain annihilation was in store for the Israelites when suddenly the waters parted, forming two solid walls. In between lay a dry path through which the Israelites passed in safety. To dramatize the event and to impress it upon all future generations, the Masoretes instructed all scribes to write the *Song at the Sea* in a special manner to simulate the two walls between which the Children of Israel passed.

The song is to be written in thirty lines, neither more nor less. The first line is to be full. The second line is to be divided into three written sections, with open space in between. The third line is to have two written sections, with white space in between. The fourth line is to be written as the second line, the fifth line as the third line, and so on. The visual effect is to be that of a brick wall.[73]

The *Song of Deborah* (Judges 5:1-31), a song of deliverance from the enemy, is recited as part of the prophetic reading when the *Song at the Sea* is read from the Torah. It is written in the same brick wall-like style. And the prophetic portion for the seventh day of Passover (II Samuel 22:1-51), which is also a song of deliverance, is written so as to have a wall-like effect as well.

Why was a special style established for the writing of the *Song of Moses*?

The Masoretes considered the *Song of Moses* (Deuteronomy 32:1-43) to be making an extremely important religious statement. They therefore mandated that it be written in a distinctive style.[74]

The Talmud[75] indicates that the *Song of Moses* is to be written in seventy lines, each line to have open space in the middle.

On the Sabbath when the *Song of Moses* is recited, the prophetic portion (II Samuel 22) is a song of thanksgiving spoken by David on the day that God saved him from his enemies. Because this haftara expresses the same theme of redemption as the *Song at the Sea* (Exodus 15:1-19), a similar style is employed. All of the printed and handwritten texts of today display this style.

Why are letters of a newly written Torah scroll sometimes left in outline form?

When a scribe writes a Torah scroll, he sometimes only outlines the letters of the first verse or two of Genesis and of the last verse or two of Deuteronomy. These letters are left open to be filled in by members of the congregation at a Torah consecration ceremony. The letters are often "auctioned off," and the highest bidder, using the scribe's quill and ink, fills in the open letter that he has purchased (or has been awarded him if no auction has taken place).

The custom of filling in Torah letters is based on a talmudic statement by Rabbi Sheshet: "He who corrects even one letter in a *Sefer Torah* is regarded as though he himself had written the entire Torah."[76] Thus, by filling in a letter (and thus "correcting" the unfinished letter), he is making the Torah eligible for public reading.

The Torah consecration ceremony is known by several names. Most often it is simply called *siyum,* meaning "completion." It is also referred to as *Chag Ha-siyum* or *Siyum Ha-Torah,* meaning "completion celebration for the Torah." The consecration ceremony is generally followed by a collation at which fine food and wine is served.

Why are scribal errors sometimes considered minor and sometimes major?

Minor errors are so considered because they are easily corrected and do not affect the meaning of the text. These include:

• The omission or addition of a thin letter, such as a *vav* or *yod*, from a word. Thin letters can be inserted into or removed from a line without greatly affecting the line's appearance.

For example, in the Torah the name Aharon (Aaron) is always spelled *alef hay resh nun*. It is never spelled with a *vav* after the *resh*. However, if a scribe should mistakenly spell the name with a *vav*, the error is considered minor, for the *vav* does not affect the meaning or the pronunciation of the word and it is easily removed.

• An improperly formed letter that can easily be made right. This would include a *vav*, *yod*, or final *nun* that is written shorter or longer than it should be.

• A word in which letters have been reversed without a resulting change in meaning. For example, if *kesev* is written instead of *keves*, the content of the text is not changed, since both words mean "lamb."

Major errors generally involve variations from the traditionally accepted text and in most cases affect the textual meaning. These include:

• The omission or misspelling of God's name, which is the most serious of all scribal errors. (See the next question.)

• The omission from a word of one or more full-width letters, such as an *alef* or *bet*. To correct such errors, letters would have to be squeezed into lines, with the result that the scroll would become blotchy and unattractive.

• The misspelling of a word that affects the meaning of a sentence. For example, if the Hebrew word *ve-nimtza* in the phrase *ve-nimtza damo* (Leviticus 1:15), meaning "its blood [blood of the sacrifice] shall be drained [on the side of the altar]," is spelled with an *alef* instead of a *hay*, the meaning is altered. *Ve-nimtza* when spelled with an *alef* means "found" and when spelled with a *hay* means "drained."

If a scribal error is discovered during the course of a Torah reading service, the procedure to be followed depends on the nature of the error found.[77] See Chapter Five, Reading the Torah, for further discussion.

Why may a Torah scroll not be corrected if the scribe has misspelled God's name?

In the Bible, God is referred to by seven names: *Yehova* (Jehova), *Adonai, El, Eloah, Elohim, Shaddai,* and *Tzevaot.* Should a scribe make an error in the writing of any of these names, the error may not be erased. The entire sheet of parchment must be rewritten.[78] In earlier centuries, defective parchments were stored away in a *geniza,* awaiting eventual burial, thus according them the same respect shown a human being.

In Jewish law erasing God's name is an affront to God. Its prohibition is derived from the Book of Deuteronomy (12:1-3) where the Israelites are commanded to obliterate the name of all idolatrous gods. The Rabbis are careful to add that such treatment may not be accorded the name of God.[79] In order to reduce the possibility of making an error when writing God's name, complete concentration is required. This is accomplished by requiring the *sofer* to say aloud before writing the name, "I intend to write the name of God." If he does not follow this procedure, the scroll is deemed invalid *(pasul)* and unfit for public reading.

Why is the number of scribal errors in a Torah a factor in determining whether it must be buried?

Several views are held by the Rabbis of the Talmud about how many errors a Torah scroll may contain before it is considered invalid *(pasul)* and must be buried in a cemetery.[80] One view is that if any column within the scroll contains three or more errors, the errors may not be corrected and instead the entire Torah is to be buried. Another view is that this applies only if there are four errors in a column.

For obvious economic reasons, it is current practice not to bury an entire Torah regardless of the nature or quantity of errors in a column. Rather, the defective section *(yeria)* of the scroll is removed and replaced with a newly written unit.

Why is a Torah scroll considered invalid if letters touch each other?

The Rabbis of the Talmud[81] ruled that if the letters of a Torah scroll touch, the scroll is not kosher because this type of writing might lead to a misreading of the text by the *baal koray*. For the same reason, the Talmud declared that a scroll is invalid if the scribe leaves too much space between letters, making one word look like two words. In either of these cases, the invalid scroll must be corrected before it can be considered fit for use at a synagogue service.

Not all commentators agree with this talmudic view. Some are of the opinion that if the words are recognizable and readable, a new scroll need not be substituted.[82]

Why must errors in a Torah be corrected within thirty days?

The third-century C.E. Palestinian talmudic scholar Rabbi Ammi warned that the owner of a Torah is behaving disrespectfully if he permits errors in a scroll to remain uncorrected for thirty days.[83] Moses Maimonides, in his *Mishneh Torah*,[84] repeats this caveat and instructs that if errors are not corrected within that time frame, the Torah should be stored in a *geniza*.

Why is it permissible to piece together a Torah scroll using parchment sheets from various Torot?

A Torah scroll need not be entirely the writing of one scribe, although this is the customary practice. It is proper, especially in view of the costliness of handwritten scrolls, to salvage correctly written sheets *(amudim)* from an otherwise invalid Torah and to combine them with valid sheets from other Torot, thus making up one complete, valid scroll.

Why was it once common practice to call a child to the pulpit to determine the validity of a Torah?

In the past, when errors of a minor nature appeared in a Torah scroll, it was customary to call upon children with some schooling to help determine the gravity of the error.

Children were called upon primarily when a question arose about letters such as *vav, za'yin,* or *nun* that were not perfectly shaped. For example, the vertical line of a *vav* may not have been extended downward sufficiently, and the letter could have been mistaken for a *yod.* Or, the vertical line of a *za'yin* may not have been sufficiently curved, in which case it would resemble a *vav.* Or the base of a *nun* may not have been fully formed, and the *nun* may have appeared to be a *vav.*

If, when a child was called to the pulpit to read words with such imperfections, he was able to read the words correctly, the imperfections were not considered serious and the reading was allowed to continue without replacing the scroll.[85] However, the Torah did have to be corrected as soon as possible.

Today, this practice is rarely followed.

Why are some torn Torah scrolls not fit for use?

According to the *Code of Jewish Law,*[86] compiled by Joseph Caro in the sixteenth century, a Torah may be repaired if it contains a sheet of parchment with a tear that extends only through one or two lines of the script. Such a tear is mended by sewing the torn parchment or by patching it on the reverse side. However, should the tear extend through three or more lines of script, the scroll is considered invalid and the sheet may not be mended but must be replaced.

The reasoning behind this view is that a Torah scroll must be a thing of beauty, and when a tear is so extensive, the parchment will appear unsightly even if repaired.

Not all authorities were in agreement with this reasoning. Three centuries earlier, Rabbi Meir of Rothenburg (1215-1293) was asked by his disciple Rabbi Asher ben Yechiel whether a Torah scroll may be mended by gluing a patch to the reverse side if the tear extends through three (or more) written lines. His response was that since the glue might not be strong enough to create a permanent bond and the tear might reappear, the entire sheet (amud) should be rewritten.[87]

Why may a scroll containing the Torah, the Prophets, and the Holy Writings not be used for a public Torah reading?

While it is permissible for a scribe to include in one scroll all three parts of the Bible, the Rabbis ruled that the sanctity of the Torah is diminished if it is written together with the Prophets (Neviim) and Holy Writings (Ketuvim) and that such a scroll may not be used at a public reading.[88]

Chapter 5

Reading the Torah

INTRODUCTION

The first recorded law pertaining to the time and manner in which the Torah is to be read publicly is found in Deuteronomy 31:10-12. After Moses wrote down the words of the Torah, he instructed the Priests as follows:

> [At the end of] every seventh year [the *shemita* year] at the Feast of Booths [Sukkot] . . . you shall read this Torah aloud in the presence of all Israel . . . that they may hear and so learn to respect the Lord your God and to observe faithfully every word of this Torah.[1]

Neither the Torah itself nor later Rabbis explain why the Torah was to be read publicly only once every seven years, but the very fact that the seventh year was to be a sabbatical year offers a reasonable explanation. In the sabbatical year the land was to be left fallow, and farmers therefore had little work to do. Thus, greater numbers of Jews were able to make the annual pilgrimage to the central sanctuary in Jerusalem without the pressure of having to return home to tend to their farms. They had ample time to listen to a public Torah reading.

It is not known how diligently the commandment to read the Torah every seven years was followed. Nor is it clear when more frequent public Torah readings were introduced. According to Maimonides, who codified the laws that appear in the Talmud, it was Moses who established the morning Torah readings for Sabbaths, Mondays, and Thursdays and Ezra who established the Sabbath afternoon service.[2]

One can easily understand why the Torah was read on the Sabbath, the seventh day of the week. The Sabbath was a day of rest and people had a great deal of leisure time. But why was it felt that the Torah must be read on the second and fifth day of the week as well?

One theory ascribes this practice to Ezra the Scribe (fifth century B.C.E.). The Talmud[3] portrays Ezra as having explained that just as water is absolutely essential to the survival of the human body, so is the continued study of Torah a necessity for the growth and spiritual sustenance of Jews and the Jewish people. Ezra based his assertion on Exodus 15:22, which describes how the Israelites in the desert were unable to find water for three days. They complained to Moses, and Moses appealed to God. God promised them relief if they would observe His commandments.

A second theory also ascribes the introduction of Monday and Thursday morning readings to Ezra, but offers a different reason. In ancient Palestine Monday and Thursday were market days when Jews came to Jerusalem to sell their wares. Since large numbers of people were assembled on these days, Ezra took advantage of the opportunity to read the Torah to them.

A third theory, put forth by Rabbi Israel Meir Ha-kohayn (1838-1933), author of the *Mishna Berura,* suggests that the Torah is read on Mondays and Thursdays because these are especially propitious days for supplication *(y'may ratzon):* According to tradition it was on Thursday that Moses went up to Mount Sinai to receive the Ten Commandments, and he returned with them on Monday.[4]

By the time the Talmud was finalized around the year 500 C.E., the exact days of the year when the Torah should be read were established. In addition, rules were laid down pertaining to the number of persons who were to be called to read from the Torah and which portions were to be read on various occasions. This chapter describes and explains the reasons behind talmudic and post-talmudic Torah reading practices.

———————— ▭ ————————

Why does the Torah reading in some synagogues follow a triennial cycle?

The earliest reference to the traditions that had been established with regard to the weekly Torah reading cycle is found in the Talmud.[5] In Palestine in the early centuries of the Common Era, it was customary to follow a triennial cycle. The entire Torah was divided into 154 or 155 weekly portions, depending on the calendar, and was read over three years. Each weekly reading was called a *seder* (plural, *sedarim*).[6]

At about the same time, among the Jews of Babylonia a different tradition—referred to as the "annual reading cycle"—evolved. The Pentateuch was divided into 54 portions, all of which were read in the course of one year. Each weekly reading was called a *sidra* (plural, *sidrot*).

The annual reading cycle, as contrasted with the triennial reading cycle, became the standard for world Jewry. After the ninth century, the annual cycle was adopted for the most part in Palestine as well.[7]

Today, some Conservative and Reform[8] congregations follow the triennial cycle. However, all Orthodox and most Conservative congregations follow the annual cycle.

Why is the Torah portion read on a Sabbath sometimes referred to as a *sidra* and sometimes as a *parasha*?

The terms are interchangeable. The word *sidra* (plural, *sidrot*) is used today mainly by Ashkenazim while the word *parasha* (plural, *parashot* or *parashiyot*) is used mostly by

Sephardim. In fact, some Sephardim, particularly the Spanish-Portuguese, call the Pentateuch *The Parasha Book*.

The term *sidra*, meaning "order" or "arrangement," is frequently used in the Talmud to denote a part of the Bible either read in the synagogue or studied in school. Rashi explains that in the talmudic statement "Rav read a *sidra* before Rabbi [Judah]" *sidra* means a section of the Prophets or the Hagiographa.[9] At a later date, Ashkenazim began using the term *sidra* to refer to the weekly Sabbath reading from the Torah, while the Sephardim preferred the word *parasha*, meaning "selection, division."[10] A *sidra* or *parasha* consists of one or more chapters from the Pentateuch.

In scholarly works *parashiyot (sidrot)* are usually referred to as pericopes, a word derived from the Latin and meaning "sections."

Why is the entire Pentateuch but not the entire Bible read aloud in the synagogue in the course of each year?

Although in Jewish tradition the whole of the Bible is considered the word of God and hence sacred, its first five books, known as the Pentateuch (Chumash), are considered more sacred than the Prophets and the Holy Writings.[11] For this reason, the Pentateuch is read publicly in its entirety in the course of a synagogue year, while only selected portions of the Prophets and Holy Writings are read.

Why are some Torah readings considerably longer than others?

The length of the Sabbath Torah reading varies from week to week,[12] but in every case the Sabbath reading is much longer than holiday readings. This is so because on Sabbaths the full sidra of the week and sometimes a double sidra must be read (see the next question). On holidays, however, only special selections describing the essence of the holiday are read.

No reason can be found to explain why some Sabbath portions are longer than others. Precisely where each reading ends and each new one begins was decided by rabbinic authorities and scribes in talmudic times.[13] No strict pattern seems to have been followed, but once the length of each reading was decided, tradition dictated that no changes be made.

Why are two Torah portions read on some Sabbaths?

In some years, there are occasions when two sidrot rather than one are read in the synagogue on a Sabbath. These double readings are:

From the Book of Exodus:
   Va-yakhel/Pekuday (35:1-40:38)

From the Book of Leviticus:
   Tazria/Metzora (12:1-15:33)
   Acharay Mot/Kedoshim (16:1-20:27)
   Be-har/Be-chukotai (25:1-27:34)

From the Book of Numbers:
   Chukat/Balak (19:1-25:10)
   Matot/Masay (30:2-36:13)

From the Book of Deuteronomy:
   Nitzavim/Va-yaylech (29:9-31:30)[14]

The reason why certain portions are combined in certain years but not in others is rather complicated. Basically, the combining is done in order to be sure that all 54 portions into which the Pentateuch is divided are read within a one-year time frame so that the annual Torah reading cycle can be completed on Simchat Torah. The fact that in the Jewish calendar there is a leap year seven times in every nineteen years, and that in those years an additional Adar month is added to the calendar, affects the combination or separation of sidrot. Linked to this are rules which dictate that certain portions must be read before or after certain holidays.

Maimonides offered the following general rules:

- The sidra Be-midbar (Numbers 1:1-4:20) is always to be read (one or two weeks) before Shavuot.
- The sidra Va-etchanan (Deuteronomy 3:13-7:11) is to be read after Tisha B'Av.
- The sidra Nitzavim (Deuteronomy 29:9-30:20) is to be read before Rosh Hashana.
- The sidra Tzav (Leviticus 6:1-8:36) is to be read before Passover in regular (nonleap) years.

In order to accommodate all of these requirements, sidrot such as Tazria and Metzora, Acharay Mot and Kedoshim, and Be-har and Be-chukotai are combined in all regular years and separated in leap years so that the annual cycle of Torah readings will be performed in its proper time.

Why are there occasions unrelated to the calendar when two sidrot are read on one Sabbath?

As pointed out in the previous answer, on certain Sabbaths two sidrot are combined, depending on the calendar year.

There are, however, other circumstances which would make it necessary to read two portions on one Sabbath. This would happen, for example, when for one reason or another the Torah cannot be read on a particular Sabbath—perhaps because no one is present who is able to read the Torah or because a serious error is found in the one Torah owned by the congregation. In such cases, on the Sabbath that follows, both the Torah reading for the current Sabbath and the reading of the previous Sabbath are read in full.[15]

This rule does not apply when two portions are scheduled for that second Sabbath, as dictated by the calendar. It also does not apply if the sidra that was missed was the last sidra in one of the five books of the Torah—for example, Va-yechi (the last portion of Genesis) and Shemot (the first portion of Exodus) would not be read together.

Why are Torah portions in the Book of Genesis never combined?

The sidrot in the Book of Genesis (Bereshit) are particularly lengthy compared to those in the other four books of the Pentateuch, and to avoid extending the service unduly two portions from Genesis are never combined during a Sabbath reading. The principle of *tircha de-tzibura*, "public inconvenience," is at work here. Jewish law is careful to avoid imposing upon the public unnecessary inconvenience.

Why does Jewish law prescribe that Torah readings not be selected at random?

Two great second-century C.E. Palestinian scholars, Rabbi Meir and Rabbi Judah ben Ila'i, disciples of the renowned Rabbi Akiba, were disturbed over the haphazard way in which the Torah was read at public gatherings. No specific sequence was followed; the reader would often skip sections within a sidra; the leader of the congregation *(Rosh Ha-keneset)* or the invited preacher of the day would decide on the reading to be done.

Rabbi Meir was of the view that the reading for the Sabbath afternoon *(Mincha)* service should begin at the point where the Sabbath morning reading ended; that the Monday morning reading should begin at the point where the Sabbath afternoon reading ended; that the Thursday morning reading should begin at the point where the Monday morning reading ended; and, finally, that the reading for the next Sabbath should begin at the point where the Thursday morning reading ended.

Rabbi Ila'i disagreed. He believed that for each Sabbath

the Torah reading should begin at the point where the reading ended the previous Sabbath morning.[16]

The view of Rabbi Ila'i prevailed and was established as law *(halacha)*, thus making it possible to divide the portions so that the reading of the Five Books of Moses would be finished within a fixed time frame. Selected, random readings were permitted only on holidays in order to offer better instruction to the congregation on the theme of the holiday.[17]

Why must some sections of the Torah be read from beginning to end without interruption?

Certain sections of the Torah are considered by tradition to be sufficiently significant that they must be read in toto, without a break.

The fourteenth-century Rabbi David ben Yosef Abudraham (also referred to as Abudarham)[18] pointed out that the entire *Song at the Sea* (Exodus 15:1-19), the entire Ten Commandments (Exodus 20:2-14 and Deuteronomy 5:6-18), and the listing of the forty-two desert stations from Egypt to the Plains of Moab (Numbers 33:1-49) must be read in their entirety, without being subdivided to accommodate several aliyot.[19]

Why were laymen once permitted to interrupt the Torah reading service?

Before modern times it was common practice that at some point during the Sabbath or holiday service, particularly during the Torah reading, a person would mount the pulpit and interrupt the proceedings in order to express a grievance against a community leader or a synagogue member.[20]

Rabbi Gershom Meor Ha-gola (tenth to eleventh century) ruled that a congregant had the right to delay the service and lodge a complaint if he had requested a fellow congregant to appear in court in order to adjudicate a matter but the person had refused to appear.

In the fifteenth century the German authority Rabbi Israel Isserlein also ruled that it was permissible for an individual to interrupt a public Torah reading and to demand a public apology of a fellow Jew who had offended or injured him.

The apology ran as follows:

> I have sinned against the God of Israel and against you. I have placed a stain upon the holiness of the synagogue and the sacred commandments. I have also transgressed the warning of the Torah not to strike or do bodily injury to anyone ... I humbly seek your pardon and atonement ...[21]

Modern congregations no longer permit the interruption of the Torah reading service.

Why have Reform congregations abbreviated the Torah reading service?

As a reaction to the restlessness and disorderliness found in many traditional synagogues during the lengthy Torah reading service, the Reform movement, in the middle nineteenth century, changed the entire system of aliyot. In some Reform congregations only one aliya is awarded,[22] while in others two or three are assigned. Quite often, instead of calling members of the congregation to the Torah, aliyot are given only to the rabbi, the cantor, and the synagogue officers seated on the pulpit.

The number of Torah verses read for each aliya varies, and occasionally only a single verse is read. It should be noted, however, that in recent years there has been a trend in Reform synagogues toward awarding more Torah honors to members of the congregation, some even offering the full minimum of seven that Jewish law requires for the Sabbath morning service.

Why are rabbinic authorities opposed to holding Torah readings at night?

With the exception of Simchat Torah, Jewish law and

tradition oppose holding public Torah readings at night. Nonetheless, in Reform practice the Torah is usually read on Friday nights, and some Conservative and Reconstructionist congregations do likewise.

Although neither the Talmud nor the codes discuss this question directly, it is likely that the Torah was not read at night owing to poor lighting conditions. Jewish law mandates that he who reads the Torah must see each word as he reads it, otherwise the reading is invalid. When candles were the only source of light, the Torah was not read at night on the Sabbath or holidays because it would have been necessary to move the candles around, which would be a violation of Jewish law.

With the introduction of electricity, the problem no longer existed. Nevertheless, traditionalists insist that since the time to read the Torah had always been during daylight hours, no change in practice should be made.[23]

Why is it required that a minyan be present when the Torah is read at a religious service?

The Rabbis believed that there is a biblical basis for the requirement that a quorum of ten adults (minyan) be present whenever a public Torah reading is held. The verse cited is Leviticus 22:32, which speaks of sanctifying God's name "in the midst of the Children of Israel." The phrase "in the midst" (in Hebrew, be-toch) is taken to mean that when God's name is invoked in public—at a public prayer service or at a public reading of the Torah—a quorum must be present.[24]

Why is the Torah sometimes read even though the required quorum is not present in the synagogue?

If a Torah reading begins with ten adults present, it may be completed even if some of the adults have left the synagogue during the course of the reading.[25]

In the view of some scholars the justification for continuing with the Torah reading in the absence of a minyan is to counter the possibility of the Torah being forgotten (neglected) by the people.[26] They caution, however, that those who receive an aliya when a quorum is not present should omit the Torah blessings.

In one of his responsa, Rashi condemns those communities who consider a minyan present and read from the Torah when there are actually only nine men and a boy present (the boy is given a *Sefer Torah* to hold).[27]

Why might it occur that the Torah may not be read even though the required quorum is present?

In a responsum,[28] the great thirteenth-century scholar Rabbi Meir of Rothenburg points out that in a situation where a minyan consists only of Kohanim (descendants of the priestly family), and no one else is present, the Torah may not be read at all. This is because a Kohayn is not eligible to receive the third, fourth, fifth, sixth, or seventh aliya, which are reserved only for Yisraelim (the masses, those who are not descendants of the Priests or Levites). Were a Kohayn to be awarded one of these aliyot, the impression might be given that his priestly lineage is questionable or that he is "tainted,"[29] for otherwise he would not have been awarded an aliya reserved for a Yisrael.

Why do some authorities maintain that a minyan need not be present when the last portion of the Torah is read?

Despite the fact that Jewish law requires a minyan to be present whenever the Torah is read, Maimonides and other authorities believe that the last eight verses of the Torah (Deuteronomy 34:5-12) may be read even in the absence of a minyan. In his code,[30] Maimonides writes that although Jewish tradition considers every word of the Torah sacred, having been dictated by God to Moses, the events described in the last eight verses transpired after the death of Moses and are therefore in a separate category. For this reason, says Maimonides, the quorum of ten need not be present when these verses are read.

Not all authorities are in agreement with Maimonides.[31]

Why is the congregation *not* required to remain standing throughout the reading of the Torah?

Although it is customary for the congregation to rise and remain standing when the Torah is removed from the ark, during the actual reading of the Torah the congregation is seated.[32]

Aside from the practical consideration that it would be a hardship for congregants to stand for the duration of the Torah reading, standing is not required because the reading of the Torah is considered a form of study. Since students normally sit when they study Torah, the congregation sits during the reading of the Torah.

For this same reason, in Orthodox synagogues congregants do not rise when the *Shema*, which is a selection from the Torah, is recited. Most non-Orthodox congregations stand when the first verse of the *Shema* is chanted because they consider the concept of One God, which is expressed in that verse, to be deserving of special recognition.

Rabbi Moses Isserles, in his Notes to the *Code of Jewish Law*, reported that the famous twelfth-century German scholar Rabbi Meir of Rothenburg (the Maharam) would stand when the Torah was being read. (The *Code* makes no such demand.)

Why do some people stand when the Torah is being read?

The practice of standing while the Torah is being read has its origin in the Book of Ezra. Describing Ezra's reading the Torah to the people, the Bible (Nehemiah 8:5) says, "And Ezra opened the book in the presence of all the people ... and when he opened it, all the people stood up." Some scholars have taken this to mean that one *must* stand when the Torah is read.

Other scholars, however, remind us that the term "to stand" also means "to be silent," and the word should therefore not be taken literally. They call attention to Job's three friends who, after much argumentation, finally remain silent. The Book of Job (32:16) uses the expression "... they stand still and answer no more."

Based on the verse in the Book of Job where "to stand still" means "to be silent," most authorities conclude that one may not converse while the Torah is being read. However, the verse is not interpreted to mean that congregants must stand during the reading.[33]

Why does the congregation stand when certain portions of the Torah are read?

Although customs vary with regard to the practice of standing when certain prayers and portions of the Torah are read, all congregations consider the Ten Commandments (Exodus 20:1-14 and Deuteronomy 5:6-18) and the *Song at the Sea* (Exodus 15:1-19) to be of exceptional importance, and most require members to stand during their recitation. For these portions, persons of exceptional learning and piety are generally awarded aliyot.[34]

Likewise, all congregations consider the reading of the last portion of each of the Five Books of Moses to be a significant occasion, and the congregation rises when the last verse of each of these books is chanted. As soon as the Torah reader concludes the reading, the congregation sings out in unison: *Chazak, chazak, ve-nitchazek*, meaning "Be strong, be strong, and let us be strengthened."

Why were early authorities opposed to the practice of standing during the reading of the Ten Commandments in the synagogue?

While most authorities favor standing when the Ten

Commandments are read, others share the view of Maimonides that this custom should be discontinued because it might lead people to think that not all parts of the Torah are of equal importance, that only the Decalogue was revealed to Moses on Mount Sinai.[35] There is a historical basis for Maimonides' view.

In Second Temple times, after the Priests offered the daily morning sacrifice (Sabbath included), a prayer service was held. During this service the Ten Commandments (Decalogue) was recited as a reminder of the Revelation on Sinai.[36] This was not the only selection from the Torah that was recited at the service.

After the destruction of the Temple in the year 70 C.E., the Decalogue was transferred to the liturgy of the synagogue. The Samaritans and the emerging Christian community expressed the opinion that the sole reason for having included the Ten Commandments in the Temple service or the synagogue liturgy was because it was the only part of the Torah that had been revealed on Mount Sinai and that it alone was sacred.[37]

To discredit this thesis and to make the point that all parts of the Torah were revealed on Mount Sinai, the Rabbis of Palestine eliminated the Ten Commandments from the liturgy. Around 400 C.E. Rav Ashi enacted a similar ruling for Babylonian Jewry. Other communities throughout the world followed suit, the Jews of Egypt being the last to remove the Ten Commandments from the prayerbook. Nevertheless, isolated congregations continued to recite it as part of the prayer service.[38]

Why is the Torah reader called a baal koray?

The person designated to read the Torah for all members of the congregation who are honored with aliyot is referred to as the baal koray, meaning "master of the reading."[39] Originally, in Temple times and in early talmudic times, each person called to the Torah read his own portion. Later, when the majority of people were not proficient in reading the unvocalized Torah text, one trained person, the *baal koray,* read the Torah portions for all. This included even those who were knowledgeable enough to read from the Torah.[40]

Today, the *baal koray* serves the same basic function except for those individuals—especially the Bar and Bat Mitzva—who choose to read their own portions. The Torah reader nowadays is generally an adult, but in the Middle Ages it was not uncommon for a minor to serve in this capacity.[41]

Why must the Torah reader look at each word as it is being read from the Torah?

Jewish law forbids the *baal koray* from reading the Torah without looking at the actual words in the scroll. The Rabbis established this rule to be in compliance with the admonition in Deuteronomy 4:2: "You shall not add anything to what I command you, nor shall you omit any part of it, but you shall keep the commandments of the Lord ..."

By being compelled to look at each word of the Torah as he recites it, there is less likelihood that a Torah reader will add, omit, or mispronounce words, thus changing or distorting the meaning of the text.[42] He will also be able to spot scribal errors or fading letters.

Why was it once customary for the *baal koray* to sit down after he read each portion from the Torah?

The Talmud[43] indicates that at the time in Jewish history when it was customary for each person called to the Torah *(oleh)* to read his own Torah portion, the first honoree recited the first Torah blessing and the last honoree recited the last blessing. None of the other aliya recipients recited Torah blessings.

When one person, the *baal koray,* was designated to read all Torah portions, it became customary for this reader to sit down after each portion was read. This would draw attention to the fact that a new *oleh* was being called up.

In post-talmudic times the practice changed, and each honoree recited both Torah blessings. At that point the Torah reader no longer took his seat between aliyot.

Why is it generally assumed that a woman may not serve as a Torah reader?

While the law explicitly states that a woman may not *write* a Torah scroll for public use,[44] it is quite clear that she may *read* the Torah at a public service. Nevertheless, many authorities, particularly Maimonides (twelfth century), found such permissiveness objectionable and ruled that a woman should not read the Torah publicly because it would be offensive to the congregation, which is not accustomed to having women officiate.[45]

Another argument advanced for denying women the privilege of reading the Torah publicly is that menstruants are sometimes in a state of ritual impurity. This reasoning is not valid, however. The Talmud[46] is quite explicit in stating that "the words of the Torah are not subject to ritual impurity." No one can render a Torah impure by touching it. See pages 45-46 for a further discussion.

Why may an inexperienced congregant read the Torah?

Both Joseph Caro and Moses Isserles were of the opinion[47] that if an experienced *baal koray* is not present to read the Torah, an inexperienced member of the congregation may be called upon to perform the task, despite the fact that many errors will be made. The synagogue officials (*gabbaim;* singular, *gabbai*) who stand at his side are expected to guide the reading and correct any errors that are made.

Why does the *baal koray* stand to the left of the Torah when reading from it?

Some scholars[48] cite Deuteronomy 33:2 as the scriptural basis for this practice. In this verse Moses begins his farewell blessing to the Israelites:

> The Lord came from Sinai ... [to reveal Himself] lightning flashing at them [the Israelites] from His right.

Here and throughout Scripture the right hand denotes strength, as in Exodus 15:6: "Your right hand, O Lord, is glorious in power; Your right hand, O Lord, crushes the enemy."

Since most persons are right-handed, by standing to the left of the Torah the *baal koray* is able to hold the Torah pointer in the right hand and point to the words of the Torah when reading them.[49] Because Hebrew is read from right to left, the *oleh* stands to the right of the *baal koray*, and his view of the Torah is unobstructed as the Torah pointer is moved from word to word.

See pages 44 and 155 for more on the significance of the right hand and right side in Jewish tradition.

Why does a member of the congregation stand on either side of the Torah reader?

The Talmud[50] notes that it would be demeaning for the Torah to be resting on the reading table without being flanked by an honor guard. It was therefore ruled that a *gabbai* (synagogue official) should stand on either side of the reading table while the Torah is read. The Torah reader and the officials who stand beside him are said to represent the three patriarchs—Abraham, Isaac, and Jacob—whose names are often invoked during prayer.

The Jerusalem Talmud[51] explains that just as at Sinai God, Moses, and the congregation of Israel were present when the Torah was transmitted to Moses, so at every reading must this trio be represented. Hence, the Torah reader, who represents Moses (the transmitter), is flanked by two *gabbaim,* who represent God and Israel.

The two officials serve a practical function as well. They follow the reading in a printed Chumash and quietly correct any errors in pronunciation or cantillation made by the reader.

In some congregations, one of the *gabbaim* is assigned the task of calling out the aliyot and/or making the *Mi Shebayrach* prayer, although these tasks are often performed by the rabbi, the sexton, or the *baal koray* himself. At times when the scroll must be covered, such as between aliyot or before the maftir is called, one of the *gabbaim* attends to this chore.[52]

Why do synagogue officials in some congregations make hand signals while the *baal koray* is reading the Torah?

The Torah reader must read the scroll in accordance with the established cantillation. In some Sephardic congregations, particularly among Yemenites, an official who stands next to the *baal koray* indicates through hand movements when the reader's voice should rise or be lowered, when a note should be extended and when curtailed.

Rashi (eleventh century) mentions this practice in his commentary on the Talmud. He recalls seeing Jews from Palestine who had settled in France motioning with the right hand to indicate the melody when the Torah was being read.[53]

The custom of using hand movements is not widespread today, but it is still practiced in the synagogues of Rome and at times can also be observed in synagogues that follow the Moroccan and Yemenite rituals.[54]

Why do congregants sometimes shout out corrections to the Torah reader?

If the *baal koray* makes even the slightest error that

changes the meaning of a word or sentence—such as reading *hu*, meaning "he," for *hi*, meaning "she"—then the reader must return to the word and pronounce it correctly before proceeding with the reading. If, however, the error does not change the meaning of the text, the reader may continue without repeating the word.[55]

If an error is made in cantillation or pronunciation, the reader does not have to repeat the word. In either case, though, the congregation is duty bound to call the error to the reader's attention by shouting out the correction.[56]

Why doesn't everyone who receives an aliya mouth each word along with the Torah reader?

Jewish law requires that after pronouncing a blessing, one should follow through by performing the act. Thus, after one recites the *Kiddush,* he immediately drinks the wine; after he pronounces the *Ha-motzi* prayer, he immediately eats the bread. Likewise, when one recites the Torah blessings, he should follow through by reading from the Torah as was the original practice. However, since today a *baal koray* does the reading for all who receive aliyot, the law prescribes[57] that the honoree should read along silently, mouthing the words being read by the Torah reader. By so doing, the honoree is considered to have performed the act of reading from the Torah, and the blessing he recited cannot be considered a *beracha le-vatala,* a "wasted blessing."

This ruling is generally not followed. In fact, very few people who receive aliyot are able to read or even follow the unvoweled words of the Torah scroll. The more liberal view that applies to the reading of the Purim Megilla was applied to the Torah reading. In connection with the Megilla the rule is that he who hears the scroll read has fulfilled the requirement of reading it aloud.[58]

Why did the *meturgeman* serve an important function at the Torah reading service?

So that members of the congregation, who were generally not well versed in Hebrew, would understand the meaning of the Hebrew Torah text as it was read aloud, the position of *meturgeman* was introduced into Jewish life in the time of Ezra and Nehemiah (fifth century B.C.E.). The Torah reader would read a Hebrew verse and then pause while the verse was translated by the *meturgeman* (an Aramaic word meaning "translator") into the vernacular. Aramaic was the vernacular in Palestine and Babylonia in biblical and talmudic times.[59]

The earliest reference to this verse-by-verse translation for the benefit of the masses is found in Nehemiah 8:1-8. Here we are told that as Ezra read the Torah to the public, Levites stood by his side and "caused them [the public] to understand the reading."

Why did the *meturgeman* do his translation extemporaneously?

The translator of the Hebrew Torah text was not permitted to write out and read his translation to the public because it was feared that people might be misled into thinking that the words being spoken by the translator were actually written in the Torah scroll. The rule was therefore established that a *meturgeman* must speak extemporaneously.[60]

Why did the *meturgeman* omit certain portions when translating the Torah text?

From early biblical times Judaism displayed a strong aversion to the use of foul language and the recounting of incidents involving immorality. The Talmud,[61] for example, cautions that the episode of Reuben and his illicit relationship with his father's concubine (Genesis 35:22) as well as the second account of the Golden Calf (Exodus 32:21-25) be read aloud in Hebrew but not be translated into the vernacular.

Another category of Hebrew text to be left untranslated covers sections that are considered especially sacred. One such example is the priestly benediction, *Birkat Kohanim* (Numbers 6:24-26), the words of which are to be pronounced by Priests only.[62]

It should be noted that the Rabbis ruled that no part of the Torah reading may be skipped by the *baal koray*, but this does not apply to the *meturgeman*.

Why was the use of the *meturgeman* abandoned?

The employment of a translator at public readings of the Torah was discontinued for a very practical reason: it lengthened the service unduly.

The problem was not terribly acute for the Jews of Palestine, who read the Torah over a period of three years (triennial cycle). But the Jews of Babylonia and the Jews of the Diaspora employed the annual cycle of Torah reading, which meant that the Sabbath readings were often very long. It was therefore decided to dispense with the services of the *meturgeman* and to require the members of the congregation to review the Hebrew text and its translation in advance of the Sabbath reading.[63]

There is one exception to the above: Yemenite synagogues in Israel today continue to use a *meturgeman*, who stands beside the *baal koray* and translates each verse into Arabic.

Why do many Jews review the weekly Torah portion three times before the Sabbath on which it is read?

In the middle of the second century C.E. the Aramaic translation of the Torah by Onkelos, known as Targum Onkelos, was adopted in Babylonia as the official translation of the Bible. Since by that time the *meturgeman* was no longer widely employed and since many Jews were not well versed in Hebrew, the Rabbis of the Talmud required all Jews to review in advance of the Sabbath the Torah portion that was to be read that week. Each person was to read the whole text twice in Hebrew and once in the Aramaic translation.[64]

This procedure is followed by many Jews to this day despite the fact that in the early Middle Ages Aramaic ceased to be the vernacular of the Jews.

Why was a Torah reader excommunicated when he refused to pronounce words as established by tradition?

According to tradition, the manner in which each word of the Torah is to be written and read was established by Moses based upon instructions he received directly from God on Mount Sinai. Accordingly, any deviation from the established way of spelling or vocalizing a word of the Torah is a gross violation of biblical law.

Thus, the Hebrew name Yisachar (Issachar) is actually spelled Yi-sas-char, with the Hebrew letter *sin* repeated. Despite the spelling, the name is to be pronounced Yisachar, as if only one *sin* appeared in the spelling.[65]

The *Code of Jewish Law* relates an incident in which a Torah was read before a congregation comprised of great scholars, and the *baal koray* did not follow the reading that tradition demanded as established by the Masoretes. The reader was warned that he must follow the Masoretic tradition even if the pronunciation runs counter to the actual spelling of the words.[66] In this particular case the reader defied the scholars even after being warned. He was therefore excommunicated and denied the right to continue to serve as a *baal koray*.

Why must a Torah scroll sometimes be replaced in the middle of a Torah reading service?

While the Rabbis considered it demeaning to a congregation for a reading to be conducted from a defective scroll, they did draw a distinction between minor errors and major ones.

As discussed in Chapter Four, Writing the Torah, minor errors include those that do not change the meaning of the text and can easily be corrected without spoiling the appearance of the parchment sheet. Major errors, on the other hand, include the omission of an entire word, a misspelling that changes the meaning of the text and, most serious of all, the misspelling or omission of God's name.

Although there are many divergent views among authorities[67] as to the procedure to be followed when an error is discovered in a Torah scroll during a public reading, the consensus is that if the error is minor, the reading is continued until its completion, and the scroll is then taken out of service. However, if a major error is discovered, the reading is immediately halted and the defective scroll is replaced. In either case errors must be corrected within thirty days.

Why is a Torah reading not completely invalidated if a serious error is discovered in the course of the reading?

If a serious error is found in a scroll as it is being read, the scroll must be replaced with another. The reading that had been in progress until the point that the error was discovered is considered to have been valid because the first scroll was a valid scroll until the moment that the error was discovered.

When the second Torah is placed in service, the reading continues from the verse where the Torah reading was stopped.

There is no legal requirement that the *oleh* repeat the first Torah blessing before the reading commences from the second Torah scroll, because up until the point that the error was discovered, the first scroll was presumed to be kosher. The blessing that had been recited over the first scroll is therefore considered valid and carries over to the second scroll.[68]

However, scholars such as the famous Rosh (Rabbi Asher ben Yechiel) and Rashba (Rabbi Solomon ben Adret) were of the opinion that all of the reading that had been done from the first scroll and all of the Torah blessings that had been pronounced are invalid and must be repeated with a new scroll. The reasoning is that since the first Torah is invalid (pasul), whatever verses were read from it do not count and whatever blessings were pronounced by the olim are considered wasted (berachot le-vatala).[69]

Why do some authorities require an honoree to repeat the first Torah blessing if the baal koray has indicated the wrong starting place for the reading?

Before the person called to the Torah recites the first Torah blessing, it is customary for the Torah reader to point to the word in the scroll where the reading is to begin. The oleh then touches that word with a talit or some other religious article and kisses the object. According to some authorities, if it then becomes apparent that the reader has inadvertently pointed to the wrong column in the scroll, the oleh is required to repeat the first Torah blessing. However, if the reader merely pointed to the wrong word in the correct column, the blessing need not be repeated.[70]

Why does the Torah reader read some portions in hushed tones?

Verses in the Torah describing unpleasant events are traditionally read rapidly or in quiet, hushed tones. The reason for this is based on the superstition that a mere mentioning of the event might invite its recurrence.

Sections of the Torah that are thus glossed over include the curses found in verse 17 of Deuteronomy 11, verses 14-39 of Leviticus 26, and verses 15-68 of Deuteronomy 28.

Portions of Exodus 32 describing the events relating to the Golden Calf are also read unceremoniously.

Why are the musical notes in the printed text of the Bible known as *te'amim?*

The cantillation notations found in printed copies of the Bible indicate the melody that the Torah reader must follow when chanting the words of Scripture, particularly at public readings. This system of musical notation was employed as far back as talmudic times[71] but was not perfected until the ninth century as a result of the work of Aaron ben Asher. Because the work was done primarily by the Ben Asher family of Tiberias, the system of cantillation in general use became known as the Tiberian System.

מֵרָא מֻנַּח זַרְקָא מֻנַּח סָגוֹל מֻנַּח ׀ מֻנַּח רְבִיעִי מַהְפַּךְ
פַּשְׁטָא זָקֵף קָטֹן זָקֵף־נָּדוֹל מֵרְכָא טִפְּחָא מֻנַּח אֶתְנַחְתָּא
פָּזֵר תְּלִישָׁא־קְטַנָּה תְּלִישָׁא־נְדוֹלָה קַדְמָא וְאַזְלָא
אַזְלָא־נֵרֵשׁ נֵרְשַׁיִם דַּרְגָּא תְּבִיר יְתִיב פְּסִיק ׀ סוֹף־פָּסוּק
שַׁלְשֶׁלֶת קַרְנֵי־פָרָה מֵרְכָא־כְפוּלָה יֵרַח־בֶּן־יוֹמוֹ׃

These are the names of the cantillation notes. The symbols above and below the words are the notes themselves. These symbols appear in printed copies of the Pentateuch and the rest of the Bible, but not in handwritten Torah scrolls read in the synagogue.

The Hebrew word for the musical notations is *te'amim* (singular, *taam*), which literally means "tastes" or "flavors." (The Yiddish term is *trop* or *trope*.) The name is appropriate because when the Torah and haftara selections are chanted in accordance with the notes established for each word and phrase, they add flavor to the words and one is better able to comprehend the ideas which the words express.

Why do Ashkenazim and Sephardim maintain different ways of chanting the readings from the Torah?

As stated above, the manner in which the words of the Torah (and haftara) are to be chanted was perfected in the ninth century by the Ben Ashers of Tiberias.[72] The Ben Asher style was accepted in most Jewish communities throughout the world, primarily among Ashkenazim. However, different melodies developed among Jews of the Sephardic communities, particularly those of the Eastern world (including Iraq [formerly Babylonia], Syria, Yemen, Iran [formerly Persia], Egypt, and India). These tunes showed an Arab influence.

Both Ashkenazim and Sephardim have remained loyal to their traditional styles of cantillation. To deviate from them, said the Rabbis, would be a serious breach of the scriptural injunction (Deuteronomy 19:14), "You shall not move your neighbor's landmarks [traditions] established by previous generations."

Why is the Torah chanted with a different melody on Rosh Hashana and Yom Kippur?

The Maharil (Rabbi Jacob Halevi Mollin), leading fifteenth-century Ashkenazic authority on matters of custom and liturgy, suggested that the melody for the Torah reading on the High Holidays be different from the melody employed throughout the year so as to remind the public that these are special days in the Jewish calendar, days calling for serious introspection.[73]

Apparently, it was considered unnecessary to introduce a new melody for the reading of the haftara.

Why is the Torah scroll generally placed horizontally on the reading table?

Representations of the Torah ark are found on the walls of the Jewish catacombs of Rome, which date back to the third and fourth centuries C.E. In these depictions, the

Torah scroll is shown positioned horizontally on shelves in wall niches. Since this was the way in which Torah scrolls were kept in early times, it is only natural that today scrolls be placed horizontally on the reading table for the Torah reading service.

Why in some synagogues is the Torah read from an upright position?

Sephardic congregations whose members have their roots in Eastern countries follow the tradition of standing the Torah vertically on the reading table and reading from it while it is in that position. The origin of this custom is not known, and it may have simply evolved out of a practical need, since their Torah scrolls were encased in permanent wooden or metal containers.

Each container was hinged, and when it was opened, the portion of the Torah to be read was exposed. Handling the Torah and its heavy casing was much easier when the scroll stood upright. The Torah parchment was rolled from section to section by manipulating two finials *(atzay chayim)* that protruded from the top of the case.

The practice of standing scrolls upright may also have come about because in earlier centuries congregants did not have individual copies of the Pentateuch, and the only way they could follow the Torah reading was by standing close to the upright scroll on the reader's table. The upright position made it easier for congregants to see the text.

By far the more common procedure today is to lay the Torah flat on the reading table. This procedure is followed by all Ashkenazic congregations and by those Sephardic congregations whose roots are not in the East.

Why must three columns of writing be exposed when the Torah is read?

As explained earlier, the number three is beloved in Jewish tradition, and many customs and practices revolve about it. Thus, according to the Talmud[74] at least three columns must be written on each sheet of parchment; and while the Torah is being read, three columns must be exposed to prove that the scroll was properly written.

Why is the Torah read on the Sabbath in some houses of mourning?

The Sabbath is a day on which all mourning rites are canceled. Mourners do not sit *Shiva* on the Sabbath, and generally they attend services in the synagogue.

A Torah may be brought into a house of mourning, but it must be read on three consecutive Torah reading days, and one of these must necessarily be the Sabbath. If this requirement cannot be fulfilled, a Torah may not be brought into a house of mourning because, said the Rabbis, it would be disrespectful to move the scroll from a synagogue to private quarters and not read from it on three consecutive Torah reading days.[75]

Mourners have the option of holding the Sabbath Torah reading service in the morning or the afternoon or at both times.

Why is the expression *Chazak chazak ve-nitchazek* recited by the congregation?

It is customary in all synagogues, after the last verse of each of the Five Books of Moses is read, for the congregation to recite aloud the three words *Chazak chazak ve-nitchazek,* meaning "Be strong, be strong, and let us be strengthened."

In the view of some scholars, these words were selected because in II Samuel 10:12, where the warriors of Israel promise to help each other if attacked by an enemy, the words *chazak ve-nitchazek* are used. Joab, the commander-in-chief, says to his brother Abishai:

> Be of good courage, and let us prove strong for our people. . .

In Jewish tradition, the completion of the reading of

each book of the Torah is a victory in the battle to keep God's word strong and alive.

The reason for the recitation of the three-worded expression *Chazak chazak ve-nitchazek* is traced to the Book of Joshua (1:6-9) where the expression *Chazak ve-ematz* ("Be strong and of good courage") appears three separate times. One of them (verse 7) refers directly to the importance of observing the laws of the Torah: "Be strong and brave that you may observe all the laws of the Torah that Moses My servant commanded you."

Why do some congregations repeat the word *chazak* three times upon completing each of the books of the Torah?

Although it is the more common practice for congregants to call out the words *chazak chazak ve-nitchazek* upon completing the reading of each of the Five Books of Moses, some communities follow a different practice. Instead, they call out the words *Chazak chazak chazak,* meaning "Be strong, be strong, be strong."

Those who follow the latter practice do so because they find it a more direct way of associating each book of the Torah with Moses. They discovered that the numerical value of the three Hebrew letters in the name Moshe (the Hebrew form of Moses) is 345. (*Mem* equals 40, *shin* equals 300, and *hay* equals 5.) The word *chazak* has a numerical value of 115 (*chet* equals 8, *za'yin* equals 7, and *kuf* equals 100). Therefore, the word *chazak,* when repeated three times, applauds Moses, through whom the Torah was given to Israel.[76]

Chapter 6

Aliyot

INTRODUCTION

Prior to the return of the exiled Jewish people to Palestine from Babylonia in 520 B.C.E., the Torah was not read publicly on a regular basis. On those occasions when it was read, a king, elder, or High Priest did the reading while the assembly listened.

When Ezra the Scribe assumed leadership of the Jewish people in the middle of the fifth century B.C.E., he introduced a new concept: individual Jews were to be called on to read portions of the Torah to the assembly at prescribed times, principally on the Sabbath.

Initially, the honor of reading from the Torah was reserved for the "seven illustrious members of the community," and for that reason seven Torah honors (aliyot; singular, aliya) were awarded each Sabbath. The first person called to read from the Torah was a Priest (Kohayn); the second a Levite (Levi), a member of the family of priestly assistants; and the others were Israelites (Yisraelim), general members of the community. Now as then, except in Reform congregations,[1] the first three aliyot are considered "aliyot of distinction," and those who receive them are referred to in Jewish literature by the Aramaic term *telata gavray* ("the three gentlemen"), a phrase based on Daniel 3:24 and referring to the three courageous friends of Daniel: Shadrach, Meshach, and Abed-Nego. The number three figures prominently in the awarding of aliyot, as it does in the whole process of Torah reading.

What becomes apparent as we study the manner in which aliyot were distributed from earliest times to this day is that Jewish communal life was founded on a strong democratic base, although in many cases there was a strong bias in favor of the learned, more educated class. The right of the Kohayn and Levi to the first and second aliya respectively was inviolable. But more broadly, the right to an aliya of any congregant celebrating or observing a special occasion—a bridegroom, the father of a newborn, a member observing Yahrzeit—had to be respected. These rights regarding the distribution of Torah honors apply today even as they did twenty centuries ago.

Since the early 1920s when the first girl was called to the Torah as a Bat Mitzva, many non-Orthodox congregations have reintroduced the practice of offering aliyot to women, a practice that was actually in effect in talmudic times.[2] This controversial issue is explored in this chapter.

Also discussed in this chapter is the complete aliya process: who is called to the Torah, the manner in which the honoree approaches the Torah, where he stands, the blessings that are recited, and so on. Note that the maftir aliya, a Torah honor awarded in addition to those prescribed by law for Sabbaths and festivals, is treated in Chapter Seven, Maftir and Haftara.

Why is the honor bestowed upon a person who is called to the Torah termed an *aliya*?

In ancient times, when the Temple was still in existence, the bringing of sacrifices was the highlight of the religious service. The sacrifices were offered on the Temple altar, which was located in the center of the sanctuary on an elevated platform.

After the destruction of the Second Temple in 70 C.E., the synagogue, which was already in existence while the Temple stood, became the spiritual center of Jewish life. Since sacrifices could no longer be offered, the reading of the Torah became the highlight of the religious service, and appropriately the reading was conducted from an elevated area.

Because the Torah is read from a raised platform, everyone who receives a Torah honor must "ascend" the platform to recite the blessings and at times to read from the Torah. The honor therefore came to be known as an *aliya* (plural, *aliyot*), meaning "ascent," and the honoree came to be called an *oleh* (plural, *olim*), meaning "one who ascends."

In the Sephardic tradition an aliya is often referred to as a *mitzva* (plural, *mitzvot*), meaning "commandment," for the study (reading) of the Torah is a primary obligation in Jewish law.

Why do Sephardim, when calling up persons for an aliya, use the words *likro ba-Torah?*

When calling an honoree to the Torah, Sephardim use the words *"Ya'amod* (so-and-so) *ben* (so-and-so) *likro ba-Torah,"* meaning "(So-and-so) the son of (so-and-so) may rise and come forward to read from the Torah." Ashkenazim simply say, *"Ya'amod* (so-and-so) *ben* (so-and-so)," omitting the words "to read from the Torah."

The longer Sephardic phrasing is the original, dating back to the time when persons receiving aliyot actually read their own Torah portions. Today, although practically all Sephardic congregations employ an official Torah reader, the original phrasing has been retained.[3]

See page 133 for a discussion of the institution of the *baal koray,* the official Torah reader.

Why is the phrase *ben Avraham avinu* often used to call a proselyte to the Torah?

Although in some respects a proselyte, a convert to Judaism, does not have full equality under Jewish law,[4] the spirit of the law demands that once a non-Jew enters the Jewish fold he is to be considered equal and is not to be reminded of his former status.

Since when he converts, a "Jew by choice" severs almost all religious ties with his biological family, he is often, though not always, given the patronymic *ben Avraham* (for example, Yitzchak ben Avraham).[5] The name Avraham was selected not only because Abraham *(Avraham)* was the first Jew (or "Hebrew" as was the original designation) but also because he was reputed to be a person who befriended strangers.

If by chance the convert also selects Avraham as his first name, he will then be called Avraham ben Avraham *avinu.* The word *avinu,* meaning "our father" (Abraham our father), was appended to identify him as a proselyte.[6]

Why has the tradition of calling an individual to the Torah by his personal name fallen into disuse, particularly in non-Orthodox congregations?

When the Torah reading was first introduced, it was decided that to call persons to the Torah by simply announcing "Kohayn, please rise [and approach the Torah]" or "Levi, please rise," or "Yisrael, please rise," would be confusing, since there were many individuals in the synagogue who belonged to each category. It therefore became accepted to call each person honored with an aliya by his own first name followed by his father's first name—for example, Yitzchak ben ("son of") Avraham ha-Kohayn if he is a Kohayn, or David ben Moshe ha-Levi if he is a Levi, or simply Shimon ben Yaakov if he is a Yisrael.[7]

In more recent times, particularly in non-Orthodox synagogues, this practice has been abandoned because many of the congregants are strangers, having come specifically to attend a celebration such as Bar or Bat Mitzva or the naming of a baby. The reader or sexton who announces the aliyot does not know these individuals and therefore calls the honorees to the Torah without using their personal names.[8]

In most congregations, before the Torah is removed from the ark, persons are advised by the *gabbai* (usher) that they will be called to the Torah. In a number of congregations "aliya cards" indicating which honor is being bestowed on an individual are handed out in advance, and before each aliya an announcement is made. For a Kohayn the Hebrew words used are *Yaamod Kohayn* ("Kohayn, please rise"); for a Levi, *Yaamod Levi* ("Levi, please rise"); for the third aliya, *Yaamod shelishi*, "Third honoree, please rise"; and so on through the last aliya.[9]

Why do some congregants in Sephardic congregations stand when a person is called up to the Torah?

To show respect for a grandfather, father, brother, son, or other relative, it is common in Sephardic congregations for all members of the honoree's immediate family to rise when the individual receives an aliya. The family members generally remain standing during the opening Torah blessing, the reading of the Torah, and for the closing Torah blessing. They then resume their seats. In some congregations the family stands only during the recitation of the opening Torah blessing. There are many diverse customs among Sephardim in this regard.

Why do Sephardim wave the fringes of their *talitot* toward one who has just received an aliya?

Among Sephardic Jews there is a custom of waving at a Torah as it passes in procession, especially when the congregants are not close enough to the scroll to touch it and kiss it.[10] It is also customary for congregants to hold up the fringes of their *talitot* and wave to a person who is returning to his seat after receiving an aliya. The recipient of the Torah honor reciprocates by holding up the corner of his *talit*. Those close enough to the honoree will offer congratulations by means of the usual handclasp.

Primo Levi, the late Italian Jewish chemist whose antecedents came from Spain, explains that the *talit* gesture is a sentimental expression of profound mystical and religious significance.[11]

Why do Orthodox authorities deprecate the custom of kissing friends and relatives after receiving an aliya?

Rabbi Ovadya Yosef, former Sephardic Chief Rabbi of Israel, was asked about the practice of kissing relatives after an aliya, a custom prevalent especially among Jews whose roots are in North Africa, especially Morocco. (We refer here to males kissing each other on the cheek, not to males kissing females.)

Drawing upon the views of other authorities for support, Ovadya Yosef deprecates this practice on the grounds that kissing relatives and friends after one has received an aliya and has returned to one's seat is a display of affection which detracts from the affection that at this moment should be reserved for God. It is imperative, he maintains, that one never forget that there is no love equal to the love of God.

Ovadya Yosef concludes his responsum by urging that this widespread custom be discouraged. He does, however, believe that it is quite proper and important to continue the custom of kissing the hand of the rabbi, of one's father, and of other relatives whom one is obligated to honor.[12]

Why does tradition demand that a Torah honoree ascend the pulpit from one direction and leave it from another?

The Rabbis ruled[13] that, when called to the Torah, one

should approach the pulpit to recite the blessings via the shortest path and return to one's seat via the longest path. Before leaving the pulpit, it is always proper for the recipient of the aliya to greet the rabbi, cantor, and other dignitaries.

Tradition demands that one take the shortest route when going up for an aliya so as to avoid delaying the progress of the service, for to do so would be an affront to the assembly. (The Hebrew term used is *mipnay kevod tzibur.*)[14]

Another explanation is that in Jewish tradition one should show eagerness to perform a religious duty *(mitzva)*—in this case, recite the Torah blessings—and reluctance to conclude it. By approaching the pulpit via the shortest route and departing via the longest, one is giving expression to this tradition.

If both paths to the pulpit are equidistant, it is proper for the *oleh* to ascend the pulpit via the path to his right and leave via the other path to his left. The right side is favored in Jewish tradition, a concept derived from Exodus 15:6, which states, "Thy right hand, O Lord, is glorious in power." It is also associated with the verse in Deuteronomy (33:2) which implies that the Torah was received by Moses in his right hand.

Why does the person who has completed an aliya wait until the next aliya is over before leaving the pulpit?

It is considered an indignity to the Torah to recite the concluding Torah blessing and then depart immediately. Some authorities base this on Deuteronomy 5:28, where God says to Moses, "Stand there before me . . ."

Abraham Gombiner, in his commentary on the *Shulchan Aruch,*[15] notes that it is customary for one receiving an aliya to remain on the pulpit until his successor has pronounced the opening Torah blessing. But, he adds, an individual who wants to be especially careful to avoid missing any of the Torah reading as he is leaving the pulpit should remain on the pulpit until the next Torah portion has been read in its entirety. It has thus become customary for one called to the Torah to leave the pulpit only after the final Torah blessing has been recited by his successor.

In the Sephardic tradition, an *oleh* does not always remain on the pulpit while the Torah reading for the next aliya is recited. Among Jews of Syrian extraction it is customary to leave the pulpit immediately before the next honoree recites the first Torah blessing. In the Spanish-Portuguese tradition, it is customary for the Torah honoree to remain on the pulpit until the next *oleh* has recited the first Torah blessing, after which he returns to his seat (while the Torah is being read). Those who follow the tradition of Turkey and other Ottoman Empire countries leave the pulpit just before the next *oleh* completes the recitation of the concluding blessing (after the Torah has been read).

Why is a congregant greeted with the Hebrew words *yishar kochacha* after having received an aliya?

In Ashkenazic synagogues, when a person returns to his seat after having had an aliya, fellow congregants generally greet him with the phrase *Yishar kochacha,* meaning "May your strength be firm" or "May you grow in strength."

These Hebrew words (sometimes pronounced *yiyasher kochacha* and sometimes colloquially as *yasher koiach*) are of talmudic origin.[16] They were first used by Resh Lakish (Simon ben Lakish), the third-century C.E. Palestinian scholar renowned for his great strength, in connection with his interpretation of two Hebrew words in Exodus (34:1), *asher shibarta,* meaning "which you have broken." The reference here is to Moses, who had come down from Mount Sinai with the two Tablets of the Law. When he finds the Children of Israel worshiping the Golden Calf that they had made in his absence, Moses hurls the tablets from his hands and shatters them at the foot of the mountain (32:19).

God then tells Moses to prepare new tablets of stone to replace the broken ones, and Resh Lakish records God's approval of the action by Moses and quotes God as saying to Moses, "May your strength be increased [congratulations] for breaking them" (in Hebrew, *yishar kochacha she-shibarta*).[17]

A second rabbinic explanation for greeting a person after an aliya with the phrase "May you grow in strength" is that it was believed that intense study of Torah (symbolized by the Torah reading) saps a person's strength,[18] and the greeting expresses the hope that the recipient of the aliya will be reenergized as a result of the honor just bestowed upon him.

When congratulating a person who has had an aliya, the custom among Sephardim is to use the expression *Chazak u-varuch*, meaning "Be strong and be blessed,"[19] or *Baruch tihiyeh*, meaning "May you be blessed." The honoree responds *Chazak ve-ematz*, "Be strong and of good courage."

In synagogues where the Persian rite is followed, a person returning to his seat after an aliya is greeted by congregants who raise the fringes *(tzitziot)* of their prayer-shawls *(talitot)*. The honoree in turn raises the *tzitziot* of his *talit* and touches his fringes to those of the congregants nearby.

Why do some women in Sephardic congregations issue a wailing sound after certain celebrants have received an aliya?

A common practice among Sephardic women, primarily those from Eastern countries (including Syria, Iran [Persia], and Iraq) is to issue a wailing sound after a Bar Mitzva, bridegroom, or other celebrant has pronounced the concluding Torah blessing or after he has left the pulpit to take his seat. The wail is believed to ward off evil spirits that are anxious to disturb happy occasions. (Creating noise is the original reason for breaking a glass at the conclusion of the wedding ceremony.)[20]

Visitors to the Western Wall, where many Bar Mitzva ceremonies are held by Oriental Jews, often hear shrieks and wails emanating from the women's section.

Why are Torah honors sometimes auctioned off to the highest bidder?

In the Middle Ages it was common for Torah honors to be auctioned off during the service and sold to the highest bidder in order to earn income for the synagogue. Today, this is still done, particularly among Sephardic congregations with Eastern origins. The honors that are generally auctioned off include the taking of the Torah from the ark, the *hagbaha* (elevating the Torah scroll), carrying the Torah in procession, and the maftir aliya.[21] Sephardic Jews refer to honors that are auctioned off as *mitzvot,* the same term used by them to designate aliyot.

In some Ashkenazic Orthodox congregations, the practice of selling aliyot and other honors exists today to a very limited extent. In both Sephardic and Ashkenazic congregations, one of the most coveted of the honors that are auctioned off is the maftir Yona (the Book of Jonah), read on the afternoon of Yom Kippur.

In auctioning off honors, Sephardim, particularly those who follow the Syrian tradition, use figures such as 26, 101, and 202 (two times 101) in bidding. Twenty-six is the numerical value of the letters in Yehova, while 101 is the numerical value of Michael, the guardian angel of Jews who is mentioned three times in the Book of Daniel in this capacity.

Why is a *Mi She-bayrach* prayer sometimes recited during the Torah reading service?

Many synagogues follow the established practice of offering a special *Mi She-bayrach* ("May He [God] who blessed") prayer for the well-being of the *oleh* or for others whom he may designate. The *baal koray* or sexton recites the prayer after the Torah honoree has pronounced the concluding Torah blessing. So as not to extend the service unduly, some congregations recite one collective *Mi She-bayrach* prayer when the Torah reading has been concluded.

The *Mi She-bayrach* prayer reads, "May He who blessed our fathers Abraham, Isaac, Jacob ... send His blessings upon (so-and-so) *ben* (so-and-so). May the Holy One bless him, and protect him, and deliver him from all trouble and illness. May He send a blessing and success to all his efforts and to those of the whole household of Israel. And let us say, Amen."

If a *Mi She-bayrach* is being made for the welfare of a woman, the names of the matriarchs Sarah, Rebecca, Rachel, and Leah are substituted for those of the patriarchs.

Persons for whom the *Mi She-bayrach* prayer is generally recited include the *oleh* himself; a Bar or Bat Mitzva celebrant; a groom on the Sabbath before his wedding (in non-Orthodox congregations, the bride often joins the groom on the pulpit); a newborn girl who is being named at the service; and those who are ill or who have just recovered from an illness.

In some Sephardic congregations, a *Mi She-bayrach* is recited after the ark is opened and before the Torah is removed for the reading service.

Why is the word "shnudder" used in connection with aliyot?

After the *Mi She-bayrach* prayer is recited, the *oleh* may show gratitude by announcing a donation to the synagogue, to members of the clergy, or to a charitable institution. An individual making such a donation is said to "shnudder" money. The word "shnudder" actually derives from the Hebrew word *she-naddar* in the phrase *ba-avur she-naddar,* meaning "because he has pledged," which is found in the *Mi She-bayrach* prayer.[22]

Why is eighteen dollars frequently pledged by those for whom the *Mi She-bayrach* prayer is recited?

The Hebrew word *chai,* meaning "life," has the numerical equivalent of eighteen. (The letter *chet* equals 8, and the letter *yod* equals 10, totaling 18.) Since the *Mi She-bayrach* prayer expresses the hope for renewed or continued well-being, *"chai"* has always been considered an appropriate amount to donate.

Why is the name of the mother invoked when making a *Mi She-bayrach* for a sick person?

Generally, when a special blessing is pronounced for a person who has just received an aliya, the form used is, "May He who blessed our fathers Abraham, Isaac, and Jacob send His blessings upon . . ." At this point the name of the *oleh* and his father's first name are generally mentioned. However, when a blessing is recited in behalf of a sick person, the name of the mother is used. Thus, for example, instead of referring to the ailing person as Gershom ben Moshe, he would be referred to as Gershom ben Tzipora.

Mystics (kabbalists) explain this practice by saying that greater pity will be shown to an individual if the appeal to God is made through the mother. This contention is based on the words used in Psalms 86:16: "O turn unto me and be gracious unto me . . . and save the son of Thy handmaid."

Why do Orthodox congregations award aliyot to persons who may not be Sabbath observers?

It is accepted practice in all congregations never to question a person about his religiosity before awarding him an aliya. Even the late Rabbi Moshe Feinstein, spokesman for the ultra-Orthodox community, expressed the opinion that transients who appear in a synagogue may be called to the Torah without being questioned.[23]

Why do authorities consider it justifiable to deny an aliya to a member of the Jewish community under certain circumstances?

As far back as the fourteenth century, scholars have issued responsa dealing with the question of whether a sinner may be accorded a Torah honor. Most authorities agree that a congregation has the right to deny an aliya to a person who is known to be a sinner. However, the definition of sinner is not clear.

In the Sephardic tradition, particularly among Syrians, if a Kohayn has violated the law by marrying a divorcee, all the offspring of the marriage are disqualified from the priesthood and may not assume any priestly functions. (They are called *chalalim* in Jewish law.) The Kohayn who has thus sinned is never given an aliya and is permitted to sit only in the rear of the synagogue. His sons are no longer considered Kohanim and are assigned only such aliyot as are granted to an ordinary Jew (Yisrael).[24]

The question has been debated as to whether one may be granted an aliya if it is not known whether he is a Sabbath observer. Most authorities agree with Rabbi Moshe Feinstein, who ruled that the individual may be granted an aliya. However, if it is generally known that an individual is a Sabbath violator, he is not to be accorded a Torah honor. Rabbi Feinstein, like many of his predecessors, emphasized that what is involved here is "the honor of the Torah [*kevod ha-Torah*]." He points out that one may not denigrate the status of the Torah by calling a sinner to read from it or even to recite a blessing over it.[25]

Other authorities, less stringent, argue that since the *baal koray,* not the *oleh,* now reads from the Torah, one need not worry about the honor of the Torah being at stake. They would caution, however, that a person known to be dishonest (one guilty of giving or accepting bribes, for example) should not be called up if the Torah portion to be read speaks of honesty or the pursuit of justice (such as is read for the first aliya for the portion Shofetim [Deuteronomy 16:18-20]).[26]

Why do Orthodox congregations deny women the right to aliyot?

In early talmudic times (from approximately 100 B.C.E. to 200 C.E.) women as well as men were called to the Torah, and all read their own Torah portions.[27] On occasions when a congregation consisted of very few males who were knowledgeable enough to read the unvocalized Torah script, most of the aliyot were given to women. This proved embarrassing to the male population and was probably one of the factors that led to the appointment of the *baal koray*, "master of the reading," who read all Torah portions.

At this same time, in what has been interpreted as a move to insure male dominance in Jewish life, another change was put into effect by the Rabbis. Women, who originally had *read* from the Torah, were now denied the right to even ascend the pulpit and recite the Torah blessings. The reason for this was given as *mipnay kevod ha-tzibur*, because of the "dignity of the congregation." The Rabbis felt that since the presence of women on the pulpit would be distracting to men, females should be banned from all participation in the synagogue service.

Non-Orthodox congregations have rejected this reasoning and to one degree or another permit participation by women in the Torah reading service and in other phases of synagogue ritual.

Why do some congregations award women aliyot but do not count women as part of a *minyan*?

Congregations that award women aliyot argue that a woman's right to be called to the Torah is specified in the Talmud[28] and, as discussed above, it was only later that she was denied this privilege, as the Rabbis put it, "out of respect for the congregation."

The Talmud, however, never mentions whether a woman may be counted as part of a minyan. It is only in the codes that appeared many centuries later that she is denied this right.[29] The reason given is that women have important responsibilities toward home and family that exempt them from attending public prayer services. Since women are not required to attend prayer services, they are ineligible to be counted as part of the quorum *(minyan)* for a prayer service.

In 1973 a majority of the Rabbinical Assembly Committee on Jewish Law and Standards (Conservative) voted in favor of counting women as part of a minyan. However, the rabbi of each Conservative congregation was granted the option of following the majority or minority view. The Reform movement, since its inception, has granted women full equality with men. In Orthodox congregations women are neither granted aliyot nor counted as part of a minyan.

Why do certain individuals receive preferential treatment when Torah honors are distributed?

According to tradition, there are occasions in an individual's life that entitle him to an aliya upon demand. Not all authorities are agreed on the precise order in which these honors are to be awarded, but the following is the generally accepted sequence:

1. A groom on the Sabbath before his marriage, an occasion generally known by its German name, *Aufruf.*
2. A groom on the Sabbath following his wedding.
3. A Bar Mitzva (and today in Conservative and Reform congregations, a Bat Mitzva).[30]
4. The father of a newborn child.[31]
5. One observing a Yahrzeit.
6. One who is obligated to recite the *Ha-gomel* prayer after emerging unscathed from a life-threatening situation.
7. Visiting dignitaries.

Why does a bridegroom have an *Aufruf?*

Aufruf is a German word meaning "calling up." On the Sabbath before his marriage, the bridegroom is called up to the Torah in honor of the important event that is about to take place. This affords the community as a whole an opportunity to wish him and his new bride well.

In many non-Orthodox congregations today, the bride accompanies her husband-to-be to the pulpit and sometimes recites the Torah blessings with him.

Why, in some congregations, was a reading done by a bridegroom from a second scroll?

On ordinary Sabbaths, only one scroll is removed from the ark for the Torah reading. However, from a responsum of Rabbi Simon ben Zemach Duran, the leading rabbi of North African Jewry in the fourteenth century, we learn that in Algeria it was customary on the Sabbath following a marriage to remove a second scroll from the ark and to have the bridegroom read a selection from Genesis 24, which relates to the betrothal of Rebecca to Isaac.

Rabbi Simon suggests that this custom developed so that grooms who were not learned would have to practice the reading of this special section, thus being compelled to spend time in study.[32]

In the Middle Ages, it was also customary on the Sabbath after a wedding for the groom, after completing his aliya and returning to his seat, to be greeted by the congregation joyfully singing Hebrew songs. One such song began:

> Rejoice, O bridegroom, in the wife of your youth.
> Let thy heart be merry now and when you grow old...

This practice prevails to this day in many Sephardic congregations and in some Ashkenazic ones.

Why do congregants sometimes shower *olim* with candy?

Some communities still follow an old tradition of filling small bags with candy, nuts, raisins, or other sweets and throwing them at a Bar or Bat Mitzva or at a groom who has been called to the Torah on the Sabbath before his wedding. This is done following the recitation of the closing Torah blessing as an expression of hope that a sweet life will be the lot of each celebrant.

Why do some people who have survived a hazardous experience receive an aliya and recite a special prayer?

In Temple times, a person who survived a life-threatening experience would express thanksgiving by bringing a sacrificial offering. When the Temple was destroyed and individuals could no longer offer sacrifices, thanksgiving was expressed through prayer. Synagogue officials became obliged to call to the Torah (within three days of the event if possible) anyone who had emerged safely from a perilous predicament and wished to express his thankfulness.

Today, an *oleh* who has recently survived a hazardous experience pronounces a special thanksgiving prayer after reciting the closing Torah blessing. The prayer is known in Hebrew as *Birkat Ha-gomel*,[33] "Prayer of Salvation," and the act of reciting it is referred to in Yiddish as *benshn goiml.* The honoree thanks God for "granting favors to people as unworthy as he." The congregation responds by saying, "May He who was good to you continue to bestow His goodness upon you."[34]

Why does the father of a Bar Mitzva recite a special blessing after his son has recited the closing Torah blessing?

An old tradition, practiced in Orthodox synagogues, has the father pronounce a prayer after his son recites the final Torah blessing at his Bar Mitzva. The prayer, *Baruch She-petarani,* thanks God "who has freed me [the father] from the obligation [burden] of this one [child]."

The prayer was dropped by most non-Orthodox congregations because of its negative connotation: it seems to express relief at being free from responsibility for one's son. Congregations who have retained the prayer view it as an expression of joy over a son's having reached the age of accountability rather than a parent's having reached a point of nonaccountability.

In many Conservative and Reform congregations today, instead of the *Baruch She-petarani,* parents together with their child recite the *She-hecheyanu* prayer after the Bar/Bat Mitzva has recited the second Torah blessing. This prayer expresses thanks for having lived to enjoy this day.

Why does the natural father have a greater claim to an aliya at the Bar Mitzva of his son than the child's adoptive father?

Where a woman has remarried and her child has been reared by a stepfather, the natural father retains all religious rights and obligations pertaining to the child. The aliya generally awarded to the father of the Bar Mitzva boy is given to him rather than the stepfather, and when the traditional *Baruch She-petarani* blessing is recited, it is he who does so.[35] (See preceding question.)

Even where there is great love between child and stepfather, the legal relationship between the natural father and the child does not change. The child is legally bound to respect and honor the natural father, and whereas the honor and respect he bestows upon the stepfather is praiseworthy, it is not mandatory under the law.

Why may the father of a Bar Mitzva sometimes be denied an aliya?

If the father of a Bar Mitzva is not Jewish (but the

mother is), Jewish law does not permit the father to be called to the Torah even if he has learned to recite the blessings. The reason: the Torah blessings refer to "granting *us* the Torah," meaning to the *Jewish* people. A person who is not Jewish cannot honestly pronounce such blessings. In Jewish law, all benedictions that are untrue or unnecessary are termed *berachot le-vatala,* "wasted blessings."[36]

Aside from this objection, many traditionalists are of the opinion that allowing a non-Jew to recite a Jewish prayer at a Jewish service would lead an observer to mistakenly conclude that the individual reciting the prayer (the non-Jew) is in fact a Jew.

However, many congregations feel that it is proper to show consideration for the non-Jewish father by permitting him to ascend the pulpit and stand near his son without actively participating.

Why do some congregations prohibit the calling of two people to the Torah for the same aliya?

Jewish law[37] requires that members of a congregation be able to hear every word of the Torah as it is being read. When two persons chant the words of the Torah in unison, it is often difficult to hear the words distinctly. Therefore, the Rabbis forbade the practice.

Orthodox congregations have interpreted this ruling to mean that two people are not to be called up to the Torah together even if they are not to read from the Torah but merely to recite the blessings. They indicate that Jewish law prohibits the simultaneous recitation of the Torah blessings because if the two voices are not heard distinctly, the members of the congregation would be unable to honestly answer "Amen" and the blessings would therefore be construed as *berachot le-vatala,* "wasted blessings."

In many non-Orthodox congregations today, namely those that do not give the *beracha le-vatala* concept credence, two people occasionally are called up for the same aliya. At times the *olim* recite the blessings in unison, and at other times one person recites the first blessing and the other recites the concluding blessing.

Why is the recitation of the Torah blessings by two Bar Mitzva boys at the same service prohibited in some congregations?

Rabbi Moshe Feinstein[38] was asked how to handle a situation in which two boys are celebrating a Bar Mitzva on the same Sabbath and each wishes to recite the full maftir, haftara, and accompanying blessings independently. Rabbi Feinstein ruled that this is forbidden, because the repeating of blessings unnecessarily is a breach of Jewish law. (See above.)

In a situation where each family insists that it wants its child's Bar Mitzva to be held on that particular Sabbath, Rabbi Feinstein suggests that first one boy should be called to the Torah. But before he begins to chant the blessings, ten men must leave the synagogue and wait outside. When this first Bar Mitzva boy has completed the recitation of the haftara, the ten men who have left the synagogue return and the second Bar Mitzva is then called to the Torah and he repeats the full performance. Since these ten men had not yet heard the blessings pronounced, they are considered to be a new minyan. Rabbi Feinstein is aware, of course, that this procedure may represent an inconvenience to the congregation, but he considers it a necessary inconvenience inasmuch as it will avoid a situation in which enmity might develop between families should only one Bar Mitzva celebration be permitted on that Sabbath.[39]

Why does a mourner generally receive an aliya on the Sabbath after he concludes observing the *Shiva* period?

During the first week of mourning *(Shiva)*, one who has lost a loved one is not called to the Torah because to be

honored with an aliya is a joyous experience that symbolizes an individual's association with the community of
Israel. By offering the mourner an aliya on the Sabbath after
the *Shiva* period, the congregation is in effect welcoming
the mourner back to the community.

In the event that a mourner is inadvertently offered an
aliya during *Shiva* (because the individual who distributes
the aliyot is unaware of his status), he is obligated to accept
it. To do otherwise would appear to the congregation to be
an act of disrespect.[40]

Why may a mourner sometimes accept an aliya on a Sabbath during *Shiva?*

As explained above, a mourner should not be offered an
aliya on a Sabbath that falls during the *Shiva* period. However, many authorities are of the opinion that a mourner
may accept an aliya on a Sabbath that coincides with the
seventh (last) day of *Shiva.*[41]

This view is founded on the principle that in Jewish law
part of a day is equivalent to a whole day.[42] Just as the first
day of mourning is counted as a full day even if the mourner
arrives home from the funeral only moments before nightfall, so is the last day counted as a full day if a mourner sits
for only a short time after the conclusion of the morning
(Shacharit) service.[43]

The mourner may receive an aliya at the Torah reading
service that follows the *Shacharit* because the Torah reading service, considered a study period in Jewish tradition, is
totally independent of the morning service.

Why is it contrary to Jewish law to offer certain aliyot to handicapped persons?

In order to spare handicapped persons embarrassment,
Jewish law demands that they not be called to the Torah if
the portion to be read will refer to their infirmity.[44]

It is for this reason, for example, that

• Blind persons are not called to the Torah when the

portion describing Isaac's blindness is to be read (Genesis 27).
- Crippled persons are not called to the Torah when the portion describing Jacob's injury after wrestling with an angel is read (Genesis 32).
- Those who stutter are not called to the Torah when the portion that refers to the stuttering of Moses is read (Exodus 4:10-17).

Why in early times were blind persons not awarded aliyot?

From the first public reading of the Torah through talmudic times, the person who received an aliya not only recited the Torah blessings but also read a portion from the Torah. When doing so, the individual was required to look at each word in the scroll as he chanted it. Since it was not permissible to recite the Torah portion from memory, a blind man could not receive an aliya.[45]

In post-talmudic times (after the sixth century C.E.), when a special reader (the *baal koray*) was introduced to read all the Torah portions, there no longer was any reason to deny aliyot to the blind.[46] As far as the haftara is concerned, the view of most authorities[47] is that a blind person who becomes a Bar Mitzva may recite the prophetic portion from memory or from a Braille text.[48] However, he may not recite the Torah portion.

Why was it once possible for one person to receive all the aliyot?

Moses Maimonides states that in a congregation where there is only one individual present competent enough to read the Torah, that individual is to proceed to the reading table, read a section, return to his seat, then repeat the procedure as many times as necessary until all of the aliyot to be awarded that day have been completed.[49]

This may have been necessary in the twelfth century of Maimonides, when individuals called to the Torah still read their own Torah portions. In later times, however, this situation could not obtain because those receiving aliyot were called upon only to recite the Torah blessings, not to actually read from the Torah, a function carried out by the *baal koray.*

Why are congregants reluctant to accept certain aliyot?

Some portions of the Torah contain descriptions of unpleasant situations and conditions. Despite the fact that it is generally considered disrespectful to refuse an aliya (see page 169), it has become traditional for more knowledgeable congregants to refuse aliyot for which these unpleasant selections are read. In early times the poor, who were infrequently called to the Torah, were willing to accept even these "undesirable" aliyot.[50]

Among the sections of the Torah that are considered undesirable are the *Tochacha,* meaning "reprimand." These sections list the curses that will befall those who disobey the commandments, and the Talmud therefore refers to them as Chapters of Curses. One is Leviticus 26:14-39; the other is Deuteronomy 28:15-68.[51]

In recent times, the fear associated with being called to the Torah when unpleasant portions are read has diminished, and most people will not refuse such an aliya. Nevertheless, it is still customary in some congregations for such aliyot to be awarded to the rabbi, sexton, or the Torah reader himself. Even so, the old tradition continues of not calling by name those persons who receive these aliyot.

Why are blood relatives not given consecutive aliyot?

Although there is no talmudic law banning two brothers or a father and son from receiving consecutive aliyot, Joseph Caro's *Code of Jewish Law*[52] prohibits it out of fear that the evil eye *(a'yin ha-ra)* might cast a spell upon a family receiving too many blessings. Other prominent scholars add that on the Sabbath a person may not be awarded maftir and be called to the Torah by his personal name if his blood relative has received the previous aliya. Here, too, the reason for the proscription is to avoid the evil eye.[53]

A more rational explanation relates this ban to the demand of Jewish law that the testimony of two nonblood-related witnesses is required to substantiate evidence in a court of law.[54] Since when one pronounces the Torah blessings he is in effect giving testimony to God and to the Jewish people that he accepts the sovereignty of the Torah and its teachings, blood relatives should not follow one another as recipients of Torah honors.

Why is the same number of aliyot not awarded every time the Torah is read?

The Rabbis of the third century C.E., led by Rabbi Gamaliel, began editing and formalizing the synagogue liturgy. The practice of reading the Torah on Mondays, Thursdays, Sabbaths, and holidays was already central, and there existed a tradition, traceable to Ezra (fifth century B.C.E.), that seven people were to be called to the Torah on Sabbath morning, six on Yom Kippur morning, five on festivals and on Rosh Hashana, four on the intermediate days of festivals and the New Moon (Rosh Chodesh), and three on Monday, Thursday, and Sabbath afternoons.

Since the Rabbis did not know how these numbers were arrived at, they offered fanciful explanations, often based on a verse of Scripture. They said, for example,[55] that three, five, and seven aliyot are awarded on certain occasions in order to create a correspondence with the number of words in the priestly benediction (Numbers 6:24-26): the first of the three blessings in the benediction consists of three Hebrew words; the second, five; and the third, seven. This, of course, does not explain why six persons are called to the Torah on Yom Kippur morning and four are called on other occasions.

The eighth-century minor talmudic tractate Soferim

offers a more legalistic interpretation for the various numbers of aliyot awarded and relates them to the degree of punishment imposed for violating the holiness of the day.[56] The more holy the day, the more severe the punishment. The more severe the punishment, the more aliyot awarded.

Why are seven aliyot awarded on the Sabbath, more than on any other occasion?

The Talmud[57] specifies that a minimum of seven aliyot are to be awarded on a Sabbath. As mentioned in the previous answer, it is understandable that more honors were to be distributed on the Sabbath than on any other day: the Sabbath, the seventh day of the week, is the most holy day in the calendar.

Like the number three, seven figures prominently in Jewish tradition. Its preeminence was highlighted early in the Bible, when the seventh day was consecrated as holy, climaxing the six days of Creation.

Additionally, both Passover and Sukkot were declared to be seven-day festivals, and the seven weeks after the first day of Passover were to be counted day by day, culminating in Shavuot, the holiday celebrating the Revelation on Mount Sinai.

The Book of Deuteronomy (31:10-13) declares that at the end of every seven-year period the Torah was to be read to all the Children of Israel. This is also mentioned in the Book of Nehemiah, where we are told that Ezra read the Torah to all the people on the first day of the seventh month and then again on each of the seven days of Sukkot (Nehemiah 8:2 and 8:18).

Because of the many ways in which the number seven is associated with the Torah, it is understandable why it became sacred and was selected as the number of aliyot to be awarded on the most sacred day in the Jewish calendar.[58]

Why are extra aliyot sometimes awarded at Sabbath morning services?

As stated above, not less than seven aliyot are to be awarded at a Sabbath morning service, although that number may be increased.[59] Some synagogues add aliyot known in Hebrew as *hosafot,* "additional ones," so that more people can be honored on a particular Sabbath. This is done on occasions such as a Bar or Bat Mitzva, when many guests are present at the synagogue service. Generally, and particularly among Sephardim, from the sixth aliya *(shishi)* onward Torah portions are subdivided, with not less than three verses being read for each person honored. (More than three verses are read when the third verse ends on an unsavory note.)

In many synagogues subdivisions begin much earlier, sometimes as far back as the first aliya. Also, in some congregations the last verses of the final aliya are repeated one or more times in order to accommodate additional *olim.*

Why are four honorees called to the Torah on certain occasions?

The Rabbis of the Talmud ruled that Rosh Chodesh (New Moon) and the intermediate days (Chol Ha-moed) of Sukkot and Passover are half-holidays despite the fact that a *Musaf* (additional) service is part of the liturgy. Since such days are not full festivals, four persons rather than five— not more, not less—are called to the Torah.[60]

Why are more than five aliyot occasionally awarded on festivals in some synagogues and not in others?

Although the Talmud as well as the codes of Moses Maimonides and Joseph Caro permit more than five aliyot to be awarded on the major holidays (Rosh Hashana, Pesach, Sukkot, and Shavuot), Ashkenazic authorities follow the view of Moses Isserles, who considered it inappropriate to grant more than five Torah honors on these occasions. The only exception is Simchat Torah. Reflecting the mood of his coreligionists in sixteenth-century Poland and Germany, Isserles considered it contrary to the joyous holiday spirit to keep the congregation in the synagogue for a longer time than necessary.[61]

Limiting the number of Torah honorees on major holidays became the universal Ashkenazic practice. Some Sephardic congregations do at times offer more than five aliyot on holidays.

Why are three aliyot allocated at the Monday and Thursday morning and Sabbath afternoon services?

The early Rabbis of the Talmud ruled that on Monday and Thursday mornings and on Sabbath afternoons three persons—not more, not less—are to be called to the Torah.[62]

Various reasons for the ruling are offered.[63] Some authorities suggest that since there are three classes of Jews—Kohanim, Leviim, and Yisraelim—at least three aliyot be awarded at the Torah reading service so that each class can be represented. Others relate the three aliyot to the threefold division of the Bible: Torah, Prophets, and Holy Writings.

As stated earlier, there have also been fanciful reasons offered by scholars to explain the awarding of three aliyot. One, for example, relates it to the threefold priestly benediction (Numbers 6:24-25), the first of which consists of three Hebrew words.

Why was three established as the *maximum* number of aliyot to be awarded at the Monday and Thursday morning and Sabbath afternoon services?

The reading of the Torah on Monday and Thursday mornings was probably instituted because these were market days, when many Jews journeyed to Jerusalem from various parts of the country. Ezra the Scribe ruled that on these occasions an abbreviated portion of the Torah be read and that only three aliyot be assigned so as not to extend the morning service, thus allowing as much time as possible for the pilgrims to attend to their business.

A probable reason for awarding a maximum of three aliyot on Sabbath afternoons was to curb the length of the service and to allow time for preachers and teachers to deliver sermons and teach their classes.[64]

Why are more than three aliyot sometimes awarded at the Monday and Thursday morning and Sabbath afternoon services?

In special situations more than three aliyot may be awarded at a Monday morning, Thursday morning, or Sabbath afternoon service. This view was first expressed by Rashi, who said that four honors may be granted if a congregation is amenable to it.[65]

The thirteenth-century German talmudist Rabbi Meir of Rothenburg was probably the first to allow four aliyot in order to accommodate two bridegrooms present at a service. In the view of Rabbi Moses Isserles, the same holds true when two fathers of newborn children are present. If both fathers are Yisraelim, he wrote, each may be given an aliya. The reason given for allowing the number of aliyot to exceed three is that the occasion is a holiday to these celebrants, and on holidays more than three aliyot are always allocated.[66]

In his Magen Avraham commentary on the Shulchan Aruch, Rabbi Abraham Gombiner disagrees. He says that the proper procedure is to call no more than three aliyot.[67] This view is shared by other authorities.

Why was ten established as the number of verses to be read at a public Torah reading at which three aliyot are awarded?

In the Talmud[68] Rabbi Huna, the third-century C.E. Babylonian scholar, established the rule that on those occasions (such as Monday and Thursday mornings and Sabbath afternoons) when three aliyot are awarded, neither less nor more than ten verses should be read from the Torah. Rabbi Hezekiah explained that the number ten was selected because it is the number of commandments in the Decalogue.[69]

The Rabbis of the Talmud were not agreed on how to distribute the ten verses that are read when only three people are called to the Torah. The *Code of Jewish Law* suggests that four verses may be read for any of the three *olim,* and "whoever is lucky will have four verses read for him, and he is praiseworthy."

Nevertheless, in actual practice it became customary to read the extra verse only for the first or third honoree.[70]

Why is the first aliya assigned to a Kohayn?

The Kohanim and Leviim who ministered in the Tabernacle in the desert and later in the Temples of Jerusalem were all descendants of the tribe of Levi. Levi was the third of Jacob's twelve sons.

Moses and his brother, Aaron, were the foremost members of the tribe of Levi, but since Moses was preoccupied with the task of leading the Children of Israel, it became the duty of his brother to conduct the religious affairs of the tribes. And thus it was that Aaron became the first High Priest (Kohayn Gadol), with other members of his family serving as ordinary Priests (Kohanim) and managing the sacrificial system. The rest of the tribe of Levi, the Levites (Leviim), assisted the Priests in various ways, their rank being secondary.

The Bible itself does not explain why Aaron and his family were assigned this primary role in Jewish life. The

Book of Deuteronomy (10:8) merely notes that while the Israelites were in the desert, God separated the tribe of Levi and assigned to it the task of "carrying the ark and ministering to Him." One tradition, however, notes that the tribe of Levi was chosen to minister to God because they alone, of all tribes, did not worship the Golden Calf (Exodus 32:1-33:6).[71]

When the reading of the Torah was introduced in Temple times and persons were called upon to read from the Torah, the question arose as to who was to be called first and who second. Since, unlike the other tribes, the tribe of Levi had not been given a portion of land when Canaan was conquered, the Rabbis decided to reward its members by assigning to them special religious rewards. The Kohanim, being the most important members of the tribe, were awarded the first aliya. This right was reinforced when the Rabbis of the Talmud laid down the law that an illiterate Kohayn should not be denied the first aliya even if a great scholar is present at the service.[72]

Why, after a Kohayn receives the first aliya, must a Levi be awarded the second aliya?

The Talmud[73] specifies that a Kohayn is called up to the Torah to read first and that he is to be followed by a Levi and then a Yisrael (Israelite). This rule was established "in the interest of peace," explains the Talmud.

Some Rabbis of the Talmud[74] found a biblical basis for the rule: They interpret the verse in Deuteronomy (31:9), "And Moses wrote this law and gave it to the Priests, the sons of Levi," to mean that "Priests come first [as *olim*] and other sons of Levi come [immediately] after them."

If no Levites are present, the Kohayn who received the first aliya is awarded the second aliya as well.

Why may any member of the congregation receive the first aliya if a Kohayn is not present?

The awarding to a Kohayn of the first aliya, to a Levi the

second, and to a Yisrael the third[75] is a procedure that has been followed unfailingly over the centuries. However, there has been much discussion among authorities as to who is to be awarded the first aliya when a Kohayn is not present at the service. Should a Levi or a Yisrael be called in place of the absent Kohayn? The consensus is that either may be offered the honor. The Rabbis did insist, however, that when a substitute for a Kohayn is called, an announcement be made that the individual is being awarded the aliya "in place of the Kohayn."[76]

The general principle at work in this regard was characterized by talmudic authorities by the Hebrew term *nitparda ha-chavila,* meaning "the bond has been broken." In other words, the whole "package" has come apart (that is, the package involving the system of priorities established with regard to the Kohayn, Levi, and Yisrael). Since the Kohayn is not present at the service, the Levi no longer has a claim to the second honor, for only by virtue of the Kohayn's status did the Levite enjoy his secondary position.[77]

Why, if a Levi is present at a Torah reading service, does he not necessarily receive the second aliya?

If a Kohayn receives the first aliya and a Levi is present at the service, the Levi must be given the second aliya. However, if a Kohayn is not present at the service, a Levi may be given the first aliya (although this is not mandatory), but in this event neither he nor another Levi may be given the second aliya. As discussed above, the Rabbis of the Talmud made it clear that once a Kohayn is not present to receive the first aliya the entire procedure of Kohayn first, Levi second, and Yisrael third is upset.

Why is a Yisrael sometimes given the first aliya even though a Kohayn is present?

In the unusual event that except for one Yisrael all those

present at a service are Kohanim, the first aliya is awarded to the Yisrael, not to a Kohayn. The reason is *mipnay darkay shalom,* "to keep the peace."[78] If one particular Kohayn were to be singled out for the honor of being called first, the other Kohanim might become resentful. By choosing to honor the lone Yisrael with the first aliya, the difficulty is resolved.

Not all authorities would permit the Torah to be read under these circumstances, since a Kohayn may not receive the third aliya or any of the other mandated aliyot that may follow.[79]

In another circumstance, when only one Kohayn is present at a service and he is engaged in reciting the *Shema* (or the *Shemoneh Esray*), he is not to be disturbed, and a Yisrael may be called in his place. It would be an act of disrespect to keep the whole congregation waiting until the Kohayn has finished his prayers.[80]

Why may a Levi not be called to the Torah for the second aliya if a Yisrael is called for the first?

When a Yisrael is called for the first aliya, it is clear that a Kohayn is not present at the service, otherwise the Kohayn would be called first. The Rabbis felt that if a Yisrael is called for the first aliya, he should not be followed by a Levi lest latecomers or members of the congregation who may not have been paying close attention be led into the mistaken belief that the first *oleh* is a Kohayn when he is in fact a Yisrael.[81]

Moses Maimonides summarizes the law clearly. He says that if a Kohayn is *not* present, a Yisrael takes his place, and following the Yisrael (who has received the first aliya) another Yisrael is called for the second aliya *(sheni).*[82]

To avoid any misunderstanding, a Levi is never called for the second aliya unless a Kohayn has received the first aliya.

Why must a Kohayn sometimes purposely leave the synagogue before the Torah reading begins?

Although the law mandates that when a Kohayn is present at a service he is to receive the first aliya, there are times when many honors must be awarded to Yisraelim who are entitled to be called to the Torah because of special occasions in their lives (see page 179). In such instances it has become customary to give the first aliya to someone other than a Kohayn so that all people due honors may receive them without extending the service and thereby inconveniencing the congregation.

Since the law[83] mandates that when a Kohayn is present he must always be awarded the first aliya, should a Kohayn be attending that service, he must leave the synagogue before the first honoree is called up to the Torah. By this voluntary action, the Kohayn expresses his agreement with the procedure and allows the aliya that rightfully belongs to him to be assigned to a non-Kohayn.

Why does a Kohayn sometimes receive two consecutive aliyot?

When a Levite is not present at the Torah reading service, the rule is that the Kohayn who received the first aliya is awarded the second aliya as well. Neither a different Kohayn nor a Yisrael may be called up for the second aliya in such a case.[84]

This rule was established so that those unaware that a Levi is not present to receive the second aliya should not be misled into thinking that a second Kohayn was called up for the second aliya because a doubt has been cast upon the legitimacy of the first Kohayn. It might be perceived that someone in the congregation had called into question the lineage of the first Kohayn. Or it might be perceived that someone had charged that the first Kohayn is "tainted,"[85] necessitating a second Priest being called to the Torah to correct the error.

A Yisrael may not be awarded the second aliya after a Kohayn has received the first one because this might lead someone entering the synagogue late to conclude that the first *oleh* was not a Kohayn. If the first *oleh* were a Kohayn, he would have been followed by a Levi, or he would have repeated the blessings for the second aliya himself.

Why may two Leviim not receive consecutive aliyot?

Two Leviim may not be called to the Torah consecutively for the same reason that two Kohanim may not be called up one after the other: members of the congregation might be led to the erroneous conclusion that the first Levi called up to the Torah was flawed and that a legitimate Levi was now being called up to correct the situation.[86]

Why may a Kohayn and Levi sometimes be awarded aliyot other than the first and second ones?

Even though the Kohayn and Levi enjoy a preferred status when it comes to the awarding of aliyot, in Ashkenazic rites they may not be granted those honors that are specifically reserved for Yisraelim. These include the third, fourth, fifth, sixth, and seventh aliyot on Sabbaths; the third, fourth, fifth, and sixth on Yom Kippur; the third, fourth, and fifth on holidays; the third and fourth on Rosh Chodesh and the intermediate days of Passover and Sukkot; and the third (last) aliya on Mondays, Thursdays, Sabbath afternoons, and fast days.

This, however, does not take into consideration the category of aliyot known as *hosafot*, "additional ones," which may be awarded in addition to mandated aliyot. Included in this category of additional aliyot is the maftir, which may be assigned to a Kohayn or Levi.[87]

In Sephardic congregations, a Kohayn is given an aliya normally reserved for a Yisrael. He may be called for any aliya beginning with the fourth *(revii)*. When this is done, the *gabbai* announces that the *oleh* is being called up *af al pi she-hu Kohayn,* "despite the fact that he is a Kohayn." The same applies to a Levi.

Why has Reform Judaism abolished the distinction between Kohayn, Levi, and Yisrael?

Reform as well as some liberal Conservative congregations take the position that because today no one can be certain of the lineage of any Jew, it is not valid to classify Jews as Kohanim, Leviim, and Yisraelim. They also argue that in a democratic society all people are equal, and special rights and privileges should not accrue to any one group.[88]

Why is the third aliya regarded as the most coveted honor accorded a Yisrael?

The number three has assumed a sacred character in Jewish tradition, and it is for that reason that the third aliya *(shelishi),* the first honor awarded to a Yisrael, is cherished. The third Torah honor is generally awarded to a member of the congregation who has achieved a degree of distinction in the community.

Joseph Caro's *Code of Jewish Law*[89] lists in order of priority those to whom the third aliya should be assigned. First are scholars who also serve as synagogue functionaries (such as the rabbi or cantor). Second are distinguished scholars who are members of the congregation. Third are the children of scholars who serve as congregation officials. Fourth are lay leaders of the congregation, after which follow the remaining members of the congregation.

Among some Sephardim the third aliya is awarded to the father of a Bar Mitzva.

Why does the sixth aliya have special significance?

The sixth aliya, *shishi,* is coveted because it is two times three, which, as discussed above, is a sacred number in Jewish tradition.

The number six is also important in its own right because the sixth day of the week was the day on which man was created and the day on which the Torah says God completed the task of Creation and expressed deep satisfaction with His work. The Bible (Genesis 1:31) says:

> And God saw everything that He had made and behold it was very good. And there was evening and there was morning, the sixth day.

The word "very" is used as a modifier for "good" only in connection with the sixth day.

The kabbalists believe that when God created the heavens, he combined light and darkness and fire and water and then stretched them out like a curtain, as alluded to in Psalm 104:2. This stretched-out form reminded mystics of the Hebrew letter *vav*. *Vav* thus became a holy letter, and the sixth aliya (*vav* has the numerical value of six) became a distinguished one.[90]

Probably the most convincing reason for ascribing such importance to the sixth aliya is that it was on the sixth day of the Hebrew month Sivan that the Revelation took place.

Why in Jewish tradition is the last aliya considered prestigious?

The last aliya before maftir, known as *acharon* by Ashkenazim, has traditionally been considered a highly desirable one, probably because of its association with the expression *acharon acharon chaviv*, "the last [one] is most beloved."

This phrase was first used in the Midrash[91] in a comment made on the verse in Genesis (33:2) which describes the order in which Jacob arranged his family when he anticipated a confrontation with his brother, Esau. Jacob placed Rachel and her son Joseph at the very end of the formation, says the Midrash, because he loved them most, thus securing for them the safest position.

Among Ashkenazim the last aliya is generally offered to pious people, particularly when each of the Five Books of Moses is concluded and especially on Simchat Torah when the concluding portion of the entire Pentateuch is read.

Sephardim refer to the last aliya by the name *mashlim,* meaning "concluder," the one that concludes the cycle of aliyot. The honor is usually reserved for a bridegroom, for it symbolizes the hope that the man's life will now be complete and fulfilled. Among Moroccan Jews particularly, where sons are coveted, the *mashlim* aliya is reserved for the father of a newborn girl, and it is an expression of the father's hope that with the birth of this child he will have "completed" fathering daughters and will have only sons in the future.

Why are portions of the Torah reading sometimes repeated several times?

On Sabbath and holidays, before the maftir is called, the last verses of the final aliya (*shevii* on Sabbath, *chamishi* on holidays) may be repeated one or more times in order to accommodate additional *olim* who are deserving of being honored on that day. At least three verses are read for each of these extra aliyot *(hosafot).*[92]

Why does a Torah honoree touch the *talit* to the scroll before reciting the blessings?

It is considered a sign of respect and adoration to touch the Torah scroll at the place where the reading is to begin before reciting the first Torah blessing, and to then touch the scroll at the place where the reading ends before reciting the final Torah blessing. To avoid using one's fingers for this purpose, the *tzitziot* (fringes) of the *talit* are traditionally used. The fringes from one of the four corners of the *talit* are touched to the Torah by the honoree and then kissed.[93]

Although the precise origin of the fringe-touching custom is unknown, it is generally assumed to be derived from the fact that the numerical value of the word *tzitzit* (600),[94] when added to the number of knots and strings (13)[95] on each of the four fringes of the *talit,* yields a total of 613, which is equal to the number of commandments in the Torah.[96]

In congregations where women receive aliyot, women who wear a *talit* follow the same procedure, while others touch the Torah with the corner of a prayerbook or Bible.

It should be noted that there is no legal requirement that a *talit* be worn by the recipient of an aliya.

Why is a blessing recited before and after the Torah is read?

The reading of the Torah in the synagogue is considered a form of study. Since studying the Torah is a divine commandment, and since Jewish law[97] demands that a blessing be recited before a commandment is performed, a blessing is pronounced before the Torah is read.

As it was customary to recite a form of the Kaddish *(Kaddish de-Rabbanan)* at the conclusion of a Torah study session in the academies of learning, so it also became customary to recite a concluding blessing to mark the completion of the Torah reading.

From the fifth century B.C.E. through the middle of the third century C.E., when each person called to the Torah actually read his own portion, the first honoree recited the first blessing only and the last honoree recited the concluding blessing only.[98] Those who were called to the Torah for the other aliyot did not recite any blessings. They merely read a portion from the Torah.

By the end of the third century C.E. the procedure had been modified. The Talmud says, "Nowadays all [who are called to read the Torah] recite a blessing before and after they read their portions."[99] The Rabbis instituted this change because they were concerned that those who would arrive at the synagogue after the Torah reading had already begun would see that some persons were reading from the Torah without first having pronounced a blessing. The latecomers might be left with the impression that it is not necessary to recite a Torah blessing before one reads the Torah. Likewise, congregants who leave the synagogue before the Torah reading has ended, without having heard

Why do some persons lift the Torah slightly when reciting the Torah blessings?

Some Jews follow the custom of pressing down on the front Torah finials when they pronounce any form of the word Torah in the Torah blessings. Pressing down on the front finials causes the upper part of the scroll to be raised slightly. This serves as a reminder to all present that *this* is the same Torah that Moses received on Mount Sinai.

In some congregations one occasionally sees the honoree not only raise the Torah slightly off the reading table but shake[107] the scroll at the same time. The intention here, too, is to emphasize that this is the original Torah.

Why does the individual who raises the Torah not recite the Torah blessings?

Hagbaha is a Hebrew word meaning "raising [of the Torah]." The person who performs this act is called the *magbi'a*, "the one who raises."[108] Although raising the Torah scroll is considered an important honor, the *magbi'a* does not recite the Torah blessings. These are reserved only for those who actually read a Torah selection (or for whom a selection is read).

In Ashkenazic congregations the Torah is raised after the Torah reading for the day has been completed. In Sephardic synagogues it is raised before the Torah reading ceremony begins. The Hebrew term used by Sephardim for their Torah-raising ceremony is *hakama*, meaning "elevating [the Torah]." In Spanish-Portuguese synagogues the ceremony is referred to by the Spanish term *levantador*.

Why do Sephardim perform the Torah-raising ceremony *before* the Torah is read?

In Ashkenazic congregations the Torah is raised *after* the Torah reading has been completed. The *magbiha* lifts the scroll from the lectern, exposing three columns of the Torah text. He then turns around so the congregation can

anyone recite the closing Torah blessing, might be misled into believing that it is not necessary to recite a blessing after the Torah reading has been completed. It was therefore required that each person to receive an aliya recite an opening blessing before his Torah portion is read and a closing blessing after the portion is read.

The Rabbis of the Talmud were not agreed[100] upon what wording is most appropriate for the opening blessing, but the view of Rabbi Hamnuna prevailed. He favored the following:

> *Baruch ata Adonai, Elohenu melech ha-olam, asher bachar banu mi-kol ha-amim, ve-natan lanu et Torato. Baruch ata Adonai, noten ha-Torah.*
> Praised be Thou, O Lord our God, King of the Universe, Who has chosen us from among all peoples and has given us His Torah. Praised be Thou, O Lord, Giver of the Torah.

The Rabbis were agreed that the following invocation be offered by the *oleh* before the first Torah blessing is recited: *Barchu et Adonai ha-mevorach*, "Praise the Lord, Who is the blessed One." The congregation responds: *Baruch Adonai ha-mevorach le-olam va-ed*, "Praise the Lord, Who is blessed forever and ever." After the honoree repeats this sentence, he pronounces the opening Torah blessing. (The invocation is pronounced only when a minyan is present.[101])

Sephardim preface the invocation preceding the opening Torah blessing with the following proclamation which the honoree addresses to the congregation: *Adonai imachem*, "May the Lord be with you." To which the congregation responds: *Yevarechecha Adonai*, "May the Lord bless you."

After the reading of the Torah portion for each aliya, the closing Torah blessing is recited:

> *Baruch ata Adonai, Elohenu melech ha-olam asher natan lanu Torat emet, ve-cha'yay olam nata betochenu. Baruch ata Adonai, noten ha-Torah.*

Praised be Thou, O Lord our God, King of the Universe, Who has given us a Torah of truth, thereby implanting within us the seed of eternal life. Praised be Thou, O Lord, Giver of the Torah.

Sephardim have modified the second Torah blessing slightly by adding the words *et Torato* ("His Torah") before the words *Torat emet* ("a Torah of truth"). The reading is thus . . . *asher natan lanu et Torato, Torat 'emet, vecha'yay olam . . ,* ". . . Who has given us His Torah, a Torah of truth, thereby implanting within us . . ." This formula has been ascribed to Maimonides.

Why did Reconstructionists change the wording of the first Torah blessing?

The first Torah blessing includes the words *asher bachar banu,* meaning "Who [God] has chosen us." Reconstructionists reject the idea that Jews have been "chosen" by God and substitute the words *asher kervanu la-avodato,* meaning "Who has brought us closer to His service." In their view, this modification in the prayer expresses the idea of responsibility rather than superiority.[102]

Only the Reconstructionist Movement has made a change in the traditional blessing.

Why is it customary in many congregations for a Torah scroll to be rolled closed while the Torah blessings are being recited?

The Talmud[103] describes two procedures followed by *olim* in this regard. According to the second-century Palestinian scholar Rabbi Meir, a person called up to the Torah should open the scroll, look at the words where the reading is to begin, roll the scroll closed, recite the first Torah blessing, and then unroll the scroll for the reading to begin. After the portion is read, the scroll is once again rolled closed, and the *oleh* recites the final blessing.

Rabbi Meir believed that the scroll should not be left

open while the Torah blessings are recited because eyes of the honoree should be cast downward, towa open scroll, people might assume that the blessings a ing read from the Torah itself, when in fact the blessir not written in the Torah.

Rabbi Judah did not believe that the Torah scroll be rolled closed when the blessings are recited. He wa vinced that no one would ever think that the Torah ings are written in the Torah scroll.

Although Rabbi Judah's procedure was the mo cepted one, both practices have been followed by dif communities over the centuries. Ashkenazic Jews g ally follow the precise procedure as outlined by Rabbi although some cover the Torah either with the mantl special Torah cover when the Torah blessings are re Sephardic Jews generally do not roll the Torah scroll c when the blessings are recited, nor do they cover it.

Why do some people close their eyes or tu their heads to one side when reciting the Tor: blessings?

Although it would appear that individuals close eyes when reciting the Torah blessings in order to inte concentration, the true purpose is to indicate to tl watching that they are not reading the Torah blessings the Torah itself.[104]

The same reasoning applies to those who turn t heads to the side when reciting the blessings.[105]

Why is it customary to take hold of the Tora finials *(atzay chayim)* when reciting the bless ings?

The Torah is compared to a tree of life. Proverbs (3: says, "It [the Torah] is a tree of life to those who take hol it." This verse became the basis for the practice of hold the *atzay chayim* (finials) of the Torah when reciting Torah blessings.[106]

see the words of the open scroll. The congregation recites, "This is the Torah that Moses set before the Children of Israel at the command of the Lord by the hand of Moses."[109] The Torah is then rolled up and prepared for its return to the ark.

In Sephardic congregations, whether Eastern or Western, *before* the reading of the Torah begins, a person raises the scroll, revealing all or part of three columns of the Torah text. He shows the script to the people standing to his right, then to those to his left. Next he faces front and then turns and faces toward the rear so persons in every part of the synagogue can see the words on the parchment. (In some Sephardic congregations the procedure is to turn clockwise—east, south, west, north—when displaying the Torah.) The Torah reader *(baal koray)* turns with him and with a Torah pointer *(yad,* literally "hand") indicates where the reading will begin. The congregation then recites "This is the Torah . . ." (Deuteronomy 4:44), as do the Ashkenazim at the conclusion of the Torah reading.[110] Sephardim, however, omit the final phrase: "at the command of the Lord by the hand of Moses" (Numbers 9:23).

Why Sephardic and Ashkenazic practices differ is not readily explained, but it is quite clear that the Sephardic custom is older.

The Talmud itself makes no mention of a *magbi'a* and exactly when it became customary to designate a special person to raise the Torah is unknown.

The laws of *hagbaha* are given in the *Shulchan Aruch,* Orach Chayim 134, and these precede the laws pertaining to the actual reading of the Torah, which begin section 135. This was probably the order in which things happened in the sixteenth century, although Isserles does add that the custom as he knows it (in Poland and surrounding areas) is to have *hagbaha* after the Torah reading.

Rabbi Solomon B. Freehof pointed out that the Turkish talmudist Chayim Benveniste (1603-1673) was of the opinion that *hagbaha* was transferred from *before* the Torah reading to *after* the Torah reading so as to discourage persons from leaving the synagogue early. Many ignorant people, said Benveniste, believe that *hagbaha* is more important than the Torah reading itself and would therefore leave the synagogue immediately after the Torah was raised. With *hagbaha* transferred to the end of the reading, people would stay and listen to the reading, waiting for *hagbaha*.[111]

Why are Torah blessings not recited by the golel?

Gelila is Hebrew for "rolling up."[112] The person who performs the honor of rolling up the Torah scroll is called the *golel,* meaning "the one who rolls up." The Talmud[113] says that the "senior" person among all who have received an aliya at a particular service is to be the *golel,* and this honor is equal in importance to all Torah honors combined.

Today, only Ashkenazic congregations call up an individual formally for the *gelila* honor. In Sephardic congregations the task is performed routinely by one of the *gabbaim* who flank the Torah reader. *Gelila,* like *hagbaha,* is not one of the aliyot prescribed for any of the various Torah reading occasions. And, because no Torah portion is read for these honorees, they do not recite Torah blessings.

The term *gelila* has a secondary meaning as well. It is used to refer to the act of "covering" or "dressing" the Torah.[114]

anyone recite the closing Torah blessing, might be misled into believing that it is not necessary to recite a blessing after the Torah reading has been completed. It was therefore required that each person to receive an aliya recite an opening blessing before his Torah portion is read and a closing blessing after the portion is read.

The Rabbis of the Talmud were not agreed[100] upon what wording is most appropriate for the opening blessing, but the view of Rabbi Hamnuna prevailed. He favored the following:

> *Baruch ata Adonai, Elohenu melech ha-olam, asher bachar banu mi-kol ha-amim, ve-natan lanu et Torato. Baruch ata Adonai, noten ha-Torah.*
>
> Praised be Thou, O Lord our God, King of the Universe, Who has chosen us from among all peoples and has given us His Torah. Praised be Thou, O Lord, Giver of the Torah.

The Rabbis were agreed that the following invocation be offered by the *oleh* before the first Torah blessing is recited: *Barchu et Adonai ha-mevorach,* "Praise the Lord, Who is the blessed One." The congregation responds: *Baruch Adonai ha-mevorach le-olam va-ed,* "Praise the Lord, Who is blessed forever and ever." After the honoree repeats this sentence, he pronounces the opening Torah blessing. (The invocation is pronounced only when a minyan is present.[101])

Sephardim preface the invocation preceding the opening Torah blessing with the following proclamation which the honoree addresses to the congregation: *Adonai imachem,* "May the Lord be with you." To which the congregation responds: *Yevarechecha Adonai,* "May the Lord bless you."

After the reading of the Torah portion for each aliya, the closing Torah blessing is recited:

> *Baruch ata Adonai, Elohenu melech ha-olam asher natan lanu Torat emet, ve-cha'yay olam nata be-tochenu. Baruch ata Adonai, noten ha-Torah.*

Praised be Thou, O Lord our God, King of the Universe, Who has given us a Torah of truth, thereby implanting within us the seed of eternal life. Praised be Thou, O Lord, Giver of the Torah.

Sephardim have modified the second Torah blessing slightly by adding the words *et Torato* ("His Torah") before the words *Torat emet* ("a Torah of truth"). The reading is thus . . . *asher natan lanu et Torato, Torat emet, ve-cha'yay olam* . . , ". . . Who has given us His Torah, a Torah of truth, thereby implanting within us . . ." This formula has been ascribed to Maimonides.

Why did Reconstructionists change the wording of the first Torah blessing?

The first Torah blessing includes the words *asher bachar banu,* meaning "Who [God] has chosen us." Reconstructionists reject the idea that Jews have been "chosen" by God and substitute the words *asher kervanu la-avodato,* meaning "Who has brought us closer to His service." In their view, this modification in the prayer expresses the idea of responsibility rather than superiority.[102]

Only the Reconstructionist Movement has made a change in the traditional blessing.

Why is it customary in many congregations for a Torah scroll to be rolled closed while the Torah blessings are being recited?

The Talmud[103] describes two procedures followed by *olim* in this regard. According to the second-century Palestinian scholar Rabbi Meir, a person called up to the Torah should open the scroll, look at the words where the reading is to begin, roll the scroll closed, recite the first Torah blessing, and then unroll the scroll for the reading to begin. After the portion is read, the scroll is once again rolled closed, and the *oleh* recites the final blessing.

Rabbi Meir believed that the scroll should not be left

open while the Torah blessings are recited because if the eyes of the honoree should be cast downward, toward the open scroll, people might assume that the blessings are being read from the Torah itself, when in fact the blessings are not written in the Torah.

Rabbi Judah did not believe that the Torah scroll has to be rolled closed when the blessings are recited. He was convinced that no one would ever think that the Torah blessings are written in the Torah scroll.

Although Rabbi Judah's procedure was the more accepted one, both practices have been followed by different communities over the centuries. Ashkenazic Jews generally follow the precise procedure as outlined by Rabbi Meir, although some cover the Torah either with the mantle or a special Torah cover when the Torah blessings are recited. Sephardic Jews generally do not roll the Torah scroll closed when the blessings are recited, nor do they cover it.

Why do some people close their eyes or turn their heads to one side when reciting the Torah blessings?

Although it would appear that individuals close their eyes when reciting the Torah blessings in order to intensify concentration, the true purpose is to indicate to those watching that they are not reading the Torah blessings from the Torah itself.[104]

The same reasoning applies to those who turn their heads to the side when reciting the blessings.[105]

Why is it customary to take hold of the Torah finials (atzay chayim) when reciting the blessings?

The Torah is compared to a tree of life. Proverbs (3:18) says, "It [the Torah] is a tree of life to those who take hold of it." This verse became the basis for the practice of holding the atzay chayim (finials) of the Torah when reciting the Torah blessings.[106]

Why do some persons lift the Torah slightly when reciting the Torah blessings?

Some Jews follow the custom of pressing down on the front Torah finials when they pronounce any form of the word Torah in the Torah blessings. Pressing down on the front finials causes the upper part of the scroll to be raised slightly. This serves as a reminder to all present that *this* is the same Torah that Moses received on Mount Sinai.

In some congregations one occasionally sees the honoree not only raise the Torah slightly off the reading table but shake[107] the scroll at the same time. The intention here, too, is to emphasize that this is the original Torah.

Why does the individual who raises the Torah not recite the Torah blessings?

Hagbaha is a Hebrew word meaning "raising [of the Torah]." The person who performs this act is called the *magbi'a,* "the one who raises."[108] Although raising the Torah scroll is considered an important honor, the *magbi'a* does not recite the Torah blessings. These are reserved only for those who actually read a Torah selection (or for whom a selection is read).

In Ashkenazic congregations the Torah is raised after the Torah reading for the day has been completed. In Sephardic synagogues it is raised before the Torah reading ceremony begins. The Hebrew term used by Sephardim for their Torah-raising ceremony is *hakama,* meaning "elevating [the Torah]." In Spanish-Portuguese synagogues the ceremony is referred to by the Spanish term *levantador.*

Why do Sephardim perform the Torah-raising ceremony *before* the Torah is read?

In Ashkenazic congregations the Torah is raised *after* the Torah reading has been completed. The *magbiha* lifts the scroll from the lectern, exposing three columns of the Torah text. He then turns around so the congregation can see the words of the open scroll. The congregation recites, "This is the Torah that Moses set before the Children of Israel at the command of the Lord by the hand of Moses."[109] The Torah is then rolled up and prepared for its return to the ark.

In Sephardic congregations, whether Eastern or Western, *before* the reading of the Torah begins, a person raises the scroll, revealing all or part of three columns of the Torah text. He shows the script to the people standing to his right, then to those to his left. Next he faces front and then turns and faces toward the rear so persons in every part of the synagogue can see the words on the parchment. (In some Sephardic congregations the procedure is to turn clockwise—east, south, west, north—when displaying the Torah.) The Torah reader *(baal koray)* turns with him and with a Torah pointer *(yad,* literally "hand") indicates where the reading will begin. The congregation then recites "This is the Torah . . ." (Deuteronomy 4:44), as do the Ashkenazim at the conclusion of the Torah reading.[110] Sephardim, however, omit the final phrase: "at the command of the Lord by the hand of Moses" (Numbers 9:23).

Why Sephardic and Ashkenazic practices differ is not readily explained, but it is quite clear that the Sephardic custom is older.

The Talmud itself makes no mention of a *magbi'a* and exactly when it became customary to designate a special person to raise the Torah is unknown.

The laws of *hagbaha* are given in the *Shulchan Aruch,* Orach Chayim 134, and these precede the laws pertaining to the actual reading of the Torah, which begin section 135. This was probably the order in which things happened in the sixteenth century, although Isserles does add that the custom as he knows it (in Poland and surrounding areas) is to have *hagbaha* after the Torah reading.

Rabbi Solomon B. Freehof pointed out that the Turkish talmudist Chayim Benveniste (1603-1673) was of the opinion that *hagbaha* was transferred from *before* the Torah reading to *after* the Torah reading so as to discourage persons from leaving the synagogue early. Many ignorant people, said Benveniste, believe that *hagbaha* is more important than the Torah reading itself and would therefore leave the synagogue immediately after the Torah was raised. With *hagbaha* transferred to the end of the reading, people would stay and listen to the reading, waiting for *hagbaha*.[111]

Why are Torah blessings not recited by the golel?

Gelila is Hebrew for "rolling up."[112] The person who performs the honor of rolling up the Torah scroll is called the *golel*, meaning "the one who rolls up." The Talmud[113] says that the "senior" person among all who have received an aliya at a particular service is to be the *golel*, and this honor is equal in importance to all Torah honors combined.

Today, only Ashkenazic congregations call up an individual formally for the *gelila* honor. In Sephardic congregations the task is performed routinely by one of the *gabbaim* who flank the Torah reader. *Gelila*, like *hagbaha*, is not one of the aliyot prescribed for any of the various Torah reading occasions. And, because no Torah portion is read for these honorees, they do not recite Torah blessings.

The term *gelila* has a secondary meaning as well. It is used to refer to the act of "covering" or "dressing" the Torah.[114]

Chapter 7

Maftir and Haftara

INTRODUCTION

The word *maftir* and its variant form *haftara* mean "conclusion." Both derive from the root *patar,* meaning "to be rid of, to be free of, to end or complete a situation." A person whose life has ended is called a *niftar,* "deceased."

The person who is awarded the last aliya of the day is called the *maftir* ("concluder"), and the portion that he reads from the Torah (or that is read for him by the *baal koray*) is also called the *maftir.* After the maftir portion has been read, the Torah scroll is removed from the reading table and the maftir honoree recites the *haftara,* a selection from the Prophets.

According to the most widely accepted theory,[1] the introduction of the haftara reading dates back to the second century B.C.E. Palestine and many of the countries bordering it had been conquered by Antiochus, ruler of Syria and Greece. Antiochus wished to impose idolatrous practices on the people of Judea, hoping to win them over to a pagan lifestyle. To achieve this during his reign in the years prior to 165 B.C.E., Antiochus tried to weaken Judaism by banning many basic Jewish practices, one of which was the public reading of the Torah.

Being in a weak military position, Jews had no choice but to obey this ban. However, since a prohibition had not been placed on other types of public reading, synagogues replaced the Torah reading with selected readings from the

Prophets. Because the Rabbis did not want the Torah lesson of each week to be forgotten, they took great pains to select as the prophetic reading of the week a portion directly or tangentially related to the theme of the Torah reading that would normally have been read on that particular Sabbath or holiday.

After the Hasmoneans defeated the armies of Antiochus, and the Jews regained their independence, the regular Torah reading was restored, but the reading of the haftara was retained.

This chapter deals with the laws, customs, and practices relating to these two "concluding" readings. The precise thematic relationship between the maftir and haftara read on each Sabbath and festival will be found in Chapter Nine, Week by Week, and Chapter Ten, Holiday by Holiday.

———— ☐ ————

Why was the practice of reading a maftir selection instituted?

After the Hasmonean revolt of the second century B.C.E. succeeded in freeing Palestine from the domination of the Syrian-Greeks, the practice of reading the Torah in public, which had been suspended, was resumed. At the same time, the custom of reading a selection from the Prophets, which had been introduced to replace the Torah reading, was retained. To accommodate this new situation, the Rabbis ruled that before the haftara (selection from the Prophets) is read on Sabbaths, the last verses of the Torah reading of the day should be repeated, and this added aliya became known as the *maftir* (literally, "conclusion [of the Torah reading]"). On holidays, the maftir consisted of a completely different reading from a second scroll.

The maftir honor was not considered particularly prestigious in the post-Hasmonean period (after the first century B.C.E.), and the Rabbis raised its status by declaring that the person honored with the maftir and the haftara should also be accorded the privilege of leading the congregation in the reading of the very important *Shema* (and *Shemoneh Esray*) prayer.[2]

Why are the last verses of the Sabbath Torah reading repeated before the prophetic selection is read?

The fourth-century Palestinian scholar Ulla explains that these verses are repeated so that the person who will be reciting the prophetic portion will first have an opportunity to accord the Torah ample respect. By following this procedure, he is reaffirming the fact that the Torah is greater in sanctity than the writings of the Prophets.[3]

Why is the maftir not counted as one of the prescribed number of aliyot?

The maftir aliya is not counted as one of the seven aliyot mandated for the Sabbath, as one of the six for Yom Kippur, or as one of the five for holidays because the primary purpose for honoring a maftir is so that an individual will read a selection from the Prophets. As explained in the previous answer, the reading from the Torah is done solely to acknowledge its primacy.

An exception to the above is the maftir who is honored on Yom Kippur afternoon. This person is called to the pulpit primarily as the third Torah honoree *(shelishi)*, not as one whose chief function is to read from the Prophets. The fact that this honoree also recites the Book of Jonah (maftir Yona) is secondary.[4]

Why is the Torah scroll sometimes covered between the final aliya and the maftir aliya?

Following the last aliya *(acharon)* of the Torah reading service, there is an extended period during which prayers unrelated to the Torah reading are recited. These include prayers for the good and welfare of the individual (*Mi She-*

bayrach prayers) and culminate in the recitation of the *Kaddish,* which is followed by the maftir.

Out of respect for the Torah, during these and other extended gaps in the Torah reading service it is customary to keep the scroll covered.[5]

Why is Kaddish recited before the maftir is called to the Torah?

Originally, the Kaddish prayer was recited after a period of study.[6] Since the Torah reading service itself was considered a study period, once all the aliyot (except maftir) had been awarded, it became common practice to recite the Kaddish.

Maftir is considered an "extra" aliya. It is not one of the prescribed seven Torah honors that must be awarded on a Sabbath or one of the five that must be awarded on festivals. Once the prescribed number of honorees has been called to the Torah, the reading is legally complete. It is at this point, therefore, that the Kaddish must be recited.

When the maftir is read from a second scroll, Kaddish is recited after the second scroll has been placed on the reading table, before it is opened for the reading. When three Torot are read, the Kaddish is recited after the reading has been completed from the second scroll. The maftir portion is read from the third Torah scroll.

Why is the Half-Kaddish, not the full Kaddish, recited after the Torah reading is concluded?

The full Kaddish, consisting of six short paragraphs, is recited only when a major portion of the prayer service has been concluded, such as after *Shacharit* or *Musaf*. The Torah reading service itself is actually a form of divine worship but not a regularly constituted liturgical service. Therefore, only the Half-Kaddish *(Chatzi Kaddish)* is recited after the Torah has been read.

Maimonides (twelfth century) points out[7] that "in some communities it is customary to recite the Kaddish after the maftir has been read." Current practice, however, is to recite the Kaddish before the maftir is called to the Torah, since at that point all the mandated aliyot have already been awarded.

In some Sephardic congregations, when readings are conducted from two scrolls, it is customary for the *oleh* to recite the Half-Kaddish[8] after the second Torah has been read and the final Torah blessing has been recited.

Why is the Half-Kaddish not recited at the conclusion of all Torah reading services?

Although after the reading of the Torah has been completed the Half-Kaddish is generally recited, there are occasions when it is not. Since on Sabbath afternoons and fast days the Half-Kaddish is to be recited momentarily—prior to the recitation of the Silent Devotion—there is no need to recite it immediately following the conclusion of the Torah reading.

Why is a second scroll sometimes used for the maftir reading?

Normally, when the Torah is read on a Sabbath or on weekdays, only one scroll is removed from the ark for the public reading. However, should a new Hebrew month (Rosh Chodesh) begin on a day when the Torah is to be read, an additional scroll is removed from the ark, and the maftir portion, containing material relevant to the occasion, is read from that Torah.

Likewise, a second Torah is used for the reading of maftir on all major holidays. On the intermediate days of Passover (but not on the intermediate days of Sukkot) the reading from the second scroll is for the fourth aliya.

A second Torah is also removed from the ark for a maftir reading on four special Sabbaths that occur around the Purim-Passover season. These include Shabbat Shekalim, Shabbat Zachor (immediately prior to Purim), Shabbat Para, and Shabbat Ha-chodesh. (See Chapter Ten, Holiday by Holiday, for elaboration on the four Sabbaths.)

In all of the above instances a second scroll is used for the reading of maftir so as not to burden the congregation by keeping it waiting unnecessarily while the first scroll is rolled to that part of the Torah where the maftir portion is to be found.

The principle of Jewish law[9] which stipulates that it is improper to burden a congregation unnecessarily is based on a procedure established by the High Priest, who in Temple times read aloud Leviticus 16 followed by a selection from Leviticus 23 (26-32). The Mishna[10] says that after reading the two selections, the High Priest rolled up the scroll, placed it under his arm, and proceeded to recite from memory a selection from the Book of Numbers (29:7-11).

The Talmud asks, "Why did he recite the selection from memory? Why did he not roll the scroll from Leviticus to Numbers and read from it?" Rabbi Huna replies, "Because it is not proper to roll the scroll in public" and thereby keep the congregation waiting unduly.

To this day, except in emergencies such as when a congregation has only one Torah scroll, synagogue etiquette demands that two or three scrolls be used when readings are done from different parts of the Pentateuch.

Why are there occasions when a maftir portion is not read on Sabbath?

If a congregation has only one Torah scroll and an error is found in it at any point during the course of the Sabbath reading, in the view of the thirteenth-century German talmudic authority Rabbi Meir ben Baruch of Rothenburg (the Maharam), only the seven mandated aliyot are awarded. This means that there is to be neither a maftir reading nor a haftara reading[11] that day, thereby making the point that the Torah that had been read from contained an error.

Even when a congregation has more than one Torah, some authorities believe that there are times when the maftir may be omitted so as not to inconvenience the congregation by causing them to wait while a new Torah is taken from the ark. This type of situation could occur if an error is discovered when the seventh (and last) aliya, *shevii*, is being read on a Sabbath.

Rabbi Abraham Gombiner, in his commentary on the *Shulchan Aruch*,[12] indicates that some scholars are of the opinion that in such a case it is proper for the reading to be completed to the end of the sidra, at which point the *oleh* recites the second Torah blessing. This same *oleh* then proceeds immediately to read the haftara, omitting the haftara blessings. A separate maftir is not called to the Torah in the usual manner, thus avoiding the need for Torah blessings to be recited over an invalid scroll.

Why does the selection from the Prophets usually contain at least twenty-one verses?

The practice of reading a selection from the Prophets, the haftara, dates back to the time of King Antiochus, a second-century B.C.E. Syrian-Greek ruler who forbade the reading of the Torah by the Jews of Palestine. Reading from the Prophets was permitted because, unlike the Torah, these books were considered secular.

During this period, as a substitute for the Sabbath Torah reading, each week a selection from the Prophets was read. Since it had been customary to read a minimum of three verses for each of the seven *olim* at a Sabbath Torah reading service, it was established that a minimum of twenty-one verses be divided among the seven honorees called to read from the Prophets.[13]

After the Maccabean (Hasmonean) victory in 165 B.C.E., the reading from the Torah was resumed. Nevertheless, the practice of reading from the Prophets continued, with only one person rather than seven called to do the entire prophetic reading.

The earliest reference to the actual reading of a haftara is found in the New Testament (Book of Acts 13:15), where Paul is invited to deliver a sermon "after the reading from the Law [Torah] and the Prophets." There is also a reference in Luke (4:17) to Jesus reading from the Book of Isaiah during a Sabbath service in Nazareth.

Why do some prophetic portions contain less than twenty-one verses?

Although it had become traditional, particularly among Ashkenazim, for the haftara to consist of a minimum of twenty-one verses (as explained above), in post-Hasmonean and talmudic times it was not uncommon for as few as three[14] verses to be read. The Talmud[15] explains that the minimum of twenty-one verses applied to synagogues in which the Torah reading was not accompanied by translation into the vernacular or by commentary from a scholar. In these synagogues, since the Torah reading service was shorter, the congregation did not object to hearing a lengthier reading from the Prophets.

However, in cases where the Torah text was accompanied by translation and exposition, thus extending the service, the maftir read "three, five, or six verses from the Prophets, and this sufficed."

In the Sephardic tradition, it is quite common for the haftara to consist of less than twenty-one verses, and in many Conservative and Reform congregations today the length of the haftara is often curtailed.

Why are festival prophetic portions generally shorter than those read on Sabbaths?

As stated above, twenty-one was set by the Rabbis as the minimum number of verses for Sabbath haftarot. This corresponds to the minimum number of verses read from the Torah for all seven Sabbath aliyot.[16] On festivals, the requirement is to read a minimum of fifteen verses from the Prophets since fifteen is the minimum number of verses that must be read from the Torah for the five persons honored with aliyot.[17]

Why is a portion from the Prophets not read every time the Torah is read?

A haftara reading is omitted on Mondays and Thursdays because people must go to work after services, and to read a prophetic portion on these days would prolong the service, thus inconveniencing the congregation unduly. The Aramaic term for such inconvenience is *tircha d'tzibura*, "public inconvenience." This principle of Jewish law is often invoked when establishing religious and social communal practices.

A haftara selection is not recited at the Sabbath afternoon *Mincha* service in part because a selection from the Prophets had already been read that morning. But perhaps the primary reason can be traced to earlier times, in Europe in particular, when it was customary for a preacher (*magid* in Hebrew) to deliver a sermon on Sabbath afternoon. To extend the Torah reading section of the service by reciting a haftara as well would have used up time needed by the preacher.

Why is a minor sometimes awarded the maftir aliya?

Although a boy is considered a minor under Jewish law until he has reached the age of thirteen (actually, thirteen and one day), it is permissible to call a pre-Bar Mitzva to the Torah as maftir and to permit him to recite the haftara.[18] (In congregations that award aliyot to women, this would apply to pre-Bat Mitzva girls.)

In some Sephardic congregations it is not unusual for a child as young as age seven to be permitted to recite the haftara, although an adult is called for maftir.[19]

As pointed out earlier, the maftir aliya is an additional one, not one of the seven prescribed for the Sabbath Torah reading or the five for festivals. As such, the Rabbis considered it appropriate to award this concluding aliya to minors in order to encourage them to pursue their Torah studies diligently. To be able to display one's accomplishments in public by reading from the Torah and reciting the haftara was a great honor.

In the Middle Ages it was not uncommon for minors to read the Torah and to lead the whole service. The leading fourteenth-century rabbi of North Africa, Rabbi Simon Duran, observes in one of his responsa that maftir was auctioned off each week at the Sabbath service, and he who made the largest offer would bestow the haftara honor upon a minor so that he might gain experience.[20]

There are authorities, however, who limit this practice and prohibit the calling up of a minor for maftir on Shabbat Chazon, Shabbat Shuva, the seventh day of Passover, Shabbat Zachor, Shabbat Para, and on the first day of Shavuot. The haftarot selected for these occasions contain subject matter more appropriately read by adults.[21]

Why was the practice instituted of awarding the Sabbath maftir and haftara to a Bar Mitzva?

The Bar Mitzva ceremony marks the passage of a boy into manhood. In the fourteenth century it became customary to celebrate the occasion on the Sabbath by honoring the Bar Mitzva boy with the maftir aliya and by granting him the privilege of reciting the prophetic portion.

When the Bar Mitzva is honored with an aliya, he is still legally a minor. It is therefore appropriate that he be awarded the maftir aliya, which is an *additional* Torah honor, rather than awarding him one of the seven aliyot prescribed for adults at a Sabbath Torah reading.

At the Monday or Thursday morning service in advance of the Sabbath on which a boy is to become a Bar Mitzva, it is customary in many Sephardic congregations to call the boy to the Torah. At that time the boy puts on *tefilin* and receives an aliya. On the Sabbath of his Bar Mitzva the boy is awarded the fifth aliya or the sixth aliya, depending on the congregation. He does not receive the maftir aliya and does not recite the haftara.[22]

Why was the practice instituted of awarding the maftir and haftara to a Bat Mitzva?

In 1922, Rabbi Mordecai Kaplan, founder of the Reconstructionist Movement, introduced a Bat Mitzva ceremony to correspond to the Bar Mitzva celebration enjoyed by boys. He felt that just as boys are called to the Torah for the maftir aliya and to recite the prophetic portion, so should girls. He believed it would encourage young girls to pursue Jewish studies and would also restore some of the equality denied Jewish women under Jewish law.

Rabbi Kaplan's daughter, Judith, was the first girl to become a Bat Mitzva. The ceremony was held in New York City at the Society for the Advancement of Judaism, the "mother synagogue" of the Reconstructionist movement.

Bat Mitzva girls are generally one year younger than Bar Mitzva boys, the age of maturity for a girl being twelve years and one day according to Jewish law.

Why do some traditional synagogues permit a Bar Mitzva to read a haftara when the celebration is held on a Monday or Thursday morning or on a Sabbath afternoon?

Jewish law calls for a reading from the Prophets accompanied by the appropriate haftara blessings only at Sabbath and festival morning services and at the morning and/or afternoon services of the various fast days. To recite haftara blessings, in which God's name is mentioned, at times not specifically mandated constitutes a violation of law, and the blessings themselves are considered *berachot le-vatala,* "wasted blessings."

To satisfy families who would prefer a short, simple service for a Bar or Bat Mitzva child but nevertheless want the child to chant a haftara, many synagogues permit the prophetic portion to be read without the recitation of the haftara blessings. Thus, the *beracha le-vatala* proscription is avoided and the family is able to hold the celebration at a convenient time.

Bar or Bat Mitzva ceremonies at which the haftara is recited without the accompanying blessings are generally held on Monday or Thursday morning or Sabbath afternoon.[23] A number of Conservative congregations do celebrate Bar or Bat Mitzva ceremonies on Friday nights, and some Reform congregations hold them on Sunday mornings as well as on Friday nights.[24]

Why is the haftara sometimes read by a Bat Mitzva on Friday night?

Congregations that favor calling women to the Torah generally conduct the Bat Mitzva ceremony during the Sabbath morning service. The young lady being inducted into the Jewish fold receives an aliya and often reads from the Torah. She also reads the haftara of the day.

Congregations that do not honor a woman with an aliya often hold the Bat Mitzva celebration at the Friday evening service, when the Torah is not normally read. At such Bat Mitzva celebrations, the young lady chants from the prophetic portion scheduled to be read the next morning.

Some Conservative rabbis who conduct a Friday night Bat Mitzva do not permit the haftara blessings to be recited, arguing that these would be wasted blessings, as discussed above. In Reform congregations, where the Torah itself is read on Friday night, the Bat Mitzva reads from the Torah and from the Prophets.

Why is the Sabbath haftara preceded by one blessing and followed by four blessings?

On Sabbath morning, the person who is called as maftir and who later chants the haftara portion pronounces a total of seven blessings: two in conjunction with the Torah reading itself and five in conjunction with the haftara. Of the five blessings, one is recited before the prophetic portion and four upon its conclusion.

The Rabbis of the Talmud[25] explain that this procedure was established so that the total number of blessings recited by the maftir honoree would correspond with the prescribed number of aliyot (seven) that must be awarded at the Sabbath morning Torah reading service.

These seven blessings, however, are also recited by a maftir on festivals and, for an unexplained reason, were not made to correspond to the number of aliyot awarded on such occasions. The only difference between the Sabbath and festival haftara blessings is in the wording of the last haftara blessing, which begins with *Al ha-Torah* ("For the Torah"). On festivals this blessing makes special reference to each holiday and the nature of the occasion. On Sabbaths it refers to the holiness of the Sabbath.

Why are the haftara blessings that are recited on the Sabbath of the intermediary days of Passover different from those recited on the Sabbath of the intermediary days of Sukkot?

The final haftara blessing recited on the Sabbath of Chol Ha-moed Passover, unlike the final blessing recited on the Sabbath of Chol Ha-moed Sukkot, does not mention the holiday by name. The blessings recited after the haftara on the Sabbath of Chol Ha-moed Passover are identical in content with those recited on any ordinary Sabbath, while those recited on the Sabbath of Chol Ha-moed Sukkot are the same as those recited on the first and last days of every major festival plus several insertions referring to the Sabbath.

The reason for this unusual arrangement is that in ancient times each day of the Sukkot holiday was treated as a festival day. The intermediary Sabbath of the holiday was treated not as an ordinary Sabbath but as a festival day.

In the case of Passover, only the first day of the holiday was considered a full festival day; the other days of the holiday being less important. For this reason, the Rabbis ruled that it was more important that *matza* be eaten on the first day of the holiday than on any other day (although *chametz* was not allowed throughout the holiday). In addition, the *Hallel* prayer, recited on all holidays, was *originally* recited only on the first day of Passover (at the Seder), not on the other days of Passover.[26]

It is therefore understandable why the haftara blessings recited on the Sabbath of Chol Ha-moed Passover should be the same as those recited on any ordinary Sabbath, while the final haftara blessing recited on the Sabbath of Chol Ha-moed Sukkot should be the same as that recited on regular festival days plus the special Sabbath insertions.

Why is the last haftara blessing omitted on fast days?

The fifth and concluding haftara blessing (beginning with the words *Al ha-Torah ve-al ha-avoda*), recited on Sabbaths and all festivals, is omitted on fast days because it makes reference to periods of joy and peace, and quite clearly such a description cannot apply to fast days, which commemorate the most devastating events in Jewish history.

Why are different chants used to read the Torah and haftara?

So that a congregant who arrives late for the synagogue service will recognize immediately whether the Torah or haftara portion is being read, a distinct chant was created for each.

This was particularly important in earlier centuries when books were scarce and the readings could not be followed from a printed text as they are today. The musical notations (cantillation) found in today's Torah and haftara texts are identical, but they are sung differently. Distinctive chants were also created for the selections read on the High Holidays and for each of the five *megillot*, which are read on various holidays. In all cases, the cantillation symbols employed are the same.

Why are selections from the Hagiographa not used as selections for haftara readings?

The Bible consists of three parts: the Torah (Pentateuch or Chumash), the *Neviim* (Prophets), and the *Ketuvim* (Hagiographa or Holy Writings). The Torah is of primary importance and sanctity; the *Neviim* rank second, and the *Ketuvim*, third. When the reading of the haftara was introduced in the second century B.C.E. to replace the Torah reading that had been banned by the Syrian-Greeks, the Rabbis found an ample supply of selections in the Prophets and therefore had no need to draw from the third biblical source.

Why do Ashkenazim and Sephardim read different prophetic portions on certain Sabbaths?

In the early centuries of the Common Era, the choice of haftarot for the Sabbath was not firmly fixed, and congregations made their own selections. We find in the Talmud,[27] for example, a discussion of whether on a given Sabbath the story of David and Bathsheba (II Samuel 11:1-17) or the story of Amnon (II Samuel 13:1ff.) should be read.

As late as the eighth century, the haftarot varied in content from locality to locality. Thereafter, Ashkenazim and Sephardim—each separately—standardized the portions to be read. Sephardim generally opted for shorter readings.

Why are there more haftara readings from the Book of Isaiah than from any other book of the Prophets?

Isaiah, the largest of the Books of the Prophets, consists of sixty-six chapters and hence contains a large pool of themes from which selections might be made.

Actually, there are two prophets named Isaiah. The ministry of the first Isaiah (740-701 B.C.E.) extended over almost forty years, longer than any other prophet. He lived through a crucial period in Jewish history during which the Kingdom of Israel was decimated (721 B.C.E.).

The Second Isaiah, whose prophecies are recorded in Chapters 40 to 66 of the Book of Isaiah, lived in Babylonia during the years of the Babylonian Exile in the sixth century B.C.E., some two hundred years after the First Isaiah.

Second Isaiah, who is generally referred to as Deutero (Greek for "second") Isaiah, preached a message of hope to his fellow Jews enslaved in Babylonia. His language is among the most imaginative and beautiful in biblical literature. The New Testament (Luke 4:16-21) records that when Jesus once visited a synagogue and was asked to read a haftara, he selected Isaiah 61 for his reading.

Why, in some congregations, is the haftara read from a handwritten scroll?

Some authorities are of the opinion that just as the Torah must be read from a handwritten scroll, so must the Prophets. While this was considered laudatory, it is not mandatory.[28] It is known that the famous Gaon of Vilna (1720-1797) followed this practice.

The custom of reading the haftara from a handwritten scroll never took root because, for one thing, most congregations could not afford the high cost of such scrolls. Secondly, it limited the number of people who could be honored with maftir, since chanting the haftara from the unvoweled script of a handwritten scroll required considerable expertise.

While today the overwhelming majority of congregations in Israel and the Diaspora read the haftara from a printed book, a number of Eastern Sephardic as well as ultra-Orthodox congregations still read the haftara from handwritten scrolls. Persians (Iranians) always read from a scroll that stands erect on the reading table. This scroll, called a *navi*, is carried in the Torah procession behind the Torah itself.

Why are verses sometimes repeated at the end of a haftara reading?

An old Jewish tradition frowns upon ending a Torah or haftara reading on a sad or discouraging note. Hence, there are occasions when the next-to-last verse in a prophetic reading is repeated after the last verse has been recited. Such, for example, is the case when reading the haftara for the Sabbath of the New Moon (Shabbat Rosh Chodesh). The reading is from Isaiah 66. The last verse (24) of the chapter is unpleasant, and to avoid ending on this note, the reader repeats verse 23 and thus concludes the reading on a hopeful note. The same is true of the last verse in the books of Malachi, Lamentations, and Ecclesiastes.

See page 225 regarding the acronym *yitakak* in this connection.

Why are isolated verses sometimes added to conclude a haftara reading?

As explained above, every effort was made to avoid ending a Torah or haftara reading on an unpleasant note, and in a number of cases the next-to-last verse of a haftara is repeated so as to conclude the reading on a hopeful note.

In some instances it was found necessary to append to the haftara reading an extra verse or two from a following chapter. One such case is the haftara for the sidra Masay (Numbers 33:1-36:13).[29] Here, in addition to the reading from Jeremiah 2:4-28, one verse is added from Jeremiah 3 (verse 4) and two verses (1-2) are added from Jeremiah 4, bringing the reading to a hopeful conclusion.

Why do some congregations prohibit a blind boy from reciting the haftara?

While practically all congregations permit a Bar Mitzva boy who is blind to celebrate his Bar Mitzva exactly as a sighted boy does,[30] there are still a few among the ultra-Orthodox who do not permit the boy to recite the haftara.

These congregations insist that the haftara must be read from a handwritten scroll with unvoweled letters, written exactly in the style of a Torah scroll. And since, the reasoning goes, the one who reads from a Torah scroll must *see* every word that he recites, the same rule applies when the prophetic portion is read from a scroll.[31]

Those who agree with this view will not permit a Bar Mitzva boy to recite the haftara but will permit him to be called to the Torah for the maftir aliya. When called up as maftir, the young man is only required to recite the blessings, not read from the Torah. Since the Torah blessings may be recited from memory, no objection can be made to calling up the youngster to the Torah.

Most authorities permit the haftara to be read from a printed book and therefore do allow a blind boy to conduct his Bar Mitzva exactly as a sighted boy does. The prophetic portion may be transcribed into Braille and be "read" just as one reads from a printed book.[32]

Chapter 8

The Masoretic Text

INTRODUCTION

The standard version of the Hebrew Bible used today is known as the Masoretic Text. Scholars refer to it as *textus receptus,* meaning "received text," the text received by one generation from an earlier one. Today's text is the result of a process that began some 2,400 years ago with Ezra, the first scribe.

The work of the early scribe *(sofer),* as discussed in Chapter Four, Writing the Torah, was not confined to writing copies of the Torah but included counting letters and words of the finished scrolls to ascertain whether anything had been omitted from or added to the text. (The actual meaning of the word *sofer* is "counter, one who counts.")

Over the centuries thousands of Torah manuscripts were written by countless scribes, and many variations appeared in the texts. In the post-talmudic period (after 500 C.E.) the importance of establishing a single, normative text of the Torah and of the Bible as a whole became obvious. The scribes who set out to achieve this were called Masoretes, a form of the word *masora,* meaning "tradition" or "that which has been transmitted." Their purpose was to determine and preserve the authentic text of the Bible.

Ascertaining which of the numerous biblical texts in existence was the true original turned out to be a monumental task. Over a period of several centuries, particularly from the eighth through the tenth centuries, Masoretes were actively engaged in sorting through manuscripts and in establishing authenticity. In the great Babylonian cities of Sura and Pumpedita, Masoretic schools were established within the academies of higher learning. There, scholars devoted themselves almost exclusively to purging the biblical text of errors that had crept in as a result of the work of inefficient copyists.

At the same time, in Tiberias, Palestine, two great Masoretic schools appeared on the scene. One was made up primarily of the Ben Asher family and the other of the Ben Naftali family. By the ninth century, the Ben Asher school emerged as the dominant force, and its text became the accepted one.

Besides establishing the content and form of the handwritten scrolls to be used for public readings in the synagogue, the Babylonian and Palestinian Masoretes devoted their attention to the preparation of Bible manuscripts to be used by students. These editions, usually handwritten on both sides of single sheets of parchment, were known as codices (singular, codex). The margins of the codices often contained notations on the spelling, writing, pronunciation, and cantillation of given words. These Masoretic notes are found in most printed Hebrew Bibles in use today.

The oldest text containing the Masoretic alterations is the St. Petersburg Codex of 916 C.E. What is sometimes considered the official Masoretic Text was firmly established by the middle of the sixteenth century when a Hebrew Bible that had been edited by Jacob ben Chayim was published in Venice by Daniel Bomberg, a Christian printer. This Bible, which appeared in 1525, became the model for all future editions. Most contemporary biblical scholars are of the opinion that there is no one version of the Bible that can accurately be labeled *the* Masoretic Text.

———————□———————

Why is it said that all copies of the Torah have derived from one master copy?

According to tradition, not only were the Ten Commandments given to Moses on Mount Sinai, but the entire contents of the Torah were dictated by God to him at that time. This Torah, the Rabbis taught,[1] was transmitted to Joshua, who transmitted it to the elders, who transmitted it to the prophets, who transmitted it to the members of the Great Assembly. Thus, the Torah that was read and studied in later generations was believed to be one and the same as the original Torah of Moses.

This has been the traditional view despite the fact that the whereabouts of the Torah of Moses were unknown for many centuries. From the time of the Revelation at Sinai, dated around 1250 B.C.E., until the reign of King Josiah in the early part of the seventh century B.C.E.—a span of 600 years—no mention is made of such a Torah scroll.

Not until Chapter 22 of the Second Book of Kings do we hear of the existence of a Torah scroll. At this point the High Priest Hilkiah tells the scribe Shafan that he has discovered a scroll of the Torah in the Temple. Shafan tells King Josiah about the discovery, and the king is ecstatic. The king then summons all the people to appear at the Temple in Jerusalem, and he reads to them the entire text of the scroll that had been found in the Temple (II Kings 23:1-2). (Scholars believe that the scroll was the Book of Deuteronomy.)

The next reference made to a public reading from a Torah scroll is to one held some two hundred years later, when Ezra, in the middle of the fifth century B.C.E., reads the Torah to the people (Nehemiah 8).

Was the Torah used by Ezra the actual Torah dictated by God to Moses? The Talmud[2] refers to many copies of the Torah that apparently were in existence at that time. However, one Torah scroll—the scroll from which the High Priest read to the public on Yom Kippur—was considered to be the authentic Moses scroll.

This scroll, known as the Azara Scroll (*Sefer Ha-azara*)

and also as the Ezra Scroll *(Sefer Ezra)*,[3] was the official Temple scroll. It was never removed from the Temple precincts and was considered to always be in a state of purity. It is the text of this Torah scroll that tradition says was handed down from Ezra the Scribe to future generations and that eventually became the master from which all scrolls and codices were copies. This master scroll, although referred to, apparently was never found, and thus the trueness of current texts to the Torah of Moses is taken by traditionalists as an act of faith.

Other Torah scrolls kept in the Temple at that time were probably used for study purposes.[4] But these were not guarded as was the *Sefer Ha-azara*. They were kept in the storage area of the Temple together with gifts of food known as heave-offerings *(terumot)* that were brought for the Priests by pilgrims to Jerusalem. Since the Priests devoted their time exclusively to Temple work, this was their only means of sustenance (Leviticus 22:10-16 and Numbers 18:8ff.).[5]

Why was the master scroll theory abandoned in the post-Ezra period?

While at one point in Jewish history the Torah scroll used by the High Priest in Temple times was considered the official Torah scroll, and at a later period the scroll employed by Ezra was so considered, the Rabbis of the Talmud became aware of many discrepancies in the existing Torah manuscripts. They were thus unable to declare any one copy as authentic.

Resh Lakish, the prominent third-century C.E. Palestinian Talmud scholar, noted that "three scrolls [or codices] of the Torah were found in the Temple Court [*Azara*] which contained variant and even conflicting readings."[6] (Actually, there were more than just three scrolls in the Temple precincts. See the previous answer.)

Over the centuries numerous Torah manuscripts with countless variations were written. In the post-talmudic period (after the sixth century) it became clear that a standard text ought to be established, and it was then that the work of the Masoretes (derived from *masora,* meaning "tradition" or "that which has been transmitted") began in earnest. When scrolls did not agree, the Masoretes adopted the text of the majority. However, the text of the minority was not ignored. Differences were recorded as variant readings in the margins of the normative text, and in this way the historical record was preserved.[7]

Why did the Ben Asher family emerge as the dominant Masoretes?

Although many scholars in Babylonia and Palestine, particularly from the eighth through the tenth centuries, devoted themselves to establishing an authoritative text of the Bible, the two most prominent schools of Masoretes were the Ben Asher school and the Ben Naftali school. Both carried on their work in Tiberias, Palestine.

Moses ben Asher and his son were the two most illustrious members of the Ben Asher family. Moses the Elder prepared a codex of the second and third parts of the Bible, the Prophets and Holy Writings. His manuscript, which today is in the possession of the Karaite community in Cairo, is dated 895 C.E. (actually, the date given is "the year 827 after the destruction of Jerusalem," which is about 895). A copy of this codex was purchased in 1530 by Rabbi Moses Isserles. As of World War II it was located in his synagogue in Cracow, Poland.

The younger Ben Asher also edited the Hebrew Bible, furnishing it with vowel-points, accents, and Masoretic notes. However, his codex contained the entire Bible, Torah included, and was therefore of greater importance. This codex became the possession of the Jewish community in Aleppo, Syria, and is therefore known as the Aleppo Codex, although it was originally housed in Jerusalem and later in Cairo before being deposited in Aleppo.

The pre-eminent member of the Ben Naftali school of Masoretes was the tenth-century scholar Moses ben David ben Naftali. His work and the other edited versions of the

Bible produced by the Ben Naftali school have for the most part disappeared. Only fragments have been discovered, and these reveal differences in the system of punctuation and accentuation advocated by the Ben Ashers.[8]

The Bible editions of the Ben Ashers were adopted by the Jewish community at large. The fact that Moses Maimonides, in the twelfth century, made his own copy of the Torah from a Ben Asher model was more than enough to establish the prestige of the Ben Asher Masoretic Text for all time.

Why was a Torah codex named after a Roman emperor?

When Jerusalem was conquered by the Romans in the year 70 C.E., a copy of the Pentateuch was removed from the Temple by Vespasian, commander of the Roman forces. He took this codex with him to Rome later that year and deposited it in the royal palace.

In the year 220, Severus, emperor of Rome, built a synagogue for the Jews of the city, and he transferred the codex from the royal palace to the new Severus Synagogue. From that time on the codex carried his name as well.

Both the synagogue and the codex bearing the name of Severus have long disappeared, but not before a list had been made of thirty-two ways in which the text of the Severus Codex differs from other codices. A copy of the list is to be found in the Paris National Library.[9]

Why is the system of "pointing" the Hebrew text of the Bible known as the Tiberian System?

Before the fifth century C.E., vowel-points (*kamatz, patach,* and so on) were not found under or above the Hebrew letters in texts of the Bible used either for synagogue or for study use. The absence of vowel-points made it difficult to pronounce words correctly. Proper pronunciation of words was passed on orally from teacher to student, from one generation to the next.

Masoretes known as *nakdanim* set out to correct this deficiency by creating a system of vowel-pointing *(nikud)*. Over a period of several centuries, different systems were developed by the Masoretes of the East (Babylonia) and the Masoretes of the West (Palestine), and by the tenth century one system was universally accepted. This method, developed by the Masoretes in Tiberias, Palestine, became known as the Tiberian System.[10]

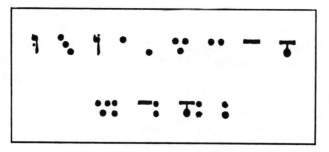

Hebrew vowel-points.

Why is God's name not pronounced as it is spelled?

The principal name of God in the Hebrew Bible is *Yehova,* spelled *yod hay vav hay.* This is often referred to as the Tetragrammaton, which in Greek means "four-lettered word."

In Jewish tradition the name of God, when written *yod hay vav hay,* is sacred and is not to be abused or used indiscriminately. Its sanctity was first emphasized in Exodus 3:13-14, where Moses is advised by God that His name is *E'he'yeh Asher E'he'yeh,* meaning "I am that I am." *E'he'yeh* is a form of *Yehova.* And in Exodus 6:2 Moses again is told that God's name is *Yehova,* an appellation so sacred that it was not revealed even to the patriarchs. Finally, the sanctity of *Yehova* as the Divine Name is reaffirmed in the third of the Ten Commandments, which cautions that we should "not utter God's name [*Yehova*] in vain" (Exodus 20:7).

To safeguard against the violation of this principle, the Tetragrammaton is never pronounced *Yehova*, as it is written. Rather, it is pronounced *Adonai*, which has the secondary meaning of "lord" or "master."

The taboo against pronouncing the actual Divine Name was emphasized by the Rabbis, who in talmudic times stressed that "among those who will have no share in the world-to-come are those who pronounce the Tetragrammaton as it is written [as *Yehova* rather than as *Adonai*]."[11] They felt so strongly about this ban that they attributed it to God himself. They said: "The Holy One, Blessed be He, said, 'I am not to be read [pronounced] as I am written. I am written with a *yod hay* [the first two letters of Yehova], but I am to be pronounced as if these two letters were *alef dalet* [the first two letters of Adonai].' "[12]

In time pronouncing the name *Adonai* was banned for casual use. *Ha-Shem* (the Name) or *Adoshem* (a contraction of *Adonai* and *Ha-Shem*) came to be used in secular contexts.

Why is a Torah scroll invalid for public reading if it contains Masoretic notations?

From the very beginning, Torah scrolls were written without vowel-points, cantillation or punctuation marks, or other grammatical notations. Reading from a scroll without such notations became a sacred tradition that has been preserved to the present time. This is based on the admonitions in Deuteronomy 31:9 and 31:19 that the Torah must be transmitted from generation to generation in the form that it was received by Moses from God.[13]

The extensive biblical notes prepared by Masoretes were intended to help the scholar and layman read the text correctly and better comprehend its meaning. Manuscripts with these Masoretic notations were designed for study purposes only and were not permitted to be used at public Torah reading services.

Why were cantillation symbols introduced by the Masoretes?

The Masoretes became aware that the vowel-points that had been added to student copies of the Torah did not always adequately serve the needs of the student or Torah reader. Although one might be able to pronounce a single word, one might still not know how to accent a word or, for that matter, know where a sentence begins or ends. To help solve this problem, cantillation marks were introduced.

Cantillation symbols, first introduced in talmudic times,[14] were finally perfected by the Palestinian Masoretes of the ninth century. They not only guided students in pronouncing words and punctuating sentences correctly, but also indicated to the Torah reader the musical patterns to be used when chanting words and phrases. These cantillation markings are widely referred to by the Yiddish term trop(e).

Why does one find Hebrew words in small type around the perimeter of the text in many editions of the Bible?

In addition to introducing vowel-points and cantillation symbols, the Masoretes inserted notations around the body of the Torah study text to explain the manner in which specific words are to be spelled, pronounced, and accented. The Masoretes would not take the liberty of changing the sacred text, which they believed to have been dictated to Moses by God, and instead used marginal notes to make their observations known.[15]

In 1524, when the first Torah text was prepared for the printer in Venice, Italy, by Jacob ben Chayim, it was the Ben Asher text that served as the model. Notes appeared in the four margins of the text: top, bottom, and both sides.

Notes on the top and bottom margins of the page are called *Masora Magna,* meaning "Large Masora," while notes in the side margins (sometimes also written in the space between columns) are referred to as *Masora Parva,* meaning "Small Masora." Printed Bibles in current use generally carry notes only in the bottom margin, under the text.[16]

Why are some words in the Torah not read as they are written?

In addition to the notes referring to pronunciation and accentuation discussed in the previous answer, the Masoretes inserted marginal notations dealing with misspelled words in the text that obviously convey the wrong meaning. For example, in Exodus 21:8 and Leviticus 11:21 the word *lo* is spelled *lamed alef,* giving it the meaning "no, not," instead of *lamed vav,* which would mean "to him, to it." The latter is the obvious intent of the texts.

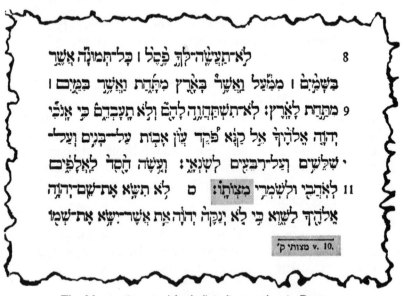

The Masoretic note (shaded) indicates that in Deuteronomy 5:10 the word spelled as *mitzvotav* (the *ketiv*) is to be read aloud by the Torah reader as *mitzvotai* (the *keri*).

To call such errors to the reader's attention, the Masoretes introduced the notation system of *ketiv* ("writing") and *keri* ("reading") whereby the incorrect text remained intact but a marginal note was inserted to indicate the correct form of the word.[17]

מוֹשִׁיעַ לָהּ: ס כח כִּי־יִמְצָא אִישׁ
נַעַר נערה קרי בְתוּלָה אֲשֶׁר לֹא־
אֹרָשָׂה וּתְפָשָׂהּ וְשָׁכַב עִמָּהּ
וְנִמְצָאוּ: כט וְנָתַן הָאִישׁ הַשֹּׁכֵב
עִמָּהּ לַאֲבִי הַנַּעַר הנערה קרי חֲמִשִּׁים

The Masoretic notes (shaded) indicate that the written words *naar* and *ha-naar* (the *ketiv*) are to be read aloud respectively as *naara* and *ha-naara* (the *keri*). Note that unlike the excerpt on the facing page, in which the Masoretic notes appear under the text, this illustration is taken from an edition of the Pentateuch in which Masoretic notes appear in small type in the body of the text.

Another example of the *ketiv* and *keri* notation involves the Hebrew word for girl, which is normally spelled *nun a'yin resh hay* and is pronounced *naara*. In Chapter 22 of the Book of Deuteronomy, this word appears thirteen times without the *hay* at the end and is spelled *nun a'yin resh*, which would normally be pronounced *naar*, meaning "boy." The text, however, refers to a girl. The Masoretes did not change the text and instead in a marginal note remind the student and reader that the *keri* (reading) of this word, regardless of its spelling, is *naara*.

The *Code of Jewish Law*[18] declares that a *baal koray* must follow the *keri*, not the *ketiv*, when reading the Torah. He is obligated to study the Masoretic notes contained in codices or printed texts of the Torah and to be aware of them when he reads from the Torah scroll itself, which does not contain notations. The *keri* and *ketiv*, say the Rabbis, originated on Mount Sinai and are not subject to alteration.

Why did the Masoretes require that certain words be substituted for others when the Torah is read in the synagogue?

To avoid reading aloud what were considered indelicate, uncouth, or derogatory words or expressions that occasionally appear in the Torah, the Masoretes substituted for them euphemistic expressions. This concept dates back to an admonition of the Rabbis that declares, "Wherever an indelicate expression is written in the text, we must substitute for it a more polite and delicate reading."[19]

An example of a word in the Torah text that must be pronounced in a totally different manner from the way it is written is located in the Book of Deuteronomy 28:27. There, in the written text (the *ketiv*) appears the word *afolim,* which means "hemorrhoids." The scribes considered this Hebrew word too coarse to be pronounced in the

In verses 27 and 30 of Deuteronomy 28, the Masoretes substituted delicate expressions for indelicate (shaded) ones in the text.

synagogue, and so in a marginal note they inform us that the word *techorim* is to be substituted for it when the Torah is read in public. Both words have the same meaning, but apparently to the ancients the word *afolim* had a bad connotation with which we are no longer familiar.[20]

Another example of a word that was changed to a euphemistic form is found in Deuteronomy 28:30. Here, among the long list of curses that will befall one who does not observe the commandments, appears the word *yishgalena*, meaning "violate her, have intercourse with her." The verse reads, "You will betroth a woman, but another man will have intercourse with her." As indicated in the marginal note, when the Torah is read, the *baal koray* substitutes for *yishgalena* the word *yishkavena*, meaning "he will lie with her." The Masoretes considered this a more delicate way of referring to sexual intercourse, so they established *yishgalena* as the written form and the euphemistic *yishkavena* as the spoken form.[21]

Why did the Masoretes sometimes include incomplete sentences in the Torah?

As pointed out in the previous answer, the Rabbis went to great lengths to avoid the use of unsavory words and expressions in the Torah. They were also anxious to avoid reporting fully, whenever possible, unseemly episodes that occasionally appear in the Torah and other parts of the Bible.[22]

One such case, found in Genesis 35:22, is called to our attention via the Masoretic note *piska b'emtza pasuk*, meaning "there is a pause [or gap] in the middle of the verse." This verse starts out with a description of how Reuben, Jacob's eldest son, has sexual intercourse with Bilhah, the concubine of Jacob. But the story ends abruptly with the words "and Israel [Jacob] heard." The verse never tells us what Jacob did after hearing about the incident, thus sparing the listener the sordid details.

The Masoretes wanted it to be known that the conclusion of the story is missing from the text, and they therefore required scribes to leave empty space when writing a Torah scroll.[23]

Why did the Masoretes make three drastic changes in the Torah text?

The Masoretes, while assuming the obligation of transmitting to future generations an exact copy of the Torah as dictated to Moses by God, nevertheless found it necessary in three instances to make modifications in the actual Torah text.[24] These alterations, referred to as *tikunay soferim*, "corrections of the scribes," were made by the Masoretes to eliminate what they considered language that was offensive or indiscreet. Two cases (Genesis 18:22 and Numbers 11:15) involve references to God, and one case (Numbers 12:12) involves a statement thought to be derogatory to the mother of Moses, Aaron, and Miriam. These modifications in the text are indicated by the Masoretes in some of the marginal notes that appear in some present-day editions of the Torah. These notes carry the designation *tikunay soferim*.

The first instance of a scribal correction is found in Genesis 18:1, which says, "The Lord appeared to him [Abraham] by the terebinths of Mamre; he [Abraham] was sitting at the entrance of the tent." A series of events is described in the next twenty verses. Genesis 18:22 then continues: "Abraham remained standing before the Lord."

Early students of the Bible questioned how the Torah could say that Abraham *remained* standing before the Lord when the first verse clearly states that it was God who had been standing before Abraham, not the reverse. This inconsistency was noted in the Midrash[25] where Rabbi Simon remarks, "This [verse 22] contains a correction made by the *soferim*, for it is clear from the text [verse 1] itself that it was God who was actually standing before Abraham." Some of the earliest Torah manuscripts corroborate this view, stating very clearly that the original reading of the text was that God stood before Abraham, and because it smacked of irreverence to have the Superior Being standing while Abraham sat, the scribes changed the written text to its present form.[26]

Similarly, Numbers 11:15 was altered by the scribes to avoid disrespect toward God. Moses pleads with God that he cannot bear the heavy burden of leadership alone. Verse 15 in our text has Moses addressing God, saying, "Kill me rather, I beg You, and let me no longer experience my wretchedness." Early manuscripts present the original text as reading "*Your* wretchedness" and not "*my* wretchedness." To ascribe to God "wretchedness" (or "evil," as given in some translations) was considered derogatory, and so the text was altered to its present form.[27]

The third of the *tikunay soferim* in the Torah appears in Numbers 12:12. Here, Miriam had been afflicted with leprosy, and Aaron pleads with Moses, "Let her not be as one dead, who emerges from his mother's womb with half his flesh eaten away." According to the Rabbis, this verse originally read "*our* mother's womb," but out of respect for Jochebed, the mother of Miriam, Moses, and Aaron, the scribes altered the text and made it impersonal.[28]

Why does the acronym *yitakak* appear as a Masoretic note in some editions of the Bible?

In some editions of the Hebrew Bible the acronym *yitakak (yod tav kuf kuf)* is to be found. It appears at the end of the last chapter of the following books: Yesha'yahu (Isaiah),[29] Malachi,[30] Aycha (Lamentations),[31] and Kohelet (Ecclesiastes).[32]

The first of the acronym's four letters, the *yod,* stands for Yesha'ya(hu); the second letter, the *tav,* stands for Tray Asar (Twelve Prophets) of which Malachi is the last book; the third letter, the *kuf,* stands for the word *kinot,* which is another way of referring to Aycha; and the fourth letter, the second *kuf,* stands for Kohelet.

The acronym *yitakak* appears to remind the reader that he must conclude the portion by repeating the next-to-last verse of the chapter. The last verse in each case expresses an unhappy sentiment, and the Masoretes wanted to avoid ending readings on a sour or despairing note.

Why does the Masoretic note *sevirin* appear?

Sevirin (also spelled *sebirin*), a Hebrew word derived from the Aramaic root *savar,* meaning "to suppose," appears as a Masoretic notation to call attention to a word that is to be read as written but is to be understood in a different light. Otherwise the text would not be comprehensible. In essence, *sevirin* are a variation on the *keri,* discussed above. That which one school of Masoretes notes as *sevirin* another school sometimes notes as *keri.*

In the Torah itself the *sevirin* notation appears twenty times.[33] One such notation refers to Genesis 19:8 and 19:25, where the last letter *(hay)* of the word *ha-eleh* is omitted. The text reads *ha-el,* and the *sevirin* note reminds one to read the word as written but to think of it *as if* it did end with the letter *hay.* Similarly, a *hay* was omitted from the word *ha-hu* in Genesis 19:33. The text reads *hu* but must be understood *as if* the word was written *ha-hu.*

Verse 31 of Exodus 26 contains an example of *sevirin.* The text uses the word *yaaseh* (shaded), meaning "he shall make." The Masoretic notation in small type (shaded) indicates that when the word *yaaseh* is pronounced, it should be understood to mean *taaseh,* "it shall be made."

Two *sevirin* notations refer to grammatical errors in Exodus 11:6. The word *kamohu,* which appears twice in the verse, should have been written as *kamoha,* the feminine form required by the context of the verse.

A significant error exists in Genesis 49:13. The *sevirin* says that the word *al* should be thought of as *ad. Al* means "on" and *ad* means "until" or "to." The text speaks of a border, and there is a large difference between a border extending *to* a place as opposed to *on* (meaning onto) a place. This particular instance of a *sevirin* appears in early Bible manuscripts but for some reason has been omitted from current Hebrew editions of the Bible.

A striking example of *sevirin* is to be found in Deuteronomy 17:19, where the word *bo,* meaning "it," is used in the Hebrew text, although the correct word is *ba. Bo* is a masculine form; *ba* is a feminine form. The Masoretes remind the Torah reader to pronounce *bo* as *ba,* because the subject to which it is referring is Torah, a feminine noun.

Why did the Masoretes use the words *malay* and *chaser* in their marginal notes?

Many words in the Bible are spelled either with a superfluous letter or a missing letter. When a superfluous letter is present, the word is said to be plene (*malay,* literally "full"). When a letter is missing, the word is said to be defective (*chaser,* literally "missing, absent").[34]

The Masoretes called attention to a plene or defective word by indicating in a marginal note that the word marked in the study text (not in the Torah scroll itself) with an asterisk or a bold dot is *malay* or *chaser.*[35] They thus served notice on scribes that these words are not spelled in a conventional fashion.

An example of a *malay* word is found in Genesis 31:35. Normally the word *lo,* meaning "no" or "not," is spelled *lamed alef,* without a *vav.* Here it is spelled *lamed vav alef.* Another example of a *malay* form is found in Isaiah 54:3 (the haftara for No'ach) where the word *semol,* meaning "left," is spelled *sin mem alef vav lamed.* Normally the word is spelled without a *vav.*

Examples of *chaser* words are *may-chato* in Genesis 20:6, which is spelled *mem chet tet vav*, with the *alef* missing; *ha-yotzet* in Deuteronomy 28:57, spelled *hay yod vav tzadi tav*, with the *alef* missing; *tomim* in Genesis 25:24, spelled *tav vav mem mem*, with the *alef* or *yod* missing.

The word *ve-nitmaytem* (shaded word on fourth line) is defective (*chaser*). The correct spelling is with an *alef* after the *mem*. The Masoretic note in small type calls this to our attention. It also indicates that the *vav* in the word *gachon* (verse 42) is to be written in large script because it is considered to be the middle letter of the Torah.

Only four letters in the Hebrew alphabet apply to *malay* and *chaser* words: *alef, hay, vav,* and *yod.* The *vav* and the *yod* are most frequently involved.

Why are some words in the Torah sometimes spelled *malay* and at other times spelled *chaser*?

The traditional belief is that the Torah was dictated by God to Moses, including those words that are sometimes *malay* and sometimes *chaser*. The noted Spanish Bible commentators and linguists Jehuda ben David Chayug (Hayyuj) (c. 945–c. 1000) and Abraham ibn Ezra (1089–1164) were the first to note that plene and defective spellings were the creation of individual copyists. It was their view that sometimes a scribe would write a word plene if he thought it would help in the understanding of the text, while another scribe might write the same word defective in order to conserve space.[36]

Why are scribal errors relating to plene and defective words not considered serious?

Rabbi Moses Isserles, in his Notes on the *Shulchan Aruch*,[37] ruled that should a scroll be discovered in which a *malay* word is written *chaser* or a *chaser* word is written *malay*, this is not sufficient cause to halt a Torah reading. Only after the entire Torah reading is concluded is it mandatory to remove the scroll from service for correction.

Malay/chaser errors are not considered as serious as other types of scribal errors because scholars cannot say with certainty that a particular spelling is absolutely correct while another is absolutely wrong. Early manuscripts contained a variety of readings.[38]

Why has the exact number of letters in the Torah been difficult to ascertain?

In order to establish an exact count of the number of letters in the Torah, scholars would have had to agree on the correct spelling of all words. This was not possible because early manuscripts followed different traditions. Particular words were often spelled defective in one place and plene in another.[39] It is estimated that there are more than 1,300 plene and defective words in the Bible.[40]

In addition, some manuscripts included words that others omitted. An example of this is found in Genesis 29:28 where the word *lo*, meaning "to him," is used twice, the second usage obviously superfluous. The Masoretic note on this word indicates that in some manuscripts this second *lo* is deleted.

The letter count of the Torah, accepted today as normative, is 304,805.[41]

Why does the word *chol* appear in the margin of some Pentateuchs?

There are words in the Bible that are used as names for God but that also have secular meanings. For example, *Adonai* is the Divine Name, but in Genesis 19:2 *adonai* appears as a secular word meaning "lord." Other instances of the Divine Name being used in a secular context are the words *elohay, elohim,* and *el,* which are found in Genesis 31:53, Deuteronomy 32:17, and Deuteronomy 32:21.

Throughout the Torah, wherever any of God's names is used in a secular sense, the Masoretes advise the reader of this by placing the word *chol* ("secular, ordinary") in the margin of the text, thus indicating that the word is not deserving of special reverence.

Why does the term *kuf devuka* appear as a Masoretic note?

The Rabbis of the Talmud declared that a Torah scroll in which two individual letters touch each other is invalid for public readings.[42] This ban was extended to cover strokes within a letter. Yet, despite this ban, there are two instances where the vertical stroke of the letter *kuf* must touch the horizontal bar of the letter.

The first such instance is in Exodus 32:25, and the word involved is *be-kamayhem,* meaning "to those who oppose them." The second instance is in Numbers 7:2, and the word involved is *ha-pekudim,* meaning "those who were numbered." In each case, in the Masoretic Text an asterisk appears over the letter *kuf,* and the marginal note says *kuf devuka,* meaning "the strokes of [the letter] are joined [rather than having a space between them]."

This method of fashioning the letter *kuf* undoubtedly appeared in the very earliest manuscripts. The reason for its introduction is unknown, but that it was retained by the Masoretes is an indication of their reluctance to make changes in the written text as it was received by them.

Why do some letters in the Hebrew Bible have dots over them?

Fifteen words or phrases in the Bible are marked with one or more dots. Ten of these are in the Torah; the other five are in the Prophets and the Holy Writings.[43]

A marking may consist of one dot over a single letter (as in Numbers 9:10, where the *hay* in *rechoka* is dotted) or of as many as eleven dots extending over three words (as in Deuteronomy 29:28, where the words *lanu u-le-vanenu ad* have three dots over the first word, seven over the second word, and one over the first letter of the last word).

These diacritical markings appear not only in Torah manuscripts used for study but also in handwritten scrolls designed for public readings in the synagogue. It is not known with certainty when the markings were first introduced, but they do appear in the very oldest Bible manuscripts, and the tractate Avot d'Rabbi Natan, Chapter 34, attributes their origin to Ezra the Scribe of the fifth century B.C.E.

The dots are thought to have been placed over words or phrases that carry an ethical or moral lesson or over incorrect or doubtful words or phrases that crept into the Hebrew text. It is known that the scribes of Alexandria in the third century B.C.E., who had come under the influence of the Greeks, had used dots for such a purpose. By dotting words or phrases but not altering them, the ancient text was preserved, but notice was given that a commentary was called for.

An example of dots noting that a moral teaching can be found hidden in the text are the six dots over the word *vayishakayhu* ["and he kissed him"] in Genesis 33:4. Esau's kissing of Jacob was considered to be insincere. The Rabbis said that he approached Jacob with hate in his heart and that he intended to bite Jacob rather than kiss him. However, at the last moment Esau felt remorse and his hatred turned to love. The intended bite became a kiss. The diacritical markings remind us that a change may occur even in the most hardened person.[44]

An example of dots indicating that the Rabbis found a problem with a word or phrase are those that appear over the word *ve-Aharon* in Numbers 3:39. This verse says that Moses *and* Aaron (*ve-Aharon* means "and Aaron") were commanded by God to take a census of the tribe of Levi, whereas verse 14 says that *only* Moses was so commanded.

The Rabbis apparently noticed this discrepancy and saw fit to call it to our attention by placing dots over each letter of the word *ve-Aharon*. This indicates, say the Rabbis, that although Aaron did not participate in conducting the census, he was nevertheless a special person. He was the first High Priest and as such is to be remembered and respected by the entire community.[45]

The Rabbis considered it extremely important that the ancient tradition of placing dots over certain letters be maintained, and they ruled that a scroll is invalid for synagogue use if these diacritical markings do not appear over the designated letters.

Why are some letters in the Torah written larger than others?

The precise reason why certain letters in the Torah (and in the rest of the Bible) are written larger than others is unknown. Most explanations are homiletical.

According to the Masoretic count, there are thirty-two large letters in the Bible, of which sixteen are in the Torah. These include:[46]

- The *bet* of the word *be-reshit* in Genesis 1:1.
- The final *mem* of *shileshim* in Genesis 50:23.
- The *za'yin* of *ha-chezona* in Genesis 34:31.
- The *tzadi* of *tzay* in Exodus 11:8.
- The *nun* of *notzer* in Exodus 34:7.
- The *resh* of *acher* in Exodus 34:14.
- The *vav* of *gachon* in Leviticus 11:42.
- The *gimmel* of *ve-hitgalach* in Leviticus 13:33.
- The *samech* of *va-yahas* in Numbers 13:30.
- The *yod* of *yigdal* in Numbers 14:17.
- The final *nun* of *mishpatan* in Numbers 27:5.
- The *a'yin* of *shema* and the *dalet* of *echad* in the *Shema* prayer in Deuteronomy 6:4.
- The *tav* of *tamim* in Deuteronomy 18:13.
- The *lamed* of *va-yashlichem* in Deuteronomy 29:27.
- The *hay* of *ha-l'Adonai* in Deuteronomy 32:6.[47]

The *bet* of bereshit is written in large script.

The *gimmel* of *ve-hitgalach* is written in large script.

The *yod* of *yigdal* is written in large script.

The *vav* of *gachon* is written in large script.

In some instances the introduction of a large letter was nothing more than the innovation of an individual scribe, and some of these innovations have been accepted by tradition. It should be noted, however, that Masoretes were never in complete agreement on which letters in the Torah should be written large.[48] In fact, not all of the letters listed above appear in all modern printed editions of the Pentateuch.

See the two questions that follow for specific information on some of the large letters referred to above.

Why is the *vav* in the word *gachon* written in large script?

To indicate the midpoint of all the letters in the Pentateuch, the Rabbis ruled that in a properly written Torah scroll the scribe must render in large script the *vav* of the Hebrew word *gachon* ("belly") in Leviticus 11:42.[49] It was believed that the number of letters from the beginning of the Pentateuch to the *vav* in *gachon* equals the number of letters from the *vav* to the end.

Indicating the middle letter of the Torah makes it possible for anyone to verify the accuracy of a scroll by counting its letters from the beginning to the midpoint and from the midpoint to the end.

Why, in the *Shema* prayer, is the *a'yin* of the word *Shema* and the *dalet* of the word *echad* written in large script?

According to tradition the last letter of the first word of the *Shema* prayer (Deuteronomy 6:4), the *a'yin*, and the last letter of the last word of the *Shema*, the *dalet* in the word *echad*, are written in large script.[50] The two letters when combined spell *ayd*, meaning "witness." The *Shema*

expresses the purpose of Israel's existence: to serve as a witness to God's primacy as the one and only Master of the universe.

The Talmud reports that as Rabbi Akiba was led away by Romans to be executed publicly for continuing to teach the Torah even after such activity was banned, his flesh was flayed with combs of iron. Watching him endure this pain with fortitude, Akiba's students shouted, "Enough! You have suffered enough!"

Rabbi Akiba replied, "All my life I have regretted that I have not been able to show my love for God in the manner prescribed by the Torah, which commands that one should love the Lord with all his soul. Now that I have the opportunity, shall I not do so?"

He then recited the *Shema,* dwelling on and prolonging the word *echad* ("one") until he expired.[51]

When reciting the *Shema* prayer, some Jews cover their eyes so that they can concentrate on the words without distraction, and as they do, they prolong the *echad* as did Rabbi Akiba.

Why are some letters in the Torah written in small script?

There are twenty-eight small letters in the entire Bible, nine of them in the Torah itself.[52] These are:

- The *hay* of the word *be-hibaram* in Genesis 2:4.
- The *kaf* of *ve-livkota* in Genesis 23:2.
- The *kuf* of *katzti* in Genesis 27:46.
- The *kuf* of *be-kamayhem* in Exodus 32:25.
- The *alef* of *va-yikra* in Leviticus 1:1.
- The *mem* of *mokda* in Leviticus 6:2.
- The *yod* of *Pinchas* in Numbers 25:11.
- The *mem* of *mamrim* in Deuteronomy 9:24.
- The *yod* of *teshi* in Deuteronomy 32:18.

Why these, rather than other letters, were written by scribes in small script is difficult to ascertain. Homiletical explanations have been offered in some cases. See the two

The *mem* of *mokda* is written in small script.

The *yod* of *Pinchas* is written in small script.

The *alef* of *va-yikra* is written in small script.

questions that follow for specific information on some of the small letters referred to above.

Why is the *hay* of *be-hibaram* written in small script?

The Baal Ha-turim commentary explains that the letter *hay* of *be-hibaram* (Genesis 2:4), meaning "when they [heaven and earth] were created," is written in small script to serve as a reminder that heaven and earth were created because of the merit of Father Abraham, whose name consists of the same letters as the word [*be*]*hibaram*.[53] The letter *hay* was added to Abraham's name when it was changed from Avram to Avraham.

Why is the *alef* of *va-yikra* written in small script?

The letter *alef* appears in the Torah 27,057 times, but in only one instance, in Leviticus 1:1, is it written in small script. This occurs in the word *va-yikra*, the first word of the third book of the Torah.

The nineteenth-century Italian Bible scholar Samuel David Luzzatto explains that originally the Torah was written without leaving space between words. When a scribe found that the last letter of one word and the first letter of the next word were the same, he might choose to omit one of the repeated letters in order to conserve space. At a later time, when it became customary to write out every word in full, one of the repeated letters was written in small script to indicate that originally it had not appeared in the text at all.

The letter *alef,* with which the word *va-yikra* in Leviticus 1:1 ends, is a case in point. The word *el,* which follows it, begins with an *alef,* and the letter *alef* in *va-yikra* is written small as an indication that at one time this repeated letter did not appear.[54]

Why is the letter *vav* in *shalom* written with a broken stroke in Numbers 25:12?

When they reached Shittim, the last stop in the desert before crossing the Jordan (Numbers 25:1-9), many Israelites were persuaded by the women of Moab and Midian to join in idolatrous worship and to engage in the licentious conduct associated with this activity.[55] This angered God and He sent a plague upon the Israelites, which took the lives of 24,000 people.

Zimri, a leader of the tribe of Simeon, was one of the offenders. He carried on flagrantly in a sexually explicit manner with Kozbi, a Midianite woman, in full view of Moses and all Israel. Phineas, the Priest, was so enraged by this conduct that he murdered both Zimri and Kozbi. His action stunned the Israelites. Whereupon the immorality ceased and the plague ended.

Verse 12 of Chapter 25 notes that because of his courageous act, God promised Phineas the "covenant of peace"
(brit shalom), and as a reward he was elevated to the High
Priesthood.

Apparently, the Masoretes were concerned about the
violence perpetrated by Phineas, and they wanted to make
the point that violence and peace are not compatible. They
accomplished this by establishing the practice that scribes
should leave a break in the vertical line that forms the *vav* in
shalom in Numbers 25:12.[56]

Why does the letter *nun* appear inverted in two places in the Torah?

Verses 35 and 36 of Chapter 10 in the Book of Numbers
contain prayers uttered by Moses when the ark was carried
forward at the head of the column of Israelites as they made
their way through the desert. The text reads:

> When the ark was set out, Moses would say:
> "Rise up, O Lord, and let Thine enemies be
>   scattered,
> And may Thy foes flee from Thee."

> And when it rested he would say:
> "Return, O Lord, unto the tens of thousands
>   of the families of Israel."

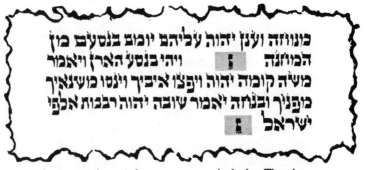

An inverted *nun* is known as a *nun hafucha*. The above
shows how the scribe writes the inverted *nun* in a Torah
scroll.

The first word of verse 35 is preceded by an inverted *nun*, and the last word of verse 36 is followed by an inverted *nun*.[57] The Rabbis of the Talmud[58] explained that these inverted letters are intended to call attention to the fact that the two verses are out of place, that they really should follow verse 17 of the second chapter of the Book of Numbers. And, they add, it was God Himself who instructed that these inverted letters be placed before verse 35 and after verse 36.

Rabbi Judah the Prince went on to explain that these two verses in the Book of Numbers should really be considered a separate book of the Bible. This, in effect, means that the Book of Numbers would consist of three separate books, bringing the total number of books in the Pentateuch to seven. The Book of Numbers would be divided as follows:

- Chapter 1 to Chapter 10, verse 34 would constitute one book.
- Chapter 10, verses 35 and 36 would comprise a second book.
- Chapter 10, verse 37 to the end of the book (Numbers 36:13) would be a third book.

To justify the legitimacy of this approach, Rabbi Jonathan brought the verse in Proverbs 9:1 to bear witness: "Wisdom has built her house, she has hewn her seven pillars." That this verse speaks of wisdom as being built on seven pillars, says Rabbi Jonathan, justifies the view that the Torah, which contains *supreme* wisdom, must likewise be thought of as consisting of seven parts.

Why does a final *mem* appear in the middle of a word in the Book of Isaiah?

Verse 5 of Isaiah 9, the haftara for the sidra Yitro, reads:

For a child has been born to us,
A son has been given us.
And authority has settled on his shoulders.

He has been named
"The mighty God is planning grace;
The Eternal Father, a prince of peace."

Verse 6 continues:

That the government may be increased,
And of peace there is no end.

The first Hebrew word of verse 6 is *le-marbe*, meaning "increase." The spelling of the word is peculiar in that its second letter, the *mem*, is closed on all sides, shaped like a *mem* that appears at the end of a word instead of a *mem* that appears in the middle of a word.

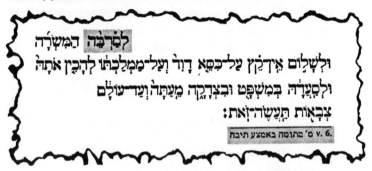

The first word of verse 6 in Isaiah 9, *le-marbe*, is written with a final *mem* in the middle of the word.

In a note, the Masoretes remind us that this is the way tradition demands that the word be spelled, and they therefore retained the traditional orthography here, as they did with other letters in many other parts of the Bible.[59]

Why were "open" and "closed" sections introduced into the Torah text?

Dividing the Torah into "open" and "closed" sections was a very ancient practice, as evidenced from references in the Talmud and Midrash.[60] Precisely what guidelines were followed in determining where a given type of section was to begin or end is not known, nor is any pattern discernible. Sections do not always reflect the beginning or end of a theme, nor do they appear to be connected with the assignment of aliyot. At times the Torah text runs on for long stretches without spacing, and at other times the spacing is frequent.[61]

A probable explanation for the introduction of these sections is that all of the earliest manuscripts of the Torah (and Bible) contained no vowels, no punctuation marks, and no cantillation symbols. The text ran on endlessly, without pause, posing difficulties for the student and the Torah reader. The ancients therefore introduced breaks in the Torah text.

Why do the letters *pay* and *samech* appear in the Hebrew text of printed copies of the Torah?

The letter *pay* is the first letter in the word *petucha,* meaning "open." When it appears in a printed Hebrew

9 שָׁנִים לְרֵעֵהוּ: ‏ ס ‏ כִּי־יִתֵּן אִישׁ אֶל־רֵעֵהוּ חֲמוֹר אוֹ־שׁוֹר
אוֹ־שֶׂה וְכָל־בְּהֵמָה לִשְׁמֹר וּמֵת אוֹ־נִשְׁבַּר אוֹ־נִשְׁבָּה אֵין
‏10 רֹאֶה: שְׁבֻעַת יְהֹוָה תִּהְיֶה בֵּין שְׁנֵיהֶם אִם־לֹא שָׁלַח יָדוֹ
‏11 בִּמְלֶאכֶת רֵעֵהוּ וְלָקַח בְּעָלָיו וְלֹא יְשַׁלֵּם: וְאִם־גָּנֹב
‏12 יִגָּנֵב מֵעִמּוֹ יְשַׁלֵּם לִבְעָלָיו: אִם־טָרֹף יִטָּרֵף יְבִאֵהוּ עֵד
הַטְּרֵפָה לֹא יְשַׁלֵּם: ‏ פ
‏13 וְכִי־יִשְׁאַל אִישׁ מֵעִם רֵעֵהוּ וְנִשְׁבַּר אוֹ־מֵת בְּעָלָיו אֵין
‏14 עִמּוֹ שַׁלֵּם יְשַׁלֵּם: אִם־בְּעָלָיו עִמּוֹ לֹא יְשַׁלֵּם אִם־שָׂכִיר
‏טו הוּא בָּא בִּשְׂכָרוֹ: ‏ ס ‏ וְכִי־יְפַתֶּה אִישׁ בְּתוּלָה

The shaded letter *samech* on the first and last line indicates the beginning of a *closed* section. The shaded letter *pay,* four lines from the bottom, indicates the beginning of an open section. The letters *samech* and *pay* appear only in printed Bibles, not in handwritten scrolls read in the synagogue.

242 •

וַיַּעֲשׂוּ כָּל בְּנֵי יִשְׂרָאֵל כַּאֲשֶׁר צִוָּה יְהוָה אֶת מֹשֶׁה
וְאֶת אַהֲרֹן כֵּן עָשׂוּ   וַיְהִי
בְּעֶצֶם הַיּוֹם הַזֶּה הוֹצִיא יְהוָה אֶת בְּנֵי יִשְׂרָאֵל
מֵאֶרֶץ מִצְרַיִם עַל צִבְאֹתָם
וַיְדַבֵּר יְהוָה אֶל מֹשֶׁה לֵּאמֹר קַדֶּשׁ לִי כָל בְּכוֹר

In handwritten scrolls read in the synagogue a minimum
of nine letter-spaces is left to indicate the beginning of
a closed section (see second line above). Open sections
always begin on a new line with blank space left on
the previous line (see fourth line).

Pentateuch, it indicates that the section that follows is an
open section, a *parasha petucha* (plural, *parashiyot petuchot*).

Open sections must always begin on a new line, with
enough open, white space left on the preceding line to accommodate a minimum of nine full-sized letters, such as the
mem or the *alef*. If there is insufficient space for nine letters
on the previous line, an entire line must be left blank.

The letter *samech* is the first letter of the Hebrew word
setuma, meaning "closed." When it appears in the Pentateuch, it indicates that the section that follows is a closed
section, a *parasha setuma* (plural, *parashiyot setumot*).

Closed sections do not have to begin on a new line.
However, the scribe must leave a minimum of nine spaces
before beginning the next section. After leaving the minimum nine spaces, the scribe must write at least one complete word at the end of the line.

Why was the amount of space required to be left before writing an open section increased from three to nine letter-spaces?

According to the Talmud,[62] for a section of the Torah to
be identified as open *(petucha)* it must start at the beginning of a line, and sufficient open space must be left on

the previous line to accommodate a word of at least three letters. Maimonides[63] did not agree with this ruling, and he declared that the amount of space to be left must be sufficient to accommodate a minimum of nine letters.

The reason for the Talmud specifying three letter-spaces and Maimonides requiring nine letter-spaces is never clearly indicated. It is known, however, that the Rabbis of the Talmud always favored the number three, and Maimonides, by increasing the talmudic requirement threefold, might have been emphasizing the number's significance.[64]

Why did Maimonides create a list of every open and closed section in the Torah?

There are 379 closed sections in the Torah and only 290 open sections.[65] Because Jewish law deems a Torah scroll invalid if open sections are written as closed ones or closed sections as open ones, Maimonides (1135-1204) considered it extremely important that scribes comply with what he considered to be the correct tradition. He therefore listed in his code of Jewish law the opening word or words of each and every open and closed section, explaining that he went to these lengths because varying views existed as to which sections should be open and which closed.[66] He writes:

> The copy on which I relied is the well-known Egyptian codex which contains the twenty-four books of the Scriptures and which had been in Jerusalem for several years, where it was used as the standard text for the checking of scrolls. Everyone relied upon it because it had been examined by Ben Asher, who closely studied it for many years and examined it again whenever it was being copied. This codex was the text on which I relied in the Torah scroll that I wrote.[67]

Why does a triple *pay* or a triple *samech* appear at the beginning of most sidrot in printed Pentateuchs?

Before the opening verse of almost every sidra in the Torah, the letter *pay* or the letter *samech* is repeated three times. These Masoretic notations, which appear in printed Hebrew Pentateuchs but not in synagogue scrolls, were probably instituted by the Rabbis of Babylonia to indicate

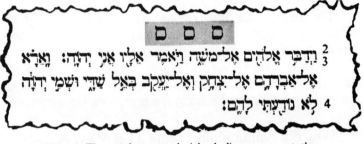

(Above) The triple *samech* (shaded) appears at the beginning of the sidra Va-ayra (Exodus 6:2).

(Below) The triple *pay* (shaded) appears at the beginning of the sidra Mishpatim (Exodus 21:1).

where weekly Torah readings began in accordance with the annual cycle. More space was left between weekly portions when the letter *pay* was used than when the *samech* was used (see earlier questions).

The significance of repeating the *pay* or *samech* three times as opposed to two times or four times is obscure. However, the choice of three may be related to the popularity of that number in Jewish tradition.

Why does the triple *pay* or the triple *samech* not appear at the beginning of some Torah portions in printed Pentateuchs?

The Rabbis[68] required that in Torah scrolls scribes leave four blank lines at the beginning of each of the books of the

Pentateuch. In these cases, it therefore became unnecessary to indicate how much space was to be left. Triple-letter markings were thus not included in printed editions of the Torah.

The only other portion in the Torah that is not preceded by a triple-letter marking is the sidra Va-yechi in the Book of Genesis.[69] Since no indication is given in the Masoretic Text as to whether this sidra is to begin with an open or closed section, Torah scribes allot only a single letter-space between it and the preceding sidra, Va-yigash.

Although no definitive reason has been given, commentators have tried to explain why the Masoretes did not call for extra spacing to be left before Va-yechi. Rashi,[70] for example, explains that there is less space here because Jacob wanted to reveal to his children what the future had in store for them and thus forewarn them, but this avenue was "closed" to him (*nistam* is the word used, which is equivalent to *setuma*). Therefore even less space than normally precedes a closed section is allocated here.

Why is it often impossible to correct scrolls in which the proper spacing for open and closed sections has not been allowed?

The ruling of the Talmud[71] is that a Torah scroll is invalid for a public reading if the proper spacing is not left for open and closed sections.

In order to correct such scrolls it would be necessary to change many lines of text. While some authorities say that this may be done (and it sometimes is done because synagogues are not always in a financial position to discard an expensive sheet of parchment), if God's name should appear in the text it may not be erased, thus making it impossible to salvage that piece of parchment.[72]

Why was it necessary to divide the text of the Torah into verses and chapters?

The scrolls used today for public Torah readings are written in the same manner as those of earliest times. The text runs on with few breaks and with no indication of where verses or chapters begin or end.

To make it easier for students to refer to particular passages, in talmudic times[73] the Rabbis divided the biblical text into verses. Such Torah texts, however, were prepared for study purposes only. Verse breakdown was not indicated in scrolls used at public worship services.

Modern Jewish scholars are agreed that the introduction of *chapter* numbering was a Christian innovation, specifically the work of Stephen Langton (1150-1228), the Archbishop of Canterbury. His goal was to enable Christians to identify passages more readily when engaged in debates with Jews. A century later this idea was accepted by most Jewish Bible scholars.[74]

Why was there disagreement in talmudic times as to which is the middle verse of the Torah?

It is quite evident from statements in the Talmud[75] that a variety of versions of the Torah existed in early times. The scholars of the East (Babylonia) were not always in agreement with the scholars of the West (Palestine) as to which version represented the authentic tradition. We therefore find that in discussing which is the central verse of the Pentateuch, some Rabbis selected Leviticus 8:8, some Leviticus 8:15, some Leviticus 8:23, and some Leviticus 13:33.[76] The final count of the number of verses in the Torah ranged from 5,845 to 5,888—a difference of 43.

An example of how differences in tradition were reflected in verse count can be seen by examining verse 9 of Exodus 19. The tradition in Babylonia was to regard this as one verse, as it appears in present-day Bibles. In the Palestinian tradition, this verse appears as three verses.[77] The fact that some long verses in the Babylonian texts were presented as two or more shorter verses in the Palestinian texts resulted in a higher verse count in the Western tradition.

The final count of verses in the Pentateuch, accepted today as normative, is 5,845, with Leviticus 8:8 considered to be the central verse.

Why was there disagreement in talmudic times as to the word count of the Torah?

Just as there were varying traditions as to the verse count of the Torah (see previous answer), so were there varying views as to the number of words in the Torah. Some sources list the number of words as 79,847 while others indicate the number as 79,976.[78]

One example of how a difference in count resulted is evident from Genesis 29:28, where the marginal note of the Masoretes states, "In some editions [of the Torah text] the word *lo* is not repeated."

According to the Masoretic tradition that has been accepted as normative, the Hebrew words *darosh darash* in Leviticus 10:16 are the midpoint of all words in the Torah, as indicated in a marginal note in Torah texts. *Darosh* is the last word of the first half of the Torah and *darash* is the first word of the second half.[79] For this reason, scribes must write *every* scroll in such a manner that *darosh* is the last word on a line and *darash* is the first word of the next line, thus making it easy to find the midpoint.

Why do some editions of the Pentateuch contain vital statistics at the end of each of the five books?

Printed Hebrew editions of the Torah generally contain, at the end of each of the five books, vital statistics pertaining to the weekly Torah readings in that book. These include: the number of chapters, the number of verses, the number of open and closed sections, the middle verse of each book, and other such information.[80]

This practice was introduced so that anyone could check the accuracy of scribes who produce scrolls or codices for private use. These statistics do not appear in handwritten parchment scrolls prepared for synagogue use.

Why are some Bibles called "Rabbinic Bibles"?

"Rabbinic Bibles" is the English term for what in Hebrew literature is called *Mikraot Gedolot,* literally meaning "Great Bibles," or "Large Bibles." The reference is undoubtedly to the scope of the Bible, not to its physical appearance.

The main feature of Great Bibles is that they contain on the same page as the text itself a large number of classical commentaries by eminent rabbis (hence the name Rabbinic Bibles). Among the commentaries usually found in these editions are those of Rashi (Rabbi Solomon ben Isaac, 1040-1105), Radak (Rabbi David Kimchi, 1160-1235), Rabbi Abraham ibn Ezra (1089-1164), and Ramban (Rabbi Moses ben Nachman, 1194-1270). Also included are one or more of the three Aramaic translations of the Bible, most often Onkelos.

The first Rabbinic Bible was edited in 1506 by an apostate Jew, Felix Pratensis, the son of a rabbi, and was published in 1517 in Venice by David Bomberg, a Christian printer. Pratensis, a philologist, devoted many years to the study and scrutiny of a variety of biblical manuscripts in order to prepare the first Great Bible.[81] He laid the groundwork for the second Rabbinic Bible, which was prepared by Jacob ben Chayim and which was published in Venice in 1525 by the same David Bomberg who issued the first Rabbinic Bible.

The Great Bible of Jacob ben Chayim achieved great distinction and remained unchallenged as the authoritative Masoretic Text until modern times. Aside from including the commentaries of all the great scholars of the early Middle Ages, it recorded in the margins of the text the notes of the Masoretes.

Chapter 9

Week By Week

INTRODUCTION

The Torah consists of five books: Genesis (Bereshit), Exodus (Shemot), Leviticus (Va-yikra), Numbers (Be-midbar), and Deuteronomy (Devarim).

In the days of the Second Temple (mid-fifth century B.C.E.), Ezra the Scribe introduced the practice of reading selected portions of the Torah aloud to the public. In the centuries that followed there evolved a tradition of reading one Torah portion (*sidra* or *parasha*) on each Sabbath throughout the year, completing the reading of the entire Torah by the end of the year. This procedure, followed in most communities, is called the annual cycle. As explained in Chapter Five, a triennial cycle is followed by some communities.

How did it come to pass that readings from both the Torah and the Prophets are recited on Sabbaths and festivals?

In the third and second centuries B.C.E., when the Syrian-Greeks ruled over Palestine, public readings from the Torah itself were banned. As a substitute, readings from the Prophets were introduced. Just as a minimum of twenty-one verses had been read by the seven persons called to the Torah on a Sabbath (each reading a minimum of three verses), a minimum of twenty-one verses from the Prophets were read by seven individuals.[1] When the Maccabees defeated the Syrian armies and Israel's independence was restored, the Torah readings were resumed, but the prophetic portions (haftarot) were not discontinued. However, it was no longer considered necessary to read a minimum of twenty-one verses from the Prophets, and since then many haftarot came to consist of fewer than this number. Sephardim in particular prefer shorter haftarot so as not to prolong the synagogue service unduly.

The Talmud indicates that the prophetic selection should thematically be related to the Torah reading of the day.[2] Consequently, in about two-thirds of the weekly readings we find a linkage between one or more aspects of the Torah reading and the haftara selection itself. For example, the Torah portion Shelach-Lecha (Numbers 13:1-15:41) details the story of the twelve scouts (spies). The corresponding prophetic selection from the Book of Joshua (2:1-24) describes a similar incident, one involving two men sent out by Joshua to survey the land that the Israelites were planning to invade.

Where there is no direct thematic linkage between Torah reading and haftara portion, the haftara will often be found to be related to a forthcoming holiday or historical event. This is the case with the selections read on the four Sabbaths preceding Passover.

The precise relationship between the Sabbath Torah reading and its haftara is discussed in this chapter, while the relationship between the Torah reading and prophetic reading of each holiday is covered in the next chapter.

The Book of Genesis

The name of the first book of the Bible, Genesis, derives from the Greek meaning "birth" or "origin." In Hebrew the book is called Bereshit, "beginning," and *bereshit* is in fact the word with which this first book of the Bible begins.

Bereshit, which consists of twelve sidrot (weekly portions), offers an account of the creation of the world and the early history of the Jewish people. According to Jewish tradition, the original Hebrew name of this book of the Bible was *Sefer Maasay Bereshit,* meaning "Book of the Works of Creation."

As is true for all books in the Pentateuch, this first of the Five Books of Moses carries the same name as its first sidra (portion): Bereshit. This first portion is read on the Sabbath immediately following the Simchat Torah holiday, which falls in late September or early October.

Unlike the other four books of the Torah, each of the twelve sidrot in the Book of Genesis is read on a separate Sabbath. This is because of the unusual length of the weekly portions in Genesis.

The narrative in the Book of Genesis falls into two categories. Chapters 1 through 11 deal with the early history of mankind in general. Here we find the stories of Creation, Adam and Eve, the Garden of Eden, and the Flood. Chapters 12 through 50 recount the early history of the Hebrew people in particular, beginning with Abraham and ending with the deaths of Jacob and Joseph.

The twelve sidrot in the Book of Genesis are:

- Bereshit ("In the beginning")
- No'ach ("Noah")
- Lech-Lecha ("Go forth")
- Va-yayra ("And He appeared")
- Cha'yay Sara ("The Lifetime of Sarah")
- Toldot ("The Story [of Isaac]")
- Va-yaytzay ("And he [Jacob] left")
- Va-yishlach ("And he [Jacob] sent [messengers]")
- Va-yayshev ("And he [Jacob] was settled")
- Mi-ketz ("At the end of [two years' time]")
- Va-yigash ("And he [Judah] approached")
- Va-yechi ("And he [Jacob] lived").

Note that the name of each sidra is generally the first word or one of the early significant words of the sidra itself.

Why were Chapters 42 and 43 of Isaiah selected as the haftara reading for Bereshit?

The sidra Bereshit (Genesis 1:1 to 6:8) begins with the story of Creation and proceeds to tell the familiar stories of Adam and Eve, the Garden of Eden, and Cain and Abel. The dominant theme, however, is Creation.

The Rabbis selected Chapter 42 of Isaiah as the haftara reading for this sidra because in verse 5 of this chapter there is a reference to Creation. The prophet assures his fellow Jews, who were then in Babylonian Exile, that just as surely as God created heaven and earth, so will He most certainly redeem Israel and create a new life for them, as promised in the covenant He made with them.

Ashkenazim begin the haftara reading with Isaiah 42:5 and conclude with 43:10. Sephardim have a much shorter reading: they begin with verse 42:5 and conclude with 42:21.

Why was Chapter 54 of Isaiah selected as the haftara for No'ach?

No'ach, the second sidra of Genesis (6:9-11:32), tells the story of Noah, the only righteous man on earth, and how he and his family are saved from the Flood. God promises Noah that never again will He bring such a calamity upon mankind, and the rainbow becomes a symbol of that promise.

Ashkenazim read Isaiah 54:1-55:5 as the haftara for No'ach, while Sephardim read only Isaiah 54:1-10. Isaiah 54:9 contains a reference to the Flood and to God's promise. The prophet assures his fellow Jews, then in exile in Babylonia, that just as God made a covenant with Noah, so will He honor the covenant He made with Israel and will repatriate the exiles.

Why was Isaiah 40:27-41:16 selected as the haftara for Lech-Lecha?

Lech-Lecha, the third Torah portion of Genesis (12:1-

17:27), describes the life of Abraham, the first patriarch, who is commanded by God to leave his birthplace and go to "the Land that I will show thee [Canaan]." Abraham's mission is to spread God's name throughout the world. He is promised that he and his seed will be a blessing to all mankind.

In the haftara reading, which begins with Isaiah 40:27 and ends with Isaiah 41:16, the prophet picks up on this theme and assures his fellow Jews, then suffering in exile in Babylonia, that the promise of God to Abraham will be kept. Isaiah portrays Abraham as God's beloved friend and Israel as God's chosen people.

Why was Chapter 4 of the Second Book of Kings selected as the haftara for the sidra Va-yayra?

While the major theme of this fourth sidra of Genesis (18:1-22:24) is the *Akeda* ("Binding of Isaac") and the testing of Abraham, a secondary theme relates to the good news that a son will be born to Abraham and Sara in their old age (Genesis 18:10).

Ashkenazim read II Kings 4:1-37 as the haftara for Va-yayra while Sephardim read only the first 23 verses of Chapter 4. In this passage from Second Kings, a woman from Shunem prays for a son but cannot have one because her husband is old. The prophet Elisha, through his servant Gechazi, sends a message to her, promising that "next year in this season" a son will be born to her, paralleling the theme of the sidra.

Why was Chapter 1 of First Kings selected as the haftara for Cha'yay Sara?

Cha'yay Sara, the fifth sidra of Genesis (23:1-25:18), tells of the death of Abraham's wife Sarah at age 127 and of her burial in Kiryat Arba, a city later named Hebron. It also discusses Abraham's concern, in his old age, for the purity of his family stock. Abraham does not want his son Isaac to marry a heathen woman from one of the neighboring Ca-

naanite clans and therefore sends his trusted servant (Eli-
ezer) to visit Haran, where members of his family reside.
There, the servant discovers Rebekah and selects her to be
a wife for Isaac.

This concern for maintaining an unadulterated lineage
prompted the Rabbis to select I Kings 1:1-31 as the haftara
reading for this sidra. In this prophetic portion King David is
concerned about the right of succession now that he has
reached old age. David is anxious that Solomon (the son of
David and Bathsheba), not Adoniya (the son of David and
Chagit), be his successor.

Why was the first chapter of Malachi selected as the haftara for the sidra Toldot?

The major characters whose lives are described in Toldot, the sixth portion of Genesis (25:19-28:9), are the twin
brothers Jacob and Esau. The sale of the birthright by Esau
to Jacob and the usurping by Jacob of the blessings which
their father, Isaac, intended for Esau are the highlights of
this segment.

In the opening verses of Malachi 1:1-2:7, selected by the
Rabbis as the haftara reading for Toldot, the prophet
makes reference to the brotherly relationship of Jacob and
Esau and to God's concern and love for Jacob.

Why was the twelfth chapter of Hosea selected as the haftara for Va-yaytzay?

Va-yaytzay, the seventh sidra of Genesis (28:10-32:3),
describes Jacob's life after he moves to Paddan-Aram and
takes up residence with his uncle Laban, the brother of his
mother, Rebekah. Jacob is fearful that his brother Esau will
murder him if the opportunity arises.

In the Ashkenazic tradition, the flight of Jacob becomes
the link between the Torah reading and the haftara selection, Hosea 12:13-14:10. The first verse of the reading
states: "And Jacob fled into the field of Aram . . ."

In the Sephardic tradition the haftara reading begins

with Hosea 11:7 and concludes with 12:12. Sephardim link the Torah and haftara readings through verse 4 of Chapter 12, which describes the very first incident of contention between the brothers: "In the womb he [Jacob] took his brother by the heel . . ."

Ashkenazim read Hosea 11:7-12:12 as the haftara for the sidra Va-yishlach.

Why do some congregations read as the haftara for Va-yishlach selections from the Book of Hosea while others read the Book of Obadiah?

Va-yishlach, the eighth sidra of Genesis (32:4-36:43), describes the situation after the brothers Jacob and Esau, who have not seen each other for twenty years, meet again. Jacob is unsure whether the anger that once seethed in Esau has subsided. As their paths are about to cross, Jacob is overcome by fear. Fortunately there is a softening of hearts, and a reconciliation takes place. The closing verses of the sidra provide a genealogy of Esau, in which he is referred to as Edom, a name first mentioned in Genesis 25:30. To the Rabbis of the Talmud, Esau and Edom are synonyms for the wicked Roman Empire.

In the Sephardic tradition, the entire Book of Obadiah (1:1-21) is read as the haftara for Va-yishlach because Obadiah begins his prophecy with the words "Thus saith the Lord concerning Edom . . ." (Obadiah is the only book of the Bible that consists of only one chapter, a total of 21 verses.)

Ashkenazim read Hosea 11:7-12:12 as the haftara for Va-yishlach because of its reference (12:4) to Jacob seizing the heel of Esau when leaving his mother's womb.

Sephardim read Hosea 11:7-12:12 as the haftara for the sidra Va-yaytzay.

Why is the haftara for Va-yayshev taken from the Book of Amos?

Va-yayshev, the ninth sidra of Genesis (37:1-40:23),

continues the narrative of the adventures of Jacob and his sons. Among its highlights are episodes detailing the hostile relationship between Joseph and his brothers. For twenty pieces of silver the brothers sell him to Ishmaelites who then transport the seventeen-year-old Joseph to Egypt, where he is resold as a slave.

In the haftara, which begins with Amos 2:6 and extends through 3:8, the prophet makes reference to a sin prevalent in Israel: the sale of "righteous [people] for silver" (2:6). The Rabbis took this as an allusion to the sale of Joseph.

Why is the haftara for Miketz taken from I Kings 3:15-4:1?

Miketz, the tenth sidra of Genesis (41:1-44:17), continues with the story of Joseph in Egypt, recounting his unique talent to interpret dreams, particularly those of Pharaoh. The Egyptian ruler is so impressed by young Joseph's uncanny ability that he elevates him to a position of power, second only to the king himself.

As the haftara for this sidra the Rabbis selected I Kings 3:15-4:1 because it details the dream of another king, Solomon. The haftara opens with a reference to a dream Solomon has in which he asks God to grant him the gift of wisdom. Young Joseph is rewarded for his special ability to interpret dreams, and young Solomon is rewarded for having made the choice of seeking wisdom over riches. The latter finds his reward in the acclaim he is accorded by the nation.

Why was Chapter 37 of Ezekiel selected as the haftara for Va-yigash?

Va-yigash, the eleventh sidra of Genesis, (44:18-47:27) opens with ten of Joseph's brothers appearing before him to plead for the life of their half-brother Benjamin. Benjamin had been incarcerated after it was discovered that Joseph's favorite goblet was found in Benjamin's knapsack. It had been placed there surreptitiously by Joseph himself because he wanted Benjamin to be apprehended and returned to Egypt.

Judah, speaking for all the brothers, pleads with Joseph for compassion. Judah reviews the events from the moment the brothers arrived in Egypt and concludes by emphasizing that their father, Jacob, had already lost one son (Joseph), and if the brothers did not return with Benjamin, the old man would not survive the shock. Joseph is overcome by Judah's words and finally breaks down, revealing that he is their brother, the brother who had been sold by them into slavery. They are then reconciled.

The opening verses of the haftara for this sidra (Ezekiel 37:15-28) refer to Joseph and Judah, the main characters of the Torah reading. The sixth-century B.C.E. prophet Ezekiel foretells the return of the exiled tribes from Babylonia and forecasts the reunification of all twelve tribes. In his prophecy the tribes are represented by Judah and Joseph, symbolized by two sticks. One stick, described in a parable in verse 16, represents the Kingdom of Judah, which is composed of two of the twelve tribes; the other stick represents the Kingdom of Israel, comprised of ten tribes. (In this haftara the Kingdom of Israel is often referred to as Ephraim, who was one of the two sons of Joseph.)

Why is the haftara for Va-yechi taken from Chapter 2 of the First Book of Kings?

Va-yechi, the twelfth and final sidra of Genesis (47:28-50:26), describes the last day in the life of Jacob. Jacob's children gather around his deathbed and he blesses them. Some of the Blessings of Jacob are actual benedictions, while others are mere predictions of the destiny of his children. The last chapter of Genesis describes Joseph's grief as he mourns the death of his father and ends with Joseph's own death.

The Rabbis selected the First Book of Kings 2:1-12 as the haftara for this final sidra of Genesis because it recalls the last days of another aged leader of Israel: King David.[3] David is described as leaving a spiritual legacy for his son

Solomon, just as Jacob did for his children in the Torah reading. His legacy also incorporates practical advice to Solomon on how to handle the political situation that will confront him when he takes over as king.

The Book of Exodus

The Septuagint, the third-century B.C.E. Greek translation of the Bible, refers to the second book of the Torah as Exodus. Jews, however, use the name Shemot, meaning "names." *Shemot* is the second word of the book, which begins, *Ve-ayleh shemot:* "And these are the names [of the Children of Israel]."

Although the Book of Exodus, which consists of eleven sidrot, opens with a listing of the names of the descendants of Jacob who settled in Egypt, the major part of the book deals with the enslavement of the Israelites, their suffering over a prolonged period of time, and their eventual release from bondage. This culminates in a triumphal march through a sea that miraculously divided as the Jews made their way to freedom. Appropriately, early manuscripts of the Torah refer to the second book of the Bible by the Hebrew name *Sefer Yetziat Mitzra'yim,* meaning "Book of the Departure from Egypt."

A major portion of the Book of Exodus describes the spiritual birth of the Jewish people, which took place on Mount Sinai. It was on Mt. Sinai that God revealed Himself to Moses and gave him the Ten Commandments, which he transmitted to the Children of Israel (Exodus 20:1-24:18), who willingly accepted them. A Tabernacle of elaborate design was then built in the wilderness so that the God of Israel could be worshiped properly.

The eleven sidrot in the Book of Exodus are:

- Shemot ("Names")
- Va-ayra ("And I [God] appeared")
- Bo ("Go [to Pharaoh]")
- Be-shalach ("When he [Pharaoh] sent forth [the Israelite slaves]")

- Yitro ("Jethro")
- Mishpatim ("Laws")
- Teruma ("An offering")
- Tetzaveh ("[You shall] Command")
- Ki Tissa ("When you take a census")
- Va-yakhel ("And he [Moses] assembled")
- Pekuday ("The records [of the Tabernacle]").

In certain years, dictated by the calendar, the last two sidrot, Va-yakhel and Pekuday, are combined and read on a single Sabbath.

Why do Sephardim read a haftara from Jeremiah for the sidra Shemot while Ashkenazim read a selection from Isaiah?

Shemot, the first sidra of Exodus (1:1-6:1), describes with bold strokes the oppression suffered by the Israelites at the hands of the Egyptians. It reaches its climax with God promising Moses that He will compel Pharaoh to free the Children of Israel.

As the haftara for Shemot, Ashkenazim read a selection from Isaiah (27:6-28:13) that has much in common with the Torah reading. In Isaiah's days, as in the days of Moses, Jews suffered at the hands of a powerful empire. And just as God redeemed the Israelites and led them from Egyptian bondage, so does the prophet foresee the redemption of his people in his own time. Miraculously, in 701 B.C.E. Jerusalem is saved, but not without being heavily damaged by the Assyrians. Verses 22-23 of Isaiah 29 were added to this reading so that it concludes on a pleasant note.

Sephardim chose to accentuate another theme vividly expressed in the Torah reading: the consecration of Moses and his elevation to a position of leadership (Exodus 3:4-10). Jeremiah is called to be a prophet to his people (Jeremiah 1:5) and, like Moses, balks because he feels unequal to the task. Sephardim read Jeremiah 1:1-2:3 as the haftara.

Why is the haftara for Va-ayra taken from the Book of Ezekiel?

Va-ayra, the second sidra of Exodus (6:2-9:35), describes the first seven of the ten plagues to which the Egyptians are subjected. These include blood that fills the rivers; frogs; gnats; flies that infest the land; a deadly disease (murrain) that destroys the cattle; a plague of boils that afflicts man and beast; and a downpour of hail from the heavens. Despite the humiliation to which Pharaoh is subjected, he remains determined to keep the Israelites in servitude.

Ezekiel 28:25 to 29:21 was selected as the haftara for this sidra because of its prophecy about Egypt. At this time, the majority of Jews were living in exile in Babylonia, but there also existed a community of Jews who lived in the Holy Land under Babylonian rule. The prophet Ezekiel warns his coreligionists in Palestine to abort their planned alliance with Egypt. Egypt is a "broken reed," warns Ezekiel. The Egyptians are not to be depended upon. They will be crushed just as surely as were the Egyptians of the Exodus (Ezekiel 29:12).

Why is Chapter 46 of Jeremiah read as the haftara for the sidra Bo?

The Torah reading for Bo, the third sidra of Exodus (10:1-13:16), describes the eighth, ninth, and tenth plagues that befall the Egyptians: locusts, darkness, and the death of the eldest son in every Egyptian household. When Pharaoh finds out that the heir to his throne was a victim, his heart softens and he allows the enslaved Israelites to leave the country. The second half of the Torah reading (beginning with Chapter 12) is devoted to the institution of Passover and the laws that apply to it

The haftara reading, taken from Jeremiah (46:13-28), strikes a note similar to that read the previous week, in which the prophet Ezekiel denounces Egypt. Jeremiah, an older contemporary of Ezekiel, was prisoner in Egypt when the First Temple was destroyed, and he foretells that Babylonia will crush Egypt just as Egypt was crushed in the days of Moses.

Why were the fourth and fifth chapters of the Book of Judges selected as the haftara for Beshalach?

Be-shalach, the fourth sidra of Exodus (13:17-17:16), highlights the successful crossing of the Children of Israel through the Sea of Reeds (referred to in older translations of the Bible as the Red Sea). Moses raises his staff and miraculously the waters part, forming two walls with dry land between. As the last Israelite passes through in safety, Moses again raises his staff and the waters come together, swallowing up the Egyptian army that was in pursuit.

Appreciating their new-found freedom, Moses and the Children of Israel give expression to their pent-up emotions in what has come to be known as the *Song at the Sea (Shirat Ha-yam)*.

The haftara for Be-shalach is a selection from the Book of Judges (4:4-5:31) that contains the famous *Song of Deborah*. This song celebrates the victory of the prophet-judge Deborah, who led the Hebrew nation during the unstable period when Judges ruled Israel. Together with her military leader, Barak, she crushed the warlike Canaanites in whose midst the tribes of Israel lived. Thus, both the *Song at the Sea* and the *Song of Deborah* are celebrations of triumph over an oppressive enemy.

Unlike Ashkenazim, Sephardim read only Judges 5:1-31 as the haftara for this Torah portion.

Why are selections from Chapters 6, 7, and 9 of Isaiah read as the haftara for Yitro?

Yitro, the fifth sidra of Exodus (18:1-20:23), details the preparations made in anticipation of the Revelation on Mount Sinai. Verses 5-6 of Chapter 19 stipulate the simple terms of the covenant made between God and Israel:

If you will obey Me faithfully and keep My covenant, you shall be My treasured people above all other peoples, for all the earth is Mine. You shall be to Me a kingdom of Priests and a holy people.

In Exodus 19:8 the people of Israel agree and make the following promise: "All that the Lord has spoken we will do." Moses then ascends Mount Sinai and after forty days returns with the Ten Commandments.

The haftara selection, Isaiah 6:1-7:6 and 9:5-6, describes a revelation experienced by Isaiah that parallels the one on Mount Sinai. As a young man, Isaiah, standing in the Temple in Jerusalem, hears the heavenly angels (seraphim) sing: "Holy, holy, holy is the Lord God of hosts, the whole earth is full of His glory." This statement about holiness echoes Exodus 19:5.

In the Sephardic tradition only verses 1-13 of Isaiah 6 are read as the haftara.

Why is the haftara for Mishpatim taken from Chapter 34 of Jeremiah?

Although the entire Torah is often called The Law, it is only with Mishpatim, the sixth sidra of Exodus (21:1-24:18), that the laws of the Torah begin to appear in significant numbers. (The first laws appear a few chapters earlier, in Exodus 12, with injunctions concerning the observance of Passover.)

The first law in Mishpatim ("Laws") deals with the Hebrew slave. It specifies that a male Hebrew slave may not serve his master for more than six years and that in the seventh year he is to be set free. If the slave refuses to leave (because he likes his master and enjoys his problem-free life), he may stay on as a slave for life, but first his ear must be pierced to indicate his status (21:5-6). The statement that appears later in the Book of Leviticus (25:10) that in the jubilee year "each of you shall return to his family" was interpreted by the Rabbis to mean that all Hebrew slaves must be released in that year.

The haftara, which consists of selections from the Book of Jeremiah (34:8-22 and 33:25-26), describes how the ruling class in Judea had disobeyed the Torah and kept its Hebrew slaves beyond the prescribed period. When the threat of attack from Babylonia is imminent, King Zedekiah warns the Judeans that their lives are in danger because they have violated the laws of the Torah. The frightened Judeans release their slaves, but when the threat passes, the wealthy slave-owners revert to their old ways. Jeremiah, outraged, predicts that the enemy will return and the cities of Judah will be ravaged.

Chapter 34 of Jeremiah ends on a note of catastrophe, and the Rabbis therefore added two verses (25 and 26) from Chapter 33 as a conclusion to the reading.

Why is the haftara for Teruma taken from Chapter 5 and 6 of the First Book of Kings?

Teruma, the seventh sidra of Exodus (25:1-27:19), begins with a description of the voluntary contributions made by the Israelites toward the erection of the Tabernacle. The offerings include gold, silver, and copper as well as yarns of fine linen and the hair of goats. All these materials are used in the building of the desert Tabernacle, in which an ark containing the Ten Commandments is to be placed.

The haftara for Teruma was selected from the First Book of Kings (5:26-6:13), where the building by Solomon of the Temple sanctuary in Jerusalem is described. To accomplish his goal, Solomon conscripts 30,000 men to work on the structure which, unlike the Tabernacle in the desert, is to be permanent. It is to be constructed of choice materials: quarried stone and the finest cedars of Lebanon.

Why was Chapter 43 of Ezekiel selected as the haftara for Tetzaveh?

Tetzaveh, the eighth sidra of Exodus (27:20-30:10), continues the story of the building of the Tabernacle in the desert by detailing the duties of the Priests who were to conduct its activities. A good deal of attention is paid to the vestments to be worn by the High Priest and by the ordinary Priests. There is a description of how the Priests are to be consecrated before they can assume office and perform their duties.

The sidra concludes with a summary of the daily sacrifices to be offered by the Priests in behalf of the community. It includes rules pertaining to the building of the Altar of Incense, a special structure of pure gold situated between the Holy of Holies and the court where offerings were to be brought. On the altar, incense was burned to sweeten the air that had been made foul by the burning animal sacrifices.

The prophetic portion from Ezekiel (43:10-27) picks up on the theme with which the Torah reading ends. Ezekiel has a vision of an altar being erected in the Temple, which will be rebuilt when the Babylonian Exile is over. Just as the Altar of Incense in the desert was of special construction, so the altar of the restored Temple, upon which sacrifices will again be offered, is to be specially constructed.

Why was the haftara for Ki Tissa selected from Chapter 18 of the First Book of Kings?

Ki Tissa, the ninth sidra of Exodus (30:11-34:35), begins with a description of a census that had been taken. To determine the number of able-bodied men in Israel available for military service, all males twenty years of age and older were required to pay a half-shekel, and these coins were counted.

The balance of the Torah portion is devoted to a variety of subjects pertaining to priestly duties, including the manner in which the laver (brass washing basin) was to be used by the Priests before offering sacrifices and details pertaining to the sacred oil and holy incense that were used in the Tabernacle. But the highlight of the sidra is a description of the Golden Calf incident and the apostasy of the people who persuaded Aaron to erect the idol for them (Exodus 32:1-33:6).[4]

The haftara, I Kings 18:1-39, parallels the Torah reading. In the sidra, Moses confronts the people and reprimands them for worshiping the Golden Calf. In the end they are contrite and return to the worship of God (Exodus 33:10). In the prophetic portion, the prophet Elijah reprimands King Ahab and his wife, Jezebel, for encouraging the people to engage in idolatrous worship. In the end Elijah convinces the people that the idols erected for the worship of Baal are worthless gods. The people are won over and respond, "The Lord He is God; the Lord He is God" (I Kings 18:39).

Why is the seventh chapter of First Kings read as the haftara for Va-yakhel?

In Va-yakhel, the tenth sidra of Exodus (35:1-38:20), the order is finally given to proceed with the actual construction of the Tabernacle in the desert. Bezalel, the chief architect whom Moses had selected to supervise the work, proceeds with the construction of the sanctuary that will accompany the Israelites in their travels and in which God's presence will abide.

The haftara, I Kings 7:40-50, parallels the Torah reading as it describes the construction of Solomon's Temple and the appurtenances of its interior.

In the Sephardic tradition, I Kings 7:13-26 is read. Here, the emphasis is on the construction of the exterior of the Temple, in which Hiram, king of Tyre, participated.

Why are the seventh and eighth chapters of First Kings read as the haftara for Pekuday?

Pekuday, the last sidra in the Book of Exodus (38:21-40:38), describes in great detail the final stages of the construction of the Tabernacle, including its interior. The placement of the various religious articles used in the Sanctuary is specified, and the type of gear to be worn by the

Priests is detailed. The final verses describe the cloud which always hovers over the Tabernacle and which protects the Children of Israel as they proceed on their hazardous trek through the desert. The Tabernacle is sometimes referred to as the *Ohel Moed,* the Tent of Meeting.

The haftara for Pekuday is a continuation of the selection from the First Book of Kings that was read for the sidra Va-yakhel on the previous Sabbath. It begins with I Kings 7:51 and continues through 8:21. King Solomon summons to Jerusalem the leaders of the nation to join in a gala celebration marking the completion of the Temple. The ark housing the Ten Commandments is placed in its permanent place in the Holy of Holies, and Solomon then addresses the people and blesses them.

In the Sephardic tradition, I Kings 7:40-50 is read as the haftara for this sidra.

In years when, because of the calendar, Va-yakhel is combined with the next sidra, Pekuday, the haftara for Pekuday is read.

The Book of Leviticus

Leviticus, the third book of the Torah, begins with the word *va-yikra,* meaning "and He [God] called," and consists of ten sidrot. Leviticus (which literally translates to "the Levitical book") is commonly referred to in Hebrew as Va-yikra, although the Talmud[5] calls it *Torat Kohanim,* "Law of the Priests." A large part of this book is devoted to the sacrificial system and the duties of the Priests, who were members of the tribe of Levi. It also contains the famous Holiness Code ("Love thy neighbor as thyself"), laws pertaining to marriage, the dietary laws, and laws pertaining to ritual purification.

In the Septuagint, the Greek name Leviticus was assigned to the third book of the Bible. The Vulgate, the Latin translation of the Bible, also refers to the third book as Leviticus. The Aramaic name for Leviticus is *Sefra* (or *Sif-*

ra) *D'chohanay,* meaning "Book of the Priests."
The ten sidrot in the Book of Leviticus are:

- Va-yikra ("And He [God] called")
- Tzav ("Command [Aaron and his sons]")
- Shemini ("The eighth [day]")
- Tazria ("Childbirth")
- Metzora ("The leper")
- Acharay Mot ("After the death [of the two sons of Aaron]")
- Kedoshim ("[You shall be] Holy")
- Emor ("Speak [to the Priests]")
- Be-har ("On the mountain [of Sinai]")
- Be-chukotai ("My commandments").

In certain years, dictated by the calendar, the following sidrot are sometimes combined and read on a single Sabbath: Tazria and Metzora, Acharay Mot and Kedoshim, Be-har and Be-chukotai.

Why are selections from Chapters 43 and 44 of Isaiah read as the haftara for the sidra Va-yikra?

Va-yikra (Leviticus 1:1-5:26), the first of the ten weekly portions found in the third of the Five Books of Moses, deals entirely with the various types of sacrifices brought in the Tabernacle in the desert and later in the First and Second Temples. The most popular of the sacrifices was the burnt offering or holocaust *(olah),* so named because, after the skin was removed, the entire animal was burned completely on the altar.

In addition to describing the burnt offering, the Torah reading also details other sacrifices, such as the sin offering, the peace offering, and the meal (cereal) offering.

Isaiah 43:21 to 44:23 was selected as the haftara for Va-yikra because it makes reference to the sacrificial system. The Second (Deutero-) Isaiah, author of these chapters, lived after the First Temple had been destroyed and sacrifices were no longer brought. He urges the Babylonian Jews in whose midst he lived to substitute offerings of the heart (prayer) for the sacrifices of the altar, and he assures the people that these would be as acceptable to God as the animal sacrifices offered by earlier generations of Jews.

Why were parts of Chapters 7 and 8 of Jeremiah selected as the haftara for Tzav?

Tzav, the second sidra of Leviticus (6:1-8:36), repeats much of what is contained in the sidra Va-yikra. In addition, it provides instruction on how to tend the fire on the altar and the manner in which the offerings of donors are to be shared with the Priests and their families.

The haftara for this sidra, which consists of Jeremiah 7:21 to 8:3 and concludes with Jeremiah 9:22-23, places the sacrificial rites in proper perspective. The prophet Jeremiah, who lived during the precarious years preceding the destruction of the First Temple, warns his compatriots that sacrifices alone will not assuage God's wrath. Evil actions and rebellious attitudes cannot be covered up by offering sacrifices. What is primary, if the nation is to be saved from Babylonian domination, says the prophet, is loyalty to the moral law. Jeremiah 9:22-23 was chosen to conclude this haftara so that, as is the custom, the reading would end on a pleasant note.

Why is the haftara for the sidra Shemini taken from the Second Book of Samuel?

Shemini, the third sidra of Leviticus (9:1-11:47), begins with a description of how Aaron, the High Priest, and his sons offered sacrifices on the altar. A significant portion of the Torah reading (Chapter 11), however, is devoted to the dietary laws.

A highlight of the sidra is the recounting of the unnatural death of the High Priest's two eldest sons, Nadav and Avihu. The Bible does not offer specifics except to indicate that the two men did not follow the established sacrificial rules and offered a "strange fire" on the altar. As a result of this unauthorized sacrifice, they died (Chapter 10, verse 2).

The haftara, II Samuel 6:1-7:17, parallels the Nadav and Avihu incident by describing the death of Uzza, the son of Avinadav who in the time of David mishandled the ark, which David's men had placed on a cart. God smote Uzza dead for his irreverence (Chapter 6, verse 7), just as Nadav and Avihu met death for their irreverence.

Sephardim limit their reading to 6:1-19 of the Second Book of Samuel.

Why were Chapters 4 and 5 of Second Kings selected as the haftara for Tazria?

Tazria, the fourth sidra of Leviticus (12:1-13:59), begins with a short section related to the laws of purification of women after childbirth. (The word *tazria* means "child-birth" or, literally, "to bring forth seed.") The balance of the Torah portion is devoted almost exclusively to the laws of leprosy, known in Hebrew as *tzara'at* and called *elephantiasis* by the Greeks.

In the Near East in biblical times, leprosy was widespread. The Torah is concerned with effecting a treatment for the stricken individual and with the creation of safeguards to protect the community-at-large from the disease. In talmudic times, the Rabbis associated the malady with gossip and slander, believing it to be punishment for such immoral conduct.

The haftara for Tazria, II Kings 4:42-5:19, also deals with the subject of leprosy. The prophetic portion tells the story of Naaman, who was cured of his leprosy by Elisha, who succeeded Elijah as the nation's prophet in the ninth century B.C.E. Naaman was the commanding officer of the armies of Aram (Syria).

Why was Chapter 7 of the Second Book of Kings selected as the haftara for Metzora?

Metzora, the fifth Torah reading portion of Leviticus

(14:1-15:33), continues to detail the laws of leprosy first outlined in Tazria. The function of the Priest as healer is elaborated upon: it is his duty to examine the patient, and when satisfied that the patient is healed, the Priest performs various purification ceremonies. Following these rites, several sacrifices are brought, and the leper then resumes his place in the community. The sidra concludes with a discussion of other types of defilement that require ritual cleansing.

Second Kings 7:3-20, the portion from the Prophets selected as the haftara for this sidra, relates the famous story of the four lepers facing starvation during the siege of Samaria by the Syrians (Aram). The lepers, who live outside the city gates, debate whether to break the rules and enter the city in search of food or to risk entering the camp of the Syrians in the hope of being given food. They choose the latter and to their surprise discover that the enemy has abandoned the camp, leaving food behind. In years when, because of the calendar, Tazria and Metzora are read on the same Sabbath, the haftara for Metzora is chanted.

Why is Chapter 22 of Ezekiel read as the haftara for the sidra Acharay Mot?

Acharay Mot, the sixth sidra of Leviticus (16:1-18:30), opens with a description of the High Priest's purification of the sanctuary each year on Yom Kippur. Sacrifices are offered, culminating in forgiveness being granted to the House of Israel for its sins. The High Priest then makes his annual entry into the Holy of Holies to commune with God.

The reading concludes with a listing of all prohibited marriages and an indication of the penalty to be imposed for engaging in immoral sexual conduct. This chapter is also read each year at the Yom Kippur *Mincha* service in order to emphasize the importance of family purity for the survival of the Jewish people.

Ezekiel 22:1-19 was selected by Ashkenazim as the haftara for Acharay Mot because it also emphasizes the theme of family purity and associates the loss of Jerusalem and the destruction of the Temple (in the year 586 B.C.E.) with Israel's moral degeneracy. The prophet ends on a note of hope as he assures the people that conditions will improve once they have purified themselves by listening to the voice of God and abiding by the Law.

When the blessing of the New Moon (Mevarchim Hachodesh) is pronounced on this Sabbath, Ashkenazim read the haftara for Kedoshim (Amos 9:7-15) and Sephardim read Ezekiel 22:1-16.

Why do Ashkenazim read as the haftara for Kedoshim a selection from the Book of Amos while Sephardim read from Ezekiel?

Kedoshim, the seventh sidra of Leviticus (19:1-20:27), was regarded by the Rabbis as possibly the most important sidra in the Pentateuch because it contains all the basic teachings of the Torah. The Hebrew word kedoshim, the plural form of kadosh, means "holy." All of the Ten Commandments are repeated in Chapter 19 in concise form, although not in the same order as they appear in Exodus 20 and in Deuteronomy 5. (See Leviticus 19, verses 3, 4, 11, 12, 16, 18, and 29.) The theme of holiness is emphasized throughout Chapter 19, and it is therefore often referred to as "The Holiness Code." The Golden Rule (19:18), "Love your neighbor as yourself," is undoubtedly the most widely quoted verse in this chapter.

The haftara read by Ashkenazim is Amos 9:7-15. In this selection Amos, the eighth-century B.C.E. prophet who was a shepherd and a farmer, cautions his people that if God's laws are not followed, they will become a sinful (unholy) people and will be overcome by enemies.

Sephardim read Ezekiel 20:2-20 as the haftara for Kedoshim because it recalls the impending doom of Jerusalem, which was finally destroyed by the Babylonians in 586 B.C.E. Doom was predicted because the inhabitants of the city had totally disregarded the teachings of Leviticus 19.

In years when, because of the calendar, the sidrot Acharay Mot and Kedoshim are combined on this Sabbath, the haftara for Kedoshim is read.

Why was Chapter 44 of Ezekiel selected as the haftara for the sidra Emor?

Emor, the eighth Torah portion of Leviticus (21:1-24:23), continues to enunciate the rules pertaining to the Priests and the Sanctuary. The ordinary Priest who serves in the Sanctuary as a representative of the people has to be free of physical defects, and even higher standards are set for the High Priest. The manner in which sacrifices are to be prepared by the Priests and how they are to be consumed is also discussed. Finally, the reading concludes with a review of the holidays in the Jewish calendar and a statement concerning the offerings to be brought on those days.

In the haftara (Ezekiel 44:15-31), the sixth-century B.C.E. prophet Ezekiel, who lived among the Jews in Babylonian Exile, presents a vision of the "New Jerusalem" that will be built after the exile has ended. Ezekiel foresees the building of a new Temple in which only descendants of the untainted priestly family of Zadok will officiate.

Why was Chapter 32 of Jeremiah selected as the haftara for the sidra Be-har?

Be-har, the ninth sidra of Leviticus (25:1-26:2), deals with a variety of laws pertaining to the ownership of property, the redemption of land, and the sabbatical and jubilee years. It also mandates the correct manner of conducting business, with specific attention to the charging of interest on loans and the treatment of those forced to become slaves.

The haftara (Jeremiah 32:6-27) discusses the redemption of land as it affects family inheritance. Jeremiah, who had predicted the downfall of Jerusalem and was imprisoned in 587 B.C.E. (one year before the siege of the city), declares while in prison that he has "redeemed" a piece of land so that it will remain part of his family's inheritance. Through this symbolic gesture, the prophet demonstrates that the Torah law safeguarding family property remains in effect despite foreign domination. The gesture also gives expression to the hope that redemption will come to Israel and that Jews will be restored to their homeland.

Why were selections from Chapters 16 and 17 of Jeremiah chosen as the haftara for Be-chukotai?

Be-chukotai, the tenth and last sidra of Leviticus (26:3-27:34), is in some years, depending on the calendar, combined with Be-har, the previous week's portion. For the most part, Be-chukotai consists of a listing of the blessings to be enjoyed by the Israelites if they observe the commandments and of the curses that will be wrought upon them if the laws are neglected. The wages of disobedience will be oppression by the enemy, physical suffering, and exile.

The curses enumerated, which occupy the greater part of Chapter 26 (14-39), are known by the Hebrew name *Tochacha* ("curses"). Beginning with verse 40 a new note is struck, and the promise is made that in the end God will remember His covenant with Israel at Sinai.

The blessings and the curses are reiterated in Deuteronomy 28.

The haftara (Jeremiah 16:19-17:14), like the Torah reading, explains that Israel may choose a life of blessings or curses. The prophet Jeremiah, who witnessed the destruction of the First Temple in 586 B.C.E., acknowledges that calamity has befallen Israel as a result of their immoral conduct. He assures his people, however, that their faith in the Lord will be restored and they will once again begin to enjoy His beneficence.

This haftara is read whenever Be-har and Be-chukotai are read on the same Sabbath.

The Book of Numbers

The Book of Numbers is the fourth of the Five Books of Moses.[6] For many years the Rabbis referred to this book as *Sefer Va-yedaber* because the book actually begins with the Hebrew word *va-yedaber,* meaning "and He [God] spoke."[7] However, since the word *va-yedaber* is found as the opening word of many biblical sections, it was deemed more expedient to call the book by the name Be-midbar. *Be-midbar,* meaning "in the desert of," is actually the fifth word of the first verse of the book: "And God spoke to Moses in the desert of Sinai . . ."

While Be-midbar is basically an account of the travels of the Children of Israel in the desert after the Exodus from Egypt, the Greek translation of the Bible, the Septuagint, as well as the Latin translation, the Vulgate, selected Numbers as the logical name for this fourth book of the Bible because the numbering (census) of the Israelites is detailed in its very first chapters. Although the name Numbers was never popular among Jews, its equivalent is found in the Talmud,[8] where the name *Chumash Ha-pekudim,* meaning "Book of Counting" or "Book of Numbers," is used.

The ten sidrot in the Book of Numbers are:

- Be-midbar ("In the wilderness of [Sinai]")
- Naso ("Take a census")
- Be-ha'alotecha ("When you light [the lamps]")
- Shelach-Lecha ("Send forth [men]")
- Korach ("Korah")
- Chukat ("The ritual law")
- Balak ("Balak")
- Pinchas ("Phineas")
- Matot ("[Heads of the] Tribes")
- Masay ("The itinerary of [the Children of Israel].")

In some years, dictated by the calendar, Chukat and Balak are combined and read on a single Sabbath. In some years, Matot and Masay are combined and read on a single Sabbath.

Why was Hosea, Chapter 2, selected as the haftara reading for the sidra Be-midbar?

Be-midbar, the first sidra of Numbers (1:1-4:20), which traditionally is read on the last Sabbath of the Hebrew month Iyyar or on the first week of Sivan, opens with the census Moses took of male Israelites of military age (twenty and up) and a listing of the tribal leaders. The sidra describes the status of the Levites and summarizes their duties in connection with the operation of the Tabernacle. Because of their sacred responsibility to carry and guard the Tabernacle, which contained the two tablets of the Law, the Levites were counted in a separate census and were not subject to military service.

The haftara for Be-midbar was taken from Hosea 2:1-22, the first verse of which speaks of the Children of Israel becoming "as numerous as the sands of the sea." This parallels the first two chapters of the Torah reading, which give details of the census taken by Moses.

Why was Judges 13 selected as the haftara for Naso?

Naso, the second Torah reading portion in Numbers (4:21-7:89), is the longest sidra in the Torah, containing 176 verses. The name of the sidra, taken from the first word of the second verse (4:22), literally means "to count." Moses is commanded to take a separate census of the families of Levites in order to determine who must serve in the Tabernacle. All males between ages 30 and 50 were obligated to serve.[9]

Naso also describes the Ordeal of Bitter Waters to which a married woman is subjected when accused by her husband of infidelity. Such a woman is referred to as a *sota*, "an unfaithful wife." The Torah reading also describes the *nazir*, the Nazirite, who pledges to abstain from wine and other intoxicants and who allows his hair to remain uncut as an expression of his loyalty to God. The sidra concludes with a description of the sacrifices offered by the tribal princes when the altar of the Tabernacle was dedicated.

Chapter 13:2-25 of the Book of Judges was selected as the haftara for Naso because it tells the story of the birth of the strongman Samson, who became a Nazirite.

Why are selections from Chapters 2, 3, and 4 of Zechariah read as the haftara for the sidra Be-ha'alotecha?

Be-ha'alotecha, the third sidra of Numbers (8:1-12:16), begins with a description of the duties incumbent upon Aaron and his sons with regard to the kindling of the seven lights of the *menora* in the Tabernacle. This sacred task is assigned to the most distinguished Levitical family, the family of Aaron.

This Torah reading stresses another important theme: the observance of a Second Passover *(Pesach Sheni)* for those who for any number of reasons are unable to celebrate Passover at the proper time, on the fifteenth day of the month of Nissan. Such individuals are to offer the Paschal lamb one month later (9:1-14).

The haftara, Zechariah 2:14-4:7, consists of a message proclaimed in Palestine after the Babylonian Exile. Paralleling the Torah reading, it speaks of the vital importance of the service of the Levites. In addition, the prophetic selection describes a vision of Zechariah in which he sees a candlestick, a reminder of the *menora* described in the sidra. To Zechariah this is a symbol of God's illuminating presence and a reinforcement of the prophet's conviction that victory for Israel can be accomplished only through God's help. The prophet states his thesis in these memorable words: "Not by might, nor by power, but by My spirit."

This same haftara is read on the first Sabbath of Chanuka.

Why was Chapter 2 of Joshua selected as the haftara for Shelach-Lecha?

Shelach-Lecha, the fourth sidra of Numbers (13:1-15:41), deals principally with the mission of twelve scouts, generally referred to as "spies" *(meraglim)*, who are sent by Moses across the Jordan River to survey the Promised Land, known then as the Land of Canaan. Moses requests that they report on the strengths and weaknesses of the natives and present an evaluation of the land's terrain and its natural resources. Ten of the scouts return with a negative report, and two express confidence that the Children of Israel would be victorious if they were to attempt to conquer the land.

The haftara (Joshua 2:1-24), like the Torah reading, recounts a story involving scouts. Joshua, the successor of Moses and now the leader of Israel, sends two scouts to survey the city of Jericho. Joshua's scouts are saved by Rahab, the harlot, from being taken captive by the king of Jericho. Upon their return, the two scouts declare optimistically, "The Lord has delivered the whole land into our hands; in fact, all its inhabitants stand in trepidation before us."

Why was a selection from the First Book of Samuel used as the haftara for Korach?

Korach, the fifth sidra of Numbers (16:1-18:32), focuses on the rebellion of Korach, a member of the tribe of Levi and a cousin of Moses and Aaron. Korach, together with Datan and Aviram, two leaders of the tribe of Reuben,[10] instigates a revolt against Moses because they believe that Moses and Aaron are power-hungry and inconsiderate. They demand new leadership, but their attempt to usurp power fails when God lends His support to His chosen leader, Moses.

The haftara reading for Korach, I Samuel 11:14-12:22 parallels the Torah reading in that it describes a rebellion that takes place in the days of the prophet Samuel, the last of Israel's ruling Judges. The people demand that the aging Samuel appoint a king to rule over them. At first the prophet resists their demand but, unlike Moses, he soon succumbs to pressure and appoints Saul as the first king over Israel (about 1000 B.C.E.).

Why was Chapter 11 of the Book of Judges chosen as the haftara for Chukat?

Chukat, the sixth sidra of Numbers (19:1-22:1), deals with a variety of subjects: the law of the Red Heifer; the deaths of Miriam and Aaron; the sin of Moses striking the rock and thus forfeiting the privilege of entering the Promised Land. But the historical essence of the sidra is Israel's attempt to gain entry into the Land of Canaan via the south, the most direct route. The Israelites are confronted by the Edomites (descendants of Esau), who will not allow the Children of Israel to pass through Edomite territory, compelling them to take the circuitous and more dangerous eastern route.

During their long trek, the Israelites are forced to battle many enemies. At Arad, south of Hebron (near Masada and the Dead Sea), they encounter the Canaanites, a formidable enemy. Turning to God, the Israelites vow that if He will grant them victory over the Canaanites, they will destroy the enemy cities but take no booty. Everything that is captured will be dedicated to God.

There are two links between the haftara and the Torah reading. The first is the vow made in the sidra in which the Israelites promise not to profit personally if they are victorious over the Canaanites. This is paralleled by the vow made by Jephthah in Judges 11:1-33. Jephthah, a Judge of Israel, promises that if victorious against the Ammonites, he will offer as a sacrifice to God whatever he (Jephthah) sees walking out of his house upon his return from battle. Jephthah is indeed victorious in battle, and upon his return home his daughter is the first to come out of the house to greet him. Jephthah is obliged to keep his promise, and he offers his daughter as a sacrifice.

Another link between the haftara and the Torah reading relates to the conquering of the Amorite kingdom. In the sidra this is described in Numbers 21:21-32, and it finds its parallel in the haftara (Judges 11:21-24) where Israel's victory over Sichon, king of the Amorites, is narrated.

Why were selections from the Book of Micah chosen as the haftara reading for Balak?

The famous story of Balaam and his talking donkey is featured in Balak, the seventh sidra of Numbers (22:2-25:9). So important is this tale that in early times it was believed to comprise an individual book of the Bible, separate and distinct from the other five books.

This highly unusual story involves an enemy of Israel, Balak ben Tzipor, king of Moab, and Balaam, a pagan soothsayer who is hired by the king to curse Israel. Observing how overwhelmingly victorious Israel had been in its wars with the neighboring Amorite nations, Balak is overcome with fear. He hopes that if cursed by Balaam, Israel will be contained. But Balaam's ass is a factor in thwarting Balak's plan, and in the end, instead of cursing Israel, Balaam blesses them. His memorable words have become part of the traditional morning prayer service: "How goodly are thy tents, O Jacob, thy tabernacles, O Israel" (24:5).

Micah 5:6-6:8 was selected as the haftara for the sidra Balak because it contains the verse (6:5), "O my people, remember the plot of Balak king of Moab against you, and how Balaam son of Beor responded to him." Micah, the eighth-century B.C.E. prophet, a contemporary of Isaiah, reminds Israel that God is on its side and that those who plot against Israel will have to contend with Him. To merit this, says the prophet, Israel must show its gratitude not by bringing sacrifices but by acting justly, mercifully, and humbly (Micah 6:8).

In years when the second day of Shavuot falls on a Sabbath, the sidrot Chukat and Balak are both read on the same Sabbath. Whenever the portions Chukat and Balak are combined, the haftara for Balak is recited.

Why is the haftara for the sidra Pinchas taken from the First Book of Kings?

Pinchas, the eighth sidra of Numbers (25:10-30:1), covers a variety of subjects including a military battle with the Midianites; the taking of a second census (the previous one had been taken some forty years earlier); a discussion of the laws of inheritance, with specific attention to the claim of the five daughters of Zelophehad (Tzelafchad); and laws pertaining to the daily and festival sacrifices.

The central character of this Torah reading is Pinchas (Phineas), the son of Elazar, the son of Aaron the High Priest. Pinchas is lauded for taking action against Zimri, a member of the tribe of Simeon who blatantly, publicly carried out sexual activity with Cozbi, a Midianite woman. Pinchas, indignant over what has transpired, kills Zimri and Cozbi (Chapter 25). Because of his courageous action, Pinchas is rewarded with the High Priesthood.

First Kings 18:46-19:21, the haftara for this sidra, emphasizes the loyalty shown to God by the leading character of the prophetic reading, the ninth-century B.C.E. prophet Elijah. Like Pinchas in the Torah reading, he is a devoted servant of God and His people, Israel. Just as Pinchas is rewarded for defending God's holy name, Elijah is rewarded for his advocacy of God and His teachings, which he displays by his defiance of the ruling monarch, King Ahab, and his evil wife, Jezebel, who were promoting the worship of Baal.

When, because of the calendar, the two sidrot Matot and Masay are combined, Jeremiah 1:1-2:3 (the haftara for Matot) is read as the haftara for Pinchas.

Why were readings from the Book of Jeremiah selected as the haftara for Matot?

Matot, the ninth Torah portion of Numbers (30:2-

32:42), deals with three major themes. One involves the solemnity of oaths—specifically, the individual's duty to carry out all vows made to God. The second theme involves the violent war the Israelites waged against the Midianites, a nation steeped in idol worship and immorality. The third theme relates to the agreement made between Moses and the two and one-half tribes (Reuben, Gad, and half of Manasseh) who want to settle in Transjordan, the eastern part of Palestine. These tribes are permitted to settle there only after agreeing to help the other tribes conquer the western portion of the Promised Land, the area that lay between the Jordan River and the Mediterranean Sea.

Because the Sabbath on which this sidra is read is the first of three Sabbaths that precede the Fast of the Ninth of Av (Tisha B'Av), the haftara selection (Jeremiah 1:1-2:3) is not related to the subject matter of the sidra but to the forthcoming fast day commemorating the destruction of the Temple. Jeremiah, one of a large number of Jews who had been exiled to Babylonia, lived through the two sieges of Jerusalem: the first in 597 B.C.E. and the second in 586 B.C.E., when the First Temple was destroyed.

In his preachments Jeremiah blames his sinful fellow Jews for the calamity that has come about, but he is nevertheless hopeful that through sincere repentance the Jewish state and its institutions will be restored.

The fact that the haftara for the sidra Matot contains Jeremiah's rebuke of Israel and the fact that the haftarot for the next two Sabbaths pursue a similar theme led to the three Sabbaths prior to Tisha B'Av being named *Telat* (or *Shelosha*) *De-puranuta,* an Aramaic expression meaning "Three [Haftarot] of Rebuke."

Why are readings from the early chapters of Jeremiah selected as the haftara for Masay?

Masay (Numbers 33:1-36:13), the tenth and last of the weekly portions from the Book of Numbers, is read on the last Sabbath of Tammuz or on the first Sabbath of Av. The sidra recapitulates the Israelites' forty years of wandering, from the time of their exodus from Egypt to their reaching the river Jordan. The Torah reading describes the stages of the long journey and recalls the forty-one places where the Israelites stopped and rested. It then discusses how they are to conduct themselves once they occupy the Promised Land.

Special mention is made of six cities of refuge that had been established, three on either side of the Jordan. Anyone involved in accidental manslaughter could find a haven in these cities, safe from the victim's avenging family. The idea of asylum for accidental homicide was quite advanced for this early period.

Like the haftara of the previous week, the haftara for Maşay is taken from the Book of Jeremiah. This reading (Jeremiah 2:4-28; 3:4; and 4:1-2) continues the theme of rebuke pronounced by Jeremiah. As in the prophetic portion that preceded it, the prophet foresees disaster for God's Chosen People because they have forsaken His Law and commandments.

For this second of the Three Haftarot of Rebuke, Sephardim read Jeremiah 2:4-28 and 4:1-2.

When, because of the calendar, Matot is combined with Masay and read on the same Sabbath, Ashkenazim recite Jeremiah 2:4-28 and 3:4 as the prophetic selection, while Sephardim recite these portions plus verses 1 and 2 of Jeremiah 4.

The Book of Deuteronomy

The Greek (Septuagint) and Latin (Vulgate) translations of the Bible refer to the fifth Book of the Bible as Deuteronomy, which roughly translates as "second telling [repetition] of the Law." This final book of the Pentateuch is basically a recapitulation of the first four books of the Bible.

Devarim, meaning "words," is the second Hebrew word of the first verse of Deuteronomy: "These are the words that Moses spoke to the Israelites . . ." And it is by the name

Devarim that the last book of the Bible is generally called by Jews. The older name for this book, however, is *Mishneh Torah,* meaning "recapitulation of the Torah," a Hebrew phrase found in Deuteronomy 17:18. This name was commonly used by the Rabbis of the Talmud, and Maimonides used it as the title for his classic compendium of Jewish law.

Deuteronomy is primarily a review of events that occurred during the forty years of Israel's wandering in the desert. Moses reviews all the laws that had been proclaimed during that long period of time, and in three discourses he reminds the Children of Israel that obedience to God's laws will lead to a blessed life while the penalty for disobedience will be a life of curses. The book ends with a farewell song and a farewell blessing by the great leader who brought the Israelites to the brink of the Promised Land but was not privileged to enter it.

Devarim is divided into eleven sidrot. The first of these, which also carries the name Devarim, is read in the synagogue on Shabbat Chazon, the Sabbath before Tisha B'Av. The last sidra of Deuteronomy, Ve-zot Ha-beracha, is read on Simchat Torah, which falls on the twenty-third day of the month of Tishri.

The eleven sidrot in the Book of Deuteronomy are:

- Devarim ("Words")
- Va-etchanan ("And I pleaded")
- Aykev ("Reward [of obedience]")
- Re'ay ("Behold")
- Shoftim ("Judges")
- Ki Taytzay ("When you go forth")
- Ki Tavo ("When you enter")
- Nitzavim ("[You are] standing")
- Va-yelech ("And he [Moses] went")
- Ha'azinu ("Pay heed")
- Ve-zot Ha-beracha ("And this is the blessing").

In some years, dictated by the calendar, the sidrot Nitzavim and Va-yelech are combined and read on a single Sabbath.

Why was Isaiah 1:1-27 selected as the prophetic reading for the sidra Devarim?

Devarim (Deuteronomy 1:1-3:22) contains the first of three discourses to be found in the Book of Deuteronomy. Beginning with verse 6 of Chapter 1, Moses reviews the travels of the Israelites from the time they leave Mount Sinai to the time they reach Kadesh-Barnea, where the account of the twelve scouts who are sent forth to spy out the Land of Canaan is repeated.

The sidra concludes with a description of several battles in which the Children of Israel are engaged and with a statement of conditions under which land is to be allotted to Reuben, Gad, and half of the tribe of Manasseh.

The sidra Devarim is always read on the Sabbath before Tisha B'Av, and the haftara reading, Isaiah 1:1-27, was selected to accompany it because it speaks of the catastrophe that befell Jerusalem as a result of Israel's sinfulness. The prophet foresees the possibility of redemption if Israel turns back to God in sincere repentance. This haftara is the third of the Three Haftarot of Rebuke and is chanted in the mournful style associated with the Book of Lamentations (Echa).

The Sabbath on which the sidra Devarim is read is called Shabbat Chazon because the first Hebrew word of the prophetic reading is *chazon,* meaning "the vision of [Isaiah]." Verse 1:12 of the sidra is also chanted to the Echa tune.

Why are the seven prophetic portions read on the seven Sabbaths before Rosh Hashana all taken from the Book of Isaiah?

The seven weeks between Tisha B'Av and Rosh Hashana are known as Shiva D'nechemta, the "Seven [Sabbaths] of Consolation." This seven-week period following the Three Weeks of Rebuke was instituted to offer consolation to a despondent and despairing people. The Rabbis considered the prophecies of the Second (Deutero-) Isaiah to be most suited for this purpose. From his home in Babylonia, this sixth-century B.C.E. prophet promised Israel that although God punishes His people for disloyalty, He rewards them and shows them compassion when they return to Him with renewed faith.

This message runs through each of the Haftarot of Consolation recited during the seven Sabbaths after Tisha B'Av. The seven haftarot, beginning with the Sabbath after Tisha B'Av (Shabbat Nachamu), are:

- Isaiah 40:1-26 for the sidra Va-etchanan.
- Isaiah 49:14-51:3 for the sidra Aykev.
- Isaiah 54:11-55:5 for the sidra Re'ay.
- Isaiah 51:12-52:12 for the sidra Shoftim.
- Isaiah 54:1-10 for the sidra Ki Taytzay.
- Isaiah 60:1-22 for the sidra Ki Tavo.
- Isaiah 61:10-63:9 for the sidra Nitzavim (or Nitzavim/Va-yaylech). This, the last of the seven Haftarot of Consolation, is always read on the Sabbath before Rosh Hashana.

Why is Chapter 40 of Isaiah read as the haftara for Va-etchanan?

Va-etchanan, the second sidra of Deuteronomy (3:23-7:11), presents the conclusion of the First Discourse of Moses. Here, Moses expresses the hope that the recent victories of the Israelites are a signal that God has again begun to look with favor upon Israel and that as a result he (Moses) might be privileged to enter the Promised Land.

In the balance of the Torah reading, Moses summarizes the fundamental commandments that the Children of Israel are expected to observe. He then begins his Second Discourse, in which he exhorts the people that if they obey God's commandments, all will be well with them; if not, disaster will overtake them. This Torah reading includes a repetition of the Decalogue (5:6-18), which first appeared in Exodus 20. In addition, it contains the famous declaration of faith, the *Shema* (6:4ff.)

The haftara for Va-etchanan, Isaiah 40:1-26, expands upon the theme of the sidra, emphasizing that God's love will provide comfort to Israel, now in Babylonian Exile. The prophet assures Israel that if they remain loyal to God, He will gather them into His arms like a shepherd "gathers lambs in his arms and carries them in his bosom."

The first words of Isaiah 40:1-26 are *Nachamu, nachamu ami,* "Comfort ye, comfort ye, my people." Hence the Sabbath on which this selection is recited came to be known as Shabbat Nachamu, "Sabbath of Consolation."

The prophetic selection read on Shabbat Nachamu is the first of the Seven Haftarot of Consolation taken from the Book of Isaiah.

Why was Isaiah 49:14-51:3 selected as the haftara for the sidra Aykev?

Aykev, the third sidra of Deuteronomy (7:12-11:25), discusses how the Israelites will handle their lives after they occupy Canaan, the Promised Land. Will they be strong enough in their faith to resist the idolatrous practices of the enemies whom they will conquer and who will be living in their midst?

The sidra describes the promise made to Israel that as a reward for their loyalty to God and His commandments they will be blessed, and the new land they are about to occupy will yield them material abundance. If, however, they are unloyal to God and become obstinate, stiff-necked, and self-righteous, they will suffer for their sins.

The haftara for Aykev, Isaiah 49:14-51:3, stresses that Israel will be strong and will reject the idolatrous practices of its neighbors, thus displaying loyalty to God. As a consequence, Israel may look forward with hope to a blessed future. This haftara is the second of the Seven Haftarot of Consolation that follow Tisha B'Av.

Why was Isaiah 54:11-55:5 selected as the haftara for Re'ay?

Re'ay, the fourth Torah reading portion of Deuteronomy (11:26-16:17), restates some of the laws that had been promulgated in earlier parts of the Torah. It opens with Moses presenting two options to the Israelites: to follow the laws of the Torah and enjoy a blessed life or to abandon the laws and be cursed.

Of particular significance in this Torah selection is the commandment that the Israelites establish a central Sanctuary once they are settled in the Promised Land. Only there are sacrifices to be brought, always in accordance with a prescribed procedure. This law is spelled out in detail because only a single, respected spiritual center could offset the threat of pagan influence and stem the pagan practices to which many Israelites had become addicted.

Deuteronomy 13:2-6 discusses prophecy and how to distinguish between authentic prophets and fraudulent ones. It also reminds the Children of Israel that they are to be a kingdom of Priests and a holy nation (first stated in Exodus 19:6). Previously stated laws pertaining to the observance of dietary practices, abstaining from pagan rites and rituals, and the pursuit of social justice are repeated.

The prophetic reading for Re'ay, Isaiah 54:11-55:5, is the third of the Seven Haftarot of Consolation that are read between Tisha B'Av and Rosh Hashana. Like the Torah reading, the prophetic portion emphasizes that Israel has a choice between following the good or evil path. Isaiah assures his fellow Jews that they will enjoy the rewards of life if they make the right choice.

Why was Isaiah 51:12-52:12 selected as the haftara for Shoftim?

Shoftim, the fifth sidra of Deuteronomy (16:18-21:9), concerns itself mainly with the administration of justice. Shoftim, "Judges," are to be appointed, and judicial procedures are to be established so that Israel will follow a path that will help them reach the goal of becoming "a kingdom of Priests and a holy people" (Exodus 19:6). The pursuit of justice was the essential ingredient in achieving this end, and Israel is advised to be guided by the caveat "Justice, justice shall you pursue" (Deuteronomy 16:20).

The haftara for Shoftim, Isaiah 51:12-52:12, is the fourth of the Seven Haftarot of Consolation recited in commemoration of the events that culminated in the destruction of the First Temple in the year 586 B.C.E. The prophet, speaking for God, opens his oration with words of solace. "I, I am the Lord who comforts you," he says, and then he proceeds to assure the Israelites that those who persist in persecuting them unjustly will one day find that God's justice will prevail. Israel will finally be saved and their enemies be held accountable.

Why was Isaiah 54:1-10 selected as the haftara for Ki Taytzay?

Ki Taytzay, the sixth sidra of Deuteronomy (21:10-25:19), discusses a wide range of laws, rites, and rituals, beginning with instructions on the proper way to treat a captive woman whom one wishes to marry. Among the significant subjects dealt with in this portion are the treatment of a disobedient son, the restoration of lost property, the treatment of criminals, laws of *shaatnez* (mixing fabrics), violation of marital vows, prohibited marriages, laws of divorce, kindness to animals, and laws pertaining to just dealings between human beings.

The haftara for Ki Taytzay, the fifth of the Seven Haftarot of Consolation, consists of ten verses from Isaiah (54:1-10). It is the shortest haftara read by Ashkenazim in the course of the year. (The only shorter haftara is that for Ve-zot Ha-beracha, read by Sephardim on Simchat Torah. It consists of nine verses.)

Here, the prophet promises the Jews in Babylonian Exile that God will not forsake them. He has abandoned them only temporarily and will save them if they will observe His laws (many of which are spelled out in detail in the Torah reading). God says that just as after the Flood in the days of Noah (through the symbol of the rainbow) He vowed never again to destroy mankind, so now does He promise that He will not destroy Israel (verses 9-10).

The first ten verses of Chapter 54 of Isaiah are the beginning of the haftara read for the sidra No'ach.

Why was Isaiah 60:1-22 selected as the haftara for Ki Tavo?

Ki Tavo, the seventh sidra of Deuteronomy (26:1-29:8), begins with a description of the rituals that are to accompany the sacrificial offerings to be brought when the Sanctuary is established in the Promised Land. The portion discusses the offering of first fruits and the various tithes assigned to the Levites and the poor. It then details the ceremonies to be conducted by the Israelites after crossing the Jordan.

Chapter 27 enumerates the blessings and the curses that may be expected by those who adhere to the Law and by those who violate it. The curses, or "warnings" as they are sometimes referred to, are collectively called the *Tochacha*. They are described in verses 15 to 68 of Chapter 28. The *baal koray* reads the *Tochacha* quickly and in a subdued tone.

The haftara for Ki Tavo is the sixth in the series of Seven Haftarot of Consolation. Taken from Isaiah (60:1-22), the selection expresses the assurance that despite their present state of exile, Jews will again find favor in the eyes of God. The haftara opens with words of hope and comfort. Speaking of Jerusalem, Isaiah declares: "Arise and shine for thy light has come."

Why is Isaiah 61:10-63:9 always read on the Sabbath before Rosh Hashana?

Nitzavim, the eighth sidra of Deuteronomy (29:9-30:20), is one of the shortest weekly portions (forty verses) in the annual cycle of Torah readings. Here, Moses continues to instruct the Children of Israel about their obligation to be loyal to the laws of God. He reminds them that the Covenant with God is binding upon Israel for all time. Here, in his third and final discourse to the people (Deuteronomy 30:1-10), Moses emphasizes that despite their sinfulness Israel may still hope for forgiveness if they repent.

Verses 15 to 20 of Chapter 30 are perhaps the most striking in the sidra. Verse 15 reads, "I set before you this day life and well-being, death and adversity . . ." Verse 19 continues, "I have put before you life and death, blessing and curse. *Choose life* so that you and your offspring will survive."

The haftara for Nitzavim (Isaiah 61:10-63:9) emphasizes the importance of making the right choice, of choosing God and the moral life. Thus, it sets the stage for Rosh Hashana and the Days of Awe that follow within the week.

Nitzavim, depending on the calendar, is sometimes combined with the next sidra, Va-yaylech. Normally, when two Torah reading portions are combined and read on one Sabbath, only the haftara for the second sidra is read. The only exception is Nitzavim/Va-yaylech. When these sidrot are combined, the haftara for Nitzavim is read. This prophetic reading is the last of the Seven Haftarot of Consolation and is always read on the seventh Sabbath following Tisha B'Av, which coincides with the Sabbath that precedes Rosh Hashana.[11]

Why is Hosea 14:2-10 the primary prophetic portion for the sidra Va-yaylech?

Va-yaylech, the ninth sidra of Deuteronomy (31:1-30), is the shortest sidra in the entire Torah, consisting of only thirty verses. It describes the last days in the life of Moses. He has reached the age of 120 and, although still in good health, confesses that he can no longer carry on as in past years. And Moses expresses disappointment that God has not seen fit to permit him to enter the Promised Land.

Moses appoints Joshua as his successor and places the Torah, which he had committed to writing, in the hands of the Priests and the Elders. He commands the Levites to put the Torah alongside the ark in which the Ten Commandments were kept.[12]

Whenever Va-yaylech is read by itself, the Sabbath on which it is read will fall between Rosh Hashana and Yom Kippur. The first verse of the prophetic reading for the day will begin with the words *Shuva Yisrael,* "Repent [return], O Israel" (Hosea 14:2). On all other Sabbaths when Va-yaylech is part of a Torah reading, it is combined with the sidra Nitzavim.

See the previous answer to a discussion of the Nitza-vim/Va-yaylech combination. And see page 316 in the next chapter for more information on the prophetic portion read on Shabbat Shuva.

Why was a reading from Chapter 22 of the Second Book of Samuel selected as the haftara for Ha'azinu?

Ha'azinu, the tenth sidra of Deuteronomy (32:1-52), is devoted to a second "song" of Moses. The first was uttered on the banks of the Sea of Reeds when the Israelites were saved from the Egyptians (Exodus 15:1-18). In this Second Song of Moses, the aging leader delivers his farewell message to the people whom he has served for so many years. As he peers at the banks of the Jordan, he praises God for all He has done for Israel and admonishes his fellow Israelites not to forsake God and His teachings, for "He is the Rock whose deeds are perfect" and "all His ways are just." He is a Being upon whom one can depend.

The Second Book of Samuel (22:1-51) was selected as the haftara for Ha'azinu because its theme parallels the theme of the Torah reading. King David, like Moses, utters a song of thanksgiving to God for having saved him from menacing enemies. Just as the sidra refers to God as the Rock whose acts are perfect (Deuteronomy 32:4), so does

David (II Samuel 22:3) speak of God as "the Rock in whom I can take shelter."

When this Sabbath falls between Rosh Hashana and Yom Kippur, the haftara for Shabbat Shuva is read. (See the preceding answer.)

Why is the first chapter of the Book of Joshua read as the haftara for Ve-zot Ha-beracha?

Ve-zot Ha-beracha (Deuteronomy 33:1-34:12) is the last sidra in the Torah. In it, the aged leader Moses approaches the end of his life. And just as Jacob blessed his children as he lay on his deathbed, so does Moses bless the tribes of Israel before his death. As Jacob evaluated the characters of his children, so does Moses evaluate each tribe and utter words of prophecy concerning its future.

The sidra concludes with a description of the ascent of Moses to the top of Mount Nebo, from where he can see across the Jordan River to the Promised Land, a land he is never privileged to enter.

As the last verse of the sidra is about to be chanted, the congregation rises, and when the *baal koray* has completed reading the final verse, the congregation sings out (as it does when each of the Five Books of Moses is completed): *Chazak, chazak, ve-nitchazek,* "Be strong, be strong, and let us be strengthened [by the words of the Torah]."

The haftara for Ve-zot Ha-beracha is taken from the Book of Joshua (1:1-18), the book of the Bible that immediately follows Deuteronomy and is the first book of the Prophets. Through Joshua, the handpicked successor of Moses, the saga of the Children of Israel continues.

Sephardim read only Joshua 1:1-9 as the haftara for this Torah portion.

Why, in most congregations, is the last sidra in the Torah never read on a Sabbath?

Ve-zot Ha-beracha (Deuteronomy 33:1-34:12), the last

sidra in the entire Pentateuch, is the only Torah portion that is never read on a Sabbath. It is reserved for Simchat Torah, which always falls on the twenty-third day of the month of Tishri, which can never coincide with a Sabbath.

In Israel and in Reform congregations, where Simchat Torah is observed as part of the Shemini Atzeret festival, Ve-zot Ha-beracha is read on Shemini Atzeret, which does occasionally fall on a Sabbath.

Chapter 10

Holiday By Holiday

INTRODUCTION

On each of the holidays in the calendar year, special sacrifices were brought in the Temple to commemorate the occasion. These offerings were in addition to the two regular sacrifices that were brought every day of the week. The "additional" sacrifices were called *musafim* (singular, *musaf*).

After the Temple was destroyed in the year 70 C.E. and sacrifices were no longer offered, a special maftir Torah portion was assigned to be read on holidays in order to remind future generations of the significance of the sacrificial system. The holiday maftir was almost always a selection from Chapters 28 or 29 of the Book of Numbers, chapters which detail the various types of sacrifices offered on each festival. The maftir portion is always read from a second scroll.

The practice of reading haftarot, selections from the Prophets, as supplementary readings to the Sabbath Torah portions, dates back to the second century B.C.E., the years of the Hasmoneans. It is not until the third century C.E., however, that the Talmud assigns specific haftara readings to the holidays.

This chapter discusses the Torah and haftara readings for all holidays of the year, including the four special Sabbaths that precede the great Passover festival.

Why does the maftir portion read on festivals always deal with sacrifices?

In Temple times, sacrifices were brought on the altar twice daily. On Sabbaths an additional sacrifice was brought to mark the special significance of the day. The same procedure that was followed on Sabbaths was followed on festivals, except that on the latter each person brought two additional sacrifices: a burnt offering *(olah)* and a peace offering *(shelamim)*. The two special festival sacrifices were brought by the many pilgrims who came to Jerusalem to celebrate Passover, Shavuot, and Sukkot.

The Second Temple was destroyed in 70 C.E. and the sacrificial system was discontinued. To keep alive the importance of the sacrifices that had been brought on the three Pilgrim Festivals, the practice developed of reading a special maftir on each day of each festival. These selections, which dealt with the sacrifices brought on the various festivals, were taken from Numbers 28-29 (the sidra Pinchas). Since the maftir selections were not to be found in the Torah scroll near the holiday readings for the other aliyot, a second Torah was used for the maftir portions. This would eliminate the necessity of the congregation waiting while the Torah scroll was rolled to the appropriate place.

The thirteenth-century German scholar Rabbi Mordechai ben Hillel, author of the Mordechai commentary on the Talmud, offers a simple reason for devoting the festival maftir readings to the sacrificial system. This, he says, is done so that the public will always be reminded that sacrifices were brought in Temple times. By continuing to recall the offerings through festival Torah readings, he adds, it is as if one is actually performing them.[1]

Why is a prophetic portion not read at the morning service on minor holidays?

Although on major holidays a maftir aliya is called to the Torah, on minor holidays—including Purim, Chanuka, and the intermediate days of Passover and Sukkot—a maftir is not awarded. This practice was instituted because most Jews engage in their usual business or professional activities on minor holidays.[2] Since a reading from the Prophets (haftara) always follows a maftir aliya, and since this always prolongs the synagogue service, the Rabbis chose to omit the maftir aliya on minor holidays.

Why are readings conducted from three Torah scrolls at some services?

Three Torot are used during one Torah reading service on only four occasions in the calendar year. One of these is Simchat Torah. On this holiday, first the concluding sidra of Deuteronomy is read from one scroll to complete the yearly cycle. Then Genesis 1:1-2:3 is read from a second scroll to begin the new cycle. This is followed by the reading of a relevant maftir portion (Numbers 29:35-30:1) from a third scroll.

The other three occasions on which three Torah scrolls are used at a single service are when the new Jewish month (Rosh Chodesh) falls on the Sabbath of Chanukah or on Shabbat Shekalim or Shabbat Ha-chodesh, two special Sabbaths. Three scrolls are used on these Sabbaths because the various Torah passages read are not close to each other in the scroll.

In each of the above three cases, the first reading is the regular sidra of the week. This is followed by a reading commemorating Rosh Chodesh from a second scroll, after which a third scroll is used to read a portion relating to the special Sabbath being observed.

Why is the Torah read on Rosh Chodesh?

As far back as biblical times,[3] the New Moon (Rosh Chodesh) was celebrated as a holiday. It was not a full holiday calling for abstention from work, but it was a day on which special sacrifices were offered on the altar, special prayers recited, and a reading from the Torah conducted.

When Rosh Chodesh falls on a weekday, one Torah is

removed from the ark, and four honorees are called to the Torah for readings from the Book of Numbers (28:1-15). A maftir is not called to the Torah and a haftara is not read.[4]

Why is the last verse of the haftara read on Shabbat Rosh Chodesh repeated?

When the New Moon falls on a Sabbath, two Torot are removed from the ark. The regular weekly Sabbath portion is read from the first scroll, and the maftir, consisting of seven verses from the Book of Numbers (28:9-15) that detail the sacrifices offered on Sabbath and Rosh Chodesh, is read from the second scroll.

The haftara reading for Shabbat Rosh Chodesh is taken from the last chapter of Isaiah (66:1-24). In keeping with the rabbinic tradition of not ending Torah and haftara readings on an unpleasant note, verse 23 is repeated after verse 24 (the last verse of the chapter) has been recited.

See Chapter Seven, Maftir and Haftara, for more about this tradition.

Why is a special haftara recited on the Sabbath immediately preceding a Rosh Chodesh that falls on a Sunday?

When Rosh Chodesh falls on a Sunday, instead of reciting the usual haftara on the Sabbath that precedes it, a special prophetic portion, I Samuel 20:18-42, is read. This portion is substituted for the regular haftara because it recalls an important event in the life of David before he became king. It was on a day before Rosh Chodesh that David's friend (and brother-in-law) Jonathan saved his life.

David, fearing that King Saul will make an attempt on his life, plans to absent himself from the New Moon festivities. In the opening verse of the reading, Jonathan tells him, "Tomorrow is the New Moon, and [if you do not make an appearance] you will be missed, for your seat will be empty." This haftara has become known as Machar Chodesh, which means, "Tomorrow is the New Moon."[5]

Why are special Torah selections read on four Sabbaths preceding Passover?

In anticipation of Purim and of the festival of freedom, four Sabbaths prior to Passover were designated as special Sabbaths. Specific Torah readings *(parashiyot)* were assigned to them by the Rabbis of the Talmud, each with a haftara paralleling a theme of the Torah reading.

These four Sabbaths, also referred to as Arba Parashiyot[6], are Shabbat Shekalim, Shabbat Zachor, Shabbat Para, and Shabbat Ha-chodesh. See the questions that follow for an explanation of each of the Sabbaths.

The Sabbath immediately preceding Passover, known as Shabbat Ha-gadol, is not one of the four special Sabbaths.

Why are two scrolls usually removed from the ark on Shabbat Shekalim?

Shabbat Shekalim[7] ("Sabbath of the Coin-census") is usually celebrated on the Sabbath before the New Moon of Adar, but occasionally, depending on the calendar, it is celebrated on Rosh Chodesh proper. (In leap years, when there is an Adar I and an Adar II, this applies to the latter.)

Shabbat Shekalim was introduced in Temple times to remind Jews of their obligation to support the Temple by contributing a half-shekel for its maintenance and for the purchase of sacrificial animals. Although this tax obligation is biblical, it originally had a different purpose. Exodus 30:12 tells how every Israelite twenty years and older—that is, of military age—was to contribute one half-shekel.[8] The coins were counted and thus the number of available warriors was determined.

On Shabbat Shekalim two Torah scrolls are removed from the ark for public reading. The reading from the first Torah is the regular selection for that week, which will be from one of the following four sidrot in the Book of Exodus: Mishpatim, Teruma, Va-yakhel or Pekuday. The maftir portion, Exodus 30:11-16, is read from a second scroll. This portion relates to the census that was taken to determine the number of warriors available.

On Shabbat Shekalim the Sephardic tradition is to read II Kings 11:17-12:17 as the haftara, while the Ashkenazic practice is to read II Kings 12:1-17. This prophetic selection describes the offering brought by the people to celebrate the repairs done on the Temple in Jerusalem.

Why are three Torah scrolls sometimes removed from the ark on Shabbat Shekalim?

In years when the New Moon of Adar falls on a Sabbath, three Torot are removed from the ark.[9] (In leap years this applies to Adar II, not Adar I.) The Torah readings for the first six persons honored with aliyot are from the regular weekly sidra (see the previous answer). A seventh honoree is then called for a reading from a second Torah, which is the portion regularly read on a Shabbat Rosh Chodesh (Numbers 28:9-15). Finally, a third Torah replaces the second Torah on the reading table and the maftir is called. The maftir reading is Exodus 30:11-16, a selection that discusses the contribution of the half-shekel by all males over twenty years of age.

Why was a Torah reading from Deuteronomy 25 assigned to the Sabbath before Purim?

The Sabbath immediately before Purim, which is the second of four special Sabbaths that precede the Passover holiday, is called Shabbat Zachor, "Sabbath of Remembrance." The maftir, which is read from a second scroll on that day, begins with the Hebrew word zachor ("Remember what Amalek did to you when you came out of Egypt").

The Zachor maftir reading, Deuteronomy 25:17-19, is known as Parashat Zachor, "Chapter of Remembrance." It describes how the Amalekites attacked the Children of Israel as they began to make their way through the desert toward the Promised Land after the Exodus from Egypt. Without provocation, the Amalekites attacked the weary Israelites at the rear of the marching column. Because of the savagery of the Amalekites, Israel was commanded by God not to forget this incident but to "blot out the memory of Amalek from under heaven."

The Jewish calendar was arranged so that Shabbat Zachor is observed each year on the Sabbath before Purim, when the story of Haman, the archenemy of Israel, is told. Just as the Israelites were commanded to blot out the memory of Amalek, so has tradition dictated that Jews blot out the memory of Haman.[10] This is expressed symbolically to this day when, in the course of reading the Megilla of Purim (Book of Esther) in the synagogue, the recitation of the name of Haman is greeted by congregants spinning their *groggers* (noisemakers) and stomping their feet, thus in effect "eradicating" the villain's name.

The Torah reading for Shabbat Zachor is the regular sidra of the week which, depending on the calendar, is Tetzaveh from the Book of Exodus or Va-yikra or Tzav from the Book of Leviticus.

The haftara reading for Shabbat Zachor, I Samuel 15:2-34, opens with a reference to the attack of the Amalekites upon the Children of Israel after they left Egypt.[11]

Why is Numbers 19:1-22 read as the maftir for Shabbat Para?

Shabbat Para ("Sabbath of the Cow"), the third of the four special Sabbaths that precede Passover, falls generally (but not always, depending on the calendar) on the first Sabbath after Purim.[12] Shabbat Para always falls one week before Parashat Ha-chodesh.

On this special Sabbath, the regular weekly Sabbath portion is read from the first of two Torot taken from the ark. The reading is from one of the following sidrot, depending on the calendar: Ki Tissa, Va-yakhel/Pekuday, Tzav, or Shemini.

A special maftir selection (Numbers 19:1-22) describing the little-understood ritual of the *Para Aduma*, the Red Heifer, is read from the second Torah. A red cow, free of blemish, is to be sacrificed and then burned on a pyre. Its ashes are to be dissolved in fresh water and sprinkled upon anyone who has come into contact with a corpse, thus purifying the individual. What is paradoxical about this ritual is that the ashes of the sacrificed heifer cleanse the defiled person who is sprinkled with them, but the person who actually touches the mixture and does the sprinkling is himself defiled in the process.

In Temple times, Shabbat Para served as a reminder that Passover was approaching and that Jews must prepare themselves to be in a state of ritual purity (as symbolized by the ritual of the Red Heifer) in order to be eligible to partake of the Passover sacrifice (the Paschal lamb).

The haftara reading for Shabbat Para is Ezekiel 36:16-38, a prophetic portion that emphasizes how essential it is for Israel to learn that when it regains its independence after the Babylonian Exile, it must live by a strict moral code. Sephardim read only Ezekiel 36:16-36 as the haftara.

Why is Exodus 12:1-20 read as the maftir on Shabbat Ha-chodesh?

Shabbat Ha-chodesh ("Sabbath of the New Moon"), also called Parashat Ha-chodesh, is the fourth of the special Sabbaths that precede Passover. It is celebrated on the Sabbath that is closest to the beginning of the new month of Nissan, the first month in the Jewish calendar and the month in which Passover falls.

On Shabbat Ha-chodesh two scrolls are removed from the ark. The regular weekly portion—which, depending on the calendar, is Va-yakhel/Pekuday, Va-yikra, Shemini, or Tazria—is read from the first Torah. Exodus 12:1-20 is read as maftir from the second scroll. This maftir reading emphasizes the significance of the month that will follow (Nissan), when preparations must be made for the observance of Passover.[13]

If the New Moon of Nissan falls on a Sabbath, three Torot are removed from the ark for the public reading. The regular sidra of the week is read from the first Torah, but only six aliyot, instead of seven, are awarded. (The text for the seventh aliya is added to the sixth in this case.)

A second Torah then replaces the first on the reading table, and a seventh honoree is called for the Rosh Chodesh reading, Numbers 28:9-15. Finally, a maftir is called and Exodus 12:1-20, which discusses the basic commandments pertaining to the Passover festival, is read from the third scroll.

The haftara selection for Shabbat Ha-chodesh, Ezekiel 45:16-46:18, touches upon the sacrifices offered on Passover when the Temple was in existence. The Prophet voices the expectation that the Temple will be restored when the Babylonian Exile comes to an end. Sephardim begin the haftara with 45:18 and conclude with 46:15.

Why is a selection from the Book of Malachi read as the haftara for Shabbat Ha-gadol?

Shabbat Ha-gadol means "Great Sabbath." Many reasons have been suggested for the name choice, the most obvious being that this Sabbath immediately precedes the forthcoming great festival of Passover.[14]

A second reason advanced for the choice of name is that the haftara recited on this Sabbath, Malachi 3:4-24, speaks of the "great day" that is to come, a day in which the ninth-century B.C.E. prophet Elijah, renowned as the great healer and peacemaker, will reappear. According to Jewish tradition, Elijah will herald the coming of the Messiah and will usher in an age in which the world will enjoy the blessings of freedom, peace, and love.[15]

Only one Torah is removed from the ark on this significant Sabbath, and the regular weekly portion is read. Depending on the calendar, the sidra may be either Tzav,

Metzora, or Acharay Mot, all from the Book of Leviticus, but the haftara is always from the Book of Malachi.

It is customary in some Jewish communities to recite all or part of the Haggadah during the *Mincha* service on Shabbat Ha-gadol.

Why was a selection from the twelfth chapter of Exodus chosen as the Torah reading for the first day of Passover?

Exodus 12:21-51 was selected as the Torah reading for the first day of Passover because it describes the laws of Passover as communicated by Moses to the elders. Incorporated in the instructions are statements outlining the origin and significance of the festival. Some of this wording has been incorporated into the Seder service.

Five honorees are called to the Torah when the first day of Passover falls on a weekday, and seven when the first day is a Sabbath. Because of the way the calendar is constructed, the first day of Passover can never fall on a Monday, Wednesday, or Friday.

The maftir portion, Numbers 28:19-25, details the sacrifices that were brought in biblical times up until the destruction of the Second Temple. This selection is read from a second Torah on all eight days of the holiday.[16]

The haftara for the first day of Passover is Joshua 5:2-6:1. Sephardic congregations read Joshua 5:2-6:1 and 6:27. These selections were made because they describe the observance of the first Passover after the Children of Israel, under Joshua's leadership, took control of the Promised Land.

Why is the Torah reading for the second day of Passover taken from Chapters 22 and 23 of Leviticus?

Leviticus 22:26-23:44 was chosen as the Torah reading for the second day of Passover because it specifies the compassionate treatment that must be accorded sacrificial animals and then proceeds to describe, holiday by holiday, beginning with Passover, the sacrifices to be brought on each holiday in the Jewish calendar.

The maftir portion for the second day of Passover is the same as for the first day, but the haftara is II Kings 23:1-9 and 21-25, which describes the reign of Josiah, king of Judah (637-608 B.C.E.). Josiah became king at the age of eight, upon the murder of his father, Amon. When he attained maturity, he instituted religious reforms. In the course of repairing the Temple, a Torah scroll was discovered, and on Passover of that year (621 B.C.E.) it was read before the entire people, thus beginning the process of renewing the Covenant with God that had been neglected.

Why are two scrolls used for the Torah readings on the intermediate days of Passover?

On the third, fourth, fifth, and sixth days of Passover (the intermediate days of the holiday), known as Chol Hamoed in Hebrew, the reading for the fourth aliya is taken from the Book of Numbers, Chapter 28. (This applies to the second day in Israel, where only the first day of the festival is a full holiday.) In the Torah scroll this portion is not in close proximity to the portions read for the first three aliyot each day. In order not to detain the congregation while the Torah is rolled from one portion to another, in accordance with established tradition a second Torah is used for the fourth aliya.[17]

Why is Ezekiel's parable of the Valley of Dry Bones read as the haftara on the intermediate Sabbath of Passover?

The Torah reading for this Sabbath, Exodus 33:12-34:26, concludes with verses (34:18-26) that emphasize Israel's duty to remain loyal to God. Israel, it affirms, owes its freedom, its very existence to God's beneficence. The importance of Passover and its observances are stressed as the Torah reading recalls the release of a people from bondage and its revivification.

Chapter 37 of Ezekiel, selected by the Sages as the haftara for this day, presents the parable of the Valley of Dry Bones, in which inert bones come back to life. This theme of resurrection of the dead parallels the theme of revivification that is central to the Torah reading. The Rabbis foresaw the resurrection of the dead as taking place on the Passover festival.

The maftir selection, Numbers 28:19-25, which is read from a second scroll, is the same as that read on all other intermediate days.

As on all Sabbaths, on the intermediate Sabbath of Passover seven honorees plus a maftir are called to the Torah.

On the intermediate Sabbath of Passover, immediately before the regular Torah reading, it is customary in many Ashkenazic congregations to read the Song of Songs (Shir Ha-shirim), one of the Five Megillot. In the Sephardic ritual it is often read before the *Mincha* service. In the Diaspora it is read on the afternoon of the eighth day of Passover, and in Israel it is read on the seventh day of the holiday.[18]

Why was II Samuel 22:1-51 selected as the haftara for the seventh day of Passover?

The Torah reading for the seventh day of Passover, Exodus 13:17-15:26, describes the dramatic rescue of the Israelites who, after fleeing Egypt, find themselves trapped between the pursuing Egyptian army and the Sea of Reeds. Miraculously, the sea splits and the Children of Israel pass through safely. The portion concludes (15:1-26) with Israel giving thanks, joining Moses in singing the *Song at the Sea (Shirat Ha-yam)*, also known simply as *The Song (Shira)*.

On this day five worshipers are called to the Torah, plus the maftir, whose portion is Numbers 28:19-25. If the seventh day of Passover falls on a Sabbath, seven worshipers are called and the same selections are read.

The haftara reading for the seventh day of the holiday, II

Samuel 22:1-51, parallels the Torah reading in that it also
expresses thankfulness to God for having been the instrument of man's salvation. Here, David thanks God for having been saved from the enemies who had been bent upon
his destruction.[19]

Just as the *Song at the Sea* is written in the Torah in a
special format so that the words resemble a wall, so is the
Song of David in the haftara written in an atypical manner.
This form is followed in printed Pentateuchs as well as in
scrolls.

Why was Isaiah, Chapters 10-12, selected as the haftara for the eighth day of Passover?

When the eighth day of Passover falls on a weekday, the
Torah reading is Deuteronomy 15:19-16:17, which begins
with a reminder that the firstborn of one's herd belongs to
God. The requirement that the firstborn be consecrated to
God is first mentioned in Exodus 13, where it is connected
with the events that led to the Exodus from Egypt and the
attainment of freedom for the Children of Israel.

The haftara, Isaiah 10:32-12:6, reflects events that also
led to freedom for the Jews. The Assyrians, under Sen-
nacherib, had advanced to the very walls of Jerusalem and
were about to conquer the city when, in 701 B.C.E., they met
with a crushing defeat just as the Egyptians had centuries
earlier.

Why did Shavuot become associated with the Revelation?

The Bible does not associate the holiday of Shavuot, an
agricultural festival, with the Revelation on Mount Sinai,
but the Rabbis of the Talmud did link the two when they
observed that the dates of both holidays coincide.[20]

The Torah reading of the first day of the festival con-
centrates on the events which involved the Exodus and led
to the appearance of the Children of Israel at the foot of
Mount Sinai, where they received the Torah. This occurred
on the sixth day of the third month, the month of Sivan.

The Torah reading for the second day of Shavuot describes, among other things, the establishment of an agricultural holiday that was celebrated on the fiftieth day after the first day of Passover (Deuteronomy 16:9). After seven weeks (the Hebrew word for weeks is *shavuot*) from the beginning of Passover had passed, on the sixth of Sivan, a festival was held.

As far back as the eleventh century, the association of Shavuot with the Torah was well established. Rashi's biographer describes how boys aged five and six were brought to school to begin their Hebrew studies and how on Shavuot morning a child was dressed in his holiday best, was wrapped in a *talit*, and was led to the synagogue by his father or by a scholar acting as sponsor. In the synagogue the child listened to the reading of the Law; then he was led to the house of the teacher to whom his education was to be entrusted. The teacher took him in his arms and presented him with a tablet on which was written the Hebrew alphabet and some verses from the Bible applicable to the occasion. The tablet was then spread with honey, which the child ate as if to taste the sweetness of the Law of God.[21]

The Torah reading selected by the Rabbis for the first day of Shavuot is Exodus 19:1-20:23. The reading for the second day of the holiday (except in Israel, where the holiday is celebrated for only one day) is Deuteronomy 15:19-16:17. If the second day falls on a Sabbath, Deuteronomy 14:22-16:17 is read. (The first day of Shavuot never falls on a Sabbath.) For both days of the holiday the maftir is Numbers 28:26-31. Five honorees plus maftir are called to the Torah on weekdays, and seven plus maftir are called on Sabbaths.

Why were the Torah and haftara readings for the first day of Shavuot shifted to the second day?

According to the Babylonian Talmud,[22] before Shavuot became a two-day holiday, there was a difference of opinion as to what the Torah and haftara portions should be. According to one view the Torah selection was to be taken from Deuteronomy, Chapter 16, beginning with verse 9, which describes the counting of seven weeks from Passover to Shavuot. The haftara reading was to be from Habakkuk, Chapter 3, which speaks of a future manifestation of God in which God will appear and overthrow Israel's enemy. The Rabbis associated this theophany (visible appearance of God to man) with the Revelation on Mount Sinai.

According to a second view expressed in the Babylonian Talmud, the Torah reading for the one-day Shavuot holiday was to be drawn from Exodus 19, beginning with verse 1, which describes the arrival of the Children of Israel at the foot of Mount Sinai and the preparations made in anticipation of the Revelation. The haftara portion, according to this view, was to be the first chapter of Ezekiel, which describes the "heavenly hosts" who also are supposed to have appeared on Mount Sinai.

When Shavuot became a two-day holiday in communities of the Diaspora, both readings were used. The selections from Exodus and Ezekiel were read on the first day, and the selections from Deuteronomy and Habakkuk were read on the second day. Thus, the Torah reading schedule for congregations of the Diaspora is as follows:

On the first day, the Torah reading is Exodus 19:1-20:23, and the maftir is Numbers 28:26-31. Five aliyot plus a maftir are awarded. The haftara is Ezekiel 1:1-28 and 3:12.

On the second day, the Torah reading is Deuteronomy 15:19-16:17, and the maftir is Numbers 28:26-31. As on the first day, five aliyot plus a maftir are awarded. If the second day falls on a Sabbath, the Torah reading consists of Deuteronomy 14:22-16:17, and Numbers 28:26-31 is read for maftir. Seven *olim* plus a maftir are called. The haftara selection is Habakkuk 2:20-3:19.[23]

In Israel, the Torah and haftara selections are the same as the Diaspora readings of the first day.

Why is the same Torah reading procedure not followed on all fast days?

The fast of Yom Kippur, on the tenth of Tishri, is the only fast day mentioned in the Pentateuch. Although the Fast of Esther is mentioned in the Bible (Esther 4:16), the Rabbis did not consider fasting on that day obligatory.[24]

The four minor fast days are first referred to in Zechariah (8:18-19) as "the fast of the fourth month, the fast of the fifth month, the fast of the seventh month, and the fast of the tenth month." All these are associated with the siege and capture of Jerusalem and the destruction of the First and Second Temples.

The four fast days are:

- In the fourth month of the year: the Fast of the Seventeenth of Tammuz (Shiva Asar B'Tammuz), which marks the breach of the city wall.
- In the fifth month of the year: the Fast of the Ninth of Av (Tisha B'Av), which commemorated the burning of the Temples. This is the most important of the four nonbiblically-ordained fast days and has merited the most attention in Jewish law and tradition.[25]
- In the seventh month of the year: the Fast of Gedalia (Tzom Gedalia), on the third of Tishri, which commemorates the murder of the governor of Jerusalem.
- In the tenth month of the year: the Fast of the Tenth of Tevet (Asara B'Tevet), which marks the commencement of the siege of Jerusalem by the armed forces of Nebuchadnezzar.

On Shiva Asar B'Tammuz, Tzom Gedalia, and Asara B'Tevet, the Torah is read at the morning and afternoon services, at which time three worshipers are called to the Torah. The Torah portions for the morning and afternoon services are the same: Exodus 32:11-14 for the first aliya and readings from 34:1-10 for the second and third aliyot. No haftara is read in the morning, but at the afternoon

(Mincha) service the third person called to the Torah also reads a haftara, namely Isaiah 55:6-56:8.

On Tisha B'Av, as on other minor fast days, three worshippers are called to the Torah at the morning service. However, since Tisha B'Av is the most important of these minor fast days, a special Torah reading, Deuteronomy 4:25-40, is read at the morning *(Shacharit)* service. This portion, which is a renewed warning against the practice of idolatry, was selected by the Rabbis because they believed that idolatry was responsible for the disaster that befell Israel and that Jews must be ever-mindful of its consequences. The third of the honorees called to the Torah at the Tisha B'Av morning service also recites a haftara, Jeremiah 8:13-9:23.

At the Tisha B'Av afternoon service, the Torah and haftara readings recited are the same as those recited on the other minor fast days with the exception that Sephardim read Hosea 14:2-10 and Micah 7:18-20 as the Tisha B'Av afternoon haftara.

Why did the Rabbis choose selections from two different chapters of Exodus for the Torah reading for the minor fast days?

Three honorees are called to the Torah at the morning and afternoon services on minor fast days. On each of these days, the reading for the first honoree consists of three verses, 11-14, from Exodus 32, and the readings for the other two honorees are taken from Exodus 34:1-10.

It is highly unusual to read only three verses from a single chapter in the Torah for one aliya and to then skip to another chapter for the reading of the next aliya. However, the Rabbis felt that these verses in particular express the mood of these mournful days.

The reading for the first aliya, from Exodus 32, describes God's anger at the Children of Israel for building a Golden Calf and worshiping it when they believed Moses would not return from Mount Sinai, where he had been for forty days. God threatens to destroy Israel, and Moses pleads for forgiveness. God accedes and, in the reading that follows from Chapter 34, Moses is instructed to engrave another set of Ten Commandments. The message of the minor fast days reflects the same theme: sin leads to tragedy and expressions of remorse lead to forgiveness.

Why is a haftara recited at the morning service of Tisha B'Av but not at the morning service of other minor fast days?

While the Torah is read at both the morning *(Shacharit)* and the afternoon *(Mincha)* services on all fast days, and three worshipers are called to the Torah on each of these occasions, a morning haftara (Jeremiah 8:13-9:23) is read only on Tisha B'Av.

At the afternoon service of Tisha B'Av, Tzom Gedalia, Shiva Asar B'Tammuz, and Asara B'Tevet the third person called to the Torah recites a haftara. In all cases the prophetic selection is from the Book of Isaiah.

The practical reason for reading a haftara at the morning service of Tisha B'Av but not at the morning service of the other fast days is that people generally work on the other fast days, and it is more likely that they can spare extra time in the afternoon than in the morning. To prolong the morning service by reading a haftara would be a great inconvenience to many congregants. On Tisha B'Av more people abstain from work than on the other fast days, and extending the service does not constitute as much of an inconvenience.

Why were haftara readings assigned to fast days but not to some holidays?

Only holidays and fast days mentioned in the Torah (Pentateuch) were assigned haftara readings by the Rabbis. Chanuka is not mentioned in the Bible, and Purim is mentioned only in the third part of the Bible (the Holy Writings), which is of lesser sanctity than the Torah. Hence on these days no haftara is recited.

An exception was made in the case of the fast days associated with the siege of Jerusalem, which culminated in the destruction of the First and Second Temples on Tisha B'Av. Because the Rabbis considered these days to commemorate traumatic events in Jewish history, they considered it appropriate that haftarot be assigned to Tisha B'Av, Tzom Gedalia, Shiva Asar B'Tammuz, and Asara B'Tevet.

Why do some Jews fast on Mondays and Thursdays, days on which the Torah is read?

The Hebrew word for "fast day" or "fasting" is *taanit,* a five-letter word which has as its core the letters *a'yin, nun, yod,* spelling *ani,* which literally means "poor." In early centuries mystics who were in the habit of dissecting words and looking for hidden meanings found it significant that *ani* was at the center of *taanit.* They therefore decided to empathize with the poor by fasting. They selected for the days of their abstinence Mondays and Thursdays, the weekdays on which the Torah is read and which were therefore special.[26]

Some mystics took it upon themselves to start these days of abstinence at the end of either Nissan or Tishri, months during which Passover and Sukkot are celebrated, for it is during these months that much rejoicing and food consumption takes place. Their personal fasts usually began on Mondays and ended on Mondays, extending for weeks or months. Because of this, such fasts have come to be known by the Hebrew acronym *behav* or *behab,* standing for the three letters *bet, hay, bet,* which in numerical terms is two, five, two, the equivalent of Monday, Thursday, Monday.

Why are selections from Jeremiah and Isaiah read on the three Sabbaths before Tisha B'Av?

The twenty-one-day period between the fast days of

Shiva Asar B'Tammuz (Seventeenth of Tammuz) and Tisha B'Av (Ninth of Av) is referred to in the *Code of Jewish Law* by the Aramaic-Hebrew terms *Telat De-puranuta* and *Gimmel (Shelosha) De-puranuta,* meaning "Three Weeks of Rebuke" and "Three Weeks of Disaster."[27] The haftarot read on each of these three Sabbaths are selected from the writings of Jeremiah and Isaiah, whose prophecies rebuke the Jews of Palestine, emphasizing that their misfortune is of their own making. Jeremiah (1:1-2:3; 2:4-28; 3:4) and Isaiah (1:1-27) remind their fellow Jews that Jerusalem was sacked, the Temple destroyed, and the land laid waste because of their moral folly.

The Torah portions for the Three Weeks are Pinchas, Matot/Masay, and Devarim. Occasionally, depending on the calendar, the sidrot are Matot, Masay, and Devarim.

Why was Chapter 21 of Genesis selected as the Torah reading for the first day of Rosh Hashana?

The basic theme expressed in Genesis 21:1-34, the Torah reading for the first day of Rosh Hashana, is that when man is loyal to God, God remembers. He does not forsake man. In this portion, God remembers Sarah and keeps His promise to bless her with a child. According to tradition,[28] it was on Rosh Hashana that this event occurred, and because of this association, Rosh Hashana was deemed an appropriate time to read this Torah selection.

The theme of God remembering man has been incorporated into the High Holiday liturgy as a whole. It is the part of the *Musaf* service known as *Zichronot.*

Why is the haftara for the first day of Rosh Hashana taken from the Book of Samuel?

The theme of God's remembrance, the essence of the Torah reading for the first day of Rosh Hashana, is further explored in the haftara portion of the day. In the prophetic

selection, I Samuel 1-2:10, the barren Hannah is promised
that she would mother a child, just as Sarah had been
promised in the Torah reading. As Sarah's promise is fulfilled, so is Hannah's promise fulfilled, and Hannah's grate-
fulness is expressed in a stirring song of praise to God. Jewish tradition has it that it was on Rosh Hashana that Hannah
gave birth.[29]

Why was Numbers 29:1-6 selected as the maftir reading for the first and second days of Rosh Hashana?

In biblical times, before Rosh Hashana became a two-
day holiday, the Torah reading consisted of the first six
verses from Chapter 29 of the Book of Numbers. The selection began, "In the seventh month, on the first day of the
month, you shall observe a day of holy convocation . . ."[30]

When, during the talmudic period, Rosh Hashana became a two-day holiday and Torah readings from Genesis
replaced the reading from the Book of Numbers (29:1-6),
the latter was retained as the maftir reading for both the
first and the second day of the holiday.[31] The maftir reading
appropriately emphasizes the important features of Rosh
Hashanah, particularly the law calling for the sounding of
the *shofar*.

Why was the Torah reading changed from Leviticus to Genesis when Rosh Hashana became a two-day holiday?

The Torah portions to be read on holidays and other
special occasions are listed in the Mishna.[32] The portion
assigned to Rosh Hashana in this third-century C.E. Palestinian source was Leviticus 23, beginning with verse 23,
where the character of the holiday is described. In another
early rabbinic source,[33] Genesis 21 is listed as the preferred
Rosh Hashana Torah reading of some Rabbis while others
chose Numbers 29, which also describes the nature of the
holiday and the manner of its observance.

When the Rabbis in the academies of Babylonia declared that because of the uncertainty of the calendar (it was not always possible to fix precisely when the New Moon of Tishri had appeared and the month had actually begun), Rosh Hashana should be celebrated as a two-day holiday,[34] they ruled that "since we [in the Diaspora] now observe Rosh Hashana for two days," Chapter 21 of Genesis should be read on the first day, and Chapter 22 on the second day.

As a rule, Reform Jews follow the biblical law and do not observe the second day of Jewish holidays, which are referred to as Yom Tov Sheni Shel Galuyot, "the second day of holidays of the Diaspora." In recent years, however, some Reform congregations have reinstituted the practice of celebrating Rosh Hashana for two days.

Why was Genesis 22 selected as the Torah reading for the second day of Rosh Hashana?

Rosh Hashana in Jewish tradition has been a time of testing and proving one's loyalty to God.

This concept dating back to antiquity has its roots in the twenty-second chapter of Genesis, which tells the story of the *Akeda*, "Binding [of Isaac]." In this episode Abraham's faith in God is tested. He proves his loyalty by binding his beloved son Isaac and then placing him on the altar, thereby showing a willingness to offer the child as a sacrifice. The command is rescinded at the last moment, but Abraham has already proved his loyalty to God. A ram is found by Abraham and is offered as a substitute sacrifice.

Tradition has dictated that on Rosh Hashana we blow the ram's horn as a reminder of the animal that Abraham found and sacrificed as a substitute for Isaac.[35]

Why is the haftara reading for the second day of Rosh Hashana taken from the Book of Jeremiah?

Just as the Torah reading for the second day of Rosh

Hashana (Genesis 22), which describes the *Akeda* (Abraham's binding of Isaac), proves that there is a reward in manifesting one's loyalty to God (the restoration to Abraham of his beloved son), so does the haftara selection, Jeremiah 31:2-20, propose that there is a reward for those who have faith in God. Through his prophet, God assures the Jewish people that once they have returned to Him after sincere repentance, He will restore their Temple that had been destroyed in 586 B.C.E. and He will reinstate the exiled Jews, now in Babylonia, to their homeland.

Why were selections from Hosea, Micah, and Joel chosen as the prophetic portions for Shabbat Shuva?

Shabbat Shuva, meaning "Sabbath of Return," is the name given to the Sabbath that falls between Rosh Hashana and Yom Kippur. Since the liturgical theme of the solemn ten-day period between the New Year and the Day of Atonement is repentance, it is only natural that the Rabbis would select as the haftara for Shabbat Shuva portions of the prophets that speak to this subject. Thus, for this Sabbath, which is also known as the Sabbath of Repentance (Shabbat Teshuva), special readings from Hosea (14:2-10), Micah (7:18-20), and Joel (2:15-27) were chosen. (Sephardim read only the portions from Hosea and Micah.)

These particular selections were made because the prophecies of these three eighth-century B.C.E. prophets address the repentance theme. Hosea foresees a terrible fate for Israel owing to its having forsaken God. Micah, however, holds out hope and believes that Israel may yet be saved because God forgives sinners. Joel adds the assurance that if the Israelites manifest a sincere display of contrition, God will surely pardon them.

Since the first verse of the haftara begins with the Hebrew word *shuva*, meaning "return [O Israel]," the Sabbath is commonly called Shabbat Shuva.

The sidra read on Shabbat Shuva is either Va-yaylech or Ha'azinu, depending on the calendar.

Why is the Torah reading for the morning of Yom Kippur taken from the Book of Leviticus?

Leviticus 16:1-34, the morning Torah reading for the Day of Atonement, is devoted to the Yom Kippur duties of the High Priest in Temple times. The selection describes how the High Priest offered sacrifices and performed rites of atonement, imploring God to forgive him and the whole family of Israel for their misdeeds.

After six aliyot are awarded, the maftir is called. The maftir reading, Numbers 29:7-11, recalls once again the holiday sacrifices that were brought on Yom Kippur in ancient times. The selection goes on to caution that the tenth day of the seventh month (Tishri) is to be observed as a fast day, a day on which one must cleanse oneself of sin.

Why does the biblical term *shabbat shabbaton*, found in the Yom Kippur morning Torah reading, most often refer to the Sabbath in general?

Most Jews regard Yom Kippur as the holiest day in the Jewish calendar. They support their view by pointing to the fact that Leviticus 16:31, read on Yom Kippur morning, contains the term *shabbat shabbaton*, which translates literally as "sabbath of sabbaths." This, they say, is proof that Yom Kippur is the holiest day in the Jewish calendar. However, *shabbat shabbaton* is more accurately translated as "a solemn sabbath" or "a sabbath of complete rest."

Of the seven times that the term *shabbat shabbaton* is mentioned in the Torah, only twice (Leviticus 16:31 and 23:32) does it actually refer to Yom Kippur, whereas three times (Exodus 31:15 and 35:2; Leviticus 23:3) it refers to the weekly Sabbath itself.[36]

Actually, in Jewish law the penalty for violating the Sabbath is much more severe than for violating Yom Kippur. Punishment for Sabbath violators is death whereas the penalty for violating Yom Kippur is excommunication.

Why do Reform congregations read a Torah selection from the Book of Deuteronomy on Yom Kippur morning?

Reform leaders believe that recalling the rituals performed by the High Priest in ancient times is of little significance to modern Jews. Rather than reading about sacrificial rites in Leviticus 16, as is done in traditional synagogues, they consider it more befitting the mood of Yom Kippur to read selections from Chapters 29 and 30 of the Book of Deuteronomy. In these chapters Moses renders his farewell address to the Children of Israel and emphasizes a central motif of Judaism, namely that if Israel is loyal to God, God will be loyal to Israel. The Covenant established between them in the time of Abraham will never be abandoned.

Why was the haftara for Yom Kippur morning selected from the Book of Isaiah?

Just as the Yom Kippur morning Torah reading (Leviticus 16:1-34) and the maftir portion (Numbers 29:7-11) emphasize that the tenth day of Tishri is to be observed as a day of fasting and self-denial, so does the haftara reading, Isaiah 57:14-58:14, emphasize the value of fasting provided that it does not become a superficial ritual.

Isaiah searches for deeper meaning as he examines the Torah commandment. He concludes that the Torah does not propose to teach that observing the fasting ritual is sufficient in itself. Isaiah affirms instead that the ritual must be a means to an end. God delights in the fasts of man when they are expressions of his loyalty to God. But fasting has little meaning if it does not lead man to a higher ethical standard. To be a meaningful act, says Isaiah (Chapter 58), fasting must lead to

- loosening the fetters of wickedness;
- undoing the bands of oppression;
- opening the doors of freedom to those in bondage;
- sharing bread with the destitute;

- sharing one's home with the homeless;
- clothing the naked.

Why does the Torah reading on Yom Kippur afternoon concern itself with sexual offenses?

The Torah reading assigned to the *Mincha* service on Yom Kippur is Chapter 18 of the Book of Leviticus. This selection, which discusses family morality, concerns itself especially with preserving the sacred character of the institution of marriage. Adultery and incest are strongly condemned.

The choice of this particular portion for the *Mincha* Torah reading on Yom Kippur day is directly related to activities that took place on Yom Kippur afternoon in Temple times. After the High Priest had completed his performance of the elaborate annual ritual, which culminated in his entry into the Holy of Holies, the assembled masses carried on gala celebrations which led to sexual promiscuity. Concerned with this behavior, the Rabbis introduced the reading of Chapter 18 of Leviticus, which they hoped would serve to remind Israel that their impulses must be controlled if Israel's ideals of purity and holiness are to be preserved.

In Reform synagogues Leviticus 19, the theme of which is holiness, is read instead of Leviticus 18.

Why is maftir Yona read on Yom Kippur?

Maftir Yona, which is the name given the haftara read at the *Mincha* service on Yom Kippur afternoon, consists of the complete Book of Jonah. This prophetic selection, consisting of four chapters, was chosen because of its universal messages that man must not shun his responsibilities and that man can correct the course of his life.

The prophet Jonah refuses to obey God's command to go to Nineveh and tell its inhabitants of their wickedness and of the calamity about to befall them. Jonah fears that if he delivers God's message, the inhabitants of Nineveh might repent and his own prophecy would go unfulfilled. In the end, however, Jonah is convinced that he must obey the will of God. He delivers the message, and the city abandons its evil ways and is saved. This leaves Jonah very upset, and he is reprimanded by God for not being selfless enough in his concern for human life.

So that the ending of the haftara will be a positive one, three verses from the Book of Micah (7:18-20) were appended.

Why is a Kohayn or a Levi permitted to recite maftir Yona?

Ordinarily, on any Sabbath or holiday a Kohayn or Levi may be called as maftir and recite the haftara. However, when only three aliyot are assigned, as on Yom Kippur afternoon, the third aliya must be offered to a Yisrael to complete the triad of Kohayn, Levi, and Yisrael. In practice, however, most authorities allow a Kohayn or Levi to read from the Book of Jonah provided that the Torah blessings and the haftara blessings are recited by a Yisrael.

Why is the haftara for the first day of Sukkot taken from the Book of Zechariah?

The Torah reading for the first day of Sukkot, Leviticus 22:26-23:44, discusses when and how holiday sacrifices are to be offered. Five persons are called to the Torah, unless the first day of the holiday falls on a Sabbath, in which case seven aliyot are awarded. Like the Torah reading from Leviticus, the maftir portion, Numbers 29:12-16, discusses the sacrifices to be offered on the holiday.

Zechariah 14:1-21 was selected as the haftara for the first day of Sukkot because it addresses itself to the restoration of the Temple and the sacrificial system, which had been neglected during the Babylonian Exile.

The prophet Zechariah was among the returnees from the Babylonian Exile in 537 B.C.E. when King Cyrus of Persia, the power that dominated the region, permitted the

Jews to return to Jerusalem to rebuild the Temple that had been destroyed in 586 B.C.E. In the prophetic portion, Zechariah foresees God's punishment being visited upon the heathen nations that had attacked and destroyed Jerusalem and the Temple. He further foresees the heathen nations turning to the worship of the God of Israel and all nations making an annual pilgrimage to Jerusalem, the religious center of the world, to observe the festival of Sukkot.

Why is the haftara for the second day of Sukkot taken from the First Book of Kings?

The Torah reading for the second day of Sukkot is the same as that for the first day of the holiday, namely Leviticus 22:26-23:44.

Five persons are called to the Torah. (The second day never falls on a Sabbath.) The maftir portion, as on the first day, is Numbers 29:12-16, which discusses the sacrifices to be offered on the holiday.

The haftara of the day, First Kings 8:2-21, was selected because it is devoted to a description of the dedication ceremonies that were held when Solomon's Temple was consecrated beginning on the eighth day of the seventh month (the month then called Etanim but now known as Tishri)[37] and extending over a fourteen-day period, the last seven of which coincided with the seven days of Sukkot.

The second day of Sukkot is not observed by Israelis or by Reform Jews.

Why is only one Torah scroll used for the Torah reading during the intermediate days of Sukkot, whereas two are used during the intermediate days of Passover?

On the intermediate days of Sukkot, four persons are called to the Torah, and since the Torah reading for all honorees is from the same chapter in the Book of Numbers, there is no need to use more than one scroll. This contrasts with the intermediate days of Passover, when two scrolls are used, because on that holiday the reading for the fourth aliya is not in close proximity to the portions read for the other three aliyot.

The portions read when the intermediate days of Sukkot fall on weekdays are all taken from Numbers 29, the sidra Pinchas.[38]

Why were portions of Chapters 38 and 39 of Ezekiel selected as the haftara for the intermediate Sabbath of Sukkot?

The Torah reading for the Sabbath of Chol Ha-moed Sukkot, Exodus 33:12-34:26, describes the ascent of Moses to Mount Sinai after the incident of the Golden Calf. Moses engraves a second set of stone tablets and is reassured by God that the Covenant between God and Israel has been renewed. Israel will prevail over its enemies as long as it remains loyal to God.[39]

Seven worshipers plus a maftir are called to the Torah. The maftir reading, Numbers 29:17-31, enumerates the sacrifices offered on this Sabbath. The exact verses read depend on which day of Sukkot the Sabbath of Chol Ha-moed happens to fall. If it falls on the third day of Sukkot, the maftir is Numbers 29:17-22; if on the fourth day of Sukkot, Numbers 29:20-25; if on the fifth, Numbers 29:23-28; and if on the sixth, Numbers 29:26-31.

The concept of a renewal of the Covenant between God and Israel mentioned in the Torah reading is repeated in the haftara portion, Ezekiel 38:18-39:16. The prophet foretells the restoration of Israel and its primacy among the nations by describing a great war between the powers of good and evil that will be fought prior to the coming of the Messiah. The war, says Ezekiel, will take place during the Sukkot holiday. The invasion of Israel by enemies from the North, led by the apocalyptic figure Gog, king of Magog, will be repulsed. Israel will emerge victorious, and all nations will come to recognize that God has kept His covenant with the seed of Abraham.[40]

Why was First Kings 8:54-66 selected as the haftara reading for Shemini Atzeret?

The Torah reading for Shemini Atzeret ("Eighth Day of Assembly"), Deuteronomy 14:22-16:17, emphasizes that all Israelites are required to set aside one-tenth of their annual harvest and bring it to the Sanctuary, where it is to be consumed.[41] The maftir, Numbers 29:35-30:1, discusses the sacrifices that are to be offered on this day.

First Kings 8:54-66, the haftara for this day, continues with the theme of the haftara read on the second day of Sukkot. Here, King Solomon concludes the festivities surrounding the dedication of the Temple with a prayer of thanksgiving and an offering of thousands of sacrifices. This prophetic portion was selected for Shemini Atzeret because this eighth day after the beginning of Sukkot coincides with the conclusion of the Temple dedication ceremonies when, after seven days of rejoicing, King Solomon sends the people back to their homes.[42]

In Israel the haftara read for Shemini Atzeret is Joshua 1:1-18.

Why do synagogues in Israel observe Simchat Torah on Shemini Atzeret?

Simchat Torah ("Rejoicing of the Law") is a Diaspora holiday. It is not mentioned in the Bible, and it has never been observed as a separate holiday either in the Palestine of ancient times or in the Israel of today. Instead, the holiday was integrated into the Shemini Atzeret observance.

Simchat Torah was first introduced in Babylonia during the period of the Jewish exile (after 586 B.C.E.). In Babylonia it had become customary to complete the reading of the Torah in one year (annual cycle) and to celebrate the occasion with pomp and ceremony. After the exile, adoption of the annual cycle with the accompanying day of celebration spread to the rest of the Diaspora, and by the sixteenth century it had been widely adopted.

The Jews of Palestine had long followed the triennial system of reading the Torah—that is, of reading the entire Torah over a three-year period. A Simchat Torah–type celebration could therefore not be held every year. In time, the Jews of Palestine adopted some of the Simchat Torah rituals and customs current in the Diaspora and incorporated them into their Shemini Atzeret holiday. As a result, today *hakafot* are held in Israeli synagogues on Shemini Atzeret, and the Torah reading on that day is conducted from three Torot.[43]

Why are children called to the Torah on Simchat Torah?

Minors are not permitted to be called to the Torah for any aliya except for maftir, which is not one of the mandated aliyot. However, an exception is made on Simchat Torah, when everyone is expected to rejoice in the Torah and participate in its celebration.

The custom that prevails in most congregations is to call up "all the boys" *(kol ha-ne'arim)* for the next-to-last aliya. An adult, generally the rabbi or a congregational notable, leads the children. In non-Orthodox synagogues girls are included. A *talit* is held up over the heads of all the children, and the Torah blessings are recited in unison before and after the Torah reading. In some congregations the adult recites the blessings and the children repeat them. This tradition gives symbolic expression to the importance of the link between generations and concretizes the idea that Jewish survival depends upon the willingness of the younger generation to carry on in the footsteps of the older one.

Why is the reading of the Torah permitted on the evening of Simchat Torah?

The reading of the Torah at night was prohibited by the Rabbis because Jewish law requires that a *baal koray* see each word clearly as he reads it.[44] An exception, however, was made on Simchat Torah, when it became customary to celebrate the completion of the annual Torah reading cycle. All Torot were removed from the ark on Simchat Torah night (and again the next morning) and were paraded in procession around the synagogue seven times.[45]

It was deemed inappropriate simply to replace all of the scrolls in the ark after the procession without acknowledging their content. Therefore, one Torah was withheld so that a short selection might be read from the last sidra (Ve-zot Ha-beracha) of the Pentateuch, beginning with Deuteronomy 33:1. Three persons are honored with aliyot on this occasion.

Why are three different Torah scrolls used for readings on Simchat Torah?

In celebration of the completion of the annual reading of the Torah, three scrolls are read from on Simchat Torah.

Regardless of whether the holiday falls on a weekday or a Sabbath, the last sidra in the Pentateuch, Ve-zot Ha-beracha (Deuteronomy 33:1-34:12), is read from the first of the three scrolls that have been removed from the ark. Although this is one of the shortest sidrot in the Pentateuch, it is customary for every member of the congregation to be called up for an aliya, even though this requires the rereading of the sidra several times.[46] To save time, many congregations call up members in groups. For example, all Kohanim receive the first aliya, all Leviim the second aliya, and so on. The last aliya from Deuteronomy is awarded to a *Chatan Torah*, a "Bridegroom of the Torah." (See next question.)

A second Torah then replaces the first on the reading table, and a worshiper is called for a reading from the Book of Genesis (Bereshit). Generally, Genesis 1:1 to 2:3 is read for the recipient of this honor, known as *Chatan Bereshit*, "Bridegroom of Genesis." (See later question.)

The third Torah scroll then replaces the second on the reading table, and the maftir is called up. The Torah reading for the maftir is Numbers 29:35-30:1, the same maftir portion that is read on the previous day, Shemini Atzeret.[47]

Why is a *Chatan Torah* honored on Simchat Torah?

One of the high honors on Simchat Torah is bestowed upon the *Chatan Torah*, the "Bridegroom of the Torah." This honor is generally reserved for a scholar, for he represents the community of Israel which is forever "wedded" to the Torah. The *Chatan Torah* is summoned to the pulpit by the *baal koray*, who recites a special poem *(piyyut)* in his behalf. In some congregations the honoree is escorted to the pulpit by the rabbi, cantor, and other synagogue officials.

For the *Chatan Torah* the last portion of the last sidra (*Ve-zot Ha-beracha*, Deuteronomy 33:27 to 34:12) is read. As the *baal koray* completes the reading with the recitation of the last verse in the Torah (Deuteronomy 34:12), the congregation rises and calls out *Chazak, chazak, ve-nit-chazek*, "Be strong, be strong, and let us be strengthened."

Why is a *Chatan Bereshit* honored on Simchat Torah?

So that the cycle of Torah study is never interrupted, immediately after the last verse of Deuteronomy is read for the *Chatan Torah* a second Torah scroll replaces the first on the reading table, and it is opened to the very beginning of the Book of Genesis (Bereshit).[48] An honoree is then called to the Torah as *Chatan Bereshit*, the "Bridegroom of Genesis." This is a signal honor generally awarded to an outstanding member of the congregation.

As in the case of the *Chatan Torah*, a special poem *(piyyut)* is recited in honor of the *Chatan Bereshit* as he is summoned to the pulpit. In many congregations he is escorted by an honor guard consisting of the rabbi, cantor, and other dignitaries.

The Torah portion read for the *Chatan Bereshit* is Genesis 1:1-2:3.

Why is the haftara reading for Simchat Torah taken from the Book of Joshua?

The haftara reading for Simchat Torah is the first chapter of the Book of Joshua.[49] The day's Torah reading (the last sidra of Deuteronomy) ended with a description of the death of Moses and his replacement as leader by Joshua, the son of Nun. The prophetic portion continues to tell the story of the Jewish people following the death of Moses, as they prepare for their conquest of the Promised Land. By selecting this reading, the Rabbis stress that although the great leader Moses is dead, his message must be carried on.

Why do some people crisscross their hands when they perform *hagbaha* on Simchat Torah?

The portion read from the second scroll on Simchat Torah is from the beginning of the Book of Genesis (1:1-2:3). Since at this point the weight of the Torah is all on the left side, it is difficult for the majority of people (who are right-handed) to raise the scroll. It has therefore become customary for a right-handed person who is called to raise the second scroll to crisscross his hands so that when lifting the heavy (left) roller, he is actually doing so with the strength of his right side. As the Torah is raised, the hands are uncrossed so that the heavy roller is now on the right side of the *magbi'a* and the writing in the Torah scroll is exposed to the congregation. In some congregations, persons adept at this procedure are usually called to do the *hagbaha* during the Sabbaths of October and November when the readings are from the Book of Genesis.

Why do the Torah portions read during the Chanuka festival always include excerpts from Chapter 7 of the Book of Numbers?

Chapter Seven of the Book of Numbers describes the

gifts presented by the leaders of each of the twelve tribes when the Tabernacle altar was dedicated. This chapter was selected as appropriate for Chanuka because it parallels the restoration and rededication of the Temple in 165 B.C.E., after the victory of the Maccabees over the Syrian-Greeks.

Three aliyot are awarded on each weekday of Chanuka, except those that coincide with the New Moon (Rosh Chodesh). There is no haftara reading.

The Torah reading sequence is as follows:[50]

First day	Numbers 7:1-17
Second day	Numbers 7:18-29
Third day	Numbers 7:24-35
Fourth day	Numbers 7:30-41
Fifth day	Numbers 7:36-47
Sixth day	Numbers 7:42-53
Seventh day	Numbers 7:48-59
Eighth day	Numbers 7:54-8:4[51]

When any of the above days falls either on the New Moon or on a Sabbath, additional Torah portions are read. On the Sabbath, the regular sidra is first read. On Rosh Chodesh, the regular selection for the New Moon precedes the Chanuka reading. (See next question.)

Why are there times during Chanuka when the Torah is read from two scrolls?

Chanuka is always celebrated for eight days, beginning with the twenty-fifth day of the Hebrew month Kislev, which usually falls in December. The sixth day of Chanuka always coincides with the New Moon of Tevet (the month following Kislev). Depending on the calendar, the New Moon of Tevet may be celebrated for two days, both on the sixth and on the seventh day of Chanuka.

On weekdays, when the New Moon coincides with Chanuka, two Torot are removed from the ark for public readings and four persons are called to the Torah. The reading for the first three aliyot is Numbers 28:1-15, which is the regular weekday New Moon reading, and the reading for the fourth aliya is Numbers 7:42-53 on the sixth day of Chanuka and Numbers 7:48-59 on the seventh day of Chanuka. The readings for the fourth aliya are conducted from a second scroll.

On the Sabbath of Chanuka, two Torah scrolls are also removed from the ark, the reading from the first being the regular Sabbath sidra and the reading from the second scroll (the maftir portion) consisting of the verses from Numbers 7 that are applicable to that day of Chanuka.

In years when the first day of Chanuka is a Sabbath, the last day will also be a Sabbath. The same Sabbath Torah reading procedure mentioned above is followed.

In all cases, the second scroll is used so as to avoid keeping the congregation waiting while a single scroll would have to be rolled from one place in the Torah to the next.

Why in some years are readings during Chanuka conducted from three Torah scrolls?

When the New Moon of Tevet falls on a Sabbath during Chanuka, three Torah scrolls are removed from the ark for a public reading from each.[52] Six persons are called up for the reading from the first Torah, which consists of the regular Sabbath portion for that week. For the seventh aliya a portion is read from the second Torah, which is the selection normally read on the Sabbath of Rosh Chodesh (Numbers 28:9-15). The third Torah is used for the maftir reading, Numbers 7:42-53, the selection always read on the sixth day of the Chanuka holiday. (When Rosh Chodesh Tevet falls on a Sabbath during Chanuka, it always coincides with the sixth day of Chanuka.)

The haftara reading for this Sabbath is Isaiah 66:1-24, the last chapter of Isaiah. This is the prophetic portion read whenever Rosh Chodesh falls on a Sabbath.

Why are portions from Zechariah and from the First Book of Kings considered appropriate selections for the Sabbaths of Chanuka?

When one Sabbath falls during Chanuka, the prophetic portion is Zechariah 2:14-4:7. Here, the Jews who had been exiled to Babylonia after the destruction of the First Temple are reassured that the Temple will be rebuilt and the glory of Israel restored. Speaking in the name of God, the prophet promises them that theirs will be a spiritual victory, accomplished "not by might, nor by power, but by My spirit." This parallels the view that the Chanuka victory, accomplished through God's intervention, was a spiritual as much as a military victory.

When there is a second Sabbath of Chanuka, the prophetic selection is First Kings 7:40-50. Chanuka is the festival of the rededication of the Temple, and this portion recalls the valuable appurtenances that added to the grandeur of the magnificent Temple that had been built by King Solomon.

Why is Isaiah 55:6-56:8 read on the day preceding Purim?

On the thirteenth of Adar, the day before Purim, Queen Esther of ancient Persia engaged in a daring act that could have cost the queen her life. Uninvited, she approached King Ahasueros to plead for her people, who were threatened with annihilation by Haman, the prime minister.

Before embarking on her mission, Esther begged all the Jews in the capital city, Shushan, to fast for her safety and the success of her venture. In commemoration of that fast, which has come to be known as the Fast of Esther, Taanit Esther (actually it is the fast in *behalf* of Esther), Jews to this day fast from dawn to nightfall on the day before Purim.

The regular minor fast day Torah portion, Exodus 32:11-14 and 34:1-10, is read at the morning and afternoon service. Three aliyot are awarded, but only at the afternoon

Mincha service does the third honoree also recite a haftara. The selection is Isaiah 55:6-56:8, the regular prophetic reading for every minor fast day.

Why are only three worshipers called to the Torah on Purim?

The Purim holiday, which is described in the Book of Esther (part of the Holy Writings), never achieved the status of the biblical holidays, those ordained in the Pentateuch. This minor holiday always falls on a weekday and, as with other minor holidays celebrated on weekdays, at the morning service three aliyot are awarded. A maftir is not called up, nor is a haftara read.

The Torah reading for Purim, Exodus 17:8-16, is sometimes referred to as *Parashat Amalek*, the Chapter of Amalek. This portion describes the battle in the desert between the Israelites and the Amalekites after the Exodus from Egypt.

In Jewish tradition Amalek represents Israel's archenemy. The Book of Deuteronomy (25:18) explains how Amalek attacked Israel from the rear and assaulted the weary and feeble. In the time of Mordecai and Esther, this hatred of Amalek was transferred to Haman, who not only plotted to annihilate the Jewish people for no valid reason but also was regarded in Jewish tradition as a descendant of Agag, the Amalekite king.[53]

Why does the Torah reading for Purim consist of only nine verses, whereas the minimum for all other Torah readings is ten?

The Rabbis made an exception in the case of the Torah reading for Purim and permitted nine verses rather than the required ten to be read for all three aliyot. In nine verses the Purim Torah portion (Exodus 17:8-16) fully describes the battle of the Israelites with the Amalekites. The addition of an extra verse, the Rabbis felt, would have interfered with the flow of the story.[54]

Notes to
GENERAL INTRODUCTION
Pages 1 to 15

1. Exodus Rabba 29:9.
2. See Exodus Rabba 5:9 and 28:6. See also Shabbat 88a.
3. Sifri, Ve-zot Ha-beracha, Piska 343.
4. See the statement of Rabbi Avdimi quoted in Shabbat 88a and Avoda Zara 2b.
5. See Leviticus Rabba 23 and Song of Songs Rabba 2.
6. Avot 3:13.
7. See Alfred J. Kolatch's *Second Jewish Book of Why*, pp. 260-261, 366.
8. For a concise review of the various books that constitute the Midrash, see Meyer Waxman's *History of Jewish Literature*, Volume I, pp. 136ff.
9. Bava Metzia 86b.
10. Ibid.
11. See the Shlomo Pines edition of *Guide of the Perplexed* II:42.
12. See the essay of Louis Jacobs in his *Jewish Ethics, Philosophy, and Mysticism*, pp. 121ff. and 144ff., for more on this subject.
13. Mikra Ki-pheshuto, Leviticus 19:19.
14. Yerushalmi Nedarim 9:4.
15. See Nehama Leibowitz's *Studies in the Bible*, Leviticus, Kedoshim 6.
16. Shabbat 31a.
17. Zohar, Bereshit 36. See also *The Wisdom in the Hebrew Alphabet*, pp. 175-76, for more on the number seventy as it applies to the Torah.

Notes to Chapter 1
THE TORAH AND ITS ROOTS
Pages 17 to 39

1. Zevachim 116a.
2. Midrash Tanchuma, Bereshit.
3. Yet, on the other hand, Maimonides says that if anyone denies that even one verse or word of the Torah is not from God, he is an atheist (*kofer*). See *Mishneh Torah*, Hilchot Teshuva 3:7, 8. See also the Shlomo Pines edition of *Guide of the Perplexed*, Volume II, chapter 33.
4. Hirsch's views may be gleaned from his volume *Judaism Eternal*, pp. 88ff. See also Mordecai Kaplan's evaluation of Hirsch in *The Greater Judaism in the Making*, pp. 320-21.
5. Sukka 5a.
6. Because of a stong affinity for the number three, much of Jewish law and lore is dominated by that number. In connection with the writing and reading of a Torah scroll, the number three stands out prominently.

   See Louis Ginzberg's *Legends of the Jews* III:77-80 and VI:29. See also Tanchuma, Yitro 10, Ecclesiastes Rabba 3:2, and Pesikta d'Rav Kahana, Piska 12.

   Other areas of Jewish law, history, and tradition in which the preeminence of the number three is seen are:

   a) Adam had three sons: Cain, Abel, and Seth.
   b) Noah had three sons: Shem, Cham (Ham), and Yafet.
   c) Israel has three patriarchs: Abraham, Isaac, and Jacob.
   d) Three angels, appearing as men, came to visit Abraham (Genesis 18:2).
   e) The priestly benediction is noted for its threefold repetition of God's name (Numbers 6:24-26).
   f) Daniel kneeled and prayed three times a day (Daniel 6:11).
   g) The Sanctuary (and later the Temple) was divided into three sections: the open court where the public assembled, the holy place where the altar stood and sacrifices were offered, and the Holy of Holies where the Ten Commandment tablets were kept (Exodus 26:33; 27:9).
   h) Josephus points out that the three divisions of the Tabernacle correspond to the three realms of the world: the first two are earth and sea, which belong to mankind; and the third is the heavens, which belong to God alone (*Antiquities* III 7:7).
   i) On Yom Kippur, the High Priest prostrated himself three times as he prayed for forgiveness for the three basic elements within the Jewish community: family, Priesthood, and the whole House of Israel.
   j) On both sides of the river Jordan were established three

cities of refuge to which one who had unintentionally committed a murder might flee and find safe harbor (Numbers 35:25; Deuteronomy 19:7-10).

k) Three harvest festivals are mandated in the Bible: Pesach, Shavuot, and Sukkot (Deuteronomy 16:16).

l) Prayers such as the Kol Nidre are repeated three times.

m) In the mystical tradition of Judaism, incantations to ward off evil spirits are always repeated three times.

n) Mystics believe that three hours before sunrise and/or three days before the New Moon (Rosh Chodesh) are the best times to engage in mystical acts.

o) The Oral Law consists of three parts: Midrash, Halachot, and Haggadot.

p) The day consists of three parts: evening, morning, and afternoon.

q) Sanctification (kedusha) is tripled: kadosh, kadosh, kadosh.

r) The Jewish people consists of Priests (Kohanim), Levites (Leviim), and Israelites (Yisraelim).

s) Among the Kings (Saul, David, Solomon) it was the third, Solomon, who was the most distinguished.

t) The number three figures prominently in the life of Moses. Moses was a member of the tribe of Levi, the third son of Jacob; Levi is spelled in Hebrew with three letters: lamed, vav, yod; Moses was one of three children, his siblings being Miriam and Aaron; the Hebrew name of Moses (Moshe) consists of three letters—mem, shin, hay; in infancy, Moses was concealed by his mother for three months among the reeds on the bank of the Nile (Exodus 2:3).

The kabbalists were particularly enamored of the number three, and they considered it to be a primary number. They pointed out that there are twenty-seven letters in the Hebrew alphabet (twenty-two regular, plus five final letters), and this number is divisible by three. Also, the cube of three is twenty-seven (three times three times three).

As they delved further, these mystics found that the number three possesses sacred qualities, for of all numbers it alone conveys the idea of wholeness and unity; it alone has a distinct beginning, middle, and end. They support this view by observing that the Bible describes the world created by God as consisting of three parts: heaven, earth, and the netherworld. And they also call attention to the fact that the number three symbolizes the basic unity that exists between God, the Jewish people, and the Torah: Ha-kadosh Baruch Hu, v'Yisrael, v'oraita chad hu, meaning "God, Israel, and the Torah are one." The three are an inseparable triad.

7. See Louis Ginzberg's Legends of the Jews VI:30-33. See also Joshua Trachtenberg's Jewish Magic and Superstition, pp. 98 and 249ff.

8. In the Bible, Pesach and Sukkot are seven-day holidays; seven
   weeks separate Passover from Shavuot; every seventh year is a
   sabbatical (shemita) year, and a cycle of seven sabbatical years
   ends with the jubilee year (yovel).
9. Shabbat 86b.
10. Sota 5a and Megilla 29a.
11. Numbers Rabba 1:7. See also Mechilta (Ba-Chodesh), Yitro 1.
12. Bava Batra 60b.
13. Shabbat 89a, b.
14. Midrash Tanchuma, Ki Tissa 36.
15. Menachot 99b.
16. The number forty has held special significance in Jewish history
   and folklore. Taanit 8a relates that just as Moses spent forty days
   on Mount Sinai to acquire the Torah, so did Resh Lakish repeat his
   studies forty times so as not to forget them.
      Christians have also made use of the number forty in their theo-
   logy. According to the New Testament, forty days after Easter
   Jesus assembled his disciples and told them that he must leave to
   join his Father in heaven (Acts 1:3).
17. Horayot 14a. A distinction is made here between one who is merely
   a keen dialectician (an oker harim, meaning "one who uproots
   mountains") and one who is a Sinai, an individual thoroughly
   grounded in the Bible and Jewish law.
18. Some authorities connect Exodus 19:10 with the bride's visit to a
   mikva before her wedding. They explain: Just as Israel (the bride)
   had to be in a state of purity before receiving the Torah, so must a
   bride be ritually pure before entering into a covenant with her mate.
19. See L. Ginzberg's Legends of the Jews III:84. See also Shabbat 89a.
20. See the Shlomo Pines edition of Maimonides' Guide of the Perplexed, Volume II, chapter 33.
21. See L. Ginzberg's Legends of the Jews III:205 and VI:154.
22. Pesikta Rabbati 21.
23. Pesachim 68b.
24. See The Jewish Festivals by Hayyim Schauss, p. 297. Although the
   Book of Ruth is read in many synagogues before or after the Torah
   is read on Shavuot morning, some groups also read it during this all-
   night study period. Since Shavuot was linked to Mattan Torah,
   "the giving of the Torah," it was natural on this night to recall Ruth's
   manifestation of loyalty to the Torah and Judaism.
25. See The Jewish Festivals, by Hayyim Schauss, p. 94.
26. Ibid.
27. Ibid.
28. Bava Batra 15a.
29. Bava Batra 15a, Menachot 30a, and Sifre in Ve-zot Ha-beracha 357.
30. See Encyclopaedia Judaica 12:392.
31. Exodus Rabba 29:1.
32. See The Jewish Mystical Tradition, by B. Z. Bokser, pp. 134ff.

33. Tosefta Sanhedrin 13 and Babylonian Talmud, Sanhedrin 99a. See also *Mishneh Torah*, Hilchot Teshuva 3:8.
34. See the questions that follow for the nature of these sources. See also W.G. Plaut's *The Torah*, pp. xxii-xxix, and J. H. Hertz's *Pentateuch and Haftorahs*, pp. 554-56, for more on this subject.
35. The Hebrew expression is *ayn mukdam u-me'uchar ba-Torah*. See Pesachim 6b.
36. The Hebrew expression is *dibra Torah bi-leshon b'nay adam*. See Berachot 31b.
37. See A. Cohen's critical essay "The Challenge of Biblical Criticism" in *Judaism in a Changing World*, edited by Rabbi Leo Jung, pp. 193ff.
38. See W.G. Plat's *The Torah: A Modern Commentary*, pp. xxi-xxiii.
39. D is said to be the book found by King Josiah in 621 B.C.E. (II Kings 22). Some also assign Genesis 14 to D. See Plaut, noted above.

Notes to Chapter 2
SANCTIFYING THE TORAH
Pages 40 to 63

1. See Sota 14a.
2. See Mishna Megilla 4:1 [26a].
3. *Tefilin* are higher in sanctity because they contain four passages from the Torah while *mezuzot* contain only two. Another reason is that *tefilin* make direct contact with a person's body. See *Shulchan Aruch*, Orach Chayim 38:12, and the comment of Magen Avraham.

   Regarding the principle that religious articles may only be elevated in status, not lowered (*maalin ba-kodesh v'lo moridin*), see Menachot 32a and Yoreh Deah 290:1-2. It is quite likely that the idea stems from the manner in which the shewbreads were treated in Temple times. See Mishna Shekalim 6:4.
4. Rabbi Solomon ben Adret of Barcelona, the leading Spanish rabbi of his generation (thirteenth century), writes in his responsa that many communities in Spain had no handwritten scrolls, and instead they read from handwritten codices (see page 94). See *The Responsa of Solomon ben Adreth*, by Isidore Epstein, p. 59.
5. See Rashi on Exodus 20:22 and Mishna Middot 3:4.
6. Gittin 60a. *Mipnay kevod tzibbur* is the Hebrew expression used. See also *Shulchan Aruch*, Yoreh Deah 283:1, where this law is codified, and see *Mishneh Torah*, Hilchot Sefer Torah 7:14, for Maimonides' summary of the ruling.
7. It is quite evident, however, that in Temple times smaller units of the Torah were used for public readings. We are informed that on

Yom Kippur the High Priest read to the assembled congregation two selections from the Book of Leviticus (from Chapters 16 and 23). He would then place the scroll "in his bosom" (probably under his arm) and recite a selection from the Book of Numbers by heart. Clearly, it would not be possible for him to fit the Book of Leviticus into his bosom if it were part of a complete Torah.

8. Congregations that follow a policy of reading from a different scroll each week have been known to draw lots to determine which scroll should be read on a particular Sabbath or holiday. See *Orchot Chayim*, Part I, Orach Chayim 135:2, by Nachman Kahana.

9. See note 3, above.

10. Megilla 27a.

11. Soferim 3:10. Rabbi Solomon B. Freehof has a detailed responsum on this subject in his *Current Reform Responsa*, pp. 38ff.

 Rabbi Moses Isserles in his note on *Shulchan Aruch*, Orach Chayim 134:2, quotes the Maharil (Rabbi Jacob Halevi of Mollin), the leading Ashkenazic authority of the fourteenth and fifteenth centuries, as the first to mention the custom of holding the Torah in the right hand.

12. Parashat Yitro (81a).

13. Other significant references in the Bible portraying the power of the right hand are to be found in Exodus 15:6, 15:12 and Psalms 18:36, 48:11, 121:5, 138:7, and 139:10.

14. *Shulchan Aruch*, Orach Chayim 2:4-5.

15. *Shulchan Aruch*, Orach Chayim 147:1. See also the Magen Avraham and Magen David commentaries on 147:1.

16. Berachot 22a. See also *Shulchan Aruch*, Yoreh Deah 282:9.

17. Berachot 22a.

18. *Mishneh Torah*, Hilchot Sefer Torah 10:8. For a detailed responsum on this subject, see Rabbi Solomon B. Freehof's *Reform Jewish Practice*, Volume II, pp. 58ff. See also Rabbi J. D. Bleich's essay "Teaching Torah to Non-Jews" in *Contemporary Halakhic Problems*, Volume II, pp. 311ff.

19. Mishna Megilla 1:8 and Megilla 9a. See also Bava Kama 83a, where his very warm attitude toward Grecian culture is described.

20. Yerushalmi Megilla 1:9.

21. Soferim 1:7-8.

22. *Mishneh Torah*, Hilchot Tefilin U'Mezuzot V'Sefer Torah 1:19.

23. This story about King Ptolemy and the Greek translation of the Torah is to be found in abbreviated form in Megilla 9a and in the later (eighth-century) tractate Soferim (1:7). See also C. D. Ginsburg's *Introduction to the Massoretico-Critical Edition of the Hebrew Bible*, pp. 300ff., for a full account.

24. Soferim (1:6-7) also presents an entirely different account of the origin of the Septuagint. In this second version, "five elders wrote the Torah for King Ptolemy." The number seventy-two is not mentioned.

25. Most contemporary scholars believe that the Greek translation

came about in the same natural way as did the Aramaic translation (the Targum of Onkelos) in the first century C.E. The Aramaic translation was composed because the masses of Jews living in Palestine, whose spoken language was Aramaic, were no longer able to understand the Torah reading that was conducted in Hebrew. It was therefore translated into their vernacular, Aramaic. Similarly, when the Jews of Alexandria, Egypt (whose vernacular was Greek), were no longer proficient in Hebrew, the Torah reading had to be translated for them into Greek.

26. Along with the numbers three, seven, ten, and forty, the number seventy is significant in Jewish history and tradition. Seventy persons were in Jacob's entourage when he went to Egypt (Exodus 1:5). When Jacob died, he was mourned for seventy days (Genesis 5:3). Seventy elders assisted Moses (Numbers 11:16). Gideon had seventy sons (Judges 8:30).

The *Zohar* says there are seventy facets to the Torah. See *The Wisdom of the Hebrew Alphabet*, by Michael Munk, pp. 175ff., for additional examples.

27. See *The Interpreter's Bible*, Volume I, pp. 58-59.
28. For a full discussion of this subject and for a listing of all sources see J. David Bleich's *Contemporary Halakhic Problems*, Volume II, pp. 311ff.
29. See *Shulchan Aruch*, Orach Chayim 134:4,5 and the accompanying Magen Avraham comment, note 6.
30. The Hebrew expression for the hiatus between one aliya and the next is *bayn gavra le-gavra*.
31. See Abraham Idelsohn's *Ceremonies of Judaism*, p. 84. *Tek* is a form of the Hebrew word *tik*, meaning "container." *Tik* is used in rabbinic literature (Orach Chayim 154:3) to describe the box that houses a Torah, and it is interesting that the Jews of Ethiopia call a small house a *tekel*, which may be a diminutive form of *tik*. See *The Lost Jews*, by Louis Rapoport, p. 239.
32. Shabbat 14a and *Shulchan Aruch*, Orach Chayim 147:1. See also *Mishneh Torah*, Hilchot Sefer Torah 10:6.
33. Soferim 3:13 and Shabbat 133b.
34. *Shulchan Aruch*, Orach Chayim 147.
35. Shabbat 114a reminds us that brides and grooms wear white.
36. Yerushalmi, Rosh Hashana 7b.
37. The practice of wrapping (swaddling) newborn babies with narrow bands of cloth was popular in the Middle Ages. Among the Jews of Germany, the mother of a newborn boy would come to the synagogue on the fourth Sabbath after the birth of her son and present a *gartl* fashioned from the swaddling clothes in which her son was wrapped at his *brit*. On this same fourth Sabbath, the father received an *aliya* and bestowed a secular name upon his son. The Hebrew name had already been announced at the *brit*. *Gartls* for which there was no immediate need would be stored in the synagogue's ark.

See H. Schauss's *Lifetime of a Jew*, pp. 45ff., for more on this subject.

38. From *Nehora Ha-shalem*, a comentary on the prayerbook by Aharon ben Yechiel Michl (Vilna, 1898).
39. Moed Katan 27b.
40. Megilla 27a. See also *Mishneh Torah*, Hilchot Sefer Torah 10:2.
41. Sukka 5a. The *tass* mentioned here means "plate." It is a description of the small *tzitz*, or plate of gold, worn by the High Priest on his forehead.
42. See *Shulchan Aruch*, Yoreh Deah 282:2, where this law is codified. In his Notes, Moses Isserles emphasizes that even if one does not see the Torah being carried but hears the bells tingling, it is mandatory to stand with the rest of the congregation.
43. The principle is termed *mashmia kol*, meaning "producing sounds" via instruments. The reasoning is that the instrument might break and the user would attempt to mend it, thus violating the prohibition of doing work on Sabbaths and holidays. See Alfred J. Kolatch's *Second Jewish Book of Why*, pp. 265-66 and p. 361, note 30.
44. *Shulchan Aruch*, Yoreh Deah 282:11, 12, and *Mishneh Torah*, Hilchot Sefer Torah 10:4.
45. In Ketubot 19b Rabbi Ami is quoted as saying, "A book [of the Bible] that [contains errors and] is not corrected may be kept for thirty days, and from then on it is not to be retained, because the Bible says (Job 11:14): 'Let not unrighteousness dwell in thy tents.'" See also *Shulchan Aruch*, Yoreh Deah 279:1.
46. Shabbat 115b. See also Mishna Yada'yim 3:5.
47. This is based on the ruling in Mishna Shabbat 16:1.
48. See *Shulchan Aruch*, Yoreh Deah 282:12, where the burial or *geniza* requirement is applied to everything that has been in direct contact with the Torah. This includes the ark, the reading table, and the chair upon which a Torah has rested before or after the reading. These are all referred to in Hebrew as *tashmishay kedusha*, meaning "holy appurtenances."
49. Other types of *genizot* (plural of *geniza*) have been established in the course of Jewish history. A most unusual one was the *geniza* in Marrakesh, Morocco, where a dry well was used for the purpose of storing sacred objects. Noted in *Rabbi's Rovings*, by Rabbi Israel Mowshowitz, p. 337.
50. See Megilla 26b and Soferim 5:14. See also Yoreh Deah 282:10.
51. Moed Katan 25a.
52. See *Shulchan Aruch*, Yoreh Deah 282:4 and 367:3. In talmudic times *tefilin* were often worn all day long, so those visiting cemeteries had to be careful to remove them before entering. Comparing the dead to the poor is mentioned in the Siftay Kohayn commentary on Yoreh Deah 282:4.
53. See *Shulchan Aruch*, Yoreh Deah 282:11.

54. Megilla 26b.
55. See Solomon Freehof's *Contemporary Reform Responsa*, pp. 117ff., for a detailed discussion of this subject.

Notes to Chapter 3
THE ARK AND THE PULPIT AREA
Pages 64 to 85

1. II Samuel 6:6, which is part of the prophetic reading (*haftara*) for the Torah portion (*sidra*) Shemini (Leviticus 9-11), mentions the death penalty imposed upon Uzza for touching the ark with his hands: God smote him for this act of irreverence.

   For additional information on the folklore and function of the ark, see Louis Ginzberg's *Legends of the Jews* III: 156ff. and VI: 64ff.

2. Tosefta Sota 7:18 states this as the view of Rabbi Judah ben Lakish.
3. Menachot 99a.
4. See Mishna Taanit 2:2, where the expression *yored lifnay ha-tayva* means "to go down and stand before the cabinet [and lead the prayers]." The *tayva* in which the Torot were kept was generally placed on a platform above floor level. The cantor led the congregation in prayer from a lectern on floor level, hence one would "go down" from the ark area to floor level and stand before the lectern to conduct the service.

   In many Orthodox congregations today a portion of the prayer service is still conducted from a lectern at floor level.

5. Berachot 7:2.
6. Berachot 47b.

   Rabbenu Tam, the grandson of Rashi, notes in Berachot 48a (Tosafot) that he does not approve of those who say that a minor holding a Pentateuch can be counted to a minyan. He would count the minor as the tenth person without resorting to such devices. The *Shulchan Aruch* agrees, and the law as codified in Orach Chayim 55:4 says that in the view of some authorities a *minyan* may be considered properly formed if nine adults plus a minor above age six are present. Nevertheless, some still insist that the child hold a Pentateuch.

7. The Hebrew expression is *Ha-kol taluy b'mazal, afilu Sefer Torah she-ba-haychal*, which is from the *Zohar*, sidra Naso, 134, as indicated in J. D. Eisenstein's *Otzar Maamaray Chazal*, p. 230, note 23, where he associates this aphorism with the Roman (Latin) expression *habent sua fata libelli*, "books have their own luck."

   Mazal literally means "star," and *mazal tov* means "lucky star." The Midrash (Genesis Rabba 10:6) comments: "There is not a single blade of grass that is not governed by a star that commands it and says to it, 'Grow!' "

8. This question was addressed to Rabbi Moshe Feinstein. See *Igrot Moshe*, Orach Chayim IV:38. See also the *Aruch Ha-shulchan* on Orach Chayim 154:8 for more on this subject.

9. Tosefta, Megilla 3:2.

10. Megilla 26a. The ark is more sacred than the synagogue building itself.

11. *Shulchan Aruch*, Orach Chayim 154:3-8.

12. *Responsa from the Holocaust,* by Ephraim Oshry, pp. 166-67.

13. In some congregations the *parochet* is hung in front of the ark door, while in others it is hung behind the door.

14. Makkot 22b and Kiddushin 33b.

15. This is mentioned several times in the Talmud and is codified in the *Mishneh Torah* of Maimonides, Hilchot Tefila 12:23. See also Yoma 70a.

16. Soferim 14:9-10 describes a procedure followed when the Torah is removed from the ark that includes elements no longer fully followed by Ashkenazic or Sephardic congregations.

17. See *Shulchan Aruch*, Yoreh Deah 282:1, particularly the Turay Zahav commentary. See also Yoma 53a and the *Aruch Ha-shulchan*, Orach Chayim 123:1.

18. See pages 334-35 for more on the number three.

19. Soferim 14:14.

20. Mishna Sukka 4:5 describes the ritual of Hoshana Rabba in Temple times in this manner:

> Every day [of the first six days of the festival] they went round the altar once, saying, "We beseech Thee, O Lord, save now; we beseech Thee, O Lord, make us now prosper [Psalms 118:25]." But on that [seventh] day they went round the altar seven times.

See also *Shulchan Aruch*, Orach Chayim 660:1.

21. For a full discussion of this subject see *Toledot Chag Simchat Torah,* by Avraham Yaari, p. 261. The author asserts that conducting *hakafot* on Simchat Torah was a practice totally unknown before the last third of the sixteenth century.

See also *Encyclopaedia Judaica* 14:1571, 15:1491.

22. Yoreh Deah 282:2.

23. Sukka 51b describes the huge synagogue in Alexandria, Egypt, in which the *bima* was located in the center of the sanctuary.

24. See the Notes of Moses Isserles on *Shulchan Aruch*, Orach Chayim 103, and the *Mishneh Torah* of Maimonides, Hilchot Tefila 11:3.

See also Rabbi Moshe Feinstein's *Igrot Moshe*, Orach Chayim II:41,42, for a full discussion of this subject. Feinstein sees no reason why the reading must be done from a table in the center of the synagogue if it is advisable (as in the case of small synagogues) to have the reader's desk located elsewhere in the room. He explains that the ban against moving the *bima* from the center of the room was introduced merely to offset a practice introduced by the "wicked Reformers." In general, however, he recommends that large synagogues should position the reading table in the center of the room.

25. *Shulchan Aruch,* Yoreh Deah 282:2.
26. Ibid. 242:13,18.
27. See a responsum of Rabbi Solomon B. Freehof on this subject in *Contemporary Reform Responsa,* pp. 37ff.
28. *Aruch Ha-shulchan,* Yoreh Deah 282:13.
29. This was the response of Rabbi Moses Sofer (1762-1839), the illustrious rabbi of Pressburg, Germany, when this question was addressed to him. A similar response came from Rabbi Naftali Tzevi Berlin (1817-1893) who for thirty-seven years was the head of the famous Volozhin yeshiva.

   See Meyer Waxman's *History of Jewish Literature,* p. 726. Waxman quotes the responsum of Moses Sofer in which the Pressburg rabbi, unwilling to agree to change a practice followed by German Jewry for centuries, declares that it is "biblically prohibited to introduce new practices."
30. *Tircha d'tzibura* is the Aramaic term used in the Talmud to express this important concept in Jewish law.
31. See Rabbi Moshe Feinstein's *Igrot Moshe,* Orach Chayim 2:37, where the pros and cons of this issue are discussed. He believes that either course may be followed, depending upon the attitude of the congregation.

   See also *Teshuvot Rashi,* Orach Chayim 37 (Elfenbein edition, p. 225), where the subject of the "feelings" of a *Sefer Torah* are discussed.
32. This quotation is found in Hagahot Maimoniyot, the commentary of Rabbi Meir Ha-kohayn on the *Mishneh Torah,* Hilchot Sefer Torah 10:10. Meir Ha-kohayn was a disciple of Rabbi Meir of Rothenburg, and many of his master's responsa were preserved in his commentary on the code of Maimonides.
33. This explains why Rabbenu Tam was of the opinion that when a *mezuza* is affixed to the doorpost, it should be placed horizontally rather than vertically as advocated by his grandfather Rashi. See Menachot 33a. The Maharil (Rabbenu Jacob Halevi Mollin), the fourteenth-century German authority, called attention to this in his famous book on Jewish customs and liturgy entitled *Minhagay Maharil* (section dealing with *mezuzot*). He suggested a compromise so as not to belittle either of these two authorities. He proposed that the *mezuza* be placed on a slant on the doorpost, and this has been the custom since the seventeenth century, when the Maharil's book was first published and widely distributed.
34. Megilla 27a. See also *Mishneh Torah,* Hilchot Sefer Torah 10:5.
35. *Shulchan Aruch,* Orach Chayim 154:5.
36. Bava Batra 14b.

37. Shabbat 115b and 116a. The number eighty-five was designated because there are that many letters in the Hebrew verses of Numbers 10:35-36. Verse 35 is recited when the Torah is removed from the ark before reading from it, and verse 36 is recited after the Torah is returned to the ark. See also page 60 in Chapter Two, Sanctifying the Torah Scroll.
38. Noda Bi-Yehuda, Volume I on Orach Chayim 9.
39. For a full discussion of this subject see Rabbi Solomon Freehof's Contemporary Reform Responsa, pp. 114ff.
40. Shulchan Aruch, Orach Chayim 154:3.
41. Megilla 16b.
42. See The Lost Jews, by Louis Rapoport, p. 239.
43. Avoda Zara 43a and Shulchan Aruch, Yoreh Deah 141:8.
    A facsimile of the seven-branched candelabrum may be seen in Rome, etched into the wall of the Arch of Titus as part of a bas-relief that depicts the goddess of victory crowning Titus. It portrays the march of Jewish captives bearing the Temple vessels, the shewbread table, the seven-branched candelabrum, and the trumpet.
44. Mishna Tamid 6:1. Exodus 27:20-21 and Leviticus 24:2 mention the kindling of lamps regularly "in the Tent of Meeting outside the curtain" which is over the ark.
45. In a comment on the verse in Exodus (15:2), "This is my God and I will glorify Him," the Talmud and Midrash (Shabbat 133b and Mechilta d'Rabbi Ishmael, Be-shalach 3) say: "Make a beautiful sukka in His honor; use a beautiful lulav in His honor; select a beautiful shofar in His honor; wear beautiful tzitzit in His honor; recite beautiful prayers in His honor." Based upon this, others went even further in expressing their love of God: they incorporated painted and sculptured artforms into the decor of the synagogue. By so doing, they were not deviating from tradition but rather fulfilling it. Evidence was drawn from Exodus 26:1, where the figures of cherubim are described as being woven into the fabric used for the curtains in the Tabernacle.
46. Even earlier, at the beginning of the second century, the famous Rabbi Gamaliel II patronized a Roman bath in Acre in which there was a statue of Aphrodite. He said to those who criticized him that since the statue was placed in a bath, it was obviously not meant to be worshiped, since pagans did not worship gods in baths. And he concluded, "What is regarded as a deity is prohibited; what is not regarded as a god is not prohibited." See Mishna Avoda Zara 3:3-4.
47. See Kanof's Jewish Ceremonial Art and Religious Observance, pp. 21-22, and Encyclopaedia Judaica 15:1132.
48. Menachot 28b.
49. For some of the characteristics of the lion see Numbers 23:24, II Samuel 1:23, Isaiah 38:13, Ezekiel 22:25 and Proverbs 30:30.
50. See Joshua Trachtenberg's Jewish Magic and Superstition, pp. 140-41.

Notes to Chapter 4

WRITING THE TORAH

Pages 86 to 119

1. *Shulchan Aruch*, Yoreh Deah 274:1, and the Turay Zahav commentary on this section.
2. See *Shulchan Aruch*, Yoreh Deah 274:2. In Temple times, a Torah scroll that was deemed to be one hundred percent accurate was available for consultation. That scroll was called the "Temple Scroll," and texts were examined by a group of "book correctors" in the Temple. Their wages were paid from the public funds of the Temple treasury. See Ketubot 106a.
3. Soferim 3:13.
4. Kiddushin 30a. See also Eruvin 13a, where a scribe is advised to be extra careful when transcribing sacred texts, lest he omit or add a single letter. And see *Shulchan Aruch*, Orach Chayim 31:20, where this rule is applied to the writing of *tefilin*.

   Additional information on the counting of *soferim* will be found in Chapter Eight, The Masoretic Text.
5. The expression *otiyot setam* refers to the type of script used in the writing of Torah scrolls, *tefilin*, and *mezuzot*.
6. See Shabbat 103a, where the rule is well established that the *usual* way of writing a scroll is with the right hand. For other references signifying the importance of the right hand and right side see Berachot 62a and *Shulchan Aruch*, Orach Chayim 2:4. The ancient Greeks and Romans also favored the right side.
7. Turay Zahav commentary on Yoreh Deah 271:7. See also Menachot 10a.
8. The *Shulchan Aruch* (Orach Chayim 31:5) states that an ambidextrous person must write the *tefilin* with his right hand, otherwise the *tefilin* are invalid (*pasul*). Abraham Gombiner, in his Magen Avraham commentary, disagrees.
9. Megilla 18b. The Purim Megilla, like the Torah scroll, may not be written from memory, but this rule does not apply to *tefilin* and *mezuzot*. See also Menachot 32b and *Shulchan Aruch*, Yoreh Deah 274:2.
10. *Tefilin* and *mezuzot* may be written from memory because the biblical passages are not only brief but also very familiar, and consequently the scribe is not likely to err in writing them.
11. See Exodus 21:8 and Leviticus 11:21 and 27:30.
12. The minor tractate The Fathers According to Rabbi Nathan, Chapter 34, cites ten such instances in the Pentateuch: Genesis 14:2; 20:5; 38:25; Leviticus 11:39; 13:10, 21; 20:17; 21:9; Numbers 5:13, 14.
13. Rashi to Mishna Moed Katan 3:4.

14. *Mishneh Torah*, Hilchot Sefer Torah 8:4.
15. *Shulchan Aruch*, Yoreh Deah 281:3. Rabbenu Asher ben Yechiel (the Rosh) and the Alfasi (the Rif) permit a woman to write a Torah. The same ruling applies to the writing of *tefilin* but not to the writing of *mezuzot*. See also Yoreh Deah 291:3.
16. The Talmud (Soferim 1:13) emphasizes that "whosoever cannot serve as the representative of the public in religious matters is not permitted to write a scroll of the Torah."

    In his *Mishneh Torah*, Hilchot Sefer Torah 1:13, Maimonides emphasizes that a scroll written by a woman may not be used, and this is reiterated in the *Shulchan Aruch*, Yoreh Deah 281:3.
17. Shabbat 79b.
18. See Soferim 1:4; Sefer Torah 1:4; Orach Chayim 31:7, 8; and Shabbat 79b for a review of all these rulings. See also *Aruch Ha-shulchan*, Yoreh Deah, 271:19-24.
19. Megilla 19a. See also Yoreh Deah 271:2.
20. Maimonides, in his *Mishneh Torah*, Hilchot Tefilin U'Mezuza V'Sefer Torah 1:6-7, tells us that first the hair is removed from the whole hide. The hide is then pickled in salt to which flour has been added. Later, the hide is rubbed with gallnuts or another product that will close the pores of the hide and make it durable. The hide is then split in two, and the *kelaf* and the *doksostos* are treated in the same manner.
21. Soferim 1:2. See also Sefer Torah 1:1-2, Shabbat 108a, and Yoreh Deah 271:1. One of the concerns of the Rabbis with regard to the use of the skin of an animal that had died of natural causes in the field is that the animal's heart may have been removed and used for idolatrous purposes. It was heathen practice to pierce the skin of a living animal, remove the heart, and then offer the heart as a sacrifice. Rabbinic law considered such an animal, including its skin, to be forbidden. See Avoda Zara 29b and 32a. The Rabbis, however, did not consider this possibility common enough to disallow the use of the skin of animals found dead in the field.
22. Yoreh Deah 271:1.
23. See *Mishneh Torah*, Hilchot Sefer Torah 1:11.
24. *Tefilin* and *mezuzot* parchment may also not be made from fish skin. See *Mishneh Torah*, Hilchot Tefilin U'Mezuzah V'Sefer Torah 1:9.
25. The skin of kosher birds may also be used as parchment for *tefilin* and *mezuzot*. See *Mishneh Torah*, Hilchot Tefilin U'Mezuza V'Sefer Torah 1:10.
26. See Mishna Kelim 13:2 for a description of the writing instrument known as a *machtayu*, which was used in talmudic times. It had one sharp, pointed end for writing and a broad end for erasing.
27. The minor tractate Soferim 1:5.
28. Sefer Torah 1:5 prohibits it, but 1:6 permits it. See also Eruvin 13a, where the discussion of 1:6 is repeated.

29. See Numbers 5:11-31 for the full story of the suspected adulterous woman and the Ordeal of Bitter Waters to which she was subjected.

30. A wide variety of ink preparations are mentioned in various parts of talmudic and post-talmudic literature. Here are two:

    • Rabbi Joshua ben Levi, in Shabbat 23a, was of the opinion that "all oils are fit for ink, but olive oil is the best of all [because it creates the best kind of soot]."

      This ink was made by heating a vessel containing olive oil. The soot formed on the outside of the vessel was then scraped off and mixed with oil, honey, and gallnuts. (Gallnuts are ball-like fungi that grow on the bark of oak trees and have a high tannic acid content.)

      For more on ink ingredients see Gittin 19a and *Shulchan Aruch*, Yoreh Deah 271:6.

    • In the *Mishneh Torah*, Hilchot Tefilin U'Mezuza V'Sefer Torah 1:4, Maimonides describes how he understands the ink should be prepared. He writes: "The soot of oils or of pitch, wax, or a similar substance is collected; kneaded with gum of trees and a little honey; thoroughly wetted and pounded till it is like wafers. It is then stored away. When the scribe wishes to write, he soaks it in water in which gall-apples or similar substances have been steeped, and with this fluid he writes. Such writing, when erased, leaves no mark. This is the best way to write Torah scrolls, *tefilin* and *mezuzot*."

31. Sefer Torah 1:10 and Soferim 1:9. Tractate Shabbat 103b relates the ban only to scrolls in which God's name is written with gold ink.

32. Mishna Megilla 4:8. The *Shulchan Aruch* specifies that a Torah scroll is not kosher if even one letter is written with gold or any other colored ink.

33. To be kosher, a Scroll of Esther, like a Torah scroll, must have ruled lines to serve the *sofer* as a guide (Megilla 16b, Soferim 13:2, and Yoreh Deah 271:5). The same is true of a *mezuza*. However, a scribe is not required to draw guidelines when writing *tefilin* because these parchments are enclosed in boxes, and beauty is not a factor (Megilla 18b).

34. *See* Yoreh Deah 271:5, which adds that the rules are not to be made with an instrument that may leave a colored mark. *Sirtut* is the Hebrew word for these ruled lines. For other references to *sirtut* see Megilla 18b, Menachot 32b, Gittin 6b, and Yoreh Deah 284:1.

35. Soferim 3:16 and Eruvin 98a.

36. Eruvin 13a.

37. Bava Batra 14a and Sefer Torah 2:10.

38. *Shulchan Aruch*, Yoreh Deah 272:1.

39. Ibid. See the Turay Zahav commentary.

40. See *Shulchan Aruch*, Yoreh Deah 278:1, where it is pointed out that when sewing sheets together, the stitches must not extend to the very top or bottom of the parchment, in order to reduce the possibility of the stitches tearing as the scroll is used.
41. Assyria, to the north of Israel, was the name of the area before it was conquered by the Babylonians.
42. See Talmud Yerushalmi, Megilla 1:9. See also Talmud Bavli, Sanhedrin 22a.
43. The Phoenician-Hebrew script continued to be used for secular purposes, as is evidenced by the writing found on coins unearthed from the Bar Kochba period (132-135 C.E.) and from texts discovered in the Dead Sea caves. Scrolls written in this old script were considered of lesser sanctity. See Megilla 8b-9a.
44. Shabbat 115b and Soferim 1:6. See also Sanhedrin 21b and 22a. And see *The Text of the Old Testament*, by Ernst Würthwein, pp. 5-6.
45. Some scholars suggest that the Samaritan break occurred earlier, in 332 B.C.E.
46. Menachot 29b. See also *Jewish Encyclopaedia* 11:667 and *Otzar Dinim U'minhagim*, by J. D. Eisenstein, p. 433, for a full discussion and additional source material.
47. Song of Songs Rabba 3:3 and Sanhedrin 104a.
48. Psalm 91 (which often appears in the prayerbook with the last verse of Psalm 90 as its opening sentence and opens with the words *vi-yehi noam*) lists a variety of plagues (punishments) that will befall all who are disloyal to God and promises protection for all who are faithful. Because the plagues are so pointedly mentioned in verses 1-9, this psalm is called in the Talmud (Shevuot 15b) *Shir Shel Pega'im*, meaning "Psalm of Affliction." It has also become known as the antidemonic psalm, because it was (and in some quarters still is) recited by Jews whenever they believe demons will or can attack. Saturday night is one such time. After a day of having been kept at bay by the holiness of the Sabbath, demons were expected to attack. Psalm 91 is recited to ward them off. Funerals are another occasion when demons were believed to be active, and Psalm 91 is therefore sometimes recited.

    Famous rabbis of the Middle Ages, such as Meir of Rothenburg and Jacob Weil, were known to have recited this Psalm before taking a nap. To this day it is recited each night as part of bedtime prayers.

    In Frankfurt, Germany, it was once reported that on one Rosh Hashana the blower (*baal tokaya*) could not get the sounds to come out of his *shofar*. He blamed it on evil spirits who had lodged themselves in the ram's horn. To remedy the situation, Psalm 91 was recited three times into the wide end of the *shofar*. The demons were dislodged, and the *shofar* was able to emit its beautiful sounds. See *Jewish Magic and Superstition*, by Joshua Trachtenberg, p. 113.
49. *Mishneh Torah*, Hilchot Sefer Torah 7:9.

50. Orach Chayim 36:3.
51. Menachot 29b records that Rabbi Judah said in the name of Rav that when Moses went up to heaven, he found God engaged in affixing crownlets to the letters.

Said Moses to God, "For what purpose are these?"

God answered, "There will arise a man after many generations and his name is Akiba. He will use each crownlet as a basis for interpreting many new laws."
52. Soferim 9:1.
53. The Rabbis in the Talmud wondered about the origin of these final letters, and some concluded that they were instituted by the prophets, while others believed that when he received the Torah on Mount Sinai, Moses was instructed to use them.

Mystics theorized about the origin of final letters and expressed the belief that they were created by God at the time of Creation but were stored away until the Children of Israel entered the Promised Land. They were then revealed and were added to the other twenty-two letters of the alphabet.

See Shabbat 104a. See also Talmud Yerushalmi, Megilla 1:9, which refers to the final letters of the alphabet by the acronym *menatzpach*.

C. D. Ginsburg is of the opinion that it was not until the second century C.E. that the use of final letters became a firmly established practice in writing books of the Bible. See pp. 297-99 of Ginsburg's *Introduction to the Massoretico-Critical Edition of the Hebrew Bible*.
54. For basic source material see Louis Ginzberg's *Legends of the Jews* I:5-8 and Notes to the latter in V:3-6. See also Menachem Kasher's *Encyclopedia of Biblical Interpretation* I:4-8.

See in particular Genesis Rabba 1:10. See also Yerushalmi, Chagiga 10a.
55. A more reasonable explanation for the discrepancy in the interpretation of Rabbi Levi and Bar Kappara is that each may have owned Torah manuscripts with different texts. It is known that in the early Hebrew-Phoenician script used by Jews before the Assyrian script (*ketav Ashuri*) was adopted, the *bet* did not have an open panel on its left side as it does today.
56. See the minor tractate Sefer Torah 2:9. See also *Shulchan Aruch*, Yoreh Deah 272:2.
57. Although this is the general rule today, it was not followed by Maimonides, who wrote his own Torah with lines that were six fingers (inches) wide.

It should be noted that in early Bible manuscripts *le-mish-pechotayhem* probably was written *malay* (plene), with a *vav* after the *chet*—that is, with ten letters. Today's texts spell it *chaser* (defective), without the *vav*—that is, with only nine letters. In Joshua 18:21 the spelling is *malay*.

See Chapter Eight, The Masoretic Text, for a discussion of plene and defective words.

58. Sefer Torah 2:6 and Soferim 2:6. See also *Shulchan Aruch*, Yoreh Deah 272:3.
59. Soferim 2:6. The ruling of Maimonides, however, is that a Torah scroll should contain not less than forty-eight lines or more than sixty. See *Mishneh Torah*, Hilchot Sefer Torah 7:10.
60. Soferim 2:6.
61. One reason for selecting the number seventy-two despite the fact that only seventy elders are mentioned in the Bible is that this was the number of the members of the Great Sanhedrin, the supreme tribunal established during the century or more preceding the fall of the Second Temple. The tribunal consisted of seventy-one members plus its president (*nasi*), making a total of seventy-two.

    Some scholars believe that there were two Sanhedrins, one political and one religious, and that the High Priest presided over the religious Sanhedrin while the *nasi* presided over the political Sanhedrin.
62. Sefer Torah 2:2-5 and Soferim 2:4.
63. See Yoreh Deah 272:1 and 273:1 on measurement rules.
64. The Talmud uses the term "three fingers," which equals approximately three inches.

    See also the *Mishneh Torah*, Hilchot Sefer Torah 9:9, where Maimonides identifies the middle finger as the finger on which measurements are based.
65. See Bava Batra 13b.
66. Exodus 26:1-6 describes the dimensions and design of the ten curtains that surrounded the Tabernacle.
67. There are many similarities between the terminology as applied to the Torah and the Tabernacle. The Hebrew word for curtain is *yeria* (Exodus 26:1), and the Hebrew word for a sheet of parchment is *yeria*. The Hebrew word for a column in the Torah is *amud*, and the curtains of the Tabernacle were supported by *amudim*.
68. See Hertz's *Pentateuch and Haftorahs*, p. 269, note 28, for additional commentary.
69. Ibid., p. 678, note 5.
70. In the preceding verse, Moses commands the Levites to place in the ark the Torah that he had just written. Moses anticipates that the Children of Israel at some future point will violate the precepts of the Torah and that he will have to call upon heaven and earth (which will exist for all time) to serve as witnesses that the Torah and its good teachings had been given to Israel. If tragedy were to befall the Israelites, it would be their own fault, for they would have been forewarned but nevertheless would have neglected the teachings of the Torah, which would have directed them along the path of success and joy.
71. Hagahot Maimoniyot, Hilchot Sefer Torah 7:9, note 7. Rabbi Meir Ha-kohayn calls scribes who begin columns with a *vav* ignoramuses (*burim*). He writes: "If I had to write a scroll, I would not begin even one column with a *vav*, except for *ve-a'ida* [Deuteronomy 31:28]."

72. Shabbat 103b. The Decalogue in Exodus 20 and Deuteronomy 5 are also written to have a special visual effect. The same is true for the fourteen lines beginning with Kohelet (Ecclesiastes) 3:2 ("A time to be born . . .") and for the listing of the ten sons of Haman, in the Book of Esther (9:7-9).

73. See Megilla 16b, Soferim 12:10-11, Shabbat 103b, the Jerusalem Talmud Megilla 3:7 (74b), Mishneh Torah, Hilchot Sefer Torah 8:3, and Shulchan Aruch, Yoreh Deah 275:4.

74. Soferim 12:8-12 and Sefer Torah 1:11.

75. Shabbat 103b and Shulchan Aruch, Yoreh Deah 275:5.

76. Menachot 30a.

In North African communities, especially Algeria, a siyum is called Chag Ha-siyum and also Se'udat Yitro U'Moshe. It is celebrated on the Thursday before the portion Yitro (Exodus 18-20) is read, for on that Sabbath the portion containing the Decalogue is part of the reading. Although the Decalogue would not normally be read at a Thursday morning service (not being part of the first ten verses of the weekly Torah portion), it is read on that occasion. After the service, a festive banquet meal is served.

77. Shulchan Aruch, Orach Chayim 143:4. See Isserles on this section.

78. Although the view was not unanimous, Soferim 5:6 states that one who erases a single letter of a Divine name violates the negative commandment mentioned in Deuteronomy 12:3. This is codified in the Shulchan Aruch, Yoreh Deah 276:9.

79. See Makkot 22a. See also Current Reform Responsa, by Rabbi Solomon B. Freehof, pp. 29ff., for a full discussion of this subject.

80. Menachot 29b and Shulchan Aruch, Yoreh Deah 279:3, 4. See also Maimonides' Mishneh Torah, Hilchot Sefer Torah 7:12.

81. Menachot 29a and Mishneh Torah, Hilchot Sefer Torah 10:1.

See also Chapter Eight, The Masoretic Text, for an explanation of the kuf devuka.

82. See Shulchan Aruch, Yoreh Deah 274:4, and commentaries thereon.

83. Ketubot 19b.

84. Hilchot Sefer Torah 7:12. See also Shulchan Aruch, Yoreh Deah 279:1.

85. Shulchan Aruch, Orach Chajim 32:16.

86. Shulchan Aruch, Yoreh Deah 280:1.

87. See Rabbi Meir of Rothenburg, by Irving Agus, p. 265, where this responsum is quoted.

88. See Bava Batra 13b and Mishneh Torah, Hilchot Sefer Torah 7:16. Maimonides points out here that while it is permitted to write each book of the Pentateuch in a separate scroll, these individual scrolls do not have the sanctity of a Torah scroll that is complete.

Notes to Chapter 5
READING THE TORAH
Pages 120 to 148

1. The Torah was actually read in the beginning of the eighth year, after seven years had passed. See Rashi on Deuteronomy 31:10.
2. The Sabbath morning service was held at a very early hour. To accommodate the many people who lived on the outskirts of town and were unable to reach the service on time, a Sabbath afternoon Torah reading was introduced. The Hebrew term for these merchants is *yoshvay keranot* ("those who dwell in the corners [of the city]").

    See *Mishneh Torah* Hilchot Tefila 12:1-2. See also Talmud Yerushalmi, Megilla 4:1 and Bava Kama 82a.
3. Bava Kama 82a.
4. *Mishna Berura*, Orach Chayim 134:1.
5. See Megilla 29b.
6. In many Hebrew Pentateuchs, at the end of each of the five books of the Torah the number of *sedarim* is indicated.
7. In the *Mishneh Torah*, Hilchot Tefila 13:1, Maimonides says that while the generally accepted practice in the thirteenth century was to complete the Torah reading in one year, in some places it was completed in three years. In the Palestinian synagogue of Fustat (Old Cairo), the triennial cycle was still in vogue as late as the seventeenth century.
8. In 1845 the triennial cycle was revived at the Conference of Reform Rabbis in Frankfurt am Main. *The Union Prayerbook* of the Reform movement, pp. 387-95, lists both the Torah and the haftara readings suggested for each week in accordance with the triennial cycle. See also *Gates of Understanding*, issued by the Central Conference of American Rabbis (1977), which lists additional haftara readings.
9. Yoma 87a.
10. The word *parasha* is also used to designate the "open" and "closed" portions of the Torah (*petuchot* and *setumot*). See Chapter Eight, The Masoretic Text.
11. Megilla 21b and Rashi on Megilla 23a.
12. The shortest weekly portion is Va-yaylech (Deuteronomy 31:1-30), containing only 30 verses, and the longest is Naso (Numbers 4:21 to 7:89), with 176 verses. Naso also contains the longest chapter in the Torah: Chapter 7 of the Book of Numbers consists of 89 verses.
13. Maimonides was of the opinion that Ezra the Scribe (fifth century B.C.E.) made these decisions.
14. *Mishneh Torah*, Hilchot Tefila 13:2. The Hagahot Maimoniyot commentary on the above quotes the eleventh-century Rabbi Nissim Gaon as saying that when there are two Sabbaths between

Rosh Hashana and Sukkot, the sidrot Nitzavim and Va-yaylech, even though they are brief, are read individually. And although both Matot and Masay are long, they are nevertheless combined. The reason for not combining Nitzavim and Va-yaylech is so that the curses which appear in Deuteronomy 30:17-18 (in the sidra Nitzavim) should not have to be read after Rosh Hashana, thus making it possible for the new year to begin on a positive note. The reading is therefore so arranged that Nitzavim will always be read before Rosh Hashana.

The Alfasi (Isaac ben Jacob of Fez, 1013-1103) points out that the same is true of the sidra Be-midbar (Numbers 1:1-4:20), which is always read before Shavuot so as to create a hiatus between the reading of the sidra Be-chukotai, with its list of curses, and the Shavuot holiday that follows in a week or two.

To help remember when Nitzavim and Va-yaylech are read separately, in his Baal Ha-turim commentary (on Deuteronomy 31:1 in the sidra Va-yaylech) Jacob ben Asher (1270-1343) employs the catchy phrase *bag ha-melech, pat Va-yaylech* (based on Daniel 1:5). The word *bag* consists of two Hebrew letters: *bet*, which equals two and represents the second day of the week (Monday), and *gimmel* which equals three and represents the third day of the week (Tuesday). The word *ha-melech* in the phrase *bag ha-melech* means "the king," and it is this word with which the Rosh Hashana *Shacharit* (morning) service opens.

The two words that follow *bag ha-melech* are *pat Va-yaylech.* *Pat* is a Hebrew word meaning "small piece, slice." *Va-yaylech* is the name of the sidra read on the Sabbath immediately before or after Rosh Hashana. The mnemonic device *bag ha-melech, pat Va-yaylech* makes it easy to remember that when the *ha-melech* prayer of Rosh Hashana is recited on *bag* (on Monday or Tuesday), the sidra Va-yaylech is "sliced off" (*pat Va-yaylech*) from the earlier sidra (Nitzavim) and is recited by itself on the Sabbath after Rosh Hashana.

15. See *Shulchan Aruch*, Orach Chayim 135:2, and the note of Rema on same. See also *Aruch Ha-shulchan* 135:6, where the position is taken that under all circumstances Torah portions of the week must be completed, if not on that Sabbath then on the succeeding one.

16. Megilla 31b. Codified in the *Shulchan Aruch*, Orach Chayim 135:2. See also Soferim 11:2, which states that it is permitted to skip from place to place when reading from the Prophets but not when reading from a Torah scroll, because a Torah scroll may not be unrolled in public, a rule that does not apply to the prophetic books.

17. Megilla 4a. See also 32a, where the Rabbis indicate that "Moses laid down a rule for the Israelites that they should inquire and give expositions concerning the theme of the day: the laws of Passover on Passover, the laws of Pentecost on Pentecost, and the laws of Tabernacles on Tabernacles."

18. His famous book on liturgy, published in Lisbon in 1490, is entitled *Sefer Abudarham*.

19. The importance of the *Song at the Sea* and of the Ten Commandments is quite evident from the special way in which the scribe writes these sections. See page 112 for more on this subject.

   The reason offered for reading without interruption about the places in which the Israelites rested during their trek from Egypt to the Jordan is, the Midrash says, that at these resting places instruction and guidance was offered the weary travelers. Moses and the leaders of the tribes assured them of God's everlasting concern and compassion.

20. See *Jewish Life in the Middle Ages*, by Israel Abrahams, p. 19. See also his note, which provides other references.

   The Hebrew term for interrupting or holding up a service is *ikuv ha-tefila*.

   In thirteenth-century Rome, on the eve of Yom Kippur, with the ark open, an announcement was made describing all goods stolen during the year, and a warning was issued to congregants not to buy or have any dealings with such goods. In Venice, this practice was followed at services throughout the year. The power and influence of the Torah was brought to bear in a real, practical way.

21. Quoted in *Jewish Law and Jewish Life*, by J. Bazak and S. M. Passamaneck, p. 193. Isserlein's principal work is his collection of responsa called *Terumat Ha-deshen*.

22. Justification for this practice is often grounded on the fact that in earliest times only one person read the Torah to the people. That person was either the king, a prophet, or a leader such as Ezra.

23. Rabbi Solomon B. Freehof, in his *Modern Reform Responsa*, pp. 14ff., reports on a responsum written by Rabbi Naftali Tzevi Berlin, head of the Lithuanian Volozhin Yeshiva (responsum number 16 in *Meshiv Davar*, Part I). Here the question discussed is whether the Torah may be read on Sunday morning. Rabbi Berlin's response is that since the requirement to read the Torah publicly is rabbinic rather than biblical, it is not improper to add a Sunday morning reading. Although the introduction of additional readings is not prohibited by law, Rabbi Berlin does not favor this practice because it involves reciting unnecessary blessings (*berachot le-vatala*) and also because it is contrary to the traditional attitude towards changing long-established customs and practices.

   See also Meyer Waxman's *History of Jewish Literature*, Volume III, p. 731.

24. See Berachot 21b and Sanhedrin 74b.

   Aside from the Torah reading itself, which requires the presence of a minyan, there are five other times during a public prayer service when a quorum must be in attendance. These are when the following prayers are recited: *Kaddish, Kedusha, Barchu, Birkat Kohanim,* and the *Shemoneh Esray (Amida)* when it is repeated by the cantor. In each of these liturgical portions, God's name is prominently sanctified, and therefore a quorum must be present. See page 341 for a further discussion of this subject.

25. *Shulchan Aruch*, Orach Chayim 143:1.

26. In his Magen Avraham commentary, Rabbi Abraham Gombiner specifies that when this situation develops on a Sabbath, the full seven aliyot are called, but a maftir is not called and the haftara is not read. The rule for a holiday would be similar: only five aliyot would be called and the maftir and haftara would be omitted.

27. *Teshuvot Rashi*, No. 277, p. 313.

28. Referred to in the commentary Hagahot Maimoniyot, by Rabbi Meir Ha-kohayn, a disciple of Meir of Rothenburg. See *Mishneh Torah*, Hilchot Tefila 12:19, note 200. The actual quote is: "If a city is composed only of Kohanim and not even one Yisrael lives there, it would seem to me that the Kohayn reads twice [takes the first two aliyot] and the balance is read by women [if present]. However, if women, slaves, or minors are not present, the Torah is not read at all."

   See also *Shulchan Aruch*, Orach Chayim 135:12, on this subject.

   Today on the Tunisian island of Djerba there is a community of about eight hundred Jews consisting mostly of Kohanim, with no Leviim and few Yisraelim.

29. A Kohayn is considered tainted if, for example, he marries a divorcee. The Torah (Leviticus 21:7) declares that such a Kohayn loses his priestly status. His sons would also lose their status as legitimate Priests.

30. *Mishneh Torah*, Hilchot Tefila 13:6.

31. Ibid. The primary opposing view was expressed by the twelfth-century French scholar Ravad (Abraham ben David of Posquières), one of Maimonides' greatest critics.

32. See *Shulchan Aruch*, Orach Chayim 146:4, where these laws are listed.

33. In fact, the more correct translation of the words in Job 32:16 (*ki amdu, lo anu od*) is "I have waited till they stopped speaking, till they ended and no longer replied."

   See the Magen Avraham commentary on Orach Chayim 146:4 for further discussion.

34. The Song at the Sea, or *Shirat Ha-yam* in Hebrew, is read for the fourth aliya of the sidra Be-shalach among Ashkenazim, and for the third aliya in the Sephardic rite.

35. See *Igrot Moshe* IV:22 for a detailed discussion on this subject.

36. Mishna Tamid 5:1 and Berachot 12a.

37. The same charge was not made against the *Shema* (Deuteronomy 6:4-9) and the priestly benediction (Numbers 6:24-26), and these prayers were retained in the liturgy of post-Temple times. See the discussion in *The Canonization of the Synagogue Service*, by Lawrence A. Hoffman, pp. 84-85, for the attitudes of Hai Gaon and

the Karaites toward the retention of the Decalogue in the liturgy.
38. See Alfred J. Kolatch's *Jewish Book of Why*, p. 159, and Salo W.
    Baron's *A Social and Religious History of the Jews*, Volume I,
    p. 246. See also *Jewish Worship*, by Abraham Millgram, pp. 400
    and 606.
       Pressure from scholars, such as the thirteenth-century Rabbi
    Solomon ben Adreth (Rashba) of Barcelona, Spain, to reintroduce
    the Decalogue into the daily service was of no avail. See *The Re-
    sponsa of Solomon ben Adreth*, by Isidore Epstein, p. 59.
39. *Baal koray* is the popular expression. The more grammatical form
    is *baal keria*. Similarly, the person who blows the *shofar* is popu-
    larly known as the *baal tokaya*, although the more grammatical
    form is *baal tekia*.
40. See *Igrot Moshe*, Orach Chayim IV:91, section 7, for Rabbi Moshe
    Feinstein's comment on this subject.
41. See *The Responsa of Rabbi Simon ben Zemach Duran*, by Isidore
    Epstein, p. 74.
42. Most commentators on the Bible believe that Deuteronomy 4:2
    refers only to adding to or omitting the actual commandments of
    the Torah.
       See also *Shulchan Aruch*, Orach Chayim 142:1.
43. Soferim 11:1.
44. *Shulchan Aruch*, Yoreh Deah 281:3.
45. Maimonides uses the talmudic phrase *mipnay kevod ha-tzibur*,
    meaning "because of the honor of the congregation." See *Mishneh
    Torah*, Hilchot Tefila 12:17.
46. Berachot 22a. A glaring example of this mistaken notion is con-
    veyed in the recent (1985) book *Holy Days*, by Lis Harris, p. 134. In
    describing life in the Lubavitcher community in Brooklyn, New
    York, she has the leading character, a devout chassidic woman,
    say that when Conservative and Reform synagogues hire women
    as rabbis, they violate the laws of the Torah because "the Torah
    forbids them from touching the Torah when they are menstruants,
    so how can you have a woman rabbi officiating if she can't touch the
    Torah?"
47. See *Shulchan Aruch*, Orach Chayim 142:1.
48. See *Otzar Dinim U-minhagim*, by J. D. Eisenstein, p. 375.
49. See also Berachot 62a, where a variety of other reasons are given
    for the favoring of the right hand and right side in Jewish law and
    tradition.
50. Soferim 14:14.
51. Talmud Yerushalmi Megilla 4:1. The Hebrew word for intermediary
    is *sarsur*. In early times, it was the *meturgeman* who was referred to
    as the *sarsur*. For more on this see *Aruch Ha-shulchan*, Orach
    Chayim 141:7.
52. The Chafetz Chaim explains that the covering of the Torah with a
    mantle or *mappa* is done primarily in those synagogues where a *Mi
    She-bayrach* prayer is pronounced for each person called to the

Torah. Respect is shown the Torah by not allowing it to remain uncovered and unattended while it is not in actual use. See *Shulchan Aruch*, Orach Chayim 139:5, and *Mishna Berura*, note 20 on this section, for the comment of the Chafetz Chayim.
53. Berachot 62a.
54. For illustrations of these hand movements see *Encyclopaedia Judaica* 11:1099.
55. It is customary in Orthodox synagogues for a congregant to call out the correction so the reader can hear him. The *baal koray* hears the rebuff but continues the reading without repeating the mispronounced word. Minor errors of this type include accenting a word improperly and using the wrong cantillation.
    See Isserles on Orach Chayim 142:1. See also Maimonides' *Mishneh Torah*, Hilchot Tefila 12:6.
56. Orach Chayim 142:1. In particular, see the Notes of Rabbi Moses Isserles on this section.
57. *Shulchan Aruch*, Orach Chayim 141:2.
58. See Chapter 4 of Megilla in the Yerushalmi, Halacha I. See also responsum number 1 in Rabbi Ovadya Yosef's book, *Yechaveh Daat* IV, for further discussion.
59. The most popular Aramaic translation of the Torah text, known as Targum Onkelos, was composed in the second century C.E.
    See Mishna Megilla 4:4. See also *Mishneh Torah*, Hilchot Tefila 12:10-14, and *Shulchan Aruch*, Orach Chayim 145:1-3.
60. *Mishneh Torah*, Hilchot Tefila 12:11.
61. Megilla 25a and 25b.
62. Mishna Megilla 4:10 and *Mishneh Torah*, Hilchot Tefila 12:12.
63. See *Shulchan Aruch*, Orach Chayim 145:3, for additional information.
64. Berachot 8a. The Hebrew expression is *shna'yim mikra ve-echad targum*, sometimes referred to by the acronym *shmot*. See also *Mishneh Torah*, Hilchot Tefila 13:25.
65. This practice is followed except for the first time the name occurs, when it is pronounced Yi-sas-char.
66. *Shulchan Aruch*, Orach Chayim 141:8.
67. See *Shulchan Aruch*, Orach Chayim 143:4 and Yoreh Deah 279:1. See also *Aruch Ha-shulchan*, Orach Chayim 279:4ff.
68. This is the view of Maimonides, and it is so ruled in the *Shulchan Aruch*, Orach Chayim 143:4. See also *Aruch Ha-shulchan*, Hilchot Keriat Ha-Torah 143:3, for a detailed analysis of this subject.
    If three verses had already been read when the error was discovered, the *baal koray* stops immediately and the final Torah blessing is pronounced at this point. A second Torah then replaces the first, and the reading continues.
69. See the Magen Avraham commentary on Orach Chayim 143:4.
70. *Shulchan Aruch*, Orach Chayim 140:3. See also the Magen Avraham commentary, note 4, for a complete analysis of the question.
71. See Megilla 32a.

72. A condemnation of those who chanted Scripture not in accordance with the currect cantillation was emphasized in the Talmud (Megilla 32a) by Rabbi Shefatya, a disciple of Rabbi Yochanan.
73. This reason is quoted in *Otzar Kol Minhagay Yeshurun*, by A. Hirshowitz, p. 175.
74. *Sefer Torah* 3:7 and *Soferim* 3:10.
75. See *Aruch Ha-shulchan*, Orach Chayim 135:32, and J. D. Bleich's *Contemporary Halakhic Problems*, Vol. I, pp. 67ff., for a wide-ranging discussion of this matter.
76. *Aruch Ha-shulchan* 139:15.

Notes to Chapter 6
ALIYOT
Pages 149 to 192

1. Reform Judaism rejects the traditional system whereby the Kohayn, Levi, and Yisrael are awarded aliyot in that order.
2. Megilla 23a states: "All are qualified to be among the seven [who read the Torah before the congregation on a Sabbath], even a minor and a woman. But the Sages said that a woman should not read the Torah out of respect for the congregation."
3. Not all Sephardic congregations use this wording. Moroccans and other North African congregations use the formula "*Ya'amod ha-shem ha-tov* (so-and-so) *ben* (so-and-so) *likro ba-Torah*," meaning "The honorable (so-and-so) the son of (so-and-so) may rise and come forward to read from the Torah." Often the surname is added to the personal name.

   A variety of other introductions are used by Sephardim in other parts of the world.
4. While many rabbis over the centuries did not wish to accord proselytes full equality, the majority did. Judah Halevi (1075-1141), in his famous *Kuzari* (1:95), states that although Gentiles may convert to Judaism and are welcome, they are not equal to Jews born of a Jewish mother. Maimonides (1135-1204), on the other hand, in a letter to Obadiah, a Catholic convert to Judaism, expressed the opposite view. He believed that proselytes must be accorded full Jewish status. In this famous letter he asserts the right of converts to recite the phrase "our God and God of our fathers" in their prayers, like the average Jew born of a Jewish mother.

   See Alfred J. Kolatch's *Second Jewish Book of Why*, pp. 132-33. See also Mishna Horayot 3:8, which states: "A Priest takes precedence over a Levite, a Levite takes precedence over an Israelite, an Israelite takes precedence over a bastard, a bastard takes precedence over a *natin* [a descendant of Gibeonites who in the time of Joshua became temple slaves (Joshua 9:3 and Ezra 2:70)], a *natin* takes precedence over a proselyte, and a proselyte takes precedence over a freed slave." Proselytes were not considered the equal of born Jews because, the Rabbis claimed, they came from tainted (heathen) stock. For this reason a Kohayn, who was supposed to serve in a state of purity, was not permitted to marry a proselyte, lest he become tainted by association.

5. There is no requirement in the major codes that a convert must assume a Hebrew name. In fact, one of the most famous of all converts is known simply as Onkelos the Proselyte. A pupil of Rabbi Akiba (first century C.E.), he is reputed to be the author of the Aramaic translation of the Pentateuch known as the *Targum* or *Targum Onkelos*. See Megilla 3a for more on this subject.

6. See *The Second Jewish Book of Why*, pp. 126-28 and 309-310.

7. See the note of Moses Isserles on Orach Chayim 139:3.

8. Rabbi Solomon B. Freehof points out in his *Contemporary Reform Responsa*, p. 33, that as far back as the early 1800s Rabbi Jacob Ettinger of Hamburg protested against the growing custom in Germany of not calling people to the Torah by their Hebrew names.

9. The fourth aliya is called as *revii*; the fifth as *chamishi*; the sixth as *shishi*; and the seventh as *shevii*, or *mashlim* in the Sephardic tradition. Supplemental aliyot carry the designations *hosafa*, "additional one"; *acharon*, "last one"; *maftir*, "conclusion."

10. See page 55 for a discussion of the Sephardic practice of waving at the Torah scroll.

11. See Primo Levi's *Periodic Table*, p. 5, where he indicates that it is significant that the fringes of the *talit* are regulated by number, length, and form.

12. *Yechaveh Daat* IV, responsum 12.
Moses Maimonides, in his commentary on Sanhedrin 7:4, says that although an individual does not ordinarily become sexually aroused when kissing a female relative such as one's sister, aunt, or granddaughter, such an act is disgraceful and forbidden. The sole exceptions to this rule are that a mother is permitted to kiss a son and embrace him up until his thirteenth birthday and that a father may kiss and embrace a daughter until she reaches her tenth birthday. See Kiddushin 81b.

13. *Shulchan Aruch*, Orach Chayim 141:7.

14. See *Mishna Berura* 141:9 for additional reasons. See also Alfred J. Kolatch's *Second Jewish Book of Why*, p. 244, 298, and 365, for more on the concept of *kevod ha-tzibur*.

15. See *Shulchan Aruch*, Orach Chayim 141:7.

16. Yevamot 62a. See also Shabbat 87a.

17. There is here also a play on the word *asher* in the phrase *asher shibarta. Asher* and *yishar* are similar in sound, although they are unrelated in meaning.

18. Sanhedrin 26b.

19. Moses Isserles, in his Notes on Orach Chayim 139:11, links the use of the word *chazak* in greeting one who has had an aliya to the

360 •

phrase in the Book of Joshua (1:7), "Be strong and courageous to observe the Law which Moses My servant commanded you."

20. For more on this superstition see *The Jewish Book of Why*, pp. 42-43.

21. See *The Responsa of Rabbi Simon ben Zemach Duran*, by Isidore Epstein, pp. 73ff. Duran also informs us that in North Africa in the fourteenth century, particularly on Simchat Torah, the highest bidder was given the highest honors, and those who acquired them sometimes kept them for the entire year.

We also learn from Duran that a person who paid for the writing of a Torah scroll, which he then donated to a congregation, often reserved the right to bestow aliyot as he saw fit when his Torah was used for a public reading.

In many communities, persons paid a fee for the privilege of assigning aliyot for a period of time, usually six months.

22. A pledge was often made by a person who did not really want to or could not really afford to but who was too embarrassed not to announce a donation. The individual made a pledge knowing that he would not be able to honor it.

23. See *Igrot Moshe*, Orach Chayim II:3, III:12, and IV:91, section 8. Feinstein notes that if transients happen to be Kohanim or Leviim, they *must* be called for the first and second aliyot. However, should it be known that these visitors are Sabbath violators, even if there is no other Kohayn or Levi present, they are not to be called to the Torah.

See also the analysis of this subject in *Current Reform Responsa*, by Rabbi Solomon B. Freehof, pp. 62ff.

24. See Herbert C. Dobrinsky's *Treasury of Sephardic Laws and Customs*, p. 169.

25. *Igrot Moshe*, Orach Chayim IV:92, section 8.

26. See *Current Reform Responsa*, pp. 62ff., by Rabbi Solomon Freehof, for a full discussion of whether receiving an aliya is a right that any Jew may claim. He cites the case of a Yemenite Jew in Israel who once sued the officers of his congregation charging that they were prejudiced against him and he had therefore not been called up to the Torah in a long time. He was suing for what he considered his *rights* as a Jew.

27. See Ginzberg's *Legends of the Jews* III:85-86 for *midrashim* (legends) describing how God instructed Moses to first persuade the women to accept the Torah before proposing it to the menfolk. The reason: If women accepted the Torah, they could be depended upon to transmit its message to their children.

Permitting women to have an aliya is based on a statement in the Talmud (Megilla 23a): "All are qualified to be among the seven who are called to the Torah and read a portion, even a minor and a woman. But the Sages said that a woman should not read from the Torah out of respect for the congregation."

Some scholars maintain that one cannot infer from this statement that women were or were not actually called to the Torah. See Aaron H. Blumenthal's article, "An Aliyah for Women," in the Rabbinical Assembly of America's *Proceedings 1955*, pp. 168-81, and Sanders A. Tofield's "Woman's Place in the Rites of the Synagogue," ibid., pp. 182-90, for Conservative Judaism's attitude.

See also Maimonides' *Mishneh Torah*, Hilchot Tefila 12:17, and Joseph Caro's *Shulchan Aruch*, Orach Chayim 282:3.

28. Megilla 23a.
29. *Shulchan Aruch*, Orach Chayim 55:1.
30. In many Sephardic congregations, particularly those that follow the Spanish-Portuguese ritual, the father of a Bar Mitzva is honored with *chamishi* (the fifth aliya) and a grandfather is usually called for *shishi* (the sixth aliya) or *mashlim* (the seventh aliya). The Bar Mitzva boy recites the haftara, but someone else is honored with the maftir aliya.

Among Sephardic congregations that follow the ritual once prevalent in Turkey and other Ottoman Empire countries, the Bar Mitzva is honored with *shishi* (the sixth aliya) and his father is called for *shelishi* (the third aliya).

Sephardim in general do not celebrate a Bar Mitzva in the synagogue. Some do hold lavish private parties to mark the occasion of a girl's coming of age.
31. When the child is a girl, she is named at that time. In many Conservative and Reform congregations the mother ascends the pulpit with the child at the time of the aliya, and the naming ceremony follows.
32. See *The Responsa of Rabbi Simon ben Zemach Duran*, by Isidore Epstein, p. 74.
33. The origin of the prayer is to be found in the Talmud, tractate Berachot 54b. Here the Talmud lists four hazardous situations: a sea voyage, a trip through a desert, an illness, release from prison. See Psalm 107, where reference is made to these adversities.

In recent years, authorities have debated whether one who has been on an airplane trip in the course of the preceding week is entitled to an aliya so that he may recite the *Ha-gomel* prayer. No definitive ruling has been issued. See Orach Chayim 219:9 and the comment of the Magen Avraham, note 10, where the point is made that one should pronounce *Ha-gomel* after surviving all perilous situations, and not only the four mentioned in the Talmud.
34. There have been times in Jewish history when a whole congregation recited the *Ha-gomel* prayer. One such occasion is described by Rabbi J. H. Hertz, the late Chief Rabbi of the British Empire. In *The Daily Prayerbook*, pp. 487-88, he relates that "after the bombing of a city in England, on Friday evening December 14, 1940, which resulted in 587 deaths including a number of Jews, at the Sabbath service the next morning the Jewish worshippers repeated as a body the *Gomel*-thanksgiving for their delivery and there was not a dry eye in the synagogue."

35. For a full discussion of the legal and emotional considerations involved in circumstances such as these, see the responsum of Rabbi Solomon B. Freehof in his *Reform Responsa*, pp. 32ff.
36. See Alfred J. Kolatch's *Second Jewish Book of Why*, pp. 222-23.
37. See *Shulchan Aruch*, Orach Chayim 141:2, and the Magen Avraham commentary. See also the question addressed to Rabbi Moshe Feinstein regarding two Bar Mitzva boys whom he forbids to read the maftir and haftara in unison (*Igrot Moshe*, Orach Chayim I:102).
38. *Igrot Moshe*, Orach Chayim I:102.
39. See *The Second Jewish Book of Why*, p. 241, for more on this subject.
40. See *Ach Letzara*, by Yekutiel Greenwald, p. 256, for a discussion on the subject of a Kohayn who is called to the Torah while he is observing *Shiva*.
41. Ibid.
42. The Hebrew expression is *miktzat ha-yom k'chulo*.
43. *Shacharit* ends immediately before the Torah reading service begins.
44. In Hebrew this caveat is expressed as *le-baal mum ayn kore'in parashat mumin she-lo le-hitba'yesh*, "An afflicted person is not called [to the Torah] when a portion describing [an affliction] is read, so as not to embarrass him."
45. See Chapter Five, Reading the Torah, for a discussion of the requirement that one reading from a Torah scroll look at each word as he pronounces it.
46. See Orach Chayim 139:3 and the Magen Avraham commentary.
47. See the next chapter for the ultra-Orthodox view.
48. For a full discussion of this subject see J. D. Bleich's *Contemporary Halakhic Problems*, Volume II, pp. 29-32.
49. *Mishneh Torah*, Hilchot Tefila 12:17.
50. In time, even the poor came to resent this indignity. And so the custom arose in many communities for individuals to volunteer for these aliyot. The *baal koray* would announce *Yaamod mi she-yirtzeh*, "May he who wishes come forward for this aliya," thus eliminating the stigma, since the *oleh* came forward of his own volition.
51. It is customary to read these Chapters of Curses hurriedly and in a low voice. In some synagogues the portion about the Golden Calf (Exodus 32) also is read in hushed tones.

    In Sephardic congregations it is customary for the *chazzan* to articulate every word of every prayer. When he reaches the unpleasantries in verses 16 and 17 of Deuteronomy 11 (the second paragraph of the *Shema*), he does not recite them aloud.
52. *Shulchan Aruch*, Orach Chayim 141:6.
53. This is the view of the fifteenth-century Rabbi Jacob ben Moses Halevi Mollin, who is quoted by Rabbi Moses Isserles in his note on 141:6.

54. See Alfred J. Kolatch's *Jewish Book of Why*, p. 135.
55. Megilla 23a.
56. Soferim 10:5,6. The text says that when one violates a festival, the violation of which involves only a negative precept (*mitzvat lo taaseh*), the punishment is less severe and five persons are called to read from the Torah. On Yom Kippur, when the penalty for violation is more severe (the penalty is *karet*, meaning "excommunication"), six are called to the Torah. On the Sabbath, when the penalty for violation is death (by stoning), seven are called to the Torah.
57. Mishna Megilla 3:1. See also Megilla 23a and Soferim 10:5, 6 for reasons why seven aliyot are awarded.
58. It is interesting to note that 77—the numerical value achieved when the number seven is repeated—is equal to that of the Hebrew word *mazal*, meaning "good luck." *Mazal* consists of the Hebrew letter *mem*, which equals 40; *za'yin* which equals 7; and *lamed* which equals 30—totaling 77.
59. Mishna Megilla 4:1-2.
60. Megilla 4:2 and Soferim 10:5.
61. See Megilla 21a. See also *Mishneh Torah*, Hilchot Tefila 12:16, and *Shulchan Aruch*, Orach Chayim 282:1, 2.
62. Mishna Megilla 4:1. Later authorities permit the calling of four aliyot on occasion. See Soferim 10:5.
63. Megilla 21b.
64. Soferim 10:5. See also Rashi on Megilla 21a and 22b and *Aruch Ha-shulchan* 135:3.
65. See Rashi's commentary on Megilla 21b.
66. *Shulchan Aruch*, Orach Chayim 135:1.
67. Ibid.
68. See Soferim 21:7. See also *Shulchan Aruch*, Orach Chayim 137:1, 2. This rule is not absolute. On Purim, when *parashat* Amalek is read, a total of only nine verses is read for the three aliyot.
69. See *Aruch Ha-shulchan*, Orach Chayim 135:3 and 137:2.
70. Ibid.
71. Aaron himself is exonerated from responsibility even though it was actually he who made the calf. He is generally portrayed as the victim of circumstance.

     One *midrash* does not exonerate him, pointing out that the death of Nadav and Avihu (two sons of Aaron), which occurred later, was Aaron's punishment for fashioning the Golden Calf. See Leviticus Rabba 10:1-3, where Aaron is exonerated.
72. See *Mishneh Torah*, Hilchot Tefila 12:18, and *Shulchan Aruch*, Orach Chayim 135:4.
73. Mishna Gittin 5:8 [59a].
74. Gittin 59b. See also *Shulchan Aruch*, Orach Chayim 135:3, and Mishna Berura, note 9, on Orach Chayim 135:3.
75. Mishna Gittin 5:8.
76. The Hebrew words used are *bi-mekom Kohayn*, meaning "in place

of the Kohayn." This is the view of Rabbi Moses Isserles, as stated in his Notes on Orach Chayim 135:6. The reason: If the announcement is not made when the Levi or Yisrael receives the first aliya, members of the congregation might be misled into thinking that the person who had been called to the Torah first was actually a Kohayn.

77. The expression *nitparda ha-chavila*, which is also translated as "the bundle has separated," was first used by the talmudic scholar Abaye, who said (Gittin 59b), "We assume the rule to be that if a Kohayn is not present, the arrangement [involving Kohayn, Levi, and Yisrael] is no longer in effect."

The same expression is found in Avoda Zara 10b in another context.

78. *Shulchan Aruch*, Orach Chayim 135:12. Rabbi Moses Isserles, in his Notes on Orach Chayim 135:5, states that this rule also applies if on a public fast day a Kohayn who is not fasting is present along with a Yisrael who is fasting. In this case the Yisrael is to be called up in place of the Kohayn.

79. The same approach would be followed if all except one person present were Leviim. As a general rule, however, two Leviim (or two Kohanim) are not given consecutive aliyot lest it lead people to doubt the lineage of the first honoree. See Orach Chayim 135:9.

80. See *Shulchan Aruch*, Orach Chayim 135:5.

81. Orach Chayim 135:6. See also Mishna Berura 135:13.

82. *Mishneh Torah*, Hilchot Tefila 12:19.

83. Mishna Gittin 5:8 [59a].

84. Gittin 59b. See also *Shulchan Aruch*, Orach Chayim 135:8.

85. A Kohayn is tainted if, for example, he has—contrary to biblical law—married a divorcee. The son of such a marriage is also tainted and not eligible to perform priestly functions. The Hebrew word for tainted is *pagum*.

See also Mishna Berura 135:6 for a discussion of this subject.

86. See Gittin 59b and *Shulchan Aruch*, Orach Chayim 135:9. A Levi is flawed (tainted) if his father has married a bastard. The offspring of such a marriage are disqualified from performing levitical functions. Both the *Shulchan Aruch*, Orach Chayim 135:9, and the *Mishneh Torah*, Hilchot Tefila 12:19, assert that the legitimacy of both the first and the second Levi might be in doubt.

87. Soferim 10:5, 6. On those occasions when no more than three aliyot may be awarded (such as on certain fast days), the third *oleh* is called as *shelishi*, not as maftir. This third *oleh*, who must be a Yisrael, not a Kohayn or Levi, then reads the haftara.

88. See Alfred J. Kolatch's *Second Jewish Book of Why*, p. 168, for more on Kohanim and their pedigree.

89. *Shulchan Aruch*, Orach Chayim 136:1.

90. Zohar 4:16b.

91. Genesis Rabba 78:8.

92. See earlier questions for more on the subject of *hosafot*.
93. *Aruch Ha-shulchan*, Orach Chayim 139:15, where the author indicates that it is also customary to use the Torah mantle for this purpose.
94. The word *tzitzit* consists of a *tzadi*, which has a numerical value of 90; *yod* (10); a second *tzadi* (90); a second *yod* (10); and finally *tav* (400). 90 + 10 + 90 + 10 + 400 =600.
95. Thirteen is the total number of strings and knots in each fringe. When a fringe for a *talit* is made, four threads are folded through the corner of the garment, thus yielding eight strings. One thread is longer than the rest, and it is wound around the other seven with five knots tied along the upper portion of the fringe.
96. Exodus Rabba 32:1. There are 365 negative commandments and 248 positive commandments.
97. See Megilla 21b, where Rabbi Judah says that the performance of a religious precept must be preceded by an appropriate blessing.
98. Mishna Megilla 3:1 [21a].
99. Megilla 21b. The Talmud, when saying that "nowadays all recite a blessing before and after" the Torah reading, was referring to the three who receive aliyot at the service on Sabbath afternoon or on Monday or Thursday morning. This practice did not apply to all other services.

    The Mishna Megilla (4:1) and the minor tractate Soferim (10:5), which according to most scholars was compiled in the eighth century C.E., three centuries after the Talmud was edited in its present form, indicate that on Mondays and Thursdays and at the Sabbath afternoon Torah reading service only the persons called to the Torah for the first and third (last) aliyot recite blessings, the first *oleh* reciting the first blessing only and the third *oleh* reciting the second (last) blessing only.

    It would appear that the custom of having all persons called to the Torah recite blessings before and after the reading developed after the ninth century. The reason is not clear, but it may have been introduced to afford members of the congregation an additional opportunity to respond "Amen" to important blessings.
100. Rabbi Judah suggested that the *oleh* recite, "Praised be Thou . . . Who has sanctified us through Thy commandments and commanded us to study Torah."

    Rabbi Yochanan suggested that the following benediction be adopted: "We beseech Thee to make the words of Thy Torah fill our mouths with pleasantries and sweetness."
101. Soferim 13:8. Orthodox women who conduct their own service read the Torah, but do not permit the *olah* to recite the *Barchu* when pronouncing the first blessing, since they believe that women may not be counted to a minyan.
102. To Reconstructionists the concept of Jews being a Chosen People signifies unwarranted pride, an idea that should be discarded. They

argue that we really do not know what the Bible originally meant when it used the term *am segula*, "Chosen People" (Exodus 19:5 and Deuteronomy 14:2). They also contend that it is harmful to continue to express this idea, for it invites contempt from non-Jews and contradicts the democratic ideal of equality which Judaism espouses.

See Alfred J. Kolatch's *Second Jewish Book of Why*, pp. 22ff., for a full discussion of the Chosen People concept.

103. Megilla 32a and Soferim 13:8. See also *Mishneh Torah*, Hilchot Tefila 12:5.
104. This practice is not approved of by many authorities because it gives the impression that one is flaunting piety. It falls into the same category as excessive bowing and genuflection during prayer, a practice condemned in the *Shulchan Aruch*, Orach Chayim 113:1, 3.
105. See note of Rabbi Moses Isserles on *Shulchan Aruch*, Orach Chayim 139:4.
106. *Shulchan Aruch*, Orach Chayim 139:11. Rabbi Moses Isserles, in his Notes to the above, says that the custom of holding the Torah finials is based on the verses in the Book of Joshua (1:8,9), "This Torah must ever be on your lips...be strong [*chazak*] and resolute. ..." Grasping the Torah finials is a symbol of strength. Isserles adds that this is also the reason why an individual who has completed the recitation of the second Torah blessing is greeted with the word *chazak*, "be strong."
107. See *Aruch Ha-shulchan*, Orach Chayim 139:14.
108. The word *hagbaha* is sometimes shortened and pronounced *hagba*. It is also often heard in its Yiddish form, *hagbeh*.
109. The last part of this phrase ("at the command ...") is from Numbers 9:23, and the first part from Deuteronomy 4:44. The *siddur* composed by the Vilna Gaon (1720-1797) indicates that all of Numbers 9:23 was once recited, not merely part of it as we do today.

Apparently *hagbaha* and *gelila* (the rolling of the Torah after it is raised) were originally performed by the reader himself. See the interesting comment of the Ramban on Deuteronomy 27:26: "Cursed be he who will not maintain this Torah."
110. Soferim 14:14.
111. This was stated in a private communication to the author in 1984.
112. As used in Yoma 7:1 [68b, 70a], where the High Priest is described as rolling up the Torah.
113. Megilla 32a.
114. The word *golel* is also used to mean "cover" in connection with the burial procedure. In ancient times, when persons were buried in caves, the final act was to roll a stone over the cave opening, thus "covering" the grave. Therefore the word *golel*, which in the Talmud (Shabbat 142b and Mishna Oholot 2:4) is used to mean "rock," took on the meaning of "covering." Rashi (Shabbat 152b) was of the opinion that the word *golel* (in connection with the later

burial procedure in which persons were laid to rest in coffins that were placed in the ground and covered with earth) meant the top or "covering" of the coffin itself. This view was accepted by later authorities, such as Nachmanides, who ruled that mourning (*Shiva*) actually begins when the cover of the coffin is closed.

Notes to Chapter 7
MAFTIR AND HAFTARA
Pages 193 to 210

1. This view is expressed by David ben Yosef Abudarham, the fourteenth-century Spanish liturgical commentator and author of *Sefer Abudarham*. Other scholars are of the opinion that the haftara reading was instituted to denigrate the Samaritans (and later the Sadducees), who regarded the Prophets as possessing lesser sanctity than the Pentateuch. See *Encyclopaedia Judaica* 7:1343.
2. Mishna Megilla 4:5. *Pores al Shema* is the Hebrew expression used.
3. Megilla 23a. Maimonides, in his *Mishneh Torah*, Hilchot Tefila 12:13, says that he who reads the haftara must first read at least three verses from the Torah.
4. See Megilla 31a.
5. See *Mishna Berura*, Orach Chayim 139:5, notes 21 and 22. See also Alfred J. Kolatch's *Second Jewish Book of Why*, pp. 242-43, for more on the covering of a Torah.
6. The origin of the Kaddish prayer is obscure, but most scholars believe it was instituted after the destruction of the First Temple in 586 B.C.E.. It was recited primarily after a lecture or discourse on a Torah theme had been completed.

   In its earliest form the Kaddish ended with three short sentences, the first of which began with the Aramaic word *titkabel*. The hope was expressed that the words spoken during the study period would be acceptable to God. *Titkabel* means "acceptance."

   When a study period or lecture was devoted to more scholarly or rabbinic subjects, the Kaddish prayer recited upon its conclusion included a paragraph beginning with the words "*Al Yisrael v'al Rabbanan*," meaning "Upon Israel and the Rabbis." Being a prayer for the good and welfare of scholars, the Kaddish became known as the Scholar's (or Rabbi's) Kaddish. In Aramaic it was called *Kaddish de-Rabbanan*.
7. *Mishneh Torah*, Hilchot Tefila 12:20.
8. In the Sephardic tradition, this Kaddish is called *Kaddish Le'elah* (also spelled *L'ayla*) because the last sentence of this short form of the Kaddish begins with the Aramaic word *l'ayla*.
9. See Yoma 70a and *Mishneh Torah*, Hilchot Tefila 12:23, where the

principle is referred to by such expressions as *kevod tzibur* or *kevod ha-beriyot*, meaning "the dignity of the people" or "honor of the congregation." It is sometimes referred to as *tircha d'tzibura* or *torach tzibur*, meaning "the inconvenience of the congregation." To keep a whole congregation waiting while a Torah is being rolled is an affront to its members.

See also Rashi on Yoma 70a, and see Alfred J. Kolatch's *Second Jewish Book of Why*, pp. 298 and 365.

10. Yoma 7:1[68b]. The High Priest did not use a second scroll for this second reading because the passages were so close together.

11. See Rabbi Baruch Halevi Epstein's *Torah Temima*, end of Bereshit, p. 472.

12. Orach Chayim 143:4. See also Isserles on Orach Chayim 282:5.

13. See Soferim 14:1, which points out that actually twenty-two verses were read. The extra verse, read by one of the seven, was done out of respect to the synagogue superintendent.

14. While almost all haftarot consist of at least twenty-one verses from the Prophets, some consist of fewer. The haftara of the sidra Ki Taytzay in the Book of Deuteronomy, for example, consists of only ten verses (Isaiah 54:1-10). Soferim 14:2 explains that some prophetic portions are brief because an entirely new theme is discussed in succeeding verses.

15. Soferim 14:2.

16. Megilla 23a and Soferim 14:1.

17. See Notes of Moses Isserles on *Shulchan Aruch*, Orach Chayim 284:1.

18. See Megilla 4:5-6. *See also* J. D. Bleich's *Contemporary Halakhic Problems*, Volume II, pp. 335-36, for a detailed discussion of this subject.

19. Usually these aliyot are awarded on the Sabbath when the Torah portion No'ach or Ki Taytzay is read, because the prophetic readings for these sidrot are very short.

20. See *The Responsa of Rabbi Simon ben Zemach Duran*, by Isidore Epstein, p. 74.

21. See *Shulchan Aruch*, Orach Chayim 282:4, particularly the Notes of Moses Isserles.

22. See Herbert C. Dobrinsky's *Treasury of Sephardic Laws and Customs*, pp. 30ff., for practices in various communities.

23. Some rabbis object to the Sabbath afternoon Bar Mitzva because they feel it is being held at that time only so that an elaborate reception can follow very soon afterwards, when the Sabbath is over. Other rabbis very often favor a weekday celebration of a Bar Mitzva in cases where if the celebration were to be held on a Saturday, the family members would have to violate the Sabbath by traveling.

24. See the Solomon B. Freehof responsum "Bar Mitzvah on Sunday" in *Modern Reform Responsa*, pp. 35ff.

25. Soferim 13:8-14; 14:1.

26. It was only after the third century B.C.E. that the Rabbis of Babylonia introduced the practice of reciting *Hallel* on the last six days of Passover. And, in order that a distinction be made between the new custom and the old practice, the Rabbis of Babylonia purposely omitted portions of the *Hallel* and this shortened version became known as *Half-Hallel*, although far less than half was omitted. On each day of Sukkot, *Hallel* was always recited from the very beginning.

See Alfred J. Kolatch's *Second Jewish Book of Why*, pp. 251-52, for more on this subject.

27. Mishna Megilla 4:10.

28. See commentaries on *Shulchan Aruch*, Orach Chayim 284:1-2.

29. This haftara is recited on the second Sabbath of Rebuke during the three weeks before Tisha B'Av.

30. See *Shulchan Aruch*, Orach Chayim 139:3, where Joseph Caro disallows a blind person from being called to the Torah at any time, a view not accepted by Moses Isserles and so indicated in his Notes on this section. The view of Isserles is universally accepted.

31. The minority, which is very strict in this matter and disallows the reading from anything but a handwritten scroll, follows the opinion of the Polish-born Rabbi Mordecai Jaffe (1530-1612), popularly called the "Levush" because his commentary on the *Shulchan Aruch* is named *Levush Malchut*. The Levush, who wrote the first commentary on the *Shulchan Aruch*, emphasized his disagreement with Joseph Caro and insisted that just as it is mandatory to use only a handwritten scroll at a public reading of the Torah, so is it mandatory to read the prophetic portion from a handwritten scroll.

While some modern scholars such as Yechiel Epstein (1835-1905) agree with Jaffe, the vast majority do not. See Epstein's *Aruch Ha-shulchan*, Orach Chayim 284:2-6.

32. With regard to the reading of the haftara from a printed book, see the Magen Avraham commentary on Orach Chayim 284:1.

Notes to Chapter 8

THE MASORETIC TEXT

Pages 211 to 248

1. *Ethics of the Fathers* 1:1.

2. See Mishna Kelim 15:6.

3. *Sefer Azara* and *Sefer Ezra* are almost identical in spelling except that *azara* has a *hay* as its last letter and Ezra is spelled with an *alef* at the end. The reading of the Tosefta in Kelim, Bava Metzia 5:8, is *Sefer Ezra*, not *Sefer Azara*.

For a further discussion of this subject, see *The Biblical Text in the Making*, by Robert Gordis, p. xxvi, 1971 edition.

4. See Talmud Yerushalmi, Taanit 4:2.
5. See Shabbat 14a. It was not uncommon for mice to make their homes in the bundles of grain and other foodstuffs that were kept in storage near the Torah scrolls. The mice were attracted to the food and often made contact with the scrolls, sometimes eating the parchment. It was therefore ruled that all such scrolls were ritually impure (*tamay*), and the hands of anyone who touched these scrolls became impure as well. Priests who touched them could not carry out their ritual duties without first cleansing themselves, and the scrolls of course could never be used for public readings.
6. Soferim 6:4. See also C. D. Ginsburg's *Introduction to the Masso-retico-Critical Edition of the Hebrew Bible*, pp. 408ff. See also *The Biblical Text in the Making*, by Robert Gordis, pp. xi ff., and the article on this by J. P. Siegel in *1972 and 1973 Proceedings* of the International Organization for Masoretic Studies, p. 106.

   The Talmud refers to *shelosha sefarim*, literally meaning "three books." The Soncino Talmud translates this as "three scrolls," but C. D. Ginsburg translates it as "three codices."
7. See Talmud Yerushalmi, Taanit 4:2, which reveals that three texts of the Pentateuch were housed in the Temple Court: One was called Codex *Meon*, the second Codex *Zaatutay*, the third Codex *Hi*. The first received its name because the word *meona* (Deuteronomy 33:27) appeared in two codices and the word *meon* (without the final *hay*) appeared in the third. The majority reading, *meona*, was accepted.

   The second codex received its name from the word *zaatutay*, which appeared in Exodus 24:5 in only one of the three codices. In the other two the word *naaray* was used. *Naaray* became the accepted form, and the word *zaatutay* does not appear at all in the Masoretic Text.

   The third codex was appropriately called Codex *Hi*. Although the word *hi*, meaning "she," should be spelled *hay yod alef*, it is spelled *hay vav alef* hundreds of times throughout the Torah (and the rest of the Bible). In one of the three codices of the Temple it was discovered that the word *hi* was spelled with a *yod* (*hay yod alef*) in nine verses, while in the other two codices it was spelled *hay yod alef* in eleven instances. The Masoretes favored the text of the two codices in which the *hi* was spelled with a *yod* in eleven of its verses.

   The eleven passages in which the *hi* was spelled with a *yod* are Genesis 14:2, 20:5, 38:25; Leviticus 11:39, 13:10, 13:21, 16:31, 20:17, 21:9; Numbers 5:13, 14.

   Early manuscripts preserved the text of the minority readings in marginal notes, but current editions of the Bible no longer record the variant forms of these three codices.
8. See C. D. Ginsburg's *Introduction to the Massoretico-Critical Edition of the Hebrew Bible*, pp. 241ff., for a detailed analysis of this entire subject.

9. One interesting variation appears in Genesis 3:20. In the Severus Codex the reading of verse 20 is "and the Lord God made unto Adam and his wife coats." Unlike the Bible text in use today, the verse does not specify the material from which such garments were made. Today's text reads, "and the Lord God made unto Adam and his wife coats of skin."

Another interesting difference is the rendering of verse 31 of the first chapter of Genesis. Today's accepted biblical text reads, "and behold it was very good." The Hebrew is *ve-hinay tov me'od*. The Severus Codex reads, *ve-hinay tov mavet*, meaning "and behold *death* was good." (The codex of Rabbi Meir, a disciple of the second-century C.E. Rabbi Akiba, carried the same reading as the Severus Codex.)

See C. D. Ginsburg's *Introduction to the Massoretico-Critical Edition of the Hebrew Bible*, pp. 410ff., for the complete list of the thirty-two variations and an analysis of each.

10. See C. D. Ginsburg's *Introduction to the Massoretico-Critical Edition of the Hebrew Bible*, pp. 452ff., for more on this subject.

11. Sanhedrin 90a.

12. Pesachim 50a.

To serve as a constant reminder that the word *Adonai* is a substitute for *Yehova*, the Masoretes transferred to *Yehova* the vowel-points of *Adonai*. See C. D. Ginsburg's *Introduction to the Massoretico-Criticial Edition of the Hebrew Bible*, pp. 367ff.

When the Divine Name *Adonai* precedes the name *Yehova*, the two words are pronounced *Adonai Elohim*, not *Adonai Adonai*. (An example of this is found in Genesis 15:2.) The vowel-points of *Elohim* appear under the letters of the second *Adonai*.

13. See the Turay Zahav commentary on Yoreh Deah 274:7. He says, "The Torah written by scribes for public use must be written exactly as the Torah that was given to Moses on Sinai." See also *Shulchan Aruch*, Yoreh Deah 273:7.

14. Megilla 32a.

15. Nedarim 37b and Bava Batra 15a.

16. The following are Masoretic notes most frequently found in the margins of printed Hebrew Pentateuchs. They relate mostly to pronunciation and accentuation.

a) *Kamatz b'zakef katan*, one of the most common of the Masoretic notations, indicates that the word called to our attention (usually by an asterisk placed over it) should have a *kamatz* under the letter that has the *zakef katan* cantillation mark. Thus the word in Genesis 11:3 with the *zakef katan* over it should be read *l'aven* rather than *l'even*, which is the usual pronunciation.

b) *Kamatz b'zakef gadol* indicates that a *kamatz* is to be placed under the letter over which the *zakef gadol* appears, as in Genesis 41:5. The word *va-yishan* would normally have a *patach* under the last syllable.

c) *Dalet b'zakef katan*, found in Genesis 1:11, reminds the reader that the *zakef katan* note is to be placed over the *dalet*, as in the word *desheh*, and this first syllable is to be accented.

d) *Lamed kemutza* signifies that the *lamed* of the word indicated is to have a *kamatz* under it, as in Genesis 41:50.

e) *Dalet kemutza* signifies that the letter *dalet* in the word indicated must be vocalized with a *kamatz* instead of a *patach*, as in Exodus 29:43.

f) *Ha-mem b'kamatz* indicates that the *mem* is to have a *kamatz* under it, as in Deuteronomy 5:24.

g) *Kamatz u-mil-e'ra*, a notation found in Genesis 2:22, refers to the word *ha-tzayla*. *Mi-le'ra* signifies that the last syllable of the word is to be accented, and in this case the accent is to be placed on the *la* when pronouncing the word *ha-tzayla*. This reminder also serves notice that a *kamatz*, not a *patach*, is to be placed under the *lamed*.

h) *Ha-hay b'kamatz*, which appears in Genesis 6:19 and many other places, is a reminder that under the letter *hay* is a *kamatz*. See also Genesis 10:17.

i) *Kamatz b'fashta* indicates that under the *pashta* note is a *kamatz*, as in the word *am* in Numbers 23:24.

j) *Kamatz bi-revia (bi-revii* is the more popular spelling and pronunciation) signifies that the *kamatz* vowel, not the *patach*, is to appear under the *revii* note, as in Leviticus 12:4 in connection with the word *tiga*. See also Leviticus 16:4 and Deuteronomy 13:6.

k) *Kamatz b'segolta*, which appears in Deuteronomy 31:7, indicates that the word *ve'ematz*, which has the *segol* as its cantillation note, should be spelled with a *kamatz*, not a *patach*. The word *yishkavu* in Genesis 19:4 is another such example. Other examples are found in Exodus 12:22, Numbers 21:13, and Deuteronomy 31:7, 23.

l) *Mile'el* indicates that the word should be accented on the first syllable. The word *haba'a* in Genesis 18:21 is one such example. Other examples are found in Exodus 12:11 and 19:5 and in Deuteronomy 1:38.

m) *Mi-le'ra* signifies that the last syllable of the word is to be accented, as in the word *ravu* in Genesis 26:22. Other examples are to be found in Genesis 40:15; Exodus 8:7, 18:26, 26:33; Leviticus 15:29, 22:13; Numbers 24:17; and Deuteronomy 1:28.

n) *Tzadi rafeh* indicates that in the word marked with a Masoretic asterisk the *tzadi* is to be pronounced weakly, much like an "s." This is common pronunciation among Sephardic Jews. One example is the *tzadi* in *va-yitzok* in Genesis 28:18.

o) *Patach b'etnach* indicates that the letter carrying the cantillation note *etnachta*, as the *mem* in *va-yigamal* in Genesis 21:8, should have a *patach* under the *mem*, not the *kamatz* that would be expected. (Earlier versions of the Masoretic Text used the word *etnach* for *etnachta*, the word in current usage.) The *etnachta* indicates a major pause in the text, much akin to a semicolon. Other examples are to be found in Genesis 27:2, Exodus 16:20, and Numbers 15:31.

p) *Segol b'etnach* notes that the word carrying the *etnach* (also called *etnachta*) is to be pronounced with a *segol*. Thus, in Genesis 22:6 and 22:10 the word with the *etnachta* is to be pronounced *maachelet*, not *maachalet* as would be expected. The same is true of the word *betach* in Genesis 34:25. The *segol* under the word with the *etnachta* is to be pronounced *betach*, not *batach* as is usually done at the end of a verse or at a long pause, which is what the *etnachta* represents.

q) *Patach b'sof pasuk. Sof pasuk* means "end of the sentence." Normally a *patach* is changed to a *kamatz* at the end of a sentence, but there are exceptions noted by the Masoretes. The first such instance in the Bible is in Genesis 3:6, where the final word in the sentence is to be pronounced *va-yochal*. Other examples are to be found in Genesis 19:19, 21 and in Deuteronomy 28:42 and 31:21.

r) *Segol b'sof pasuk* means that here a *segol*, instead of the usual *kamatz*, is to be used for this last word in the verse. The first instance in the Bible of this type of Masoretic note is in Exodus 22:24, where the word is to be spelled and read as *neshech*, not *nashech*.

s) *Gimmel rafeh* signifies that the *gimmel* in the word is to be pronounced softly, much like the "j" sound. This is primarily the practice in Sephardic communities that were influenced by the Arabic language.

t) *Ha-nun be-tzayreh* indicates that the *nun* is to be vocalized with a *tzayreh* rather than the expected *segol*, as per the word *t'anay* in Exodus 22:22.

u) *Kamatz bi-tevir* means that the *kamatz* vowel is to appear under the *tevir* note, as in Leviticus 5:18, where the word *shagag* is found.

v) *Sin rafeh* indicates that the letter *sin* of a particular word is to be pronounced softly, perhaps somewhere between an "s" and a "z." This was probably traditional among Jews of Eastern countries where the Sephardic pronunciation was in vogue. Examples are to be found in the Torah in Leviticus 13:10, on the word *ba'se'ayt*, and in Leviticus 14:56 on the same basic word.

w) *Kamatz be-tircha* signifies that the letter with the *tircha* cantillation note (*tircha* is an early name for what today is commonly called *tipcha*) is to be vocalized with a *kamatz*, not a *patach*. Such notations appear in the Torah on Leviticus 27:10; Numbers 9:2, 13:8, 21:6; and Deuteronomy 9:14.

x) *Tzadi petucha* indicates that the *tzadi* in the word noted must be vocalized with a *patach*, not with the usual *kamatz*, as in Numbers 10:9 on the word *ha-tzar*.

y) *Bet petucha* means that the *bet* in the word indicated carries a *patach* vowel, as in *Shabbat* in Numbers 28:10 and as in Deuteronomy 27:8 in connection with the word *ba'er*, usually spelled with a *kamatz*.

z) *L'medincha'i* refers to the traditional way of spelling a word among Easterners—residents of Palestine, Syria, Persia, Yemen, and surrounding areas. See the haftara reading for Pinchas, I Kings 19:3, where the Easterners render the word *al* with an *a'yin*, not with an *alef* as the word appears in the written text. (The Western schools of Masoretes were known as Maarva'i.) Another example is found in I Samuel 1:3 where some editions of the Bible note that Pinchas is spelled without a *yod* in the Eastern tradition.

aa) *Ha-taam nasog achor* indicates that the word is accented on the earlier syllable rather than on the syllable over which the note now appears, as in Deuteronomy 19:19 on the word *va-a-si-tem*. The cantillation note appears on the *si* syllable, but in this case the accent should be placed on the syllable preceding it. *Nasog achor* literally means "turn back."

bb) *Ha-resh b'kamatz* means that under the *resh* is a *kamatz*, as in the word *rav* in Deuteronomy 33:7.

17. Nedarim 37b.
18. *Shulchan Aruch*, Orach Chayim 141:8.
19. Megilla 25b. See also Sanhedrin 68b.

The avoidance of unsavory language is characteristic of the Torah itself, as has been noted by many commentators.

The Rabbis believed the use of foul language and the recitation of unsavory biblical tales to be out of keeping with the goal of establishing Israel as a holy people. Pointing to Leviticus, Chapter 11, where kosher and nonkosher animals are listed, the Rabbis note that the text studiously avoids using the word *tamay*, meaning "defiled, ritually unclean," using in its stead two words, *lo-tehora*, "not clean." The Bible, which is usually very sparing in its verbiage, here uses two words when one would have told the story quite adequately (Leviticus Rabba 26:1-2).

The Rabbis adopted this same attitude toward language, as is evident in their own writings. Thus, when they speak of a Torah scroll that is beyond repair and must be disposed of, the word *nignaz*, "hidden away," is used instead of the harsher term *nikbar*, "buried" (Shabbat 103b).

This desire to avoid unpleasant words led to unusual and unexpected situations. When printed books began to appear in the sixteenth century, some Jewish printers went so far as to alter the numbering of pages and chapters in order to avoid the use of letters that would spell out words with unsavory meanings. For example, we find in editions of the *Shulchan Aruch* the number 270 or 275 being altered for this reason. The number 270 in Hebrew is normally written as *resh a'yin*, the *resh* being numerically equivalent to 200 and the *a'yin* to 70. But when placed side by side, the *resh* and *a'yin* spell out the Hebrew word *ra*, meaning "bad." To avoid the use of the word *ra*, the printers reversed the letters and wrote *a'yin resh*. The same procedure was followed for number 275, which in Hebrew is *ra'a*, the feminine form of *ra*. The spelling *resh a'yin hay* was changed to *a'yin resh hay*.

We also find that actual names of books were changed in order to avoid the use of unpleasant words. Thus, the talmudic tractate on mourning, which should have properly been named Avelut, is called Semachot, meaning "joys." And the tractate Baytza (Betza) is sometimes called by its Aramaic name Baya, because Baytza in its plural form, Baytzim, "eggs," also refers to testicles.

20. The other instances in the Bible where *afolim* is the *ketiv* and *techorim* is the *keri* are to be found in I Samuel 5:6,9,12 and 6:4,5,11,17.

21. The root-word *shagol*, meaning "sexual intercourse," appears in various forms in Psalms 45:10; Nehemiah 2:6; and Daniel 5:2,3,23. In every case the *keri* is a form of the root-word *shachov*. This euphemistic form also appears in the last chapter of Zechariah (14:2), the haftara for the first day of Sukkot.

See the *Mishneh Torah*, Hilchot Sefer Torah 7:11, and the *Shulchan Aruch*, Yoreh Deah 275:6, for more on these euphemistic expressions.

22. See Megilla 25a and 25b for a full discussion of this subject.

23. In Genesis 35:22, in printed copies of the Bible, the letter *pay* (for *petucha*, "open") appears in the open space. In Deuteronomy 2:8 the letter *samech* (for *setuma*, "closed") appears in the open space. Where the *pay* appears, the next verse begins on the next line. Where the samech appears, the next verse begins on the same line. It is possible that the *pay* was used to indicate that what is being omitted is very serious and a noticeable space should therefore be left before continuing the text. The *samech* would seem to indicate a less serious omission.

See the questions in this chapter relating to the open and closed sections in the Torah.

24. It was believed that there are a total of eighteen scribal corrections found in the Bible as a whole, three of which are in the Torah.

The oldest record of these changes is found in the Mechilta on Exodus 15:7, where eleven of the eighteen are listed. Other lists are found in the Sifre, Yalkut Shimoni, and Midrash Tanchuma. Included among the eighteen cited in the various lists are: I Samuel 3:13; II Samuel 20:1; Jeremiah 2:11; Ezekiel 8:17; Hosea 4:7; Habakkuk 1:12; Zechariah 2:12; Malachi 1:13; Psalms 106:20; Job 7:20, 32:3; and Lamentations 3:20. Sources and a detailed discussion of all the various passages are to be found in C. D. Ginsburg's *Introduction to the Massoretico-Critical Edition of the Hebrew Bible*, pp. 347ff.

25. Genesis Rabba 49:7.

26. See C. D. Ginsburg's *Introduction to the Massoretico-Critical Edition of the Hebrew Bible*, p. 352.

27. Ibid., p. 353. While this is the reason most scholars give for this

scribal emendation, it is just as reasonable to assume that the change was made because the original text represented an affront to Moses.

28. Ibid. See also Sifre, Numbers, Be-ha'alotecha 105.
29. The haftara reading for Shabbat Rosh Chodesh is Isaiah 66, the last chapter of the book.
30. Chapter 3, the last chapter of Malachi, is the haftara reading for Shabbat Ha-gadol.
31. Aycha is read on Tisha B'Av.
32. Kohelet is read on the Sabbath of Sukkot.
33. Sevirin in the Book of Genesis will be found in 19:8,25,33; in the Book of Exodus in 8:20, 11:6, 14:13, 25:39, 26:31; in the Book of Leviticus in 27:9; in the Book of Numbers in 4:49, 9:6, 13:22, 32:25, 33:8, 35:5; and in the Book of Deuteronomy in 3:20, 4:23, 4:42, 17:19, 19:11.
34. See Kiddushin 30a for more on plene and defective words.
35. Very often a chaser word is classified as a keri, as in Genesis 33:4 and Exodus 35:11.
36. See C. D. Ginsburg's Introduction to the Massoretico-Critical Edition of the Hebrew Bible, pp. 137ff., for more on this.
37. Shulchan Aruch, Orach Chayim 143:4.
38. The Aruch Ha-shulchan, Orach Chayim 143:6, is quite blunt in stating that scrolls in use today are not always absolutely correct.
39. Kiddushin 30a presents a discussion that transpired in the Babylonian academy of Pumbedita during the fourth century: Rabbi Joseph asked, "Does the vav in the word gachon [Leviticus 11:42] belong to the first half of the Torah or the second half? [The vav was said to be the middle letter of the Torah.]"

His colleagues responded, "Let a scroll of the Torah be brought out and we will count them [the letters]."

At this point the Babylonian Talmud adds, "They [the scholars of Palestine] were thoroughly versed in defective and plene readings, but we are not."
40. An example of how a single word in a single chapter is sometimes plene and sometimes defective can be seen in the first chapter of the Book of Numbers where the word shaymot, "names," is spelled six times with the letter vav and seven times without it. This is also true of the word lo, meaning "no" or "not," which is spelled very often with a vav. With so many deviations in spelling it is not surprising that there was no accurate letter count. Scribes in various localities followed practices of particular Masoretic schools, each with distinctly different traditions.
41. See Baruch Epstein's Torah Temima, end of Deuteronomy, and the Even-Shoshan Concordantzya Chadasha.
42. Menachot 30a and Mishneh Torah, Hilchot Sefer Torah 10:1.
43. The ten places in the Torah where dots appear over letters are Genesis 16:5, 18:9, 19:33, 33:4, 37:12; Numbers 3:39, 9:10, 21:30,

29:15; and Deuteronomy 29:28. Elsewhere in the Bible, dots appear in II Samuel 19:20; Isaiah 44:9; Ezekiel 41:20, 46:22; and Psalms 27:13. In biblical literature, dots that appear over letters are also termed *puncta extraordinaire* or extraordinary points.

C. D. Ginsburg's *Introduction to the Massoretico-Critical Edition of the Hebrew Bible*, pp.318-34, has an in-depth treatment of the fifteen extraordinary points. See also Soferim 6:3 and Genesis Rabba 48:15 for additional basic information. Chapter 34 of The Fathers According to Rabbi Nathan offers an explanation for each of the ten biblical instances.

Only one word in the Bible has dots below as well as above each of its letters. In all other cases where dots appear they are to be found only above the letters of the words. The unusual case in question is the Hebrew word *lulay* in Psalms 27:13, which is read in many congregations at the conclusion of the daily service during the month of Elul through Shemini Atzeret. The theme of the psalm is closely linked to that which is expressed during Rosh Hashana and Yom Kippur: through faith one can be assured that he will "enjoy the goodness of the Lord."

The renowned Bible commentator S. L. Gordon believed that the Masoretes treated the word *lulay* in this most unusual way because they wanted to convey strong doubts as to the correctness of the word. They questioned whether the word actually appeared in the earliest Bible manuscripts, conjecturing that the original word in the verse was not *lulay* but *ve-lo*. When the first *lamed* of *lulay* is dropped, the word becomes *ve-lo*. *Lulay he-emanti* means "Had I not believed," while *ve-lo he-emanti* means "I did not believe." The dots placed above and below the word are to serve as reminders of how difficult it is to interpret the verse accurately.

The Talmud (Berachot 4a) mentions the dots on *lulay* and explains their appearance by saying that David, who according to Jewish tradition was the author of the book of Psalms, was not quite sure that he would merit reward in the world-to-come because of his sins. To express his apprehension he dotted the word *lulay* above and below its letters.

44. See Rashi on this verse. Esau's sincerity was doubted because he brought with him an army of four hundred. Rabbi Shimon ben Yochai, in the second century C.E., saw in the incident a positive message: an enemy can turn into a friend given the right circumstances.

See also Mishna Pesachim 9:2, where the lesson to be learned from the dot over the *hay* of the word *rechoka*, meaning "far away," in Numbers 9:10 is that one is considered to be far away from the Temple even if he has reached the Temple but did not enter it with his sacrifice. All such persons are considered to be among those who have not appeared in the Temple precincts at the proper time (on the fourteenth of Nissan), and they are obligated to offer a paschal sacrifice one month later, on Pesach Sheni (the Second Passover).

45. Bechorot 4a. See also Midrash Rabba, Numbers 3:13.
46. Most of these are mentioned in Soferim 9:3-7. Abraham Even-Shoshan's *Concordantzya Chadasha* lists all the large and small letters.
47. In the Midrash the *hay* is considered an abbreviation for a separate word. It is said to stand for *hoy*, meaning "alas." See Exodus Rabba 24:1.
48. Some would add the letter *sin* in the word *eres* in Deuteronomy 3:11 to the list of sixteen.
49. Kiddushin 30a and Soferim 9:2. See page 376 for more on this subject.
50. Soferim 9:4.
51. Berachot 61b.
52. Even-Shoshan's *Concordantzya Chadasha* lists all the small-script letters in the Bible.
53. See Rashi, who offers other explanations.
54. See *Pentateuch and Haftorahs*, by J. H. Hertz, p. 410. In his Baal Ha-turim commentary, Jacob ben Asher (1270-1343) states that the *alef* was written in small script as a compromise: Moses wanted to spell the word *va-yikra* without the *alef* entirely, which would result in the word *va-yikar*, which means "to meet by accident." This is the same word that appears in Numbers 23:4, where it is used in connection with God's meeting with Balaam. God, however, did not want his call to Moses in Leviticus 1:1 to appear to be accidental, and he insisted that the word be written with an *alef* so it would mean "and He called." Moses agreed, and as testimony to that agreement he wrote the *alef* in small script.
55. The event is known as the Sin of Baal Peor. Peor was the name of the mountain on which the idolatry was practiced.
56. The word *shalom* is spelled *shin lamed vav mem*. The broken *vav* is referred to as *vav ketia*. See Kiddushin 66b for more on this subject.
57. Inverted *nuns* are also to be found in the Book of Psalms, Chapter 107, at the beginning of verses 23 through 27 and at the end of verse 39.
58. Shabbat 115b and 116a. See also *Igrot Moshe*, Yoreh Deah 165, for a fuller analysis.
59. There is one case in the Bible where the reverse situation exists. In the Book of Nehemiah 2:13 the word *haym* is spelled with an ordinary *mem*, not with a final *mem*. Again the Masoretes called this to our attention but did not tamper with the traditional text.

It should be noted that the Christian Church has made much of the final *mem* (closed on all sides) that appears in the middle of a word in Isaiah 9:6. Just as they claim that the last two words of verse 5, *sar shalom*, meaning "prince of peace," predict the coming of Jesus, so does the closed *mem* forecast that a virgin (who is also closed and unpenetrated) will give birth to this prince of peace.

The actual dogma of the virgin birth is based on Isaiah 7:14, which is believed by Christians to be a foretelling of the event: "Behold the young woman [*alma*] shall conceive and bear a child . . ." Many scholars acknowledge that *alma* means "young woman," not necessarily "virgin." See Alfred J. Kolatch's *Second Jewish Book of Why*, pp. 66-67, for a full discussion of this subject.

60. See Shabbat 103b and Sifra, Leviticus 1:1.

61. See the Meir A'yin commentary of Meir Ish-Shalom in the Sifra, Leviticus 1, for a statement confirming this view.

Two sidrot in the Torah contain no open or closed sections whatsoever: Va-yaytzay (Genesis 28:10-32:3) and Miketz (Genesis 41:1-44:17).

No explanation has been offered for the absence of open and closed sections within the sidra Miketz, but Rabbi Asher ben Yechiel (the Rosh) offers a homiletical explanation for Va-yaytzay. Commenting on Genesis 28:10, the opening verse of Va-yaytzay, Rabbi Asher indicates that some people believe that the entire portion is presented as one uninterrupted unit because it describes a part of the life of Jacob that was shrouded in mystery and that it is therefore, in a sense, a closed chapter.

62. Soferim 1:14 requires that there be space for only three letters, but the final law as specified in the *Shulchan Aruch*, Yoreh Deah 275:2, calls for nine letter-spaces. Here, the conflicting view of the Rosh (Rabbi Asher ben Yechiel), a fourteenth-century authority, is given.

63. Maimonides' view is spelled out in the *Mishneh Torah*, Hilchot Sefer Torah 8:1. See also *Igrot Moshe*, Yoreh Deah I:169, for a responsum of Rabbi Moshe Feinstein on this subject.

64. Maimonides might have suggested that enough white space be left to accommodate nine letters because the longest word in the Bible, *le-mishpechotayhem*, has nine letters when spelled defective (*chaser*). See Genesis 8:19. See also Chapter Four, page 106, where the number of letters that a line in the Torah should accommodate is discussed.

65. This is the view of Maimonides. Not all authorities agree, however. See *Aruch Ha-shulchan*, Yoreh Deah 275:15, for variant views.

One point of disagreement concerns whether Leviticus 7:22 begins an open section. Maimonides claims yes, but others disagree. And although the views of Maimonides are generally accepted, Bible texts today do not delineate a *parasha* at this point. See the Minchat Shai commentary on this verse.

66. Rabbi Asher ben Yechiel (1250-1327), author of the Tur, did not agree with all of the designations of Maimonides. See *Shulchan Aruch*, Yoreh Deah 275:2, for more on this difference of opinion.

67. *Mishneh Torah*, Hilchot Sefer Torah 8:4. Maimonides concludes with the following summary:

The Book of Genesis: The number of open sections is 43; of closed sections 48; total 91.

The Book of Exodus: The number of open sections is 69; of closed sections, 95; total 164.

The Book of Leviticus: The number of open sections is 52; of closed sections, 46; total 98.

The Book of Numbers: The number of open sections is 92; of closed sections, 66; total 158.

The Book of Deuteronomy: The number of open sections is 34; of closed sections, 124; total 158.

The number of open sections in the entire Pentateuch is 290; of closed sections, 379; total 669.

68. Bava Batra 13b.

69. The Koren edition of the Torah, which is based on a first edition of the Vienna Bible published in 1859, is a rare exception and does have three *samechs* at the beginning of Va-yechi.

   C. D. Ginsburg, in his *Introduction to the Massoretico-Critical Edition of the Hebrew Bible,* p. 66, notes that in some early manuscripts there is no division between the end of Toldot and the beginning of Va-yaytzay.

70. Rashi notes that his observation is based on a comment in Genesis Rabba 96:1.

71. Shabbat 103b and Soferim 1:14. This ruling is codified in the *Shulchan Aruch,* Yoreh Deah 275:1. See also *Mishneh Torah,* Hilchot Sefer Torah 8:3.

72. See *Shulchan Aruch,* Yoreh Deah 275:1, where Joseph Caro and Moses Isserles disagree. Caro's ruling is that scrolls with improper spacing should not be corrected and must be stored in a *geniza,* while Isserles says they may be corrected as long as it does not involve erasing God's name or cutting and patching the parchment in any way.

73. See Mishna Megilla 4:4 and Kiddushin 30a. The Mishna, which was already in its final form by the middle of the third century C.E., contains instructions addressed to the person who translates the Torah into the vernacular during the Torah reading. He (the *meturgeman*) was to translate *each verse* immediately after the Torah reader had completed reading it in Hebrew, which of course means that by that time the Torah had already been divided into verses.

   When the haftara was read, the *meturgeman* did the translation after every three verses.

74. See Ernst Würthwein's *Text of the Old Testament,* pp. 21, 94.

75. See Kiddushin 30a, Nedarim 37b and 38a, and Soferim 3:7 and 9:3 for more on the verse count in the Torah.

76. The theory has been advanced that the *gimmel* of *ve-hitgalach* in Leviticus 13:33 is written large to call attention to the fact that the verse in which it appears is the middle verse of the Torah. See Kiddushin 30a and C. D. Ginsburg's *Introduction to the Massoretico-Critical Edition of the Hebrew Bible,* p. 69, for an elaboration on this theme.

77. Kiddushin 30a and Nedarim 38a.
78. See *Torah Temima*, Volume V, p. 524. See also Even-Shoshan's *Concordantzya Chadasha*, Introduction, p. 38.

    This discrepancy has obviously come about because the same text was not used by all scholars, proving, as Professor Harry Orlinsky maintains, that there has never been one text that can be spoken of as *the* Masoretic Text.
79. Kiddushin 30a and Soferim 9:2.
80. The statistics at the end of each of the Five Books of Moses include the number of *parashiyot* (singular, *parasha*) and the number of *sedarim* (singular, *seder*) contained in the book. These indicate the portions of the Torah that are read weekly in the synagogue.

    Parashiyot (synonymous with *sidrot* but not to be confused with *sedarim*) refer to the 54 weekly readings in accordance with the annual Torah reading cycle, the system followed today in almost all traditional synagogues. *Sedarim* refer to the 154 weekly readings in acccordance with the triennial cycle, the system in which the entire Torah is read over a period of three years.

    The following is the breakdown of the weekly Torah readings in each of the five books of the Torah. The first number represents the number of *parashiyot*, and the number in brackets indicates the number of *sedarim*.

    > Genesis (Bereshit) 12 [43];
    > Exodus (Shemot) 11 [29];
    > Leviticus (Va-yikra) 10 [23];
    > Numbers (Be-midbar) 10 [32];
    > Deuteronomy (Devarim) 11 [27].

    The number of portions into which the Torah is divided in a particular year depends on the calendar. In leap years the extra month (of Adar) must be taken into account, as must the days of the week on which holidays fall in a given year.

    Since the communities of Europe chose to follow the annual cycle that originated in Babylonia, the breakdown of the *sedarim* in the Palestinian triennial cycle was not noted in their Hebrew texts of the Bible. Although it is known that many early manuscripts of the Torah did indicate where the triennial readings began and ended, these manuscripts have disappeared.
81. For more on this subject see Ernst Würthwein's *The Text of the Old Testament*, pp. 37 and 172. See also C. D. Ginsburg's *Introduction to the Massoretico-Critical Edition of the Hebrew Bible*, pp. 26, 925, 927, and 937.

Notes to Chapter 9
WEEK BY WEEK
Pages 249 to 293

1. Soferim 14:1.
2. Megilla 29b and 30a. Reform Judaism, which follows the triennial cycle, suggests as many as four alternative haftara readings from the Prophets and Hagiographa that can be used with each Torah reading. See *Gates of Prayer*, issued by the Union of American Hebrew Congregations.
3. David was 70 years old when he died; Jacob was 147; and Joseph was 110. I Chronicles 29:28 says of David that he died *b'sayva tova*, "in the fullness of years," which led to the expression in *Ethics of the Fathers* 5:25, "At age 70 one has achieved a ripe old age."
4. The printed Chumash in common use is always marked with the words *sheni* (second aliya), *shelishi* (third aliya), and so on, to indicate where the reading for each *oleh* is to begin. This is true of the sidra Ki Tissa as well, but in Sephardic congregations the Torah reader does not stop at *sheni* (Exodus 31:18), as is the normal practice. Instead the reader continues until *shelishi* (Exodus 33:11). At that point the Levi is called to the Torah.

   This custom was instituted to pay tribute to Levites, whose ancestors did not follow the masses by contributing to and worshiping the Golden Calf, an incident described in Exodus 31:18-33:11.
5. Kiddushin 33a.
6. According to some rabbinical interpretations there are seven books in the Torah, and the Book of Numbers should be counted as three books, with Chapter 10, verses 35 and 36 constituting a separate book. See Genesis Rabba 64:8. See also page 238 for more on these two verses, which are set off by two reversed *nuns* that look like parentheses. There is also another view that asserts that the Book of Balaam (Numbers 22:2 to 24:25) was once a separate book of the Bible.
7. See Genesis Rabba 64:7 and also Rashi on Exodus 38:26.
8. Sota 36b.
9. In Numbers 8:23-26 the minimum age was set at 25 years. Compare I Chronicles 23:24-27, where the age is 20 years.

   See Rashi on Numbers 8:24 and especially Ramban (Nachmanides) for an explanation of these discrepancies.
10. Because Reuben was the eldest son of Jacob, the tribe of Reuben was the senior tribe. Its leaders believed its status had been neglected.
11. In the twenty-one-year span between 1980 and 2000, Nitzavim is combined with Va-yaylech eight times in regular years and five times in leap years. The two sidrot are read separately five times in

regular years and three times in leap years. In all instances the haftara for Nitzavim is read.

12. Scholars differ as to the exact manner in which this was arranged. Tradition has it that a ledge projected from the ark and the Torah was kept on the ledge. Other students of the Bible are of the opinion that the Torah was kept in the ark next to the Tablets of the Law (the Ten Commandments), sometimes referred to as the Tablets of Testimony (*Luchot Ha-edut*).

Notes to Chapter 10

HOLIDAY BY HOLIDAY

Pages 294 to 332

1. See Taanit 27b, where this explanation was originally offered.

   Although the sacrificial system came to an end with the destruction of the Second Temple in 70 C.E., the hope that the Temple would be rebuilt and that sacrifices would again be brought on the altar never faded. Some Rabbis felt more strongly than others about this.

   Maimonides, in his twelfth-century code, the *Mishneh Torah*, devotes much space to a recounting of the laws pertaining to the sacrificial system. However, Joseph Caro, in his *Shulchan Aruch*, does not restate these laws.

2. The complete abstention from work applies only to the Sabbath and major holidays. However, many ultra-Orthodox Jews, particularly chassidim, do abstain from work in varying degrees on the intermediate days of Sukkot and Pesach.

3. Isaiah 1:13 refers to Rosh Chodesh and the Sabbath as solemn days.

4. Mishna Megilla 4:2 and *Shulchan Aruch*, Orach Chayim 423:1.

5. It should be noted that the Machar Chodesh haftara is not read when Shabbat Shekalim is the day on which the New Moon of Adar is blessed and the following day, Sunday, will be Rosh Chodesh. In that case, instead of the Machar Chodesh haftara, the haftara of Shabbat Shekalim is recited.

6. Mishna Megilla 3:4-6 lists the various Torah readings for each of the four special Sabbaths. See also *Shulchan Aruch*, Orach Chayim 685:1-7, and Mishna Berura 685:1, note 1.

7. Mishna Shekalim 1:1.

8. See the comment of J. Hertz in *Pentateuch and Haftorahs*, p. 352.

9. *Shulchan Aruch*, Orach Chayim 685:1.

10. See also page 383, which indicates how a Torah scribe blots out the name of Amalek as he tests his quill and ink before writing a scroll.

11. Sephardim start the haftara reading with the first verse of I Samuel 15.

12. *Shulchan Aruch,* Orach Chayim 635:3,5.
13. See Megilla 3:3 for more details. See also Orach Chayim 685:4.
14. *Shulchan Aruch,* Orach Chayim 430:1.
15. The tractate Rosh Hashana (11a) indicates that in talmudic times there was a popular belief that the Messiah would appear in the month of Nissan, the same month in which the Children of Israel were released from bondage.
16. Israel observes Passover for only seven days, as commanded in the Bible. Reform Jews also observe the holiday for seven days. In some traditions, the maftir for the first and second day of the holiday is Numbers 28:16-25. Numbers 28:19-25 is read on each of the other days of the holiday.
17. The portions read on the weekdays of Chol Ha-moed are as follows:

> On the third day of Passover, which is the first day of Chol Ha-moed, the reading for the first three aliyot is Exodus 13:1-16, and the reading for the fourth aliya is Numbers 28:19-25, which describes the holiday sacrifices.
> On the fourth day of Passover, the second intermediate day, the reading for the first three aliyot is Exodus 22:24-23:19, and the reading for the fourth aliya is Numbers 28:19-25 (as on the first intermediate days).
> On the fifth day of Passover, the third intermediate day, the reading for the first three aliyot is Exodus 34:1-26, and the reading for the fourth aliya is Numbers 28:19-25 (as on the first two intermediate days).
> On the sixth day of Passover, the fourth intermediate day, the reading for the first three aliyot is Numbers 9:1-14, and the reading for the fourth aliya is Numbers 28:19-25 (as on the first three intermediate days).
> When the first day of Chol Ha-moed falls on a Sabbath, the Torah reading is Exodus 33:12-34:26 instead of Exodus 13:1-16, and the regular maftir, Numbers 28:19-25, is also read. The readings for the first and second days of Chol Ha-moed are each postponed by one day, and the reading for the third day of Chol Ha-moed is omitted.
> See *Shulchan Aruch,* Orach Chayim 490:1.

18. The Song of Songs is associated with Passover because the Rabbis saw this *megilla* as an allegory depicting the love that exists between God and Israel. Passover is the springtime of this love (2:11-13). (See also Jeremiah 2:2, which refers to the "honeymoon" of God and Israel, Israel being the bride.)

> Other practices prevail with regard to the public reading of the Song of Songs on Passover, the most popular being the reading aloud of the entire book immediately after concluding the reading of the Haggada on Seder nights. Also, some congregations read the Song of Songs before the Friday evening Sabbath service, at which time the "bride," the Sabbath, is welcomed.

19. This haftara from the Book of Samuel is also the haftara for the sidra Ha'azinu (Deuteronomy 32), in which the *Song of Moses* is recorded. Oddly, it is not the haftara for the sidra Be-shalach (Exodus 13-17), in which the *Song at the Sea* appears.
20. See Alfred J. Kolatch's *Jewish Book of Why*, pp. 213-15. It was at a later time that the liturgy established a firm relationship between Shavuot and Revelation by referring to the former as *Zeman Mattan Toratenu*," the time of the giving of our Torah."

    See Yoma 4b, where the Rabbis disagree as to whether the sixth or the seventh of Sivan is the day on which the Torah was given to Israel.
21. *Rashi*, by Maurice Liber, p. 40.
22. See Megilla 31a.
23. See *Shulchan Aruch*, Orach Chayim 494:1-2.
24. See the comment of Isserles on *Shulchan Aruch*, Orach Chayim 686:1, in which he so indicates.

    The thirteenth day of Adar (the Fast of Esther) was fixed as a fast day in the eighth century. It is *not* designated as a fast day in the Book of Esther, written centuries earlier. The Bible (Esther 9:18) speaks of the thirteenth day of Adar only as a day of assembly for battle. The Rabbis interpreted the word "assembly" to mean "assembly for prayer and fasting," and the day became known as "Taanit Esther" (the Fast of Esther).
25. See Rosh Hashana 18b and Taanit 4:6.

    According to Jewish tradition, "Many things befell our ancestors on the seventeenth of Tammuz and the ninth of Av." These include:

- The smashing of the Ten Commandments.
- The issuance of a divine decree that none of the Hebrews who left Egypt, except Caleb and Joshua, should enter the Promised Land, as indicated in Numbers 14:21-24.
- The destruction of the First Temple by the Babylonians in 586 B.C.E.
- The destruction of the Second Temple 656 years later, in 70 C.E., by the Romans.
- The fall of Betar in 135 C.E. during the rebellion against Rome, led by Bar Kochba and Rabbi Akiba.
- Jerusalem laid waste by the Romans.

Because Tisha B'Av commemorates so many major catastrophes in Jewish life, it has been called the Black Fast. Yom Kippur, on the other hand, is called the White Fast. Taanit 30b says, "Anyone who eats or drinks on the ninth of Av is as sinful as one who eats or drinks on Yom Kippur." Jewish law, therefore, regards it as the equal of Yom Kippur in the sense that the fast must last for a full twenty-four hours, and it is not to be a sunrise-to-sunset fast as are the other minor fast days.

26. See Soferim 21:3 and *Shulchan Aruch*, Orach Chayim 580:3, where the fasting on these days is said to be in commemoration of the Temple.
27. *Shulchan Aruch*, Orach Chayim 428:8.
28. Rosh Hashana 10b.
29. Rosh Hashana 11a.
30. The first reference to the celebration of the first day of the seventh month is Leviticus 23:24-25.
31. On all two-day holidays that were originally one-day holidays, the same maftir is read on both days.
32. Megilla 3:4-6.
33. Tosefta Megilla 4:6.
34. Megilla 31a. Rosh Hashana always falls on the first of the month Tishri, and to establish the precise day on which the new month began the courts depended upon witnesses who sighted the New Moon and came forward to testify in the courts of Jerusalem. This was helpful to Palestinian Jewry, who could be notified quickly that the new month was beginning, but relaying the message to distant Jewish communities often met with problems. Therefore, communities outside of Palestine (the Diaspora) added one day to the holiday, so that if the first day of observance was incorrect, certainly the second would be correct. See Betza 6a and *Mishneh Torah*, Hilchot Yom Tov 1:24.

    Since the Bible specified that Rosh Hashana should be a one-day holiday, the Rabbis had to justify the change to a two-day holiday. This was done by means of a legal fiction: they began referring to the two days of Rosh Hashana as *yoma arichta*, meaning "one long day" of forty-eight hours. The *She-hecheyanu* prayer that was already an established part of the Kiddush of the first day of Rosh Hashana would have had to be removed from the Kiddush of the second night, otherwise it could have been a *beracha le-vatala*, a "wasted [superfluous] blessing." It was therefore left in the Kiddush for the second day, and a new fruit, one not yet eaten that year, was placed on the table and was tasted after the *She-hecheyanu* prayer was recited. Thus, the *She-hecheyanu* was associated with the new fruit and not with the second day of the holiday.
35. Some commentators, including Rashi and his grandson Rabbi Samuel ben Meir (Rashbam), in commenting on Genesis 22:13, say that from the very moment of Creation this ram was designated as the substitute for the sacrifice of Isaac.
36. The other two references to *shabbat shabbaton* are in Exodus 16:23, where the meaning is doubtful, and Leviticus 25:4, where it is related to the *shemita* year.
37. Tishri is a Babylonian word and was not used to designate the seventh month in the Jewish calendar until after the Babylonian Exile, when the Jews returned to Palestine. The name Tishri is never mentioned in the Bible.

    First Kings 8:2, the opening verse of the haftara, refers to

Sukkot as *Chag*, meaning "holiday," a term often used in other parts of the Bible.

38. The readings, from the Book of Numbers, are as follows:

On the third day of Sukkot, which is the first day of Chol Ha-moed, the reading for the first aliya is 17-19; for the second aliya, 20-22; for the third aliya, 23-25; for the fourth aliya, 17-22 are repeated.

On the fourth day of Sukkot, the second day of Chol Ha-moed, the reading for the first aliya is 20-22; for the second aliya, 23-25; for the third aliya, 26-28; for the fourth aliya, 20-25 are repeated.

On the fifth day of Sukkot, the third day of Chol Ha-moed, the reading for the first aliya is 23-25; for the second aliya, 26-28; for the third aliya, 29-31; for the fourth aliya, 23-28 are repeated.

On the sixth day of Sukkot, the fourth day of Chol Ha-moed, the reading for the first aliya is 26-28; for the second aliya, 29-31; for the third aliya, 32-34; for the fourth aliya, 26-31 are repeated.

The following are the readings in Israel for the intermediate days:

First day, Numbers 29:20-22; second day, Numbers 29:23-25; third day, Numbers 29:26-28; fourth day, Numbers 29:29-31. The verses are repeated as is necessary to accommodate all those called to the Torah.

A haftara is read during the intermediate days of Sukkot unless they fall on the Sabbath.

See page 304 for a listing of the readings for the intermediate days of Passover.

39. Kohelet, the Book of Ecclesiastes, is recited on the intermediate Sabbath of Sukkot or on the eighth day of the festival (Shemini Atzeret) if the latter falls on a Sabbath. The reading immediately precedes the morning Torah service. In some Oriental Jewish communities, Kohelet is read in the *sukka* after the morning service.

According to the Talmud (Shabbat 30b), the Rabbis originally wished to exclude the Book of Ecclesiastes from the canon. They considered it unworthy because of its many negative and contradictory statements. (Compare 7:3; 2:2; and 8:15). Yet, the book was included in the Bible based on the view that Ecclesiastes is a truly religious work, as is evident from verses 1:3 and 12:13.

40. In rabbinic literature Gog and Magog are seen as two persons who join in the great battle that has become known as the War of Gog and Magog, which will precede the Messianic Age. In world literature this is called Armageddon (the Greek form of the Hebrew *Har Megiddo*, Mountain of Megiddo). According to Christian tradition (Revelations 16:16), this is to be the site of the ultimate battle between the forces of good and evil.

41. This tenth is the "second tithe," as compared with the "first tithe," which was to be given to support the Levites (Numbers 18:26).

42. See I Kings 8:65-66.
43. The *Shulchan Aruch*, Orach Chayim 668:2, indicates that where Simchat Torah is *not* observed as a separate holiday, three Torot are removed from the ark on Shemini Atzeret, and the readings for Simchat Torah are performed on Shemini Atzeret.
44. See page 128-29 for more on this subject.
45. Some congregations also remove all Torot from the ark at the Kol Nidre service. See page 76.
46. Orthodox congregations often divide the congregation into small groups, and individual Torah readings are conducted. In this way the service is not overly extended.
47. *Shulchan Aruch*, Orach Chayim 669:1. The Talmud (Megilla 31a) mentions readings from the first and second Torah but not from the third.
48. This tradition of not interrupting study applies to other religious texts. For example, at the end of each of the sixty-three tractates of the Talmud there appear words such as those surrounding the *menora* in the illustration below. Usually the wording will appear without an accompanying design.
49. Sephardim read only verses 1-9.
50. *Shulchan Aruch*, Orach Chayim 684:1.
     In Israel, the readings of the third through the seventh day follow a slightly different sequence.
51. The reading for the eighth day, Numbers 7:54-8:4, includes the phrase (7:84) *Zot chanukat ha-mizbe'ach...* ("This was the dedication offering for the altar ..."). Hence the term *Zot Chanuka* became an appellation for the final day of Chanuka.
52. *Shulchan Aruch*, Orach Chayim 684:3.
     Rosh Chodesh will fall on a Sabbath of Chanuka if in a particular year the Hebrew month Kislev has thirty days (often it has only twenty-nine) and if in that year the first day of Chanuka (which always falls on the twenty-fifth day of Kislev) comes out on a Monday. In such years, the thirtieth day of Kislev will fall on Saturday and will be the first day of Rosh Chodesh. This is the only set of circumstances under which Rosh Chodesh, the Sabbath, and Chanuka can coincide.
53. Josephus, *Antiquities* II:209.
54. See *Shulchan Aruch*, Orach Chayim 693:4, especially the note of Isserles.

Bibliography

Abrahams, Israel. *Jewish Life in the Middle Ages*. London: Edward Goldston Ltd., 1932.

Agus, Irving, *Rabbi Meir of Rothenburg*. New York: Ktav Publishing House, 1970.

Aharon ben Yechiel Michal. *Nehora Ha-shalem* (commentary on the prayerbook). Vilna, 1898.

Albeck, Chanoch. *The Mishna*. Tel Aviv: Mossad Bialik, 1957.

Amram, David. *The Makers of Hebrew Books in Italy*. London: The Holland Press Ltd., 1963.

Arzt, Max. *Justice and Mercy*. New York: Holt, Rinehart and Winston, 1963.

The Babylonian Talmud (Hebrew). Twenty volumes. Vilna: Romm, 1922.

The Babylonian Talmud (English). Thirty-five volumes. London: Soncino Press, 1935.

Baron, Salo W. *A Social History of the Jews*. New York: Columbia University Press, 1937.

Bazak, Jacob, and Passamaneck, Stephen M. *Jewish Law and Jewish Life*. New York: Union of American Hebrew Congregations, 1979.

Bleich, J. David. *Contemporary Halakhic Problems I*. New York: Ktav Publishing House, 1977.

—————. *Contemporary Halakhic Problems II*. New York: Ktav Publishing House, 1983.

Bokser, Ben Zion. *The Jewish Mystical Tradition*. New York: Paulist Press, 1981.

Caro, Joseph. *Shulchan Aruch (Code of Jewish Law)*. Eight volumes. Probably a reprint of the 1874 Vilna edition. New York: Abraham Isaac Friedman, n.d.

Cohen, A. *Everyman's Talmud.* New York: E. P. Dutton, 1949.

———. "The Challenge of Biblical Criticism." Essay in *Judaism in a Changing World.* Leo Jung, editor. New York: Oxford University Press, 1939.

Danby, Herbert. *The Mishna.* Oxford, England: Clarendon Press, 1933.

Dobrinsky, Herbert C. *A Treasury of Sephardic Laws and Customs.* New York: Yeshiva University Press/Ktav Publishing House, 1986.

Donin, Hayim. *To Be a Jew.* New York: Basic Books, 1972.

———. *To Pray as a Jew.* New York: Basic Books, 1980.

Ehrlich, Arnold B. *Mikra Kipheshuto.* Three volumes. Introduction by Harry M. Orlinsky. New York: Ktav Publishing House, 1969.

Eisenstein, J. D. *Otzar Dinim U'minhagim.* New York: Hebrew Publishing Co., 1938.

———. *Otzar Maamarei Chazal.* New York: Hebrew Publishing Co., 1929.

Elfenbein, Israel. *Teshuvot Rashi.* B'nei Berak, Israel: Yahadut Publishers, 1980.

Encyclopaedia Judaica. Seventeen volumes. Jerusalem: Keter Publishing House, Ltd., 1971.

Epstein, Baruch Halevi. *Torah Temima* (commentary on the Pentateuch). New York: Hebrew Publishing Co., 1928.

Epstein, Isidore. *The Responsa of Solomon ben Adreth.* New York: Ktav Publishing House, 1968.

———. *The Responsa of Rabbi Simon ben Zemach Duran.* New York: Ktav Publishing House, 1930.

Epstein, Yechiel. *Aruch Ha-shulchan.* Eight volumes. Warsaw, 1900-1912.

Even-Shoshan, Abraham. *Milon Chadash.* Four volumes. Twelfth edition. Jerusalem: Kiryat Sepher, 1964.

———. *Concordantzya Chadasha (Le-Tanach).* Four volumes. Jerusalem: Kiryat Sepher, 1980.

Feinstein, Moshe. *Igrot Moshe.* Six volumes. New York: Moriah Offset, 1959-81.

Freehof, Solomon B. *Contemporary Reform Responsa.* Cincinnati: Hebrew Union College Press, 1974.

———. *Current Reform Responsa.* Cincinnati: Hebrew Union College Press, 1969.

———. *Modern Reform Responsa*. Cincinnati: Hebrew Union College Press, 1971.

———. *Reform Jewish Practice*, Volumes I and II. Augmented edition. This is a revised and enlarged edition of *Reform Jewish Practice* with material from *Reform Responsa*. Ktav Publishing House, 1976.

Fox, Marvin. *Modern Jewish Ethics*. Columbus: Ohio State University Press, 1975.

Ginsburg, Christian D. *Introduction to the Massoretico-Critical Edition of the Hebrew Bible*. Prolegomenon by Harry M. Orlinsky. New York: Ktav Publishing House, 1966.

Ginzberg, Louis. *The Legends of the Jews*. Seven volumes. Philadelphia: Jewish Publication Society, 1956.

Gordis, Robert. *The Biblical Text in the Making: A Study of the Kethib and Qere*. New York: Ktav Publishing House, 1971.

Graetz, Heinrich. *History of the Jews*. Six volumes. Philadelphia: Jewish Publication Society, 1891.

Greenwald, Yekutiel. *Ach Letzara*. St. Louis, Missouri: Quality Printing and Publishing Co., 1939.

Hertz, J. H. *The Pentateuch and Haftorahs*. London: Soncino Press, 1961.

Hirsch, Samson Raphael. *Judaism Eternal*. London: Soncino Press, 1959.

Hirshowitz, Abraham. *Otzar Kol Minhagay Yeshurun*. Pittsburgh: Moinester Printing Co., 1918.

Hoffman, Lawrence A. *The Canonization of the Synagogue Service*. Notre Dame, Indiana: University of Notre Dame Press, 1979.

Holtz, Barry W. *Back to the Sources*. New York: Summit Books, 1984.

Hyamson, Moses. *The Mishneh Torah*. Two volumes. New York: Bloch Publishing Co., 1937, 1949.

Idelsohn, Abraham. *Jewish Liturgy*. New York: Henry Holt and Co., 1932.

———. *The Ceremonies of Judaism*. Cincinnati: National Federation of Jewish Men's Clubs, 1930.

The Interpreter's Bible. Twelve volumes. Nashville: Abingdon Press, 1957.

Israel Meir Ha-kohayn (Chafetz Chayim). *Mishna Berura*. Six volumes. New York, n.d.

Jacobs, Louis. *Jewish Ethics, Philosophy and Mysticism*. New York: Behrman House, 1969.

Josephus, Flavius. *The Antiquities of the Jews*. William Whiston, editor. Grand Rapids, Michigan: Kregel Publications, 1960.

Kahana, Nachman. *Orchot Chayim*. Orach Chayim, Part One. Hungary, 1898.

Kanof, Abram. *Jewish Ceremonial Art and Religious Observance*. New York: Harry W. Abrams, Inc., 1969.

Kaplan, Mordecai. *Dynamic Judaism*. Edited by Emanuel S. Goldsmith and Mel Scult. New York: Schocken Books, 1985.

Kasher, Menachem M. *Encyclopedia of Biblical Interpretation*. Seven volumes. New York: American Biblical Encyclopedia Society, 1953.

Klagsbrun, Francine. *Voices of Wisdom*. New York: Jonathan David Publishers, 1986.

Klein, Earl. *Jewish Prayer: Concepts and Customs*. Columbus, Ohio: Alpha Publishing Co., 1986.

Kolatch, Alfred J. *Complete Dictionary of English and Hebrew First Names*. New York: Jonathan David Publishers, 1984.

———. *The Jewish Book of Why*. New York: Jonathan David Publishers, 1981.

———. *The Second Jewish Book of Why*. New York: Jonathan David Publishers, 1985.

———. *Who's Who in the Talmud*. New York: Jonathan David Publishers, 1964.

Lamm, Maurice. *The Jewish Way in Death and Mourning*. New York: Jonathan David Publishers, 1972.

———. *The Jewish Way in Love and Marriage*. New York: Jonathan David Publishers, 1986.

Leibowitz, Nehama. *Studies in the Bible*. Six volumes. Jerusalem: World Zionist Organization, 1973.

Levi, Primo. *The Periodic Table*. New York: Schocken Books, 1984.

Liber, Maurice. *Rashi*. Philadelphia: Jewish Publication Society, 1938.

Lieberman, Saul, editor. *Salo Wittmayer Baron Jubilee Volume*. Jerusalem: American Academy for Jewish Research, 1974.

Maimonides, Moses. *The Guide of the Perplexed.* Two volumes. Translated by Shlomo Pines. Chicago: University of Chicago Press, 1974.

———. *The Mishneh Torah.* Five volumes. Warsaw, 1881.

Margolis, Max, and Marx, Alexander. *A History of the Jewish People.* Philadelphia: Jewish Publication Society, 1934.

Mazar, Benjamin. *The World History of the Jewish People: Patriarchs.* New Brunswick, New Jersey: Rutgers University Press, 1970.

Meir Leibush (Loeb) ben Yechiel Michael (Malbim). *Sefer Torat Elohim* (commentary on the Pentateuch). Vilna, 1928.

Midrash Rabba. Two volumes. Vilna: Romm, 1938.

Millgram, Abraham. *Jewish Worship.* Philadelphia: Jewish Publication Society of America, 1971.

Morgenstern, Julian. *Rites of Birth, Marriage, and Sex Among Semites.* Chicago: Quadrangle Books, 1966.

Mowshowitz, Israel. *A Rabbi's Rovings.* New York: Ktav Publishing House, 1986.

Orlinsky, Harry M. *Ancient Israel.* Ithaca, New York: Cornell University Press, 1954.

———. *Proceedings of the International Organization for Masoretic Studies.* New York: Ktav Publishing House, 1974.

———. *Notes on the New Translation of the Torah.* Philadelphia: Jewish Publication Society of America, 1969.

Oshry, Ephraim. *Responsa From the Holocaust.* New York: Judaica Press, 1983.

Plant, W. Gunther, *The Torah: A Modern Commentary.* New York: Union of American Hebrew Congregations, 1981.

Potok, Chaim. *Wanderings.* New York: Alfred A. Knopf, 1978.

Rapoport, Louis. *The Lost Jews.* New York: Stein & Day, 1980.

Roth, Cecil, and Wigoder, Geoffrey. The *New Standard Jewish Encyclopedia.* New York: Doubleday, 1977.

Schauss, Hayyim. *The Jewish Festivals.* New York: Union of American Hebrew Congregations, 1938.

———. *The Lifetime of a Jew.* New York: Union of American Hebrew Congregations, 1950.

Silbermann, A. M. *Pentateuch with Rashi's Commentary.* Five volumes. London: Shapiro, Valentine & Co., 1929.

Spier, Arthur. *The Comprehensive Hebrew Calendar.* New York: Behrman House, 1952.

Steinzaltz, Adin. *Madrich leTalmud.* Jerusalem: Keter Publishing House, Ltd., 1984.

Trachtenberg, Joshua. *Jewish Magic and Superstition.* New York: Behrman House, 1939.

Urbach, Ephraim E. *The Halakhah: Its Source and Development.* Jerusalem: Massada Ltd., 1986.

Waxman, Meyer. *A History of Jewish Literature.* Four volumes. New York: Bloch Publishing Co., 1941.

Würthwein, Ernst. *The Text of the Old Testament.* Grand Rapids, Michigan: Eerdmans Publishing Co., 1980.

Yosef, Ovadya. *Yechaveh Daat.* Four volumes. Jerusalem: Chazon Ovadya Rabbinical Seminary, 1937.

Zeitlin, Solomon. *Who Crucified Jesus?* New York: Harper, 1942.

Zuckermandel, Moshe. *Tosefta.* With notes by S. Lieberman. Jerusalem: Warman Publications, 1975.

Index

416 •

About the Author

ALFRED J. KOLATCH, a graduate of the Teachers' Institute of Yeshiva University and its College of Liberal Arts, was ordained by the Jewish Theological Seminary of America, which subsequently awarded him the Doctor of Divinity degree, *honoris causa*. From 1941 to 1948 he served as rabbi of congregations in Columbia, South Carolina, and Kew Gardens, New York, and as a chaplain in the United States Army.

Rabbi Kolatch has authored more than fifty books, the most popular of which are the best-selling *Jewish Book of Why* and *Second Jewish Book of Why*, *The Jewish Book of Why: The Torah*, *The Jewish Mourner's Book of Why*, *The New Name Dictionary*, *The Complete Dictionary of English and Hebrew First Names*, *The Family Seder*, and *The Jewish Child's First Book of Why*. His most recent works are *Great Jewish Quotations: By Jews and About Jews*, *The Presidents of the United States & the Jews*, *What Jews Say About God*, and *Masters of the Talmud: Their Lives and Views*.

In addition to his scholarly work, Rabbi Kolatch has served as president of the Association of Jewish Chaplains of the Armed Forces and as vice-president of the interdenominational Military Chaplains Association of the United States.